Y0-DFY-789

The Manhattan Project and the Dropping of the Atomic Bomb

The Manhattan Project and the Dropping of the Atomic Bomb

THE ESSENTIAL REFERENCE GUIDE

Aaron Barlow, Editor

ABC-CLIO®

An Imprint of ABC-CLIO, LLC
Santa Barbara, California • Denver, Colorado

Copyright © 2020 by ABC-CLIO, LLC

All rights reserved. No part of this publication may be reproduced, stored in a retrieval system, or transmitted, in any form or by any means, electronic, mechanical, photocopying, recording, or otherwise, except for the inclusion of brief quotations in a review, without prior permission in writing from the publisher.

Library of Congress Cataloging-in-Publication Data

Names: Barlow, Aaron, 1951- editor.
Title: The Manhattan Project and the dropping of the atomic bomb : the essential reference guide / Aaron Barlow, editor.
Description: Santa Barbara, California : ABC-CLIO, [2020] | Includes bibliographical references and index.
Identifiers: LCCN 2019017826 (print) | ISBN 9781440859434 (hardcopy : alk. paper) | ISBN 9781440859441 (ebook)
Subjects: LCSH: Manhattan Project (U.S.)—History. | Atomic bomb—United States—History—20th century.
Classification: LCC QC773.3.U5 M262 2020 (print) | LCC QC773.3.U5 (ebook) | DDC 355.8/25119097309044—dc23
LC record available at https://lccn.loc.gov/2019017826
LC ebook record available at https://lccn.loc.gov/2019980549

ISBN: 978-1-4408-5943-4 (print)
       978-1-4408-5944-1 (ebook)

24 23 22 21 20   1 2 3 4 5

This book is also available as an eBook.

ABC-CLIO
An Imprint of ABC-CLIO, LLC

ABC-CLIO, LLC
147 Castilian Drive
Santa Barbara, California 93117
www.abc-clio.com

This book is printed on acid-free paper ∞

Manufactured in the United States of America

To the memory of my father,
who was on Hawaii as part of the force assembling to invade
Japan when the bombs were dropped on Hiroshima and Nagasaki.
He hated that this had been done though he recognized that
the bombings may have saved his life.

Contents

List of Entries, ix

List of Documents, xi

Introduction, xv

A–Z Entries, 1

Primary Documents, 123

Perspective Essays, 313

Chronology, 325

Bibliography, 329

About the Editor and Contributors, 335

Index, 337

List of Entries

Advisory Committee on Uranium (S-1 Executive Committee)
Alamogordo Bombing and Gunnery Range
Alsos Mission
B-29 Raids against Japan
Bockscar
Briggs, Lyman
Bush, Vannevar
Byrnes, James Francis
Churchill, Sir Winston L. S.
Clinton Engineer Works
Cockcroft, John
Compton, Arthur Holly
Conant, James Bryant
Critical Mass
Development of Substitute Materials
Einstein, Albert
Einstein-Szilárd Letter
Electromagnetic Uranium Enrichment
Enola Gay
Fat Man
Fermi, Enrico
Fissile Material
509th Composite Group
Frisch, Otto
Frisch-Peierls Memorandum
Gaseous Uranium Enrichment
Groves, Leslie Richard
Gun-Type Fission Weapon
Hahn, Otto
Hanford, Washington
Hiroshima, Bombing of
Implosion-Type Nuclear Weapon
Interim Committee
Laurence, William Leonard
Lawrence, Ernest Orlando
Little Boy
Los Alamos Laboratory (Project Y)
MAUD Committee
Meitner, Lise
Metallurgical Laboratory
Nagasaki, Bombing of
National Bureau of Standards
National Defense Research Committee
Neumann, John von
Nuclear Chain Reaction
Nuclear Reactor
Oak Ridge, Tennessee
Office of Scientific Research and Development
Oliphant, Mark
Oppenheimer, Julius Robert
Pacific Theater: World War II
Pegram, George Braxton
Peierls, Rudolf
Plutonium
Potsdam Conference
Project Alberta
Quebec Conference, 1st
Roosevelt, Franklin D.
Serber, Robert
Stimson, Henry Lewis
Strassmann, Fritz
Sweeney, Charles

List of Entries

Szilárd, Leó
Teller, Edward
Thermal Diffusion Uranium Enrichment
Thin Man
Tibbets, Paul
Tinian Joint Chiefs
Tizard Mission
Transmutation of Uranium into Plutonium
Trinity Test

Truman, Harry
Tube Alloys
University of Chicago
Uranium Enrichment
Uranium-235
U.S. Army Corps of Engineers
Wendover Army Air Field
Wigner, Eugene Paul
World War II

List of Documents

1. Leó Szilárd's Letter to Hugo Hirst, March 17, 1934
2. Leó Szilárd Letter to Lewis Strauss on Discoveries Relating to Fission of Uranium, January 25, 1939
3. Albert Einstein Letter to President Franklin Roosevelt, August 2, 1939 (Received October 11, 1939)
4. President Franklin Roosevelt's Response to Albert Einstein, October 19, 1939
5. The Frisch-Peierls Memorandum
   5a. O. R. Frisch and R. Peierls "Memorandum on the Properties of a Radioactive 'Super-bomb,'" March 1940. Part 1
   5b. O. R. Frisch and R. Peierls, "On the Construction of a 'Super-bomb' based on a Nuclear Chain Reaction in Uranium," March 1940. Part 2 of the Frisch-Peierls Memorandum
6. Arthur Compton Report of the National Academy of Sciences Committee on Atomic Fission, May 17, 1941
7. MAUD Committee Report, July 1941
8. Vannevar Bush Letter to Franklin Roosevelt, March 9, 1942
9. J. Robert Oppenheimer Letter to James Conant on the Properties of Uranium, November 30, 1942
10. Leslie Groves and James Conant Letter to J. Robert Oppenheimer, February 25, 1943
11. Robert Serber's "Los Alamos Primer" from Lectures Delivered in April 1943
12. J. Robert Oppenheimer Memorandum to Leslie Groves on Los Alamos, April 30, 1943
13. Harry Truman Telephone Conversation with Henry Stimson, June 17, 1943
14. Leslie Groves Letter to J. Robert Oppenheimer on Personal Safety, July 29, 1943
15. Quebec Agreement, August 19, 1943
16. J. Robert Oppenheimer Letter to Leslie Groves on Aliases, November 2, 1943
17. J. Robert Oppenheimer Memorandum on the Test of an Implosion Gadget, February 16, 1944
18. Niels Bohr's Memorandum to President Roosevelt, July 1944
19. Franklin Roosevelt and Winston Churchill, "Aide Memoire," September 18, 1944
20. Vannevar Bush and James Conant Memoranda to Henry Stimson, September 30, 1944
21. J. Robert Oppenheimer Letter to Leslie Groves, October 6, 1944
22. Albert Einstein's Fourth Letter to President Franklin Roosevelt, March 25, 1945

List of Documents

23. Henry Stimson Letter to Harry Truman on the Manhattan Project, April 24, 1945
24. Memorandum to Leslie Groves on the Second Meeting of the Target Committee, May 12, 1945
25. Henry Stimson Memorandum to Harry Truman on the Campaign Against Japan, May 16, 1945
26. John McCloy's Memorandum on Meeting with George Marshall and Henry Stimson Regarding Objectives toward Japan, May 29, 1945
27. James Franck, Report of the Committee on Political and Social Problems: Manhattan Project "Metallurgical Laboratory," University of Chicago, June 11, 1945
28. Arthur Compton, Enrico Fermi, Ernest Lawrence, and J. Robert Oppenheimer, Report on the Use of the Atomic Bomb in Wartime, June 16, 1945
29. Undersecretary of the Navy Ralph Bard's Memorandum to Secretary of War Henry Stimson, June 27, 1945
30. Office Diary of Leslie Groves on the Setting of the Test Date, July 2, 1945
31. Leó Szilárd's Petition to Harry Truman
    31a. Leó Szilárd's First Version of His Petition to Harry Truman, July 3, 1945
    31b. Leó Szilárd's Cover Letter for His Petition to Harry Truman, July 4, 1945
    31c. Edward Teller's Reply to Leó Szilárd's Petition Letter, July 4, 1945
    31d. Leslie Groves Response to the Szilárd Petition
    31e. Oak Ridge Addendum to the Szilárd Petition, July 13, 1945
    31f. Leó Szilárd's Final Petition Regarding the Atom Bomb, July 17, 1945
    31g. Second Oak Ridge Petition, July 1945
32. Norman Ramsey to J. Robert Oppenheimer, Memorandum on Dangers from Accidental Detonations, July 9, 1945
33. War Department Press Release on Trinity, "First Test Conducted in New Mexico," July 16, 1945
34. Leslie Groves Memorandum to Henry Stimson on the July 16 Trinity Test, July 18, 1945
35. Stafford Warren Report to Leslie Groves on the July 16 Trinity Test, July 21, 1945
36. Harry Truman Diary Entry for July 25, 1945
37. Thomas Handy to Carl Spaatz Memorandum, July 25, 1945
38. Potsdam Declaration: Proclamation Defining Terms for Japanese Surrender Issued, at Potsdam, July 26, 1945
39. Leslie Groves Memorandum to the U.S. Army Chief of Staff from the Conclusions of the Trinity Test, July 30, 1945
40. Charge-Loading Checklist for Little Boy on the Enola Gay, August 1945
41. Memorandum from General Leslie Groves to U.S. Army Chief of Staff George Marshall, August 6, 1945
42. U.S. Government Press Releases on the Occasion of the Hiroshima Bombing and Public Recognition of the Manhattan Project, August 6, 1945
    42a. White House Press Release on Hiroshima, August 6, 1945
    42b. Henry Stimson's Statement as the Secretary of War, August 6, 1945
    42c. Memorandum for the Press from the War Department, August 6, 1945

List of Documents | xiii

42d. War Department Press Release on Electromagnetic Uranium Enrichment at Oak Ridge, August 6, 1945

42e. War Department Background Information Press Release on Clinton Engineer Works at Oak Ridge, Tennessee, August 6, 1945

42f. Press Release on the Gaseous Uranium Enrichment Plant at Oak Ridge, August 6, 1945

42g. Press Release on the Thermal Diffusion Plant at Oak Ridge, August 6, 1945

42h. Press Release on the Hanford Engineer Works, August 6, 1945

42i. Press Release on the Development of the Los Alamos site, August 6, 1945

43. Leaflet Dropped on Japanese Cities, Possibly Starting Slightly Prior to the Nagasaki Bombing, August 9, 1945

44. Excerpt of Assistant Chief of Staff Summary of Activities, August 9, 1945

45. Harry Truman Radio Report, August 9, 1945

46. Henry Stimson Press Release, August 9, 1945

47. Memorandum by General Leslie Groves to Chief of Staff George Marshall, with Marshall's Note to Halt Bombings, August 10, 1945

48. Press Release on Security Measures Protecting the Secret of the Atomic Bomb, August 10, 1945

49. Japanese Request for Surrender, Transmitted August 10, 1945

50. J. Robert Oppenheimer Letter to Henry Stimson, August 17, 1945

51. Norman Ramsey Undated Letter to J. Robert Oppenheimer, Probably About August 22, 1945

52. Transcript of Telephone Conversation between General Leslie Groves and Lieutenant Colonel Charles E. Rea, August 25, 1945

53. Message from General Thomas Farrell to General Leslie Groves on Nagasaki Damage, September 14, 1945

54. Press Release of President Harry Truman's Request for Press Assistance in Assuring Secrecy on the Manhattan Project, September 14, 1945

55. J. Robert Oppenheimer's Speech to the Association of Los Alamos Scientists, November 2, 1945

56. The Effects of the Atomic Bombs: Excerpt from U.S. Strategic Bombing Survey Summary Report (Pacific War), Washington, D.C., July 1, 1946

57. Eben Ayers Diary on Memories by Harry Truman of the Atomic Bomb, August 6, 1951

58. President Harry Truman's Later Thoughts in Letters, August 5, 1963 and August 4, 1964

59. Eyewitness Accounts
    59a. Trinity
    59b. Hiroshima
    59c. Nagasaki

60. War Department Press Release, Calendar of Important Events, October 30, 1946

Introduction

Imagine that the year is 1939, late summer. August, as a matter of fact. Europe is clearly on the verge of war. Though people view the international political situation with growing horror, on the positive side, the world, including the United States, is emerging from an economic depression that had pulled progress backward, not merely slowing it, for many families for a decade.

That Great Depression notwithstanding, technology continued to move forward at an incredible rate. Think about it: Just over 12 years ago, Charles Lindbergh had soloed across the Atlantic in his little *Spirit of Saint Louis*. Yet, just two months ago, the new Yankee Clipper, a recently designed Boeing B-314 flying boat owned by Pan American Airlines, had inaugurated commercial flights across the Atlantic, letting people do in comfort what Lucky Lindy had risked death to attempt.

The B-314, with a range of some 3,500 miles, a top altitude of a bit less than 20,000 feet, and a cruising speed, depending on load, of between 150 and 200 miles per hour, was a marvelous aircraft—yet even it was a slow boat compared (let's look ahead just a bit) to the B-29 Superfortress that Boeing would be building starting in 1942. The B-29, while its range was slightly less than that of the B-314, would cruise at almost 300 miles an hour and would reach over 30,000 feet with its pressurized cabin.

Other technologies, many of them with both civilian and military origins, were progressing at similar swift rates. Some of them were breathtaking, beyond what even the science-fiction writers of the time were imagining. Foremost among these was the idea of a bomb based on nuclear fission, a recently discovered (and as yet unnamed) phenomenon, a bomb that would dwarf in power anything the world had seen or anyone could imagine.

Albert Einstein, the most famous physicist in the world, had signed a letter earlier this month addressed to U.S. President Franklin Roosevelt, suggesting that the country start a program for study of the possibility of development of an atomic bomb. The suggestion was based on the premise, made probable by recent German advances in the field, that the Nazis would soon be doing the same thing, if they weren't already. This letter, composed by Leó Szilárd in consultation with Edward Teller and Eugene Wigner, a trio of expatriate Hungarian physicists, would become the trigger for Roosevelt's decisions later in the fall and over the next three years leading to the creation of the Manhattan Project.

The B-29, of course, with its large payload, would make the resulting bomb deliverable. As a result, the world, just six years from now, in August of 1945, would be unrecognizable from the world of this 1939. A new age, an atomic age, will have begun.

From August 6, 1945, through the end of the twentieth century, knowledge of the Manhattan Project was commonplace on American college campuses and even in high schools. The impact of the bomb that exploded that day over Hiroshima, Japan—and of the one three days later over Nagasaki—was felt far beyond the range of their earth-shattering power. Americans recognized this and kept its importance front and center.

Within hours of the first explosion, almost everyone in the United States knew what the previously unknown Manhattan Project had been and were aware of its result, even if they did not know the details.

Today, more than three-quarters of a century since the Manhattan Project's inception, knowledgeable comment on this critical initiative no longer rests on the tips of American tongues. Today, most of us need to be reminded both of the broad historical context of the project and the details of its inception all the way through to the terrible events of its eventual success. This is unfortunate because, after all, almost everything in our contemporary lives, even including our new digital tools, can be traced, at least in part, back to the Manhattan Project, its consequences, and the related research.

In order to provide a needed reminder of one of the twentieth century's greatest feats, this book presents an introduction to both the wide and the narrow in describing the events and personalities associated with the Manhattan Project. It is not, however, a technical manual of any sort, for it provides few details of the physics, chemistry, and engineering that culminated in development of a successful atomic bomb. In other words, this is not a book for scientists, but it does serve as a starting-point reference for college and high school students as well as for interested members of the broader public. Importantly, it includes a wide range of significant documents, allowing the interested to learn of the Manhattan Project in the words of those who participated in it.

One of the most important—and too often forgotten—details of the Manhattan Project is that it was not an exclusively American operation. Not only were some of the most important contributors of Italian, Hungarian, and other European origins, but some were from the most important wartime ally of the United States, Great Britain. More importantly, England's early work toward the atomic bomb in the years leading up to the Manhattan Project was incorporated into it, significantly reducing the time leading to the project's success. Even before the Quebec Agreement set the stage for incorporation of the British Tube Alloys project into the Manhattan Project, it was work in England that had posited the feasibility of a deliverable atomic bomb—feasibility that was brought to American attention through the MAUD Committee Report.

The 75 years since the end of World War II have constituted an atomic age, an age unlike anything imagined prior to it. Various dates can be used to denote its start, including August 2, 1939, the date on the Einstein letter to Roosevelt; December 2, 1942, the date when Enrico Fermi unleashed the first controlled atomic chain reaction at the University of Chicago; July 16, 1945, the date of the first explosion of an atomic bomb, the Trinity Test at Alamogordo, New Mexico; and, of course, August 6, 1945, the most famous of these dates, for it was the day the United States bombed Hiroshima, Japan, in the first of only two actual instances of atomic warfare (the second being the bombing of Nagasaki three days later).

As we have seen, the world was certainly in quite a different state in 1939, when what would become the Manhattan Project began, from what it would be a mere six years later when those first atomic bombs were exploded. Not only had war engulfed the planet, but advances in science and technology had propelled mankind into an entire new universe, making the artifacts of the prewar days suddenly seem quaint. The gestation of the atomic age was one of violence and of advancement based on need and, sometimes, even, on desperation. Its goal, however, was paradoxically one of peace.

There are no easy answers to the hindsight questions of whether or not the bombs should have been dropped or regarding the morality of the action. The questions, though, are worth revisiting—over and over and for each new generation. What is most important today is that discussion of the Manhattan Project commence with intelligence and knowledge of the actualities of the time.

It is also important, as we move deeper into a postatomic age whose defining feature seems, so far, to be the digital, that we remember a time when the United States, with British help, was able to create a focused and time-driven project with the potential to change the world. The United States has actually done this twice—first with the Manhattan Project and, 20 years later, with the three spaceflight programs, Mercury, Gemini, and Apollo, that culminated in human beings walking for the first time on the surface of the moon. We need, as a nation, to be able to undertake projects of similar scope today. The question is, can we?

By learning from the Manhattan Project, perhaps we will be able to find an answer to that question.

A

Advisory Committee on Uranium (S-I Executive Committee)

Meeting for the first time on October 21, 1939, under the direction of Lyman Briggs, the Advisory Committee on Uranium came into existence in response to Albert Einstein's letter to President Franklin Roosevelt in August of 1939 urging the United States to step up involvement in research on uranium. The committee initially consisted of Briggs and Lieutenant Colonel Keith Adamson and Commander Gilbert Hoover, representing the army and the navy, respectively. Also attending the first meeting were Alexander Sachs and Edward Teller, along with Leó Szilárd and Eugene Wigner, who had been involved in drafting Einstein's letter. Two government physicists, Fred L. Mohler and Richard B. Roberts, were also present. Einstein had been invited but did not attend.

The committee reported to President Roosevelt on November 1, 1939, with the statement that chain reaction, though unproven, might be possible. It concluded that the lines of possible research could lead to the development of bombs of far greater power than anything previously known and advocated for investigation along the lines first proposed by Einstein. The committee suggested that Karl Compton, Einstein, George Pegram, and Sachs be invited to participate as full members.

The next meeting of the committee was held on April 27, 1940, with Rear Admiral Harold G. Bowen also attending, in addition to Fermi, Pegram, Sachs, Szilárd, and Wigner. The committee agreed to support the research in progress at Columbia University on the possibility of creating a chain reaction. A scientific subcommittee (without the military) was created consisting of Jesse Beams, Gregory Breit, Ross Gunn, Pegram, Merle Tuve, and Harold C. Urey. Meeting on June 13, 1940, it recommended continuing the support for research on chain reaction and also on isotope separation.

When the National Defense Research Committee was constituted on June 27, 1940, under the leadership of Vannevar Bush, the Advisory Committee on Uranium was wrapped into it as the NDRC Committee on Uranium, with Beams, Gunn, Pegram, Tuve, and Urey added to the main committee while Hoover and Adamson were dropped.

In response to the MAUD Report of March 1941, Bush, now head of the Office of Scientific Research and Development with James Conant reporting to him as new head of the NDRC, reorganized the Uranium Committee as the OSRD Section on Uranium. It soon became known as the S-1 Committee (purposely less descriptive of the task at hand) and first met on December 18, 1941. Though the new committee was expanded from its earlier manifestations, it was recognized that it, alone, would not be able to handle a project of the size that would be needed to create an atomic bomb, which was now a serious goal. It was decided to coordinate with the army. This led to the creation, under General Leslie Groves, of the Manhattan Engineer District.

On June 19, 1942, Conant replaced the S-1 Committee with a smaller S-1 Executive Committee consisting of Conant himself as chairman along with Briggs, Compton, Ernest Lawrence, Eger Murphree, and Urey. It remained in active oversight of the project until all contracts were transferred to the army in March 1943, when it became inactive, though "S-1" continued to be used as a coded reference to the atomic bomb for the rest of the war.

Aaron Barlow

See also: Briggs, Lyman; Bush, Vannevar; Compton, Arthur Holly; Conant, James Bryant; Einstein, Albert; Einstein-Szilárd Letter; National Defense Research Committee; Pegram, George Braxton; Roosevelt, Franklin D.; Szilárd, Leó; Teller, Edward; Wigner, Eugene Paul

References

Conant, Jennet. 2002. *Tuxedo Park: A Wall Street Tycoon and the Secret Palace of Science That Changed the Course of World War II*. New York: Simon & Schuster.

Nichols, Kenneth D. 1987. *The Road to Trinity: A Personal Account of How America's Nuclear Policies Were Made*. New York: William Morrow and Company.

Shrader, Charles. 2006. *History of Operations Research in the United States Army, Volume I: 1942–62*. Washington, D.C.: U.S. Army.

Alamogordo Bombing and Gunnery Range (July 16, 1945)

The Alamogordo Bombing and Gunnery Range was the site of the first successful test of an atomic device. By the spring of 1945, the ongoing Manhattan Project had produced sufficient plutonium for several fission bombs, but scientists were unsure of the reliability of the implosion technique required to initiate a nuclear chain reaction and an explosion. Small-scale experiments were unrevealing, because nothing below critical mass can explode. Thus, Major General Leslie R. Groves, overall director of the Manhattan Project, authorized a full-scale test (known as Trinity) of the implosion technique.

The Jornada del Muerto (Dead Man's Trail) near Alamogordo, New Mexico, was chosen as ground zero for the explosion. Remote and ringed by high peaks, the site helped to preserve secrecy and contain radioactive fallout, the effects of which were not yet then fully known. Secured atop of a 100-foot steel tower, the device exploded at 5:30 a.m. on July 16, 1945. With a predicted minimal yield of 500 tons of trinitrotoluene (TNT) and an optimal yield of 5,000 tons if all parts functioned synergistically, the device actually produced a yield of 20,000 tons of TNT. Accompanied by a blinding flash of light, a powerful shock wave, and an awesome roar, the device vaporized the tower, creating a crater some 400 yards in diameter and 10–20 feet deep. A mushroom cloud rose to 41,000 feet; the explosion was heard 100 miles away, and the light produced was seen from 200 miles. To allay concerns of local residents, army officials reported that an ammunition dump had blown up.

Scientists were awestruck by the power of the explosion. Julius Robert Oppenheimer, a theoretical physicist who had labored for many months on the Manhattan Project, famously recalled the god Vishnu's line from the Bhagavad Gita: "Now I am become Death, the destroyer of worlds." Groves simply predicted, "The war's over."

A report on the success of the detonation was quickly passed to President Harry S.

Truman, who was then at Potsdam, Germany, meeting with newly elected British prime minister Clement R. Atlee and Soviet leader Joseph Stalin. Truman's negotiating stance with Stalin hardened considerably based on the stunning results of the Trinity Test, although Stalin certainly knew of the Manhattan Project, because his spy network had long ago penetrated the top-secret program.

The Trinity Test site is located on White Sands Missile Range. It is open to the public twice a year: the first Saturday in April and the first Saturday in October.

William J. Astore

See also: Bush, Vannevar; Einstein, Albert; Fat Man; Fermi, Enrico; 509th Composite Group; Groves, Leslie Richard; Hiroshima, Bombing of; Little Boy; Nagasaki, Bombing of; Oppenheimer, Julius Robert; Potsdam Conference; Trinity Test. Documents: 29, 32, 33, 34, 48

References

Lamont, Lansing. 1985. *Day of Trinity*. New York: Atheneum.

Storms, Barbara. 1965. *Reach to the Unknown: Part 1: Trinity. Special Twentieth Anniversary Edition of the Atom, July 16, 1965*. Los Alamos, NM: Office of Public Relations.

Szasz, Ferenc Morton. 1984. *The Day the Sun Rose Twice: The Story of the Trinity Site Nuclear Explosion, July 16, 1945*. Albuquerque: University of New Mexico Press.

Alsos Mission

An intelligence operation tasked with discovering German scientific developments, Operation Alsos was initiated in 1943 as the Allied armies progressed up Italy and began to capture Axis documents. It was an outgrowth of the Manhattan Project, whose leaders were keen to know where German progress stood and to keep German scientific advances out of the hands of the Russians, who, though they were allies, were also already seen as likely postwar rivals. The name of the mission was a tribute to General Leslie Groves (*alsos* is Greek for *grove*), head of the Manhattan Project, though he apparently thought it inappropriate.

The Alsos Mission was composed of military staff from the Office of Scientific Research and Development and the Office of Naval Intelligence and Army Intelligence (G-2), with a mandate to keep all information discovered in American hands. Its first major actions were in occupied Italy, where it managed to obtain information on German guided missiles and rockets but little about its atomic program.

A liaison office was established in England to research German activities and interview refugee scientists. With an eye toward invasion and possible Russian activities, lists of places that might be centers of German nuclear activities or storehouses of information were compiled along with names of German scientists who might be involved in such research. Several months before the Normandy Invasion on June 6, 1944, the Alsos Mission was expanded in England to follow closely in the steps of the invading Allied forces to sweep up information about German atomic activities. By August, members of the team were operating in France in cooperation with T-Force, an American-British cooperative mission to secure German technological facilities before the retreating forces could destroy them.

While in France, the Alsos officers managed to gather information on German scientists involved in nuclear research and were also able to locate uranium stored in Belgium as well as a shipment that had gone from there to France. In November, T-Force and Alsos entered Strasbourg and identified a German nuclear laboratory there along with documents that pointed to nuclear-related activities at a number of other German sites and were able to determine that the Germans had yet to develop a practical uranium-enrichment process, a necessary step to creating an atomic bomb.

In March and April of 1945, the Alsos Mission was involved in the capture of a number of German nuclear scientists, including Otto Hahn, as well as further documentation on German nuclear programs, an experimental nuclear reactor, and additional uranium. The mission's activities culminated with the capture of Werner Heisenberg on May 2, 1945, just six days before the end of the war in Europe, and the unit was disbanded on October 15, 1945.

Aaron Barlow

See also: Groves, Leslie Richard; Hahn, Otto; Office of Scientific Research and Development; Strassmann, Fritz

References

Bernstein, Jeremy. 2001. *Hitler's Uranium Club: The Secret Recordings at Farm Hall.* New York: Springer-Verlag.

Goudsmit, Samuel A. 1947. *Alsos.* New York: Henry Schuman.

Groves, Leslie. 1962. *Now It Can Be Told: The Story of the Manhattan Project.* New York: Harper & Row.

Jones, R. V. 1978. *Most Secret War.* London: Hamilton.

Pash, Boris. 1969. *The Alsos Mission.* New York: Charter Books.

B

B-29 Raids against Japan (June 1944–August 1945)

The attacks on Japan by the Boeing B-29 Superfortresses of the Twentieth Air Force, part of the U.S. Army Air Forces (USAAF), began in June 1944 and were key components in the series of shocks that produced the Japanese surrender in August 1945. The bombers burned down cities, mined waterways, destroyed major industrial targets, and eventually dropped two atomic bombs.

Planning for the use of the long-range B-29s against Japan began in early 1943. Operation Matterhorn, launching these heavy bombers from China, was finally approved at the Cairo Conference in December 1943, and the Combined Chiefs of Staff there also supported basing in the Mariana Islands. In April 1944, General Henry "Hap" Arnold established the Twentieth Air Force, to be commanded out of Washington so he could keep the B-29s under his control. The first aircraft were rushed to the Far East that month.

Primary bases for the XX Bomber Command of the Twentieth Air Force were located in India, with forward operating fields in China. Results were disappointing, even after Arnold sent his best problem

A Boeing B-29 Superfortress being prepared for a raid on Tokyo in April 1945. (Library of Congress)

solver and combat commander, Major General Curtis LeMay, to take over the troubled unit. Facilities were austere, supply lines were long, crew training was inadequate, and the hastily fielded B-29s suffered from a host of technical problems, especially with their engines. In 10 months of operations, the XX Bomber Command delivered fewer than 1,000 tons of bombs to Japan, all against targets in Kyushu.

The USAAF had greater hopes for the XXI Bomber Command based in the Marianas, which launched its first attack on Japan in late November. This unit had better logistics and more secure airfields, and it was closer to Japan than the XX Bomber Command. Arnold expected Brigadier General Haywood Hansell, one of the architects of precision-bombing doctrine, to exert decisive airpower against Japan's homeland fortress and prove the worth of an independent air service. But Hansell was unable to put his theories into effective practice. In addition to the same problems faced in Matterhorn, the XXI Bomber Command ran into a combination of cloud cover and jet-stream winds over targets that rendered high-altitude precision bombing almost impossible.

In January 1945, a frustrated Arnold decided to consolidate all B-29s in the Marianas under LeMay, who reorganized the staff, instituted new training, and improved maintenance. After a month of ineffective precision attacks, however, LeMay, on his own initiative, shifted tactics. He adopted low-level, night, aerial, incendiary attacks designed to cripple key targets by burning down the cities around them and to destroy the Japanese ability and will to carry on the war. The first raid on Tokyo on the night of March 9–10 was a spectacular success militarily, killing more than 90,000 people and incinerating 16 square miles. By the end of the war, B-29s had burned out 178 square miles in some 66 cities and killed many hundreds of thousands of people.

The Superfortresses also performed other missions against the Japanese home islands. A psychological warfare campaign to drive panicked civilians out of targeted cities caused over eight million Japanese to flee to the countryside. Mines dropped in waterways during the last five months of the war sank or damaged over 1 million tons of scarce shipping. And of course, B-29s from the 509th Composite Bomb Group dropped two atomic bombs, one on August 6, 1945, and the other on August 9. On August 15, the Japanese agreed to surrender terms. Japanese leaders and postwar bombing evaluations acknowledged that the B-29s made a significant contribution to ending the war.

Conrad C. Crane

See also: 509th Composite Group; Hiroshima, Bombing of; Nagasaki, Bombing of; Tinian Joint Chiefs

References

Crane, Conrad C. 1993. *Bombs, Cities, and Civilians: American Airpower Strategy in World War II.* Lawrence: University Press of Kansas.

Craven, Wesley Frank, and James Lea Cate, eds. 1948–1953. *The Army Air Forces in World War II.* 7 vols. Chicago: University of Chicago Press.

Hansell, Haywood S., Jr. 1980. *Strategic Air War against Japan.* Maxwell Air Force Base, AL: Airpower Research Institute.

Tillman, Barrett. 2010. *Whirlwind: The Air War Against Japan, 1942–1945.* New York: Simon & Schuster.

Werrell, Kenneth P. 1996. *Blankets of Fire: U.S. Bombers over Japan during World War II.* Washington, D.C.: Smithsonian.

Bockscar

Bockscar, or Bock's Car, was the B-29 Superfortress of Silverplate modification that dropped the bomb called Fat Man on Nagasaki, Japan, on August 9, 1945. The plane has been preserved and resides at the National Museum of the U.S. Air Force in Dayton, Ohio. Originally, another plane, called the Great Artiste, was meant to be used for the purpose of dropping the bomb, and its crew, led by Major Charles W. Sweeney, was trained for the mission. On August 6, 1945, the Great Artiste, with its normal crew, provided support for the Enola Gay when it dropped the first atomic bomb on Hiroshima. The equipment installed in it was supposed to be transferred to Bockscar, captained by Captain Frederick Bock, which would serve the same function on the second mission. However, the date of the Nagasaki raid was moved from August 11 to August 9. This made it impossible to transfer and install the equipment in time. So, it was decided to swap crews instead of equipment. The Great Artiste, then, once again served a support function, though with a different crew.

Crew of the Bockscar on April 9, 1945

Major Charles Sweeney, aircraft commander
First Lieutenant Charles Albury, copilot

The crew of Bockscar, or Bock's Car the plane that bombed Nagasaki on August 9, 1945. Seen at their base on Tinian, Northern Mariana Islands, they are, kneeling, from left, S/Sgt. John D. Kuharek; Sgt. Abe M. Spitzer, Sgt. Ray G. Gallagher, S/Sgt. Buckley, and S/Sgt. Albert R. DeHart. Standing, from left, Major Charles W. Sweeney, CO 393rd Bombardment Squadron and pilot; Lt. Charles D. Albury, airplane commander; Lt. Fred J. Olivi, co-pilot; Capt. Kermit K. Beahan, bombardier; Capt. James F. Van Pelt, navigator; and Lt. Beser. (PhotoQuest/Getty Images)

Captain James Van Pelt Jr., navigator
Captain Kermit Beahan, bombardier
Lieutenant Jacob Beser, electronic countermeasures
Staff Sergeant Ed Buckley radio operator
Sergeant Abe Spitzer, radio operator
Master Sergeant John Kuharek, flight engineer
Sergeant Raymond Gallagher, assistant flight engineer
Staff Sergeant Albert DeHart tail gunner
Commander Frederick Ashworth, USN, weaponeer
Second Lieutenant Fred Olivi, third pilot

Ground Crew

Staff Sergeant Frederick D. Clayton
Sergeant Robert L. McNamee
Sergeant John L. Willoughby
Corporal Robert M. Haider
PFC Rudolph H. Gerken

Aaron Barlow

See also: Enola Gay; Fat Man; 509th Composite Group; Laurence, William Leonard; Nagasaki, Bombing of; Sweeney, Charles. Document: 49b1

References

Campbell, Richard H. 2005. *The Silverplate Bombers: A History and Registry of the Enola Gay and Other B-29s Configured to Carry Atomic Bombs.* Jefferson, NC: McFarland & Company.

Craven, Wesley Frank, and James Lea Cate. 1953. "Victory." In *The Pacific: Matterhorn to Nagasaki.* Vol. 5 in *The Army Air Forces in World War II,* 703–758. Chicago: University of Chicago Press.

Sweeney, Charles, James A. Antonucci, and Marion K. Antonucci. 1997. *War's End: An Eyewitness Account of America's Last Atomic Mission.* New York: Avon Books.

Wainstock, Dennis D. 1996. *The Decision to Drop the Atomic Bomb.* Westport, CT: Praeger Publishing.

Briggs, Lyman (1874–1963)

Lyman Briggs was a scientist and administrator who led the U.S. federal government's National Bureau of Standards from 1933 until 1945. In 1939, he was asked by President Franklin Roosevelt to head what became the Uranium Committee and eventually the Manhattan Project. Though initially a soil scientist at the Department of Agriculture, Briggs also had a background in physics. It was this, plus his excellent record as an administrator, that let to Roosevelt picking him for the job.

Born on May 7, 1874, in Assyria, Michigan, Briggs enrolled in Michigan Agricultural College (which would become Michigan State University) when he was 15. After earning a BS degree in 1893, he continued his studies at the University of Michigan, where he completed an MS degree in physics in 1895. After that, he enrolled in the doctoral program in physics at Johns Hopkins University but switched into the agriculture program, finishing his PhD in 1903 while working as a research scientist for the Department of Agriculture, where he had taken a job in 1896.

Briggs convened the first meeting of the Uranium Committee on October 21, 1939; Eugene Wigner, Leó Szilárd, Edward Teller, and others attended. In 1940, the Uranium Committee would be renamed the S-1 Committee as a part of the new National Defense Research Committee.

Aaron Barlow

See also: Advisory Committee on Uranium; National Bureau of Standards; National Defense Research Committee; Roosevelt, Franklin D.; Szilárd, Leó; Teller, Edward; Wigner, Eugene Paul. Documents: 6, 21

References

Cochrane, R. C. 1974. *Measures for Progress, a History of the National Bureau of*

Standards. Washington, D.C.: U.S. Government Printing Office.

Lush, Tony. 1969. *Lyman Briggs*. East Lansing, MI: n.p.

Myers, Peter Briggs, and Johanna M. H. Levelt Sengers. 1999. "Lyman James Briggs: May 7, 1874–March 25, 1963." *Biographical Memoirs: Vol. 77*. Washington, D.C.: National Academies.

Rhodes, Richard. 1986. *The Making of the Atomic Bomb*. New York: Simon & Schuster.

Bush, Vannevar (1890–1974)

A U.S. scientist who was involved with the Manhattan Project to develop an atomic bomb, Vannevar Bush was born March 11, 1890, in Everett, Massachusetts. Vannevar Bush earned both bachelor's and master's degrees in engineering at Tufts College before completing a joint doctorate at the Massachusetts Institute of Technology (MIT) and Harvard University. By 1932, he was dean of engineering at MIT.

During World War I, Bush designed a device utilizing magnetic fields to detect submarines. The navy deemed it worthless for combat, which affected Bush's attitudes regarding the relationship between science and government. He was interested in machinery that would automate thinking, and by 1931, he had built the first electronic analog computer to solve, at great speed, complex differential equations.

In 1938, Bush was selected as president of the Carnegie Institution in Washington, D.C., his duties including advising the government on scientific research. He also was chairman of the National Advisory Committee for Aeronautics from 1939 to 1941. During World War II, he worked to establish relationships between scientists and government officials regarding research resources, especially those concerning defense work. He also emphasized the importance of technological innovation and proficiency to national security.

In June 1940, Bush presented President Franklin D. Roosevelt his ideas about the coordination of military research as a partnership of scientific, industrial, business, and government groups. This approach led to the establishment of the National Defense Research Committee (NDRC), with Bush as its director, in June 1941. In addition, Bush secured congressional funding to create the Office of Scientific Research and Development (OSRD), which then oversaw the NDRC.

An adroit administrator, Bush became involved in significant technological developments, particularly in putting together a team for the Manhattan Project as well as improving radar and developing radio-guided bombs. He also recruited civilian scientists to work on military projects. His July 1945 report, "Science: The Endless Frontier," advised President Harry S. Truman regarding governmental peacetime development of science and technology. The 1950 National Science Foundation incorporated many of Bush's ideas for postwar science and government cooperation for basic research and education.

In 1945, Bush's *Atlantic Monthly* essay, "As We May Think," discussed the hypothetical "memex," a machine capable of information storage and retrieval with associative linking. This automatic technology would enable humans to augment their memory technically. Computer engineers later stated that Bush's ideas influenced their digital development of hypertext and the internet. Bush died in Belmont, Massachusetts, on June 28, 1974.

Elizabeth D. Schafer

See also: Advisory Committee on Uranium; Interim Committee; National Bureau of Standards; National Defense Research Committee; Office of Scientific Research and Development; Roosevelt, Franklin D; Tizard Mission. Documents: 8, 9, 10, 14, 19, 25, 32, 40b

References

Bush, Vannevar. 1949. *Modern Arms and Free Men: A Discussion of the Role of Science in Preserving Democracy.* New York: Simon & Schuster.

Zachary, G. Pascal. 1999. *Endless Frontier: Vannevar Bush, Engineer of the American Century.* Cambridge, MA: MIT Press.

Byrnes, James Francis (1879–1972)

James Francis Byrnes was a U.S. politician, wartime "assistant president" to Franklin D. Roosevelt, and secretary of state from 1945 to 1947. Born on May 2, 1879, in Charleston, South Carolina, Byrnes went on to study law. After qualifying as a lawyer, he won election to Congress in 1910, and in 1931, he became a senator for South Carolina. A longtime friend of President Roosevelt, Byrnes used his considerable negotiating talents to steer New Deal legislation through Congress from 1933 onward. In 1941, Roosevelt appointed him to the Supreme Court.

Sixteen months later, in 1942, Byrnes left the high court to head the new Office of Economic Stabilization. The following year, he became director of the Office of War Mobilization (from 1944, the Office of War Mobilization and Reconversion). In domestic policy, Byrnes, often called the "assistant president," exercised powers second only to those of Roosevelt himself. Responsible for coordinating all domestic war agencies and federal government departments, he worked closely with both Congress and the bureaucracy to devise the most efficient arrangements to implement the war effort.

Passed over as Roosevelt's vice presidential running mate in 1944, Byrnes, already considered a hard-liner on the Soviet Union, attended the February 1945 Yalta Conference of the "Big Three" Allied leaders. Returning to Washington, he successfully lobbied Congress to support the outcome of Yalta, deliberately glossing over outstanding contentious issues dividing the Soviet Union and its allies. Still disappointed over the 1944 election, he resigned in March 1945.

Upon Roosevelt's death one month later, Vice President Harry S. Truman became president. Truman immediately appointed Byrnes as head of a top-secret committee on the employment of atomic weapons, then in their final stage of development, whose existence Byrnes recommended be kept secret even from U.S. allies until their first use in combat. He believed the United States' possession of the bomb would make Soviet behavior more malleable.

In July 1945, Truman named Byrnes secretary of state. Attending the July 1945 Potsdam Conference, Byrnes hoped the speedy employment of atomic weapons against Japan would prevent the Soviet Union from entering the Pacific war and enhancing its influence in Asia. He also helped to reach a compromise agreement on German reparations. Returning to Washington, he took part in drafting the Japanese surrender agreement in August, implicitly agreeing to retain the emperor.

As Soviet–U.S. relations became more strained after the war, Byrnes sought for several months to negotiate compromise solutions, traveling extensively to meet with other foreign ministers outside the United States. In early 1946, political complaints that he was too conciliatory led Byrnes to assume a harsher rhetorical stance toward the Soviet Union. Even so, in January 1947, Truman—increasingly irked by Byrnes's policies, his secretive diplomacy, and his condescending attitude—made George C. Marshall secretary of state in his stead.

Byrnes returned to South Carolina and wrote his memoirs. In 1948, he broke with Truman over the issue of civil rights; subsequently, he served two terms, from 1951 to 1955, as governor of South Carolina, defending segregationist policies. Byrnes died in Columbia, South Carolina, on April 9, 1972.

Priscilla Roberts

See also: Interim Committee; Potsdam Conference; Roosevelt, Franklin D. Documents: 40b, 41, 48

References

Byrnes, James F. 1947. *Speaking Frankly.* New York: Harper.

Byrnes, James F. 1958. *All in One Lifetime.* New York: Harper.

Messer, Robert F. 1982. *The End of an Alliance: James F. Byrnes, Roosevelt, Truman, and the Origins of the Cold War.* Chapel Hill: University of North Carolina Press.

Robertson, David. 1994. *Sly and Able: A Political Biography of James F. Byrnes.* New York: Norton.

Churchill, Sir Winston L. S. (1874–1965)

British political leader, cabinet minister, and prime minister (1940–1945, 1951–1955) Winston Leonard Spencer Churchill was born at Blenheim Palace, Oxfordshire, on November 30. He was the eldest son of Lord Randolph Churchill, third son of the duke of Marlborough and a rising Conservative politician, and his wife, Jennie Jerome, an American heiress. Churchill emulated his father—who attained the position of chancellor of the exchequer before a premature death ended his political career—by entering politics in 1900 as a Unionist member of Parliament. In 1904, his party's partial conversion to protectionism caused him to join the Liberals, who made him president of the Board of Trade (1908–1910) and home secretary (1910–1911) after they returned to power.

As first lord of the Admiralty (1911–1915), Churchill enthusiastically backed the campaign of First Sea Lord Admiral Sir John "Jackie" Fisher to modernize the British Navy with faster battleships and more efficient administration. He spent the six months up to May 1916 on active service on the Western Front but regained high political office in July 1917, when Prime Minister David Lloyd George made him minister of munitions in his coalition government. By 1930, Churchill was campaigning eloquently for major British rearmament, especially the massive enhancement of British airpower, to enable the country to face a revived Italian or German military threat. From 1932 onward, he sounded this theme eloquently in Parliament, but Conservative leaders remained unsympathetic. Churchill also became perhaps the most visible and vocal critic of the appeasement policies of the successive governments of prime ministers Stanley Baldwin and Neville Chamberlain, who effectively tolerated German rearmament, Chancellor Adolf Hitler's deliberate contravention of the provisions of the Treaty of Versailles, and Germany's and Italy's territorial demands on their neighbors.

When Britain declared war on Germany in September 1939, Churchill resumed his old position as First Lord of the Admiralty. He succeeded Chamberlain as prime minister on May 10, 1940, the day Germany invaded France and the Low Countries. During the next three months, Britain sustained repeated disasters as German troops rapidly overran the Low Countries and France, forcing the British Expeditionary Force to withdraw in disarray from northern France at Dunkerque during May 26 to June 4, 1940, abandoning most of its equipment. During the Battle of Britain (July 10 to September 30, 1940), German airplanes fiercely attacked Britain in an apparent prelude to a full-scale cross-channel invasion.

Besides rallying the British people to endure military defeat in France and the bombing campaign Germany soon launched against Britain's industrial cities, Churchill's speeches, which caught the international imagination, were designed to convince the political leaders and people of the United

States—the only quarter from which Britain might anticipate effective assistance—of his country's commitment to the war. U.S. President Franklin D. Roosevelt responded by negotiating the "Destroyers-for-Bases" deal of August 1940, whereby the United States transferred 50 World War I–vintage destroyers to Britain in exchange for naval basing rights in British Caribbean Islands and North America.

In August 1941, Churchill and Roosevelt met for the first time, in Placentia Bay off the Newfoundland coast, and agreed to endorse a common set of liberal war aims—the Atlantic Charter—and to coordinate their two countries' military strategies.

When the Manhattan Project in the United States was organized in 1942, and General Leslie Groves tightened security, the British scientists working on the parallel Tube Alloys project in the United Kingdom and Canada began to recognize that, on their own, they would not be able to compete with the Americans. In July, John Anderson, Lord President of the Council and a member of Churchill's war cabinet, advised Churchill to explore ways of merging Tube Alloys into the Manhattan Project. Getting no initial positive response from the Americans, the British slowed their own cooperation.

After a period of misunderstanding, bruised feelings, and negotiations, Churchill and U.S. President Franklin Roosevelt signed the Quebec Agreement on August 19, 1943, while attending what came to be called the First Quebec Conference. This paved the way for unrestricted cooperation and communications between the two allies and gave new impetus to the project. In July 1945, the British electorate voted Churchill out of office while he was attending a meeting with the new American president, Harry Truman, and Josef Stalin of the Soviet Union at Potsdam, Germany, replacing his administration with a reformist Labour government.

Churchill died in London on January 24, 1965. For many, his death marked the symbolic final passing of Great Britain's imperial age. Churchill received the first state funeral for any British commoner since the death of the Duke of Wellington over a century before. An idiosyncratic political maverick whose pre-1939 record was, at best, mixed, Churchill rose to the occasion to become the greatest British war leader since the first Earl of Chatham in the eighteenth century.

Priscilla Roberts and Aaron Barlow

See also: Potsdam Conference; Quebec Conference, 1st; Roosevelt, Franklin D.; Truman, Harry; World War II. Documents: 14, 18, 40a, 41, 48

References

Gilbert, Martin S. 1966–1988. *Winston S. Churchill.* 8 vols. New York: Random House.

Jablonsky, David. 1994. *Churchill and Hitler: Essays on the Political-Military Direction of Total War.* Portland, OR: Cass.

Jenkins, Roy. 2001. *Churchill.* London: Macmillan Publishing.

Larres, Klaus. 2002. *Churchill's Cold War: The Politics of Personal Diplomacy.* New Haven, CT: Yale University Press.

Lukacs, John. 2002. *Churchill: Visionary, Statesman, Historian.* New Haven, CT: Yale University Press.

Ramsden, John. 2002. *Man of the Century: Winston Churchill and His Legend since 1945.* New York: Harper Collins.

Stafford, David. 1999. *Roosevelt and Churchill: Men of Secrets.* London: Little, Brown.

Clinton Engineer Works

The Clinton Engineer Works (CEW) near the town of Oak Ridge, Tennessee, was comprised of 59,000 acres and was situated about 20 miles from Knoxville. Originally planned for 13,000 people, CEW had more than 80,000 people when the Manhattan Project was at its peak. It was the center of a great deal of Manhattan Project activity at its three sites, each dedicated to a particular task.

Called at that time the Manhattan District (officially, "Development of Substitute Materials"), the project headquarters were moved to the new site during the summer of 1943. Built by the Army Corps of Engineers on land appropriated from the small number of people who had lived there, CEW was a planned community—right down to segregation of housing for blacks and whites.

Early in 1943, construction had begun on a nuclear reactor at CEW, the second in the world after the University of Chicago's Pile-1. This one would be known as the Clinton Pile, X-10 Pile and, ultimately, the X-10 Graphite Reactor. The goal was to use the reactor to produce plutonium for use in atomic bombs, themselves the main goal of what would soon be called the Manhattan Project. Completed in late 1943, the reactor began producing plutonium early in 1944, supplying the testing site at Los Alamos, New Mexico.

Also early in 1943, construction began at CEW on the Y-12 Electromagnetic

This picture of one of the three production plants built for the Manhattan Project at the Clinton Engineer Works at Oak Ridge, Tennessee, shows just how massive the project was and how difficult it must have been to maintain secrecy. (Bettmann/Getty Images)

Separation Plant using calutrons combining mass spectrometers and cyclotrons. Due to problems in construction, Y-12 did not become operational at all until about the time X-10 did, though the technology was more thoroughly understood than that of the reactor. Enriched uranium-235 from the Y-12 units was used in construction of the Little Boy bomb that was dropped on Hiroshima.

The third major CEW project was the K-25 gaseous diffusion plant. Construction began in October 1943, with the plant in use by the later part of April 1944. By 1945, the plant was enriching uranium effectively and would do so for the next 40 years.

The fourth major component of the CEW project was the S-50 thermal diffusion plant; construction began in July of 1944, with operational testing starting in September. Production of uranium-235 climbed until the surrender of Japan, after which the costly plant was shut down and then demolished.

Aaron Barlow

See also: Development of Substitute Materials; Electromagnetic Uranium Enrichment; Gaseous Uranium Enrichment; Little Boy; Oak Ridge, Tennessee; Plutonium; Thermal Diffusion Uranium Enrichment; Transmutation of Uranium into Plutonium. Documents: 30g, 40b, 40d, 40e, 40f

References

Compton, Arthur. 1956. *Atomic Quest*. New York: Oxford University Press.

Freeman, Lindsey A. 2015. *Longing for the Bomb: Oak Ridge and Atomic Nostalgia*. Chapel Hill: University of North Carolina Press.

Groueff, Stéphane. 1967. *Manhattan Project: The Untold Story of the Making of the Atomic Bomb*. Boston: Little, Brown.

Groves, Leslie. 1962. *Now It Can Be Told: The Story of the Manhattan Project*. New York: Harper & Row.

Johnson, Charles W., and Charles O. Jackson. 1981. *City Behind a Fence: Oak Ridge, Tennessee, 1942–1946*. Knoxville: University of Tennessee Press.

Kiernan, Denise. 2013. *The Girls of Atomic City: The Untold Story of the Women Who Helped Win World War II*. New York: Simon & Schuster.

Nichols, Kenneth D. 1987. *The Road to Trinity: A Personal Account of How America's Nuclear Policies Were Made*. New York: William Morrow and Company.

Rhodes, Richard. 1986. *The Making of the Atomic Bomb*. London: Simon & Schuster.

Cockcroft, John (1897–1967)

Born on May 27, 1897, in Todmorden, England, John Douglas Cockcroft came from a family of cotton manufacturers. He studied mathematics at Manchester University in 1915, leaving to serve in the British Royal Field Artillery in World War I. After the war, he returned to Manchester but switched his focus to electrical engineering before moving to Cambridge for a degree in mathematics.

By the 1930s, Cockcroft was heavily involved in physics, working with Pyotr Kapitsa and then with Ernest T. S. Walton on proton acceleration. A member of the Tizard Mission to the United States in 1940, he soon became head of the Air Defence Research and Development Establishment before taking charge of the Canadian Atomic Energy Project in 1944.

Cockcroft was put in control of the Canadian Project because of American concern over security risks seen in the large number of non-British and non-American scientists involved. The Americans had gone so far as to threaten to refuse cooperation unless Hans von Halban, a French Jewish physicist and prior head of the project, was replaced. When he left, a number of others working on the project were also removed. Ironically, sometime later, one of the British scientists on the project, Alan Nunn May, did prove to be a spy for the Soviet Union.

With assistance from the Manhattan Project, the Zero Energy Experimental Pile was constructed at the Chalk River Laboratories, opening just after the end of the war as the first nuclear reactor outside of the United States.

In 1951, Cockcroft was cowinner, with Walton, of the Nobel Prize in Physics for, as the award reads, "pioneer work on the transmutation of atomic nuclei by artificially accelerated atomic particles." He died on September 18, 1967.

Aaron Barlow

See also: MAUD Committee; Tizard Mission

Reference

Cockcroft, John. 1964. "John Douglass Cockcroft: Biographical." *Nobel Lectures, Physics 1942–1962*. Amsterdam: Elsevier Publishing Company.

Compton, Arthur Holly (1892–1962)

The joint winner of the 1927 Nobel Prize in Physics, Arthur Holly Compton is best remembered for his discovery that the wavelength of X-rays changes when they collide with the electrons in metals. He explained that that change is brought about by the transfer of energy from the photon to the electron, a phenomenon that became known as the Compton effect. His finding confirmed that electromagnetic radiation occurs in both wave and particle form and was vital in the development of quantum mechanics in the 1920s.

Compton was born in Wooster, Ohio, on September 10, 1892. His father was a professor at the nearby College of Wooster and a Presbyterian minister. Compton showed a strong leaning toward science as a boy, as he read about paleontology and astronomy and even built an experimental glider. Like his two older brothers, Compton went to the College of Wooster, from which he received his bachelor's degree in 1913. A year later, he earned a master's degree from Princeton University, and in 1916, he completed his PhD there.

After he finished his doctoral work at Princeton, Compton married and took a yearlong job as a physics instructor at the University of Minnesota. From 1917 to 1919, he worked on developing airplane instruments for the U.S. Signal Corps and worked as a research engineer at the Westinghouse Lamp Company in Pittsburgh, Pennsylvania, where he received a patent for his design for a sodium vapor lamp. Working in industry, however, made Compton realize that he missed the academic world to which he had grown accustomed.

With his excellent scholastic record, Compton had little difficulty procuring a National Research Council fellowship in physics. That fellowship allowed him to study from 1919 to 1920 at the Cavendish Laboratory at England's Cambridge University, where researchers were beginning to experiment with splitting atoms. When he returned to the United States, Compton became professor of physics and chairperson of the physics department at Washington University in St. Louis, Missouri. In 1926, he left Washington University for the University of Chicago, which had offered him a post as physics professor. That year, his book *X-Rays and Electrons* was published, and he became a physics consultant for the General Electric Company, which was the epicenter of the development of the fluorescent lamp.

Meanwhile, Compton had already made the discovery about X-rays for which he would receive so much attention. He wrote *Secondary Radiation Produced by X-Rays* in 1922. Not only did the Compton effect explain the scattering effect of X-rays, it also bolstered Albert Einstein's controversial photon theory of light in which he suggested that a photon (a particle of electromagnetic radiation) has both energy and directed momentum. Compton, then 35 years old, shared the 1927 Nobel Prize for his work with a British researcher who had photographed the trails of electrons.

From 1931 to 1933, Compton continued his experiments with X-rays but also launched a worldwide cosmic ray survey and traveled to many of the world's mountains to measure the rays. His work eventually demonstrated, contrary to the accepted theory of physicist Robert A. Millikan, that at least some cosmic rays are charged particles and so are influenced by the planet's magnetic field. In 1934 and 1935, he taught at Oxford University in England.

Compton accepted an appointment as chairperson of the physics department and dean of the physical sciences division at the University of Chicago in 1941. That same year, he also became chairperson of the National Academy of Sciences' committee to investigate the use of atomic energy as a weapon. Working closely with Ernest O. Lawrence, the designer of the first cyclotron, Compton prepared a report on the feasibility of atomic weapons that was highly influential in the government's creation of the University of Chicago's Manhattan Project. From 1942 to 1945, Compton was director of the Metallurgical Laboratory at the Manhattan Project, where Enrico Fermi engineered the chain reaction in 1942 that became the basis for the atomic bomb. The laboratory is where the plutonium necessary for the reaction was first produced.

After World War II, Compton went back to St. Louis and Washington University, which had asked him to be its chancellor. He took that post despite having been offered the leadership of the University of Chicago's new Institutes for Nuclear Studies, Metals, and Microbiology, which he had helped set up. In 1953, Compton stepped down as chancellor and became the school's distinguished professor of natural philosophy, which he remained until 1961. His 1956 book, *Atomic Quest: A Personal Narrative,* quickly became one of the most popular accounts of the historic events of the Manhattan Project.

Compton died in Berkeley, California, on March 15, 1962. He and his wife had two children. His other books include *The Freedom of Man* (1935) and *The Human Meaning of Science* (1940). The scientist's favorite hobbies were astronomy, photography, tennis, and music. The National Aeronautics and Space Administration named its new orbiting gamma ray observatory after him in 1991.

Amanda de la Garza

See also: Interim Committee; Office of Scientific Research and Development; Szilárd, Leó. Documents: 6, 27, 40b

References

Asimov, Isaac. 1982. *Asimov's Biographical Encyclopedia of Science & Technology.* New York: Doubleday.

Daintith, John. 1981. *The Biographical Encyclopedia of Scientists.* New York: Facts on File.

Conant, James Bryant (1893–1978)

Though James B. Conant was a scientist in several fields, as well as a diplomat, he made his most important contribution as an educator and a researcher in American education. His studies led him to warn that the millions of unemployed youths in American cities were "social dynamite."

James Bryant Conant was born on March 26, 1893, in Dorchester, Massachusetts, a suburb of Boston. He was a precocious chemistry student at the Roxbury Latin School. He entered Harvard University at age 17 and graduated magna cum laude at age 20. He earned his doctorate in 1916. Conant taught chemistry at Harvard for 17 years, except for two years in the army's Chemical Warfare Service during World War I and a year in Germany in 1925 studying university teaching. In organic chemistry, he did important research on the structure of chlorophyll (the green color factor of plants) and of hemoglobin (the color factor in red corpuscles).

From 1933 to 1953, Conant was president of Harvard, though during World War II, he took on other responsibilities. As a firm anti-isolationist advocating international commitments, he spoke for universal military conscription and the 1941 lend-lease bill, which allowed countries vital to American defense more credit to buy or lease war supplies. And as chairman of the Office of Scientific Research and Development, he was a leading adviser on the production of the atomic bomb and witnessed its first test in the New Mexico desert in July 1945. Conant advised the American delegation to the United Nations Atomic Energy Commission in 1947, and in 1950, he had an important role in founding the National Science Foundation.

Having introduced reforms at Harvard—in admissions policies, for example, so as to admit more non-Eastern U.S. students and those of limited means; in the improvement of teacher education; and in founding the Nieman Fellowships for journalists—Conant resigned from the presidency in 1953 upon being appointed U.S. high commissioner for West Germany. When the occupation of West Germany ended in 1955, Conant became U.S. ambassador and served for two years.

With grants from the Carnegie Corporation in 1957, Conant undertook what is considered his principal contribution: a thorough study of American public high schools and teacher education. His book *Slums and Suburbs* (1961) was a groundbreaking document on the need for upgrading the education of poor children in urban areas. Conant warned that insufficient guidance for impoverished black youths would lead to social catastrophe. In *Shaping Educational Policy* (1964), he advocated decentralizing school administration while increasing cooperation between states. He advocated busing to urban high schools in order to promote integration. He continued to call for the improvement of teacher training, which he considered then to be "scandalous." For a time, Conant was chairman of the board of the Educational Testing Service in Princeton, New Jersey.

Conant, having retired in his later years, died on February 11, 1978, at age 84 in a New Hampshire nursing home.

William McGuire and Leslie Wheeler

See also: Advisory Committee on Uranium; Interim Committee; National Bureau of Standards; National Defense Research Committee; Office of Scientific Research and Development. Documents: 8, 9, 10, 14, 15, 19, 25, 29, 32, 33, 40b

References

Conant, James B. 1970. *My Several Lives.* New York: Harper & Row.

Douglass, Paul. 1954. *Six Upon the World: Toward an American Culture for an Industrial Age.* Boston: Little, Brown.

Hershberg, James G. 1993. *James B. Conant: Harvard to Hiroshima and the Making of the Nuclear Age.* New York: Knopf.

Critical Mass

Though it has become a term in popular culture for the accumulation necessary for a body of components to reach a life of its own (to become self-sustaining), "critical mass" has a specific meaning in nuclear physics, one crucial to any understanding of the development of the atomic bomb. Basically, it is the threshold amount of fissile material necessary for maintaining a nuclear chain reaction or fission. The amount depends on properties of density, shape, enrichment, purity, temperature, and the surrounding environment. Material that can sustain a chain reaction is called fissile or fissionable.

The critical state is reached in a mass of fissile material when there is no further change in power, temperature, or neutron population. A mass is considered subcritical when it has not reached this self-sustaining state. A mass is supercritical when it continues to increase in power, temperature, or neutron population. Changes in state can be manipulated externally by controlling an added amount of fuel to the mass or by changing the temperature of the fuel or the environment.

A nuclear weapon needs to be kept in a subcritical state prior to detonation (which can be effected through implosion or through bringing together separate masses each alone below critical size).

The critical mass necessary for a nuclear chain reaction was first determined by Leó Szilárd and Enrico Fermi, working at the University of Chicago. On December 2, 1942, on a squash court, they bombarded a pile of 40,000 graphite blocks embedded with 19,000 pieces of uranium with slow neutrons to the point where fission, a nuclear chain reaction, was detectable through Geiger counters. They were able to then determine that the critical mass of U-235 was about 50 kilograms, given the type (U-235 or Pu-239, which required a smaller mass for reaching critical mass) and shape of the fuel, the temperature of the reaction, and the density of the material.

This experiment provided the crucial piece of information leading to development of the atomic bomb over the next few years at Los Alamos, New Mexico.

Aaron Barlow

See also: Fermi, Enrico; Gun-Type Fission Weapon; Implosion-Type Nuclear Weapon; Los Alamos Laboratory; Szilárd, Leó. Document: 10

Reference

Serber, Robert. 1992. *The Los Alamos Primer: The First Lectures on How to Build an Atomic Bomb.* Berkeley: University of California Press.

D

Development of Substitute Materials

"Development of Substitute Materials" was the first name of the project that would eventually be known worldwide as the Manhattan Project. When it was suggested that there was a possible clue in the name to the true purpose of the project, a decision was made to follow the tradition of the U.S. Army Corps of Engineers, which named its offices for the cities in which they were based. Thus, as the first offices were in Manhattan, Development of Substitute Materials was renamed Manhattan Engineering District, which was eventually shortened as the Manhattan Project.

Though the project was first housed in Manhattan, its central administration soon moved to Oak Ridge, Tennessee, and, later, the focus of its work was in the Los Alamos Laboratory in New Mexico.

Aaron Barlow

See also: Clinton Engineer Works; Groves, Leslie Richard; Los Alamos Laboratory; Oak Ridge, Tennessee; U.S. Army Corps of Engineers

Reference

Smyth, Henry DeWolf. 1945. *Atomic Energy for Military Purposes: The Official Report on the Development of the Atomic Bomb under the Auspices of the United States Government, 1940–1945*. Princeton, NJ: Princeton University Press.

E

Einstein, Albert (1879–1955)

Albert Einstein was a physicist, Nobel laureate, and pacifist who urged the United States to begin research into the feasibility of constructing atomic bombs. Born in Ulm, Germany, on March 14, 1879, Einstein renounced German citizenship in 1896 and became a Swiss citizen in 1901. While working as a patent clerk, he developed his special theory of relativity and the famous equation $E = mc^2$ that demonstrated the equivalency of mass and energy. In 1914, he returned to Germany after being appointed director of the Kaiser Wilhelm Institute for Physics and a professor at Humboldt University, Berlin. With the rise of Nazism and Jewish persecution, he left Berlin in 1933 for the Institute of Advanced Study in Princeton, New Jersey.

In 1939, leading physicists, including Hungarian émigrés Leó Szilárd and Eugene P. Wigner, as well as Italian expatriate Enrico Fermi, concluded that Germany was working on an atomic bomb. Szilárd approached Einstein with a letter for President Franklin D. Roosevelt, urging that the U.S. government begin an atomic bomb project of its own to deter Adolf Hitler (assuming German efforts succeeded).

Einstein was apotheosized as perhaps the world's greatest physicist since Isaac Newton, and his signature on this letter carried considerable weight. Dated August 2, 1939, the letter warned it was now likely that scientists would establish and sustain a chain reaction in uranium, which could lead to the construction of "extremely powerful bombs of a new type." Einstein urged the president to form a partnership among government officials, industry specialists, and scientists to conduct feasibility studies; he also recommended securing supplies of uranium ore.

Alexander Sachs, economist and presidential confidant, delivered the letter on October 11, 1939. Sufficiently alarmed by Sachs's précis of its contents, Roosevelt appointed the Uranium Committee to begin preliminary studies, which became the basis for the Manhattan Project organized in 1942 to build atomic bombs.

Physicist Albert Einstein in 1944. His theoretical work was foundational to the development of the atomic bomb. (The Illustrated London News Picture Library)

Einstein's letter served as the catalyst for the Manhattan Project, but Einstein himself was excluded from the project. His pacifism, Zionism, and a supposedly lackadaisical attitude regarding military secrecy made him suspect to army intelligence. After the war, he campaigned unsuccessfully for a "world government" consisting of the United States, Great Britain, and the Soviet Union that would restrict further development and construction of atomic weapons. Einstein died in Princeton, New Jersey, on April 18, 1955.

William J. Astore

See also: Bush, Vannevar; Compton, Arthur Holly; Einstein-Szilárd Letter; Fermi, Enrico; Groves, Leslie Richard; Meitner, Lise; National Bureau of Standards; Nuclear Chain Reaction; Oppenheimer, Julius Robert; Szilárd, Leó; Wigner, Eugene Paul. Documents: 3, 4, 21

References

Einstein, Albert. 1954. *Ideas and Opinions*. New York: Bonanza Books.

Fölsing, Albrecht. Ewald Osers, trans. 1997. *Albert Einstein: A Biography*. New York: Viking.

Rhodes, Richard. 1986. *The Making of the Atomic Bomb*. New York: Simon & Schuster.

Einstein-Szilárd Letter

On August 2, 1939, Albert Einstein, on the advice of Leó Szilárd, Edward Teller, and Eugene Wigner, wrote to President Franklin Roosevelt to warn him that Germany could develop a bomb based on chain reaction of uranium of heretofore unimagined power and to advocate that the United States develop its own comparable program. Roosevelt took the letter seriously, quickly establishing a Uranium Committee to coordinate and explore efforts to develop such a bomb. It was, then, the spark that lit the fuse that became the Manhattan Project, leading to the development of the first atomic bombs and their use in the destruction of the Japanese cities of Hiroshima and Nagasaki.

Though the letter was sent with Einstein's signature (after all, he was by far the most famous physicist in the world), it was sparked by Szilárd, whose concerns about advances in fission by German scientists might lead to successful development of an atomic bomb. With fellow Hungarians Teller and Wigner, Szilárd recruited Einstein as their spokesperson in an attempt to warn other countries of the danger. He also contacted economist Alexander Sachs, a personal friend of Roosevelt, who suggested that the letter, first directed only to the Belgian government, also be sent to the American president. On August 15, Sachs personally took the letter to deliver it to Roosevelt but was unable to do so until October 11, probably because of the German invasion of Poland on September 1. At that time, rather than simply handing over the letter, Sachs summarized it for the president, emphasizing the possibility of atomic power in peacetime as well as war. Roosevelt acted almost immediately, starting the chain of bureaucratic events that led to the creation of the Manhattan Project and the development of a successful atomic bomb.

Aaron Barlow

See also: Einstein, Albert; Roosevelt, Franklin D.; Szilárd, Leó; Teller, Edward; Wigner, Eugene Paul. Documents: 3, 21

References

Gowing, Margaret. 1964. *Britain and Atomic Energy, 1935–1945*. London: Macmillan Publishing.

Lanouette, William, and Bela Silard. 1992. *Genius in the Shadows: A Biography of Leo Szilard: The Man Behind the Bomb.* New York: Scribner.

Electromagnetic Uranium Enrichment

Electromagnetic Separation Uranium Enrichment is expensive and energy inefficient, but it was the first method that was known to work. Enriched uranium being a necessity for the creation of an atomic bomb, development of a successful process was a critical step. The Y-12 calutrons constructed at Oak Ridge, Tennessee, used massive magnets to separate ions of uranium-235 from uranium-238.

Enriched uranium has a higher percentage of U-235 than uranium in its natural state, which is primarily U-238. As U-235 is the only natural nuclide fissile with thermal neutrons, it was a critical element for creation of the first atomic bombs. Increasing its availability in a usable form was an important step toward successful completion of Manhattan Project goals.

Called by the code name "oralloy" (from Oak Ridge alloy), enriched uranium was initially produced through gaseous diffusion, thermal diffusion, and electromagnetic isotope separation. Through a calutron, a mass spectrometer developed by Ernest Lawrence and named for his earlier cyclotron and his home institution, the University of California, electromagnetic separation at Oak Ridge produced U-235 for the Little Boy bomb that was used at Hiroshima.

Expanding on a process developed by Australian Mark Oliphant in 1934, in April 1940, Alfred Nier, working at the University of Minnesota on the basis of information provided by Niels Bohr, along with Bohr's own subsequent work, concerning Otto Hahn and Fritz Strassmann's development of nuclear fission in 1938 (and the theoretical explanation of it by Lise Meitner and Otto Frisch), managed to create a small amount of U-235 through use of a mass spectrometer. This led Leó Szilárd and Walter Zinn to postulate development of an atomic bomb and to speculate that Nazi Germany might have the know-how to create one first.

In November 1941, Lawrence, who knew Oliphant's work and Nier's small success, converted his cyclotron into a mass spectrometer that dwarfed what Nier had been working with. Its initial operation was on December 2, 1941, and Lawrence's research was soon given a boost by funding from the S-1 Uranium Committee in the amount of $400,000 (almost $7,000,000 in 2018 dollars). Lawrence was quickly able to establish that he could create a much higher percentage of U-235 than Nier had managed. It was this that led to development of the Y-12.

Aaron Barlow

See also: Clinton Engineer Works; Frisch, Otto; Gaseous Uranium Enrichment; Hahn, Otto; Lawrence, Ernest Orlando; Meitner, Lise; Oak Ridge, Tennessee; Oliphant, Mark; Strassmann, Fritz; Szilárd, Leó; Thermal Diffusion Uranium Enrichment. Documents: 35d, 40d

References

Guthrie, Andrew, and R. K. Wakerling, eds. 1949. *Vacuum Equipment and Techniques.* National Nuclear Energy Series, Manhattan Project Technical Section; Division I: Electromagnetic Separation Project. New York: McGraw-Hill.

Yergey, Alfred L., and Karl A. Yergey. 1997. "Preparative Scale Mass Spectrometry: A Brief History of the Calutron." *American Society for Mass Spectrometry* 8, no. 9: 943–953.

Enola Gay

Named after Enola Gay Tibbets, the mother of its captain, Paul Tibbets, this was the Boeing B-29 Superfortress Silverplate bomber used for dropping the first atomic bomb used in warfare on Hiroshima, Japan, on August 6, 1945. With a pressurized cabin (like all B-29s), the Enola Gay had a range of over 2,500 miles. Unlike standard B-29s, the Silverplate bombers had no gun turrets except in the tail, less armor plate, new Curtiss electric propellers, and a single 33-foot bomb bay rather than two smaller ones. Its crew was 11, one more than the 10-man complement for standard B-29s, with a weaponeer added in the cockpit.

Crew of the Enola Gay on August 6, 1945

Colonel Paul W. Tibbets Jr., aircraft commander
Captain Robert A. Lewis, copilot
Major Thomas Ferebee, bombardier
Captain Theodore "Dutch" Van Kirk, navigator
Captain William S. Parsons, USN, weaponeer and mission commander
First Lieutenant Jacob Beser, radar countermeasures office
Second Lieutenant Morris R. Jeppson, assistant weaponeer
Staff Sergeant George R. "Bob" Caron, tail gunner
Staff Sergeant Wyatt E. Duzenbury, flight engineer
Sergeant Joe S. Stiborki, radar operator
Sergeant Robert H. Shumard, assistant flight engineer
PFC Ricard H. Nelson, VHF radio operator

Ground Crew

Technical Sergeant Walter F. McCaleb
Sergeant Leonard W. Markley

The Enola Gay, a "Silverplate" Boeing B-29 Superfortress, after its bombing of Hiroshima on August 6, 1945. (Keystone/Getty Images)

Sergeant Jean S. Cooper
Corporal Frank D. Duffy
Corporal John E. Jackson
Corporal Harold R. Olson
PFC John J. Lesniewski
Lieutenant Colonel John Porter, maintenance officer

Aaron Barlow

See also: Bockscar; Hiroshima, Bombing of; Sweeney, Charles; Tibbets, Paul. Documents: 35, 39

References

Bernstein, Barton. 1995. "The Struggle Over History: Defining the Hiroshima Narrative." In Philip Nobile, ed. *Judgment at the Smithsonian*. New York: Marlowe and Company.

Campbell, Richard H. 2005. *The Silverplate Bombers: A History and Registry of the Enola Gay and Other B-29's Configured to Carry Atomic Bombs*. Jefferson, NC: McFarland & Company.

Haggerty, Forrest. 2005. *43 Seconds to Hiroshima: The First Atomic Mission. An Autobiography of Richard H. Nelson, "Enola Gay" Radioman*. Bloomington, IN: AuthorHouse.

Hoddeson, Lillian, Paul W. Henriksen, Roger A. Meade, and Catherine L. Westfall. 1993. *Critical Assembly: A Technical History of Los Alamos During the Oppenheimer Years, 1943–1945*. New York: Cambridge University Press.

Mann, Robert A. 2004. *The B-29 Superfortress: A Comprehensive Registry of the Planes and Their Missions*. Jefferson, NC: McFarland & Company.

Newman, Robert P. 2004. *Enola Gay and the Court of History*. New York: Peter Lang Publishing.

Polmar, Norman. 2004. *The Enola Gay: The B-29 that Dropped the Atomic Bomb on Hiroshima*. Dulles, VA: Brassey's.

Sweeney, Charles, James A. Antonucci, and Marion K. Antonucci. 1997. *War's End: An Eyewitness Account of America's Last Atomic Mission*. New York: Avon Books.

Thomas, Gordon, and Max Morgan-Witts. 1977. *Ruin from the Air: The Enola Gay's Atomic Mission to Hiroshima*. London: Hamilton.

Tibbets, Paul W. 1998. *Return of the Enola Gay*. New Hope, PA: Enola Gay Remembered Inc.

Wheeler, Keith. 1982. *Bombers over Japan*. Virginia Beach, VA: Time-Life Books.

F

Fat Man

Fat Man was the name given the nuclear bomb that was the second and last used at the end of World War II, on the Japanese city of Nagasaki on August 9, 1945. Earlier called the "Mark 3," the bomb had a wide, almost round profile, the inspiration for its code name. It weighed somewhat over 10,000 pounds.

The name was also a reference to Sydney Greenstreet's character Kaspar Gutman in the 1941 John Huston film, *The Maltese Falcon*. Gutman is referred to as "the fat man." Robert Serber, a physicist whose lectures on nuclear weapons were distributed to Los Alamos staff, named the bomb and also the other model, Thin Man, which had a much narrower profile. This, too, was taken from the movies, from *The Thin Man* (W. S. Van Dyke, 1934) and its sequels—appropriately, like *The Maltese Falcon*, developed from a novel by Dashiell Hammett.

An implosion-type nuclear weapon, Fat Man was built around a solid, subcritical plutonium core and was first proposed by Richard Tolman in 1942 but was initially

Fat Man, the atomic bomb that was dropped on Nagasaki on August 9, 1945. (National Archives)

put aside in favor of the gun-type Thin Man. The Fat Man was packed in high explosives weighing over 5,000 pounds designed to explode inward, forcing the core into a supercritical state creating the real blast of the bomb. The whole thing weighed about 10,800 pounds and was 10 feet, 8 inches long and 5 feet in diameter. It was first tested during the Trinity nuclear test on July 16, 1945, at the Alamogordo Bombing and Gunnery Range in New Mexico, using a model called Gadget. It was tested again after the war at Bikini Atoll during Operation Crossroads in 1946, and over 100 of the bombs were manufactured before it was discontinued in 1950, superseded by the new Mark 4 model.

Aaron Barlow

See also: Bockscar; 509th Composite Group; Hanford, Washington; Implosion-Type Nuclear Weapon; Little Boy; Nagasaki, Bombing of; Plutonium; Project Alberta; Serber, Robert; Thin Man; Transmutation of Uranium into Plutonium; Trinity Test; Truman, Harry; Wendover Army Air Field. Document: 23

References

Campbell, Richard H. 2005. *The Silverplate Bombers: A History and Registry of the Enola Gay and Other B-29s Configured to Carry Atomic Bombs.* Jefferson, NC: McFarland & Company.

Craven, Wesley Frank, and James Lea Cate, eds. 1953. *The Pacific: Matterhorn to Nagasaki.* Vol. 5 in *The Army Air Forces in World War II.* Chicago: University of Chicago Press.

Hansen, Chuck. 1995. *Volume V: U.S. Nuclear Weapons Histories. Swords of Armageddon: U.S. Nuclear Weapons Development since 1945.* Sunnyvale, CA: Chukelea Publications.

Hoddeson, Lillian, Paul W. Henriksen, Roger A. Meade, and Catherine L. Westfall. 1993. *Critical Assembly: A Technical History of Los Alamos During the Oppenheimer Years, 1943–1945.* New York: Cambridge University Press.

Sweeney, Charles, James A. Antonucci, and Marion K. Antonucci. 1997. *War's End: An Eyewitness Account of America's Last Atomic Mission.* New York: Avon Books.

Fermi, Enrico (1901–1954)

Nuclear physicist, atomic scientist, and one of the lead scientists involved in the Manhattan Project, Enrico Fermi was born in Rome, Italy, on September 29, 1901. His great aptitude for mathematics and physics manifested itself at an early age, and encouraged by his father, he received a scholarship at the age of 17 to the University of Pisa. In 1922, the brilliant Fermi earned a doctorate in physics from the University of Pisa.

Fermi went to work in Germany until 1924, then took a position as a lecturer at the University of Florence. In 1926, he discovered the statistical laws governing particles, also known as "Fermi Statistics." In 1927, he was elected to the prestigious post of professor of theoretical physics at the University of Rome. He stayed in that post until 1938, when he won the Nobel Prize in Physics. By then, Fermi was the world's undisputed expert on neutrons. That same year, he fled Fascist Italy for the United States and took a professorship at Columbia University, which he held from 1939 to 1942.

In 1942, Fermi began work on the top-secret Manhattan Project, which produced the world's first atomic bomb in 1945. Under Fermi's direction, the first controlled

Enrico Fermi (1901–1954) at the control panel of a particle accelerator. (Library of Congress)

nuclear chain reaction was achieved at the University of Chicago in December 1942. Fermi went on to help lead the quest for an atomic weapon, which was finally achieved on July 16, 1945, when the United States detonated the world's first atomic bomb at Alamogordo, New Mexico. Less than a month later, the United States dropped two nuclear bombs on Hiroshima (August 6) and Nagasaki (August 9), hastening the end of World War II.

In 1946, Fermi accepted a faculty position at the University of Chicago and turned his attention to high-energy physics. In 1946, he was appointed to a panel charged with advising the newly established Atomic Energy Commission. In 1949, he joined a number of other scientists in voicing opposition to the development of a hydrogen (thermonuclear) bomb, but a year later, he assisted in that project, although he continued to raise concerns about the efficacy of employing such a weapon. Fermi died on November 28, 1954, in Chicago.

Paul G. Pierpaoli Jr.

See also: Advisory Committee on Uranium; Compton, Arthur Holly; Critical Mass; Einstein, Albert; Hanford, Washington; Interim Committee; Meitner, Lise; Metallurgical Laboratory; National Bureau of Standards; Nuclear Chain Reaction; Nuclear Reactor; Pegram, George Braxton; Peierls, Rudolf; Plutonium; Szilárd, Leó; Teller, Edward;

Tizard Mission; Transmutation of Uranium into Plutonium; Trinity Test; University of Chicago; Wigner, Eugene Paul. Documents: 3, 6, 15, 23, 27, 32, 39c2, 40b, 49a2

References

Bernardini, Carlo, and Luisa Bonalis, eds. 2004. *Enrico Fermi: His Work and Legacy*. New York: Springer.

Segrè, Emilio. 1995. *Enrico Fermi, Physicist*. Chicago: University of Chicago Press.

Fissile Material

The three primary fissile human-made or extracted materials—uranium-233, uranium-235, and plutonium-239—are called this because they can sustain nuclear chain reaction. They are considered a subset of fissionable material, a category that includes uranium-238, which, unless enriched, can only be fissioned through use of high-energy neutrons unlike the human-enhanced types of uranium, which can also be fissioned through the use of slow neutrons. Sufficient fissile material was necessary for construction of the first atomic bombs and was created at Oak Ridge, Tennessee, Hansford, Washington, and Los Alamos, New Mexico.

The atoms of fissile materials can be split by neutrons to create self-sustaining nuclear chain reactions releasing tremendous amounts of energy—thus bombs and, later on, in more controlled and less immediate situations, nuclear power plants.

During World War II, a new and even more powerful fissile material, plutonium-239, which is quite rare in nature, was created out of uranium-238 and harnessed for nuclear weapons, but the atomic bomb dropped on Hiroshima used only fissile uranium, called Highly Enriched Uranium.

Aaron Barlow

See also: Critical Mass; Electromagnetic Uranium Enrichment; Implosion-Type Nuclear Weapon; Plutonium; Transmutation of Uranium into Plutonium; Uranium Enrichment; Uranium-235. Documents: 6, 10

References

Croddy, Eric, Jeffrey Arthur Larsen, and James J. Wirtz. 2018. *Weapons of Mass Destruction: The Essential Reference Guide*. Santa Barbara, CA: ABC-CLIO.

Reed, Bruce Cameron. 2015. *The Physics of the Manhattan Project*. Berlin and Heidelberg: Springer Berlin Heidelberg.

509th Composite Group

The 509th Composite Group was the U.S. Army Air Forces organization created for the sole purpose of delivering atomic bombs to targets in Japan. It was formed to train crews and test equipment before eventual use of the bomb. In December of 1944, it moved to Wendover Air Force Base in Wendover, Utah, for training under command of Colonel Paul Tibbets. At the time, the group consisted of approximately 1,500 men and, among various other aircraft, the 15 "Silverplate" B-29 bombers that made up its core.

This chief aircraft of the group was a modified version of the Boeing B-29 Superfortress, the first truly long-range heavy bomber ever constructed, one that had been proposed to what was then the U.S. Army Air Corps in 1940. It was meant to eventually replace what would become the Air Corps' wartime workhorses, B-17s and B-24s, and was first tested on September 21, 1942. With a top speed of 365 miles per hour, it could cruise at 220 miles per hour for 5,830 miles and reach a ceiling of 31,850 feet. The four-engine bomber was powered by 2,200-horsepower Wright Double Cyclone engines.

The B-29 was armed with a dozen .50-caliber Browning machine guns located in the nose, tail, and three plexiglass blisters in the fuselage. Early on, there was also an M2 20-millimeter cannon in the tail. Normally, the plane could carry a 20,000-pound load of bombs. Its pressurized cabin—one of the first for a military aircraft—was meant to allow for a higher cruising altitude and improved crew comfort. From 1943 until after the end of the war, almost 4,000 B-29 Superfortresses were produced. They were only used in the Pacific, where their great range could be of use.

Soon after first deployment, the role of the B-29 was changed from high-altitude missions to low-altitude night missions, and many of the bombers saw a great deal of equipment removed to increase range and payload.

A special Silverplate version of the B-29 was designed for the unique needs of the Manhattan Project. Forty-six of them were eventually completed. They were designed starting in late November 1943 at Wright Field near Dayton, Ohio, with a prototype code-named "Silver Plated." The Silverplate bombers had much less defensive firepower than the standard B-29s so that they could handle the weight of atomic bombs. They also had only a single, much larger bomb-bay door to accommodate the sheer size of the 10,000-pound new bombs and the divergent shapes of the Thin Man and Fat Man models as well as reinforced storage areas for the bombs. The prototype bomber was flown to Muroc Field in California (now Edwards Air Force Base) in February 1944.

Testing of the newly configured B-29 continued until June, when a configuration was finally worked out that would hold and

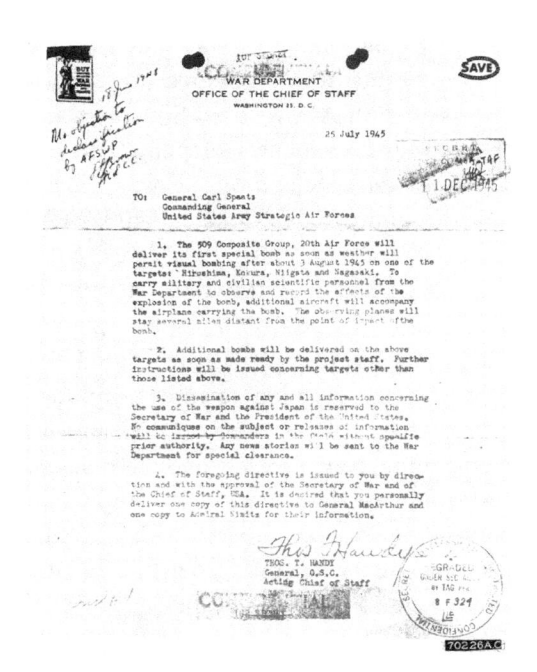

Final authorization to drop the atomic bomb on Japan. (Prisma Bildagentur/Universal Images Group via Getty Images)

release both the Fat Man and Thin Man (and its Little Boy variant) bombs, which were also being modified so that their falls would be as planned (tail boxes and drag fins needed to be appropriately configured).

By the end of the summer of 1944, 24 modified B-29s, now called Silverplates, were ordered, with 3 delivered in September to the base at Wendover, Utah, and 11 following in December. These planes were to be used for training (the remaining 10 coming later for actual combat operations). It was at Wendover in September that the 509th Composite Group was proposed by Manhattan Project head Major General Leslie Groves and Commanding General Henry "Hap" Arnold of what was now called the U.S. Army Air Force. It was activated on December 17, 1944, out of the 393rd Bomb Squadron and the 320th Troop

Carrier Squadron, the 390th Air Service Group, the 603rd Air Engineering Squadron, the 1027th Air Materiel Squadron, the 1395th Military Police Company, and the First Ordnance Squadron. It was placed under the command of Colonel Paul W. Tibbets. Training on the Silverplates commenced immediately on their arrival at Wendover. The C-54 transport planes, called "Green Hornets," from the 320th were used for ferrying scientists, military brass, and aviators between Wendover, Alamogordo, New Mexico, and other bases.

Starting in March 1945, the 509th was included in Project Alberta with the purpose of preparing the group for actual deployment of the bomb at the earliest possible time. At the same time, additional Silverplate B-29s were being added to the group for a total of what would finally be 46. The new aircraft were delivered with modifications, such as fuel injection and reversible propellers, as these technologies became available and were continually altered to reduce weight.

Starting in May 1945, the 509th began to be deployed to the island of Tinian, about 1,500 miles south-southeast of Tokyo. By July 1945, the entire group was on the island, where practice runs with both Fat Man and Little Boy took place and the 509th became combat operational.

Aaron Barlow

See also: Alamogordo Bombing and Gunnery Range; B-29 Raids against Japan; Hiroshima, Bombing of; Nagasaki, Bombing of; Project Alberta; Sweeney, Charles; Tibbets, Paul; Tinian Joint Chiefs; Wendover Army Air Field. Document: 36

References

Bowen, Lee. 1959. *Project Silverplate 1943–1946*. Vol. 1 of *A History of the Air Force Atomic Energy Program*. The U.S. Air Force Historical Division.

Campbell, Richard H. 2005. *The Silverplate Bombers: A History and Registry of the Enola Gay and Other B-29s Configured to Carry Atomic Bombs*. Jefferson, NC: McFarland & Company.

Krauss, Robert, and Amelia Krauss, eds. 2005. *The 509th Remembered: A History of the 509th Composite Group as Told by the Veterans that Dropped the Bombs on Japan*. Wichita, KS: 509th Press.

Frisch, Otto (1904–1979)

Born in Vienna, Austria, on October 1, 1904, Otto Robert Frisch, working with his aunt, Lise Meitner, in Niels Bohr's Copenhagen laboratory (she had relocated to a town in Sweden near Stockholm, about 400 miles away, due to Hitler's rise in Germany) in the 1930s, had described the process that he would call "fission," the subdivision of uranium or plutonium into two pieces of approximately equal mass, creating light nuclei where there had been heavy by splitting them in two. Frisch and Meitner were studying the implications of Otto Hahn's and Fritz Strassmann's findings of the previous year that had been shared with Meitner even before publication. This work was seminal in alerting scientists to the idea that an atomic bomb was possible.

Frisch earned his PhD in Austria in 1926 and worked in Germany until the rise of Hitler in 1933, when he moved to England before going to Copenhagen. He was back in England when war broke out, and it was there that, with Rudolf Peierls, he wrote the memorandum concluding that an atomic explosion could be generated, starting the process that led to the Manhattan Project. This led directly to the British Tube Alloys project and to Frisch's participation, as part of a British delegation, in the Manhattan Project in Los Alamos, New Mexico, where he made critical contributions to the development of the nuclear bomb.

After the war, he returned to research and teach in England. Frisch died on September 22, 1979, in Cambridge, England.

Aaron Barlow

See also: Electromagnetic Uranium Enrichment; Frisch-Peierls Memorandum; Hahn, Otto; MAUD Committee; Meitner, Lise; Nuclear Chain Reaction; Oliphant, Mark; Peierls, Rudolf; Strassmann, Fritz; Tizard Mission; Tube Alloys; Uranium Enrichment. Documents: 2, 5, 7, 39c4, 49a4

References

Bickel, Lennard. 1979. *The Deadly Element: The Story of Uranium.* New York: Stein & Day.

Dahl, Per. 1999. *Heavy Water and the Wartime Race for Nuclear Energy.* London: Institute of Physics.

Fischer, Klaus. 1993. *Changing Landscapes of Nuclear Physics: A Scientometric Study on the Social and Cognitive Position of German-Speaking Emigrants Within the Nuclear Physics Community 1921–1947.* New York: Springer-Verlag.

Frisch, Otto. 1979. *What Little I Remember.* Cambridge, U.K.: Cambridge University Press.

Gowing, Margaret. 1964. *Britain and Atomic Energy, 1939–1945.* London: Macmillan Publishing.

Frisch-Peierls Memorandum

The first detailed description of what could become a practical atomic bomb was written by Otto Frisch and Rudolf Peierls at the University of Birmingham in England in March 1940, while they were working there under the leadership of Mark Oliphant. Through the calculations presented in the memorandum, Frisch and Peierls concluded that a bomb could conceivably be constructed that could be delivered by aircraft. They presented the memorandum in two parts, an argument and outline for the nonscientist and a more detailed scientific paper.

It was this pair of papers that led to creation of the MAUD Committee in England and the English/Canadian Tube Alloys project, as well as the Manhattan Project in the United States.

The research and thought that went into the memorandum began with a visit Frisch made in 1938 to his aunt, Lise Meitner, who had fled to Sweden after Germany's annexation of Austria. She introduced him to the results of Otto Hahn and Fritz Strassmann's experiment showing that the collision of a neutron with a uranium nucleus would produce barium. Examining the results, Frisch and Meitner wondered if the uranium nucleus might have split in two. Working together just a year after the Hahn/Strassmann experiment, they developed a hypothesis based on this possibility and named the process "fission," borrowing from biology where "fission" means the division of one entity into two (or more) new entities that resemble the first. This was quickly taken up by other physicists, including Niels Bohr, who introduced American scientists to the concept.

Working at the University of Birmingham under the general supervision of Mark Oliphant but apart from Oliphant's secret work on radar (Frisch and Peierls were at first considered "enemy aliens"), Frisch began experimenting with what would become the thermal diffusion method of uranium enrichment, following work by German Klaus Clusius. Peierls was working to create a chain reaction using fast neutrons from fission, though he had earlier decided that it would take tons of uranium to create the type of reaction that would be useful for an atomic bomb.

Working with Peierls's calculation but substituting uranium-235 for uranium-238, Frisch discovered that the amount needed for a bomb could be measured in pounds instead of tons. Suddenly, construction of an atomic bomb seemed possible and even likely. Realizing the importance of this discovery, Frisch and Peierls composed a two-part memorandum, the first nontechnical and the other meant primarily for fellow physicists. They argued for the construction of atomic bombs as a deterrent, for, they stated, German scientists would be working along the same lines.

The two presented their memorandum to Oliphant, who grasped its implications and, in turn, forwarded it to Henry Tizard, chair of Great Britain's Committee for the Scientific Survey of Air Warfare. In response, CSSAW created the MAUD Committee to pursue further study. The MAUD reports of July 1941 concluded that it was, indeed, feasible to create an atomic bomb, sparking creation of the British/Canadian Tube Alloy project and accelerating American efforts in the same direction.

It is quite possible to argue that the Frisch-Peierls Memorandum speeded up creation of an atomic bomb by, at minimum, a matter of months, which, during war, can be a critical amount of time.

Aaron Barlow

See also: Frisch, Otto; MAUD Committee; Oliphant, Mark; Peierls, Rudolf; Tizard Mission; Tube Alloys; Uranium Enrichment. Documents: 5, 7

References

Bernstein, Jeremy. 2011. "A Memorandum that Changed the World." *American Journal of Physics* 79, no. 5: 441–446.

Frisch, Otto Robert. 1967. "The Discovery of Fission—How It All Began." *Physics Today* 20, no. 11: 43–48.

Frisch, Otto Robert. 1979. *What Little I Remember.* Cambridge, U.K.: Cambridge University Press.

Gowing, Margaret. 1964. *Britain and Atomic Energy, 1935–1945.* London: Macmillan Publishing.

Peierls, Rudolf. 1985. *Bird of Passage: Recollections of a Physicist.* Princeton, NJ: Princeton University Press.

G

Gaseous Uranium Enrichment

Developed as part of the British Tube Alloys project, the process of Gaseous Uranium Enrichment was used at Oak Ridge, Tennessee, through the S-50 and then the K-25 facilities. It was one of three methods of enrichment used at the Clinton Engineer Works at Oak Ridge to produce "oralloy," as it was called for reasons of secrecy during World War II (it came from "Oak Ridge Alloy"), the enriched uranium necessary for construction of the atomic bomb.

Through a process of forcing gaseous uranium hexafluoride through semipermeable membranes, uranium-235 is separated from the much more prevalent uranium-238. Through repetitions of the process, a high percentage of the uranium-235 can be extracted.

Gaseous diffusion was first developed at the Clarendon Laboratory in Oxford, England, by Francis Simon and Nicholas Kurti and became part of the Manhattan Project when the Tube Alloys project was incorporated into it after the signing of the Quebec Agreement on August 19, 1943.

The principle behind gaseous diffusion was first formulated by Thomas Graham in 1848 and is known as Graham's Law of Effusion. The upshot of the law is that the rate of effusion (escape from containment through a small hole) of a gas changes depending on molecular weight. This allows for the separation of molecules of differing weight, such as U-235 and U-238. The gas with more lighter molecules was called "enriched" and the rest "depleted." The volatile gas uranium hexafluoride was used for the process, for the weight of the fluorine was steady. That is, differences in molecular weight only occurred between molecules including U-235 and those including U-238.

Unfortunately, a single pass through a porous membrane results in very little separation, necessitating multiple passes before most of the U-238 was removed (leaving the rest as enriched uranium, that is, U-235). Not only were the multiple passes time-consuming but they required a great deal of electricity for the necessary pumping, heating, and cooling, making the process extremely expensive. Even so, it proved more efficient than the other two options (thermal diffusion and electromagnetic uranium enrichment) and continued in use after the end of the war.

Aaron Barlow

See also: Clinton Engineer Works; Electromagnetic Uranium Enrichment; Oak Ridge, Tennessee; Quebec Conference, 1st; Thermal Diffusion Uranium Enrichment; Tube Alloys; Uranium-235. Documents: 7, 40f

Reference

Cotton, Simon. 2006. "Uranium hexafluoride and isotope separation." In *Lanthanide and Actinide Chemistry*, 163–165. Chichester, West Sussex, England: John Wiley and Sons, Ltd.

Groves, Leslie Richard (1896–1970)

The U.S. Army general who oversaw the Manhattan Project, Leslie Richard "Dick" Groves was born in Albany, New York, on August 17, 1896. Groves attended the University of Washington and the Massachusetts Institute of Technology. He secured an appointment to the U.S. Military Academy at West Point, graduating in 1918, and entered the Army Corps of Engineers.

After initial training at the Engineer School at Fort Humphreys (later Fort Belvoir), Virginia, Groves served in Hawaii, Texas, Nicaragua, Washington, D.C., and Missouri. Assigned to the War Department in 1939, Groves became chief of the Corps of Engineers Operations Branch and in 1941 deputy head of the Construction Division. In these capacities, Groves oversaw the vast expansion of military camps and training facilities across the United States. He then supervised construction of the Pentagon, the world's largest office building.

Success in a variety of engineering projects led to Groves's promotion to brigadier general and assignment in September 1942 to head the Manhattan Project, charged with development and construction of an atomic bomb. Groves controlled 129,000 personnel and $2 billion in spending. He was promoted to major general in March 1944. This vast effort resulted in the explosion of the first atomic device at Alamogordo, New Mexico, on July 16, 1945. Groves advised President Harry S. Truman to employ the bomb and assisted in the selection of Japanese target cities.

After the war, Groves sought international control over atomic energy. When this did not occur, Groves organized the Army Forces Special Weapons Project to study military uses of atomic energy. Promoted to lieutenant general in January 1948, Groves retired from the army that same month and became vice president for research of the Rand Corporation. He retired altogether in 1961. Groves died in Washington, D.C., on July 13, 1970.

Ryan E. Doltz

General Leslie Groves (1896–1970) and J. Robert Oppenheimer (1904–1967) at the site of the detonation of the Trinity test near Alamogordo, New Mexico. The test, which was the first explosion of an atomic bomb, took place on July 16, 1945. (Library of Congress)

See also: Clinton Engineer Works; Hanford, Washington; Hiroshima, Bombing of; Los Alamos Laboratory; Nagasaki, Bombing of; Oak Ridge, Tennessee; Truman, Harry. Documents: 10, 11, 13, 15, 20, 23, 29, 33, 34, 38

References

Groves, Leslie R. 1962. *Now It Can Be Told: The Story of the Manhattan Project*. New York: Harper & Row.

Lawren, William. 1988. *The General and the Bomb*. New York: Dodd, Mead and Co.

Norris, Robert S. 2002. *Racing for the Bomb: General Leslie R. Groves, The Manhattan Project's Indispensable Man*. South Royalton, VT: Steerforth Press.

Gun-Type Fission Weapon

The phrase "Gun Type" is used to describe atomic bombs constructed to explode through the firing of one mass of uranium-235 into another inside the bomb casing itself. It was this type of bomb that, named "Little Boy," was dropped on Hiroshima, Japan, on August 6, 1945, in the first military use of atomic power.

A conventional explosive shoots a hollow enriched uranium "bullet" through a tube (the gun barrel) inside the bomb casing to hit a target cylinder also made of enriched uranium. The collision, if quick enough and powerful enough, creates a supercritical mass resulting in an atomic explosion. The bomb casing is necessarily long and generally slender, giving the bomb its initial nickname "Thin Man." The name was taken from a popular series of *Thin Man* movies starring William Powell and Myrna Loy and inspired by Dashiell Hammett's novel *The Thin Man*. With changes in design, the name was changed to "Little Boy."

The reason that the "bullet" uranium needs to crash quickly into the "target" uranium is that a slower collision will allow spontaneous fission instead of a chain reaction and explosion. The uranium, in this bomb, is enriched to more than 80 percent uranium-235. Initially, the Thin Man bomb was meant to use plutonium-239, but it was soon established that the spontaneous fission rate (due to the plutonium-240 also present) was so high that the bomb would likely explode prematurely and with much less force.

Aaron Barlow

See also: Hiroshima, Bombing of; Little Boy; Thin Man; Uranium-235

References

Hoddeson, Lillian, Paul W. Henriksen, Roger A. Meade, and Catherine L. Westfall. 1993. *Critical Assembly: A Technical History of Los Alamos During the Oppenheimer Years, 1943–1945*. New York: Cambridge University Press.

Nichols, Kenneth D. 1987. *The Road to Trinity: A Personal Account of How America's Nuclear Policies Were Made*. New York: William Morrow and Company.

Serber, Robert, and Robert Crease. 1998. *Peace & War: Reminiscences of a Life on the Frontiers of Science*. New York: Columbia University Press.

H

Hahn, Otto (1879–1968)

A German chemist, Otto Hahn was born on March 8, 1879, in Frankfurt. In 1901, he was awarded a doctorate in organic chemistry at the University of Marburg. Starting in 1907, he would collaborate often with Lise Meitner, who, working with her nephew, Otto Frisch, in 1939, would expand upon research by Hahn and Fritz Strassmann (which would win them a Nobel Prize in Chemistry) and call the phenomenon Hahn and Strassmann first observed "fission." Hahn and Strassmann had found traces of an alkaline earth metal in a sample where, by the theories of the time, it should not belong. On a visit to Denmark, Hahn discussed this problem with Niels Bohr, Lise Meitner, and Otto Frisch. Late in 1938, he wrote to Meitner describing having observed radium isotopes that "burst" into barium, something previous theories could not account for. The next year, Meitner and Frisch described this bursting as "fission." It was this discovery that alerted scientists to the possibility of creating an atomic bomb.

Because he stayed in Germany throughout World War II, Hahn was suspected of having worked in the Nazi nuclear program, but, as his work had purely been in chemistry and apart from research toward a bomb, he was allowed to return home to Germany after the war. He died on July 28, 1968, in Gottingen.

Aaron Barlow

See also: Alsos Mission; Frisch, Otto; Meitner, Lise; Strassmann, Fritz

References

Beyerchen, Alan D. 1977. *Scientists under Hitler.* New Haven, CT: Yale University Press.

Fermi, Laura. 1962. *The Story of Atomic Energy.* New York: Random House.

Hahn, Otto. 1970. *My Life.* London: Macdonald & Co.

McKay, Alwyn. 1984. *The Making of the Atomic Age.* Oxford: Oxford University Press.

Rhodes, Richard. 1986. *The Making of the Atomic Bomb.* New York: Simon & Schuster.

Hanford, Washington

The Hanford Engineer Works was a huge (some 600 square miles) horseshoe-shaped site along the Columbia River, not far from Yakima in South Central Washington State. Construction began soon after that of the Clinton Engineer Works at Oak Ridge, Tennessee, commencing in the early part of 1943. Colonel Franklin Matthias, a civil engineer, oversaw the building of three nuclear reactors (or "piles," as they were then often known) and four chemical separation plants. Larger than the X-10 of Oak Ridge, the reactors were known by letters B, D, and F, with construction of B commencing on August 27, 1943, though it stalled until October. It was B that would provide the bulk of the plutonium used in the Fat Man bomb that was exploded over Nagasaki on August 9, 1945.

The site was selected because it was distant from the Oak Ridge site, because it was both remote and expansive with space for keeping the reactors far from each other and from laboratories, because it was far enough from even small population centers for safety and security and was far (but not too far) from railroad lines and highways for the same reason, because it had an abundant water supply and was close to major electric supply, and because the land itself was stable enough to bear the weight of the plants. The site was quickly acquired by the U.S. Army Corps of Engineer and code-named "Site W." The 1,500 or so people living in the area, including a number of Native Americans, were relocated.

E. I. DuPont de Nemours and Company was selected for construction, eventually employing a force of almost 45,000 workers by the middle of 1944. They were housed off the site near the now-empty village of Hansford in a construction camp, while the staff of the project lived in a new town of Richland Village, where 25 dormitories and 4,300 family units were built. By the time of the dropping of the bombs on Hiroshima and Nagasaki, the Hanford Engineer Works consisted of over 500 buildings, including the three nuclear reactors and three plutonium "canyons." There were almost 400 miles of roads and over 150 miles of railway on the site, 64 underground radioactive waste tanks called "tank farms," and four electrical substations.

The B Reactor at Hanford, designed by Enrico Fermi at the University of Chicago, was the world's first plutonium nuclear reactor and the largest of the time. It was designed to produce plutonium-239 out of uranium-238, and it fueled both the Trinity Test and the Fat Man bomb that was used over Nagasaki. It was cooled by massive amounts of water pumped from the Columbia River; the water was then discharged into settling basins for cooling and initial radioactive decay of contaminated material.

The B Reactor produced its first nuclear chain reaction on September 26, 1944, followed by the D Reactor in December and the F Reactor the next February, each of which followed closely the design of the B Reactor. The reactors were designed to be independent of each other, events at one having no impact on the operations of the others. Reactor B produced plutonium starting on November 6, 1944, with the first shipment arriving at the Los Alamos, New Mexico, laboratory on February 3, 1945.

Aaron Barlow

See also: Fermi, Enrico; Los Alamos Laboratory; Plutonium; Uranium-235; U.S. Army Corps of Engineers. Document: 40h

References

Findlay, John M., and Bruce Hevly. 2011. *Atomic Frontier Days: Hanford and the American West*. Seattle: University of Washington Press.

Gerber, Michele. 1992. *Legend and Legacy: Fifty Years of Defense Production at the Hanford Site*. Richland, Washington: Westinghouse Hanford Company.

Thayer, Harry. 1996. *Management of the Hanford Engineer Works in World War II: How the Corps, DuPont and the Metallurgical Laboratory Fast Tracked the Original Plutonium Works*. New York: American Society of Civil Engineers Press.

Hiroshima, Bombing of (August 6, 1945)

The U.S. bombing of the Japanese city of Hiroshima on August 6, 1945, was the first

The atomic cloud rising over Hiroshima on August 6, 1945. (Library of Congress)

combat use of the atomic bomb. On July 25, 1945, commander of U.S. Strategic Air Forces General Carl Spaatz received orders to employ the 509th Composite Group, Twentieth Air Force, in a "special bomb" attack on selected target cities in Japan, specifically Hiroshima, Kokura, Niigata, or Nagasaki. Following rejection of conditions promulgated by the Potsdam Proclamation on July 26, a declaration threatening Japan with total destruction if unconditional surrender was not accepted, President Harry S. Truman then authorized use of the special bomb.

Assembled in secrecy and loaded on the Boeing B-29 Superfortress Enola Gay, the bomb consisted of a core of uranium isotope 235 shielded by several hundred pounds of lead, encased in explosives designed to condense the uranium and initiate a fission reaction. Nicknamed "Little Boy," the bomb possessed a force equivalent to 12,500 tons of TNT (12.5 kilotons).

The Enola Gay, commanded by Colonel Paul Tibbets, departed Tinian at 2:45 a.m. on August 6. Two B-29s assigned as scientific and photographic observers followed, and the three aircraft rendezvoused over Iwo Jima for the run over Japan. Captain William Parsons of the U.S. Navy completed the bomb's arming in the air shortly after 6:30 a.m. The flight to Japan was uneventful, and Tibbets was informed at 7:47 a.m. by weather planes over the targets that Hiroshima was clear for bombing. Japan's eighth largest city (it had about 245,000 residents in August 1945), Hiroshima was an important port on southern Honshu and headquarters of the Japanese Second Army.

The Enola Gay arrived over the city at an altitude of 31,600 feet and dropped the bomb at 8:15:17 a.m. local time. After a descent of nearly six miles, the bomb detonated 43 seconds later, some 1,890 feet over a clinic and about 800 feet from the aiming point, Aioi Bridge. The initial fireball expanded to 110 yards in diameter, generating heat in excess of 300,000 degrees centigrade, with core temperatures over 50 million degrees centigrade. At the clinic directly beneath the explosion, the temperature was several thousand degrees. The immediate concussion destroyed almost everything within two miles of ground zero. The resultant mushroom cloud rose to 50,000 feet and was observed by B-29s more than 360 miles away. After 15 minutes, the atmosphere dropped radioactive "black rain," adding to the death and destruction.

Four square miles of Hiroshima's heart disappeared in seconds, including 62,000 buildings. More than 71,000 Japanese died, another 20,000 were wounded, and 171,000 were left homeless. Some estimates place the number of killed at more than 200,000. About one-third of those killed instantly were soldiers. Most elements of the Japanese Second General Army were at physical training on the grounds of Hiroshima Castle when the bomb exploded. Barely 900 yards from the explosion's epicenter, the castle and its residents were vaporized. Also killed was one American prisoner of war in the exercise area. All died in less than a second. Radiation sickness began the next day and added to the death toll over several years.

Following three observation circuits over Hiroshima, the Enola Gay and its escorts turned for Tinian, touching down at 2:58 p.m. The bombing mission, 12 hours and 13 minutes long and covering 2,960 miles, changed the nature of warfare but did not immediately end the war. Truman released a statement on August 7 describing the weapon and calling on Japan to surrender, but his message was ignored by most Japanese leaders as propaganda. The United States dropped another atomic bomb on August 9, this time on Nagasaki.

Mark E. Van Rhyn

See also: Enola Gay; Little Boy; Nagasaki, Bombing of; Potsdam Conference; Tibbets, Paul; Truman, Harry. Documents: 40a, 40b, 40c, 41

References

Maddox, Robert James. 1995. *Weapons for Victory: The Hiroshima Decision Fifty Years Later.* Columbia: University of Missouri Press.

Nobile, Philip. 1995. *Judgment at the Smithsonian: The Bombing of Hiroshima and Nagasaki.* New York: Marlowe and Company.

Thomas, Gordon, and Max Morgan-Witts. 1977. *Enola Gay.* New York: Stein & Day.

I

Implosion-Type Nuclear Weapon

Uncertain what the best course would be, the United States, through the Manhattan Project, developed two types of nuclear weapons: gun-type and implosion-type. The more advanced and plutonium-powered implosion-type was used at Nagasaki on August 9, 1945. In it, huge amounts of explosives were packed around a plutonium core, giving the bomb the shape that inspired its name, Fat Man, after Sydney Greenstreet's character Kaspar Gutman in the 1941 Walter Huston film *The Maltese Falcon*.

Both types of bomb were fission weapons, their explosions created through quick assemblage of a supercritical mass of fissile plutonium, in the Fat Man case, or uranium, as in Little Boy. The first nuclear bomb exploded—the Trinity Test at Alamogordo, New Mexico, on July 16, 1945—was an implosion-type nuclear weapon. Both it and Fat Man exploded with the force of about 20 kilotons of TNT.

The difference in look between the bombs was necessitated by the configurations needed for their detonation processes. The functional part of an implosion-type weapon is built around a neutron initiator of polonium-beryllium in a series of spheres. The innermost of these is a plutonium sphere surrounded by uranium-238. Next is a layer of conventional explosives whose power is focused inward through lenses, forcing the uranium, the plutonium, and the initiator together to create a critical mass and explosion.

Aaron Barlow

See also: Fat Man; Little Boy; Nagasaki, Bombing of; Trinity Test

References

Croddy, Eric A., James J. Wirtz, and Jeffrey Larsen, eds. 2005. *Weapons of Mass Destruction: An Encyclopedia of Worldwide Policy, Technology, and History.* Santa Barbara, CA: ABC-CLIO, Inc.

Hoddeson, Lillian, Paul W. Henriksen, Roger A. Meade, and Catherine L. Westfall. 2004. *Critical Assembly: A Technical History of Los Alamos During the Oppenheimer Years, 1943–1945.* New York: Cambridge University Press.

Rhodes, Richard. 1995. *Dark Sun: The Making of the Hydrogen Bomb.* New York: Simon & Schuster.

Interim Committee

Established in 1945 by U.S. Secretary of War Henry Stimson, its name of the "Interim Committee" was meant to keep its purpose opaque. It met for the first time on May 9. Stimson served as chair with his aide George Harrison as alternate. Members of the committee included undersecretary of the navy Ralph Bard, assistant secretary of state for economic affairs William Clayton, Vannevar Bush, James Conant, Karl Compton, and James Byrnes representing the White House. Included in the committee was a scientific panel composed of Arthur Compton, Ernest Lawrence, J. Robert Oppenheimer, and Enrico Fermi.

The real purpose of the Interim Committee was to explore and recommend uses of the already nearly functional and practical nuclear bomb. Its report, issued on June 16, 1945, the day of the Trinity Test, concluded that the members of the committee "see no acceptable alternative to direct military use" of the atomic bomb by the United States given the military and political situations of the time.

On August 17, 1945, just two weeks before Japan's surrender and the end of World War II, the science committee of the Interim Committee sent a letter over J. Robert Oppenheimer's signature to U.S. Secretary of War Henry Stimson, the Interim Committee head, on broader questions of atomic bombs, questions muted in the earlier report because of the necessary immediate focus. The letter claimed (1) that the atomic bombs that already existed would soon be superseded; (2) that effective countermeasures against even current atomic bombs were unlikely to be found; (3) that hegemony in military atomic power would not likely last; and (4) that there would be little deterrent effect concerning war provided by atomic bombs. Though prescient, the letter would have little impact on U.S. military nuclear policy.

Aaron Barlow

See also: Bush, Vannevar; Compton, Arthur Holly; Conant, James Bryant; Fermi, Enrico; Lawrence, Ernest Orlando; Oppenheimer, Julius Robert; Stimson, Henry Lewis. Document: 28

References

Hewlett, Richard G., and Oscar E. Anderson. 1962. *The New World, 1939–1946*. University Park: Pennsylvania State University Press.

Jones, Vincent. 1985. *Manhattan: The Army and the Atomic Bomb*. Washington, D.C.: U.S. Army Center of Military History.

L

Laurence, William Leonard (1888–1977)

Born in what is now Lithuania as Leib Wolf Siew on March 7, 1888, Laurence emigrated to the United States in 1905 and became a citizen in 1913. A lawyer by training (he earned an LLB from Boston University School of Law in 1925), he soon switched to journalism with a focus on scientific issues. In 1930, he went to work for *The New York Times*, where he worked until he retired in 1964, focusing his work on scientific issues. He died on March 19, 1977, in Spain.

Laurence's reporting, though it earned him two Pulitzer Prizes, has remained controversial, with political pundits and journalists on the left like Amy Goodman complaining that he was too closely associated with the U.S. government and even on its payroll when writing the stories that earned him the prize.

With extraordinary access to top-secret operations, Laurence was the only American journalist to witness either the Trinity Test or the bombing of Nagasaki.

Aaron Barlow

See also: Bockscar; Nagasaki, Bombing of; Trinity Test. Document: 49b1

References

Keever, Beverly. 2004. *News Zero: The New York Times and the Bomb*. Monroe, ME: Common Courage Press.

Laurence, William Leonard. 1946. *Dawn Over Zero: The Story of the Atomic Bomb*. New York: Knopf.

Lifton, Jay, and Greg Mitchel. 1995. *Hiroshima in America: Fifty Years of Denial*. New York: Putnam.

Lawrence, Ernest Orlando (1901–1958)

The inventor of the cyclotron, a machine that accelerates nuclear particles so they can be smashed into their smaller constituents, Ernest Orlando Lawrence won the 1939 Nobel Prize in Physics for the invention. A major factor in the development of the nation's nuclear technology, his best-known research concerned the structure of the atom and the ways in which it changed under different conditions. The famous Lawrence Berkeley Laboratory and the Lawrence Livermore National Laboratory are both named after him.

The oldest of two sons born to parents of Norwegian descent, Lawrence was born in Canton, South Dakota, on August 8, 1901. His father was superintendent of the local school system and later became president of the state teachers' college. His mother was a former mathematics teacher. As a boy, Lawrence went to local public schools in Canton and Pierre, the state capital. He was not particularly good at anything except science, but he graduated from high school at age 16 and first attended college on a science scholarship from 1918 to 1919 at St. Olaf's College in Northfield, Minnesota. However, he transferred to South Dakota's state university later in 1919 and graduated from the school in 1922.

He earned a master's degree from the University of Minnesota in 1923, after which he spent a year studying at the University of Chicago. Lawrence enrolled at Yale University in 1924 and finished his doctorate there in 1925. A National Research Council postdoctoral fellowship allowed him to continue doing research at Yale until 1927. Most of his work at this time concerned the process of ionization, in which atoms are electrified by removing or adding one or more of their electrons. His measurements of the mercury atom's ionization potential were called the most accurate ever.

When his fellowship expired later in 1927, Lawrence started working at Yale as an assistant professor of physics. Toward the end of 1928, he moved to the University of California at Berkeley, where he took a job as associate physics professor. The following year, Lawrence got the basic idea for what would become his masterpiece: the cyclotron.

He knew from his studies of electromagnetic theory that no matter how far a charged particle has to travel in a magnetic field, its speed increases in proportion to the length of its path. Thus, it always takes the particle the same amount of time to complete a semicircular path. Lawrence's idea was to speed the particles up even more by giving them an electrical boost every time they passed a certain mark. This would allow the particles to go faster and faster without using huge amounts of electricity—only properly timed little jolts. The key to his idea was to use a D-shaped path instead of the traditional linear path to save room and electricity.

Lawrence demonstrated a miniature version of his new device at a meeting of the National Academy of Science in 1930. That year he was also promoted to full professor of physics at the University of California at the unusually young age of 29. In 1932, he founded the university's Radiation Laboratory to put his cyclotrons in, and in 1936, he became director of the facility.

Lawrence spent most of the 1930s building ever-larger cyclotrons, because the larger the machines are, the more energy they can produce to propel nuclear particles. With the help of his brother, a researcher with the Yale School of Medicine, Lawrence discovered that not only was the radiation he was dealing with very dangerous, it was also a powerful tool against cancerous tumors. This revelation helped Lawrence raise the money he needed to build his biggest cyclotron yet—a 60-inch machine with a 225-ton magnet—in 1938.

In 1939, Lawrence won the Nobel Prize for his invention of the cyclotron, but he continued his research at a furious pace. In 1940, he and his team isolated the elements plutonium and neptunium, and by 1941, he had built a cyclotron that could produce four times the power of his best cyclotron. It was this machine that produced what Lawrence called the "first man-made cosmic ray" later that year.

Lawrence was one of six scientists whom the government asked in 1941 to decide whether the country's atomic energy program was important enough to be continued and, if so, how much money to spend on it. When the Japanese attack on Pearl Harbor helped to answer this question, Lawrence was appointed one of three program chiefs for the hastily organized Office of Scientific Research and Development (OSRD). The OSRD's main purpose was to facilitate and oversee all-out work to develop the uranium fission bomb.

Lawrence was slightly ahead of the game, since he had already started work on electromagnetically separating two uranium isotopes, U-235 and U-238 (the former is the crucial ingredient in the atomic bomb). Plans for his biggest cyclotron ever were rushed to completion in 1942, and the machine was immediately put to work as a large-scale uranium isotope separator. By the end of that year, the government had authorized $350 million for what became known as the Oak Ridge Project, which featured six Lawrence cyclotrons. It was these machines that isolated the uranium 235 used in the atomic bombs dropped on Japan.

After the war, Lawrence resumed his regular research, and in 1948, he produced the first man-made mesons, a type of elementary atomic particle that had previously been found only in the cosmic rays that come to earth from space. In the last decade of his life, Lawrence worked frequently as an industrial and government consultant on the topic of nuclear energy.

Although Lawrence was a strong advocate of the use of atomic weapons against Japan during World War II, he later became an equally strong voice against the government's atomic bomb–testing programs. He died on August 27, 1958, in Palo Alto, California after surgery to alleviate his chronic ulcerative colitis. Lawrence married in 1932 and had two sons and four daughters. Among his favorite hobbies were music, boating, tennis, and skating. In 1961, element number 103 was named lawrencium in his honor.

Amanda de la Garza

See also: Electromagnetic Uranium Enrichment; Office of Scientific Research and Development; Plutonium. Document: 27

References

Asimov, Isaac. 1972. *Asimov's Biographical Encyclopedia of Science & Technology.* Garden City, NJ: Doubleday.

Childs, Herbert. 1968. *An American Genius: The Life of Ernesto Orlando Lawrence, Father of the Cyclotron.* New York: Dutton.

Mann, W. B. 1940. *The Cyclotron.* New York: Chemical Publishing.

Millar, David, ed. 1996. *The Cambridge Dictionary of Scientists.* Cambridge, U.K.: Cambridge University Press.

Williams, Trevor, ed. 1982. *Biographical Dictionary of Scientists.* New York: Harper Collins.

Little Boy

A gun-type nuclear bomb, Little Boy was the code name given to the weapon the United States exploded over Hiroshima, Japan, on August 6, 1945, effectively ending World War II. The blast was the equivalent of 15 kilotons of TNT, by far the largest explosion ever used in warfare to that point and only surpassed by the bomb used three days later over Nagasaki. The bomb itself weighed just under 10,000 pounds.

The bomb was designed and constructed at the Los Alamos Laboratory under the direction of Lieutenant Commander Francis Birch after the earlier Thin Man design had been abandoned. Thin Man had been based on the use of plutonium-239, but that had not proven practical, the bomb being too unstable to be trusted not to pre-ignite into a smaller explosion. Use of the less volatile uranium-235 necessitated changes in design leading to the new Little Boy model.

The Little Boy model was seen as a stopgap useful until the more powerful Fat Man plutonium bombs could be produced, something slow in happening because of continuing difficulty with the process of extracting plutonium from uranium. Produced in a hurry in response to perceived

Little Boy, the atomic bomb that exploded over Hiroshima on August 6, 1945, being loaded into the bomb-bay of the Enola Gay, a Boeing B-29 Superfortress. (National Archives)

necessity, it only remained in the United States arsenal until 1951.

Because it would not be using plutonium, the switch to what would become the Little Boy design allowed for a much simpler bomb, at least in terms of its construction. As it was feared that the implosion-type bomb could not be completed fast enough, it was decided that work on Little Boy would continue as well, even though the more powerful plutonium bomb was preferred.

Unlike Fat Man, which had been tested at Trinity, Little Boy was exploded for the first time in hostilities, on August 6, 1945, over Hiroshima, Japan. The bomb was 10 feet long with a diameter of two feet, four inches. Fully armed, it weighed about 9,700 pounds. Its bullet and target system forced two pieces of uranium-235 together with enough force to create a supercritical mass and, therefore, an atomic explosion. Oddly enough, the bullet was the larger of the two pieces of uranium.

Aaron Barlow

See also: Enola Gay; Fat Man; 509th Composite Group; Gun-Type Fission Weapon; Hanford, Washington; Nagasaki, Bombing of; Plutonium; Project Alberta; Serber, Robert; Thin Man; Truman, Harry; Wendover Army Air Field. Document: 39

References

Abrahamson, James L., and Paul H. Carew. 2002. *Vanguard of American Atomic Deterrence.* Westport, CT: Praeger.

Bernstein, Jeremy. 2007. *Nuclear Weapons: What You Need to Know.* Cambridge, U.K.: Cambridge University Press.

Campbell, Richard H. 2005. *The Silverplate Bombers: A History and Registry of the Enola Gay and Other B-29s Configured to*

Carry Atomic Bombs. Jefferson, NC: McFarland & Company.

Gosling, F. G. 1994. *The Manhattan Project: Making the Atomic Bomb.* Washington, D.C.: U.S. Department of Energy.

Groves, Leslie R. 1962. *Now It Can Be Told: The Story of the Manhattan Project.* New York: Harper and Row.

Hoddeson, Lillian, Paul W. Henriksen, Roger A. Meade, and Catherine L. Westfall. 1993. *Critical Assembly: A Technical History of Los Alamos During the Oppenheimer Years, 1943–1945.* New York: Cambridge University Press.

Nichols, Kenneth D. 1987. *The Road to Trinity: A Personal Account of How America's Nuclear Policies Were Made.* New York: William Morrow and Company.

Rhodes, Richard. 1986. *The Making of the Atomic Bomb.* New York: Simon & Schuster.

Serber, Robert, and Robert Crease. 1998. *Peace & War: Reminiscences of a Life on the Frontiers of Science.* New York: Columbia University Press

Los Alamos Laboratory (Project Y)

At the suggestion of physicist J. Robert Oppenheimer, who had spent time in the area in his late teens, Manhattan Project head General Leslie Groves chose Los Alamos, New Mexico, as the location for the primary laboratory for the project. The site had been a school, the Los Alamos Ranch School, since 1917. The project took over the site in February 1943. Groves had wanted an isolated site, and the school, with its existing facilities making immediate occupation possible, was surrounded by unused federal land.

Oppenheimer was appointed first director of the laboratory and remained in that position until the end of 1945. He initially focused research on the Thin Man model of a gun-type fission weapon, but this was abandoned in April 1944 on confirmation that the risks of pre-detonation due to the presence of plutonium-240 in the plutonium at hand was too great. An alternative, called "Little Boy," using uranium-235 was settled on and would become the model used in the bombing of Hiroshima, Japan, on August 6, 1945.

The main focus of research until close to the end of World War II, however, moved to the Fat Boy model, an implosion-type nuclear weapon that would be tested at the nearby Alamogordo Bombing and Gunnery Range as the Trinity Test on July 16, 1945, and that would be used in the raid on Nagasaki, Japan, on August 9, 1945. The work wasn't limited to that, however. Much of the other work at Los Alamos focused on extracting sufficiently pure quantities of fissionable uranium and plutonium for practical use in atomic bombs.

From almost the day the Manhattan Project took the site over until the end of the war, the Los Alamos Laboratory was the hub of project activities. The spokes acted as conduits to Los Alamos and included, of course, both the Oak Ridge, Tennessee, and Hanford, Washington, sites and Wendover Army Air Field as well as a number of universities, principally the University of California but including the University of Chicago and many others. Outflow from Los Alamos went to the Trinity site at Alamogordo Bombing and Gunnery Range, back to Wendover Army Air Field and, through Project Alberta, to the Tinian Islands in preparation for the raids on Japan.

Aaron Barlow

See also: Alamogordo Bombing and Gunnery Range; Fat Man; Groves, Leslie Richard; Little Boy; Oppenheimer, Julius Robert; Project Alberta; Thin Man; Tinian Joint

Chiefs; Trinity Test; Wendover Army Air Field. Documents: 10, 40i

References

Hawkins, David, Edith C. Truslow, and Ralph C. Smith. 1961. *Manhattan District History, Project Y, the Los Alamos Story.* Los Angeles: Tomash Publishers.

Hoddeson, Lillian, Paul W. Henriksen, Roger A. Meade, and Catherine L. Westfall. 1993. *Critical Assembly: A Technical History of Los Alamos During the Oppenheimer Years, 1943–1945.* New York: Cambridge University Press.

Smyth, Henry DeWolf. 1945. *Atomic Energy for Military Purposes: The Official Report on the Development of the Atomic Bomb under the Auspices of the United States Government, 1940–1945.* Princeton, NJ: Princeton University Press.

M

MAUD Committee

Chaired by George Thomson, the MAUD Committee was a subcommittee of the British Committee for the Scientific Survey of Air Warfare. Members included Mark Oliphant, John Cockcroft, James Chadwick, Philip Moon, Patrick Blackett, Charles Ellis, William Haworth, and others. The committee's name, appearance aside, was not an acronym; it was taken from what was initially an enigmatic use of the name "Maud" in a telegram from Niels Bohr to Otto Frisch. It was used because of its opaque nature, allowing the committee to operate under an indecipherable moniker.

The committee was organized in response to information coming to England about an experiment in Berlin in which Otto Hahn and Fritz Strassmann bombarded uranium with slow neutrons. They remarked that barium had been produced and speculated that the nucleus of the uranium had been split. Lise Meitner was informed of this by Hahn and, with her nephew, Otto Frisch, came up with a theoretical explanation of the result, which had implications that raised the possibility of an atomic bomb. Soon, the Committee for the Scientific Survey of Air Warfare had taken an interest and began exploring the feasibility of such a bomb. A team at Imperial College London, led by Thomson, failed to create a chain reaction and also concluded that the amount of uranium needed for a bomb would make it prohibitively heavy.

Two scientists working at the University of Birmingham, Otto Frisch and Rudolf Peierls, however, were able to calculate that a much smaller mass of uranium would be sufficient. Mark Oliphant, who directed the program they were working in, presented it to chemist Henry Tizard in March of 1940, and the MAUD Committee was created.

The committee, initially known as the Thomson Committee, met for the first time on April 10, 1940, and was limited to British scientists, excluding Frisch and Peierls, though they were eventually allowed to participate in a technical subcommittee. Eventually, the committee was split in two, the MAUD Technical Committee subsuming the technical subcommittee and the MAUD Policy Committee handling sensitive political and supervisory issues.

Two reports from the MAUD Committee were issued in July of 1941: "Use of Uranium in a Bomb" and "Use of Uranium as a Source of Power." The first report helped galvanize American researchers into developing an atomic bomb and helped move the process that led to the Manhattan Project along much more quickly.

Aaron Barlow

See also: Frisch, Otto; Hahn, Otto; Meitner, Lise; Oliphant, Mark; Peierls, Rudolf. Document: 7

References

Bernstein, Jeremy. 2011. "A Memorandum that Changed the World." *American Journal of Physics* 79, no. 5: 441–446.

Clark, Ronald W. 1961. *The Birth of the Bomb: The Untold Story of Britain's Part in the Weapon that Changed the World.* London: Phoenix House.

Farmelo, Graham. 2013. *Churchill's Bomb: How the United States Overtook Britain in the First Nuclear Arms Race*. New York: Basic Books.

Frisch, Otto Robert. 1979. *What Little I Remember*. Cambridge, U.K.: Cambridge University Press.

Gowing, Margaret. 1964. *Britain and Atomic Energy, 1939–1945*. London: Macmillan Publishing.

Paul, Septimus H. 2000. *Nuclear Rivals: Anglo-American Atomic Relations, 1941–1952*. Columbus: Ohio State University Press.

Peierls, Rudolf. 1985. *Bird of Passage: Recollections of a Physicist*. Princeton, NJ: Princeton University Press.

Szasz, Ferenc Morton. 1992. *British Scientists and the Manhattan Project: The Los Alamos Years*. New York: St. Martin's Press.

Meitner, Lise (1878–1968)

Along with Marie Curie, Lise Meitner is one of the few women to reach the top ranks in the field of nuclear physics. Born on November 7, 1878, to an intellectual Viennese family, Meitner learned to hold her own in discussions with visiting doctors and scientists. Meitner herself had a strong desire for a scientific career, but her father steered her toward becoming a teacher of French—supposedly a more "practical" career for a girl. Not satisfied with that option, Meitner persevered in her studies and entered the University of Vienna in 1901 as one of its first female students.

At Vienna, Meitner studied physics under the noted physicist Ludwig Boltzmann, earning her PhD in 1906. Meitner then met quantum physicist Max Planck and went to work in his laboratory in Berlin. There she met Otto Hahn, a chemist who was studying radioisotopes and beta radiation and who needed the help of a physicist. The two formed an effective scientific partnership despite the lab director's insistence that women were not to be allowed in the lab proper. This work garnered Meitner several awards during the 1920s.

In 1938, Hahn and Fritz Strassmann had carried out experiments with the bombarding of uranium atoms but had been unable to interpret the results, which included a surprising release of energy. Meitner, who had fled the Nazi takeover of Austria and gone to Sweden, and her nephew, Otto Frisch, came up with the key insight that the atoms had undergone splitting. Meitner applied the biological term "fission" to this process. She also realized that matter was being converted into a proportionately very large quantity of energy in the process, in accordance with Albert Einstein's equation $E = mc^2$.

Hahn received the Nobel Prize in Physics for this work, but the prize committee overlooked Meitner's contributions, an omission that many historians attribute to the rampant sexism still prevailing in science. Meitner did receive the Enrico Fermi award, given by the Atomic Energy Commission, in 1966. She died on October 27, 1968.

Harry Henderson

See also: Einstein, Albert; Frisch, Otto; Hahn, Otto; Strassmann, Fritz

References

Henderson, Harry. 1998. *Nuclear Physics*. New York: Facts on File.

Sime, Ruth Lewin. 1997. *Lise Meitner: A Life in Physics*. Berkeley: University of California Press.

Metallurgical Laboratory

Among the first actions of what would become the Manhattan Project was establishment of the Metallurgical Laboratory at the University of Chicago. Part of the project was Enrico Fermi's "Chicago Pile 1" or CP-1, which produced a self-sustaining nuclear reaction, the first ever produced by humans, on December 2, 1942. It was this that made possible the reactors at Oak Ridge, Tennessee, and Hanford, Washington, that were able to produce the fuel of the sort used at Hiroshima and Nagasaki.

Met Lab, as it was known, opened about two months after the United States entered World War II on December 7, 1941. Its primary purpose was the study of plutonium and developing ways of producing it and of separating fissile plutonium-239 from other plutonium isotopes for the purpose of creating a deliverable atomic bomb. It was at Met Lab that the designs for the X-10 Graphite Reactor at Oak Ridge's Clinton Engineer Works and the B Reactor at Hanford Engineer Works were laid out.

Among those associated with Met Lab were Eugene Wigner and Leó Szilárd, whose petition in 1945 against use of an atomic bomb was supported by a number of Met Lab scientists. The University of Chicago was chosen as the site of the new Met Lab over the University of California and Columbia University by Arthur Compton, who had been given charge of American plutonium research in the waning days of 1941. Seeing too much duplication of effort among the universities, he decided to consolidate, which led Fermi to move to Chicago from Columbia. The new lab was overseen by the Office of Scientific Research and Development.

Aaron Barlow

See also: Clinton Engineer Works; Compton, Arthur Holly; Fermi, Enrico; Hanford, Washington; Oak Ridge, Tennessee; Office of Scientific Research and Development; Plutonium; Szilárd, Leó; Wigner, Eugene Paul. Documents: 26, 27, 30

References

Anderson, Herbert L. 1975. "Assisting Fermi." In Jane Wilson, ed. *All In Our Time: The Reminiscences of Twelve Nuclear Pioneers*, 66–104. Chicago: Bulletin of the Atomic Scientists.

Compton, Arthur. 1956. *Atomic Quest*. New York: Oxford University Press.

Groves, Leslie. 1962. *Now It Can Be Told: The Story of the Manhattan Project*. New York: Harper.

Rhodes, Richard. 1986. *The Making of the Atomic Bomb*. New York: Simon & Schuster.

Salvetti, Carlo. 2001. "The Birth of Nuclear Energy: Fermi's Pile." In C. Bernardini and Luisa Bonolis, eds. *Enrico Fermi: His Work and Legacy*, 177–203. Bologna, Italy: Società Italiana di Fisica, Springer.

Szanton, Andrew. 1992. *The Recollections of Eugene P. Wigner*. New York: Plenum.

N

Nagasaki, Bombing of (August 9, 1945)

The site of the second U.S. atomic bombing of a Japanese city, Nagasaki was attacked following the Japanese refusal to surrender after the atomic bombing of Hiroshima on August 6, 1945. Twentieth Air Force headquarters on Guam issued Field Order 17 on August 8, directing that, on the following day, the second atomic bomb on Tinian Island be dropped on another Japanese city. Kokura was designated as the primary target, with Nagasaki, a city of some 230,000 persons, the alternate.

At 3:49 a.m. on August 9, Boeing B-29 Superfortress bomber *Bockscar* (sometimes written as *Bock's Car*), commanded by Major Charles Sweeney, departed Tinian. It was followed by two other B-29s as scientific observer and photographic observer aircraft. *Bockscar* carried a plutonium nuclear-fission bomb nicknamed Fat Man that was 10 feet, 8 inches long, and 5 feet in diameter, with a payload greater than that of the Hiroshima bomb. The plutonium-238 isotope core consisted of two melon-shaped hemispheres surrounded by a ring of explosive charges designed to drive the sections together, achieving "critical mass" and a chain reaction releasing 22 kilotons of energy in one-millionth of a second.

Sweeney flew to Kokura but found it overcast and circled for 10 minutes. Despite the clouds, bombardier Kermit Beahan believed they could bomb visually. Sweeney, concerned about a faulty valve that limited fuel, decided to divert to Nagasaki, which was also partly obscured by clouds. Beahan believed he could bomb by radar, but a break in the clouds allowed him to bomb visually, using the Mitsubishi shipyards as his aiming point.

Bockscar released the bomb from 31,000 feet at 11:02 a.m. local time. The bomb detonated 53 seconds later, approximately 1,500 feet over the city, destroying everything within a 1,000-yard radius. An intense blue-white explosion pushed up a pillar of fire 10,000 feet, followed by a mushroom cloud to 60,000 feet.

Although the bomb missed its intended aiming point by 8,500 feet, it leveled one-third of the city. Called the "Red Circle of Death," the fire and blast area within the Urakami Valley section destroyed more than 18,000 homes and killed 74,000 people. Another 75,000 were injured, with many of these dying from wounds or complications. Blast forces traveling in excess of 9,000 mph damaged buildings three miles away, and the concussion was felt 40 miles from the epicenter. "Ashes of Death" from the mushroom cloud spread radiation poisoning, killing all who were not killed outright within 1,000 yards of the epicenter. The bomb might have killed thousands more, but it detonated away from the city center in a heavy industrial area, vaporizing three of Nagasaki's largest war factories but "minimizing" deaths.

Sweeney made one complete circle of the city to determine damage and then left after fuel concerns and heavy smoke made other

Nagasaki after the August 9, 1945, bombing. (Andrew J. Waskey)

circuits futile. Critically low on fuel, he flew to Okinawa, landing at Yontan Field about 12:30 p.m., his gas tanks virtually empty. After refueling, he flew *Bockscar* on to Tinian, arriving there at 10:30 p.m. local time after a 20-hour flight.

Included in the instrument bundle dropped from the observation plane was a letter addressed to Japanese physicist and professor R. Sagane that urged immediate surrender and threatened continued atomic destruction of Japanese cities. Written by three American physicists, the letter was a bluff, as no other atomic bombs were then ready. Nonetheless, the second atomic attack, coupled with the August 8 declaration of war by the Soviet Union, provided Japanese Emperor Hirohito with the excuse to end the war.

Mark E. Van Rhyn

See also: Bockscar; Hiroshima, Bombing of; Laurence, William Leonard; Sweeney, Charles. Documents: 41, 49b

References

Chinnock, Frank W. 1969. *Nagasaki: The Forgotten Bomb.* New York: World Publishing.

Ishikawa, Eisei. David L. Swain, trans. 1981. *Hiroshima and Nagasaki: The Physical, Medical, and Social Effects of the Atomic Bombings.* New York: Basic Books.

Nobile, Philip. 1995. *Judgment at the Smithsonian: The Bombing of Hiroshima and Nagasaki.* New York: Marlowe and Company.

National Bureau of Standards

Headed by Lyman Briggs from 1932 until 1945, the National Bureau of Standards was instrumental in developments leading to the Manhattan Project. It was established in 1901 to provide for the standardization of weights and measures. Its laboratory served to establish these standards and for newly required ones in developing technological realms such as electricity. It also was used during World War I for the war effort and afterward worked in the area of radio and aircraft, among other things.

In the late 1920s, the bureau began to establish commercial standards for an expanding array of materials and of products, both for governmental and commercial use. Its laboratory and expertise were once again harnessed for war efforts related to scientific research even before the start of World War II.

Given the role NBS had been playing over the several preceding years, it was natural for President Franklin Roosevelt to turn to the NBS in order to explore possibilities for successful research into development of an atomic bomb. He appointed Briggs to head a new Advisory Committee on Uranium in October 1939, soon after learning of Albert Einstein and Leó Szilárd's concerns about German research on the subject and suggestion that the United States work in the same direction.

Perhaps Briggs was not the best person to be coordinating such research. Though the committee funded work by Szilárd and Enrico Fermi, coordination with the much more powerful and significant National Defense Research Committee was limited, and its top scientists, including Vannevar Bush and James Conant, were, at that early point, not convinced that resources invested in the direction of an atomic bomb was the best path for the United States to follow. However, the MAUD Committee Report and a visit to America by Mark Oliphant galvanized the NDRC to put more effort into atomic research. In July 1941, Bush replaced the Uranium Advisory Committee with the S-1 Uranium Committee and moved it from under Briggs's control, removing him and the NBS from the program and replacing them with Arthur Compton under the NDRC's replacement, the Office of Scientific Research and Development.

Aaron Barlow

See also: Advisory Committee on Uranium; Briggs, Lyman; Bush, Vannevar; MAUD Committee; National Defense Research Committee; Oliphant, Mark; Roosevelt, Franklin D.

Reference

National Bureau of Standards. 2018. *The National Bureau of Standards*. London: Forgotten Books.

National Defense Research Committee

Formed on June 27, 1940, the National Defense Research Committee (NDRC) was an American response to growing realization that a coordinated scientific effort was needed for timely and effective development of new warfare processes and devices. It was created under the umbrella of the Council of National Defense and at the insistence of Vannevar Bush, who took his argument directly to the president on June 12, 1940, and was subsequently named chairman of the NDRC.

The original members of the NDRC were, aside from Bush, Rear Admiral Harold G. Bowen, commissioner of patents Conway P. Coe, MIIT president James B. Conant, Harvard University president Frank B. Jewett, president of the National Academy of Sciences (as well as president of Bell Telephone Laboratories), Brigadier General George V. Strong, and professor of physical chemistry and mathematical physics at the California Institute of Technology Richard C. Tolman. The committee first met on July 2, 1940, and met regularly once a month for the next year.

The NDRC was involved in the creation and continuance of laboratories and projects in a variety of areas, including radar, sonar, and atomic power. In fact, it took over supervision of the work of the Advisory Committee on Uranium from the National Bureau of Standards. However, little progress was made until Bush was galvanized into action by the British MAUD Report in July 1941.

Just before the MAUD Report arrived in Washington, at Bush's request, the NDRC was superseded as a funding agency by the Office of Scientific Research and Development (OSRD), which was established through an executive order from the president on June 28, 1941. At that time, the role of the NDRC became strictly advisory.

The NDRC initially was composed of five divisions.

Five Divisions of NDRC

A. Armor and Ordnance
B. Bombs, Fuels, Gases, and Chemical Problems
C. Communication and Transportation
D. Detection, Controls, and Instruments
E. Patents and Inventions

After incorporation into the OSRD, the NDRC's responsibilities were divided into 19 divisions, two panels, and three committees.

NDRC Divisions

1. Ballistic Research
2. Effects of Impact and Explosion
3. Rocket Ordnance
4. Ordnance Accessories
5. New Missiles
6. Subsurface Warfare
7. Fire Control
8. Explosives
9. Chemistry
10. Absorbents and Aerosols
11. Chemical Engineering
12. Transportation
13. Electrical Communication
14. Radar
15. Radio Coordination
16. Optics and Camouflage
17. Physics
18. War Metallurgy
19. Miscellaneous

Panels

1. Applied Mathematics
2. Applied Psychology

Committees

1. Propagation
2. Vacuum Tube Development
3. Tropical Deterioration Administrative.

Aaron Barlow

See also: Advisory Committee on Uranium; Bush, Vannevar; Conant, James Bryant; MAUD Committee; Office of Scientific Research and Development; Roosevelt, Franklin D

References

Bush, Vannevar. 1970. *Pieces of the Action.* New York: Morrow.

Stewart, Irvin. 1948. *Organizing Scientific Research for War: The Administrative History of the Office of Scientific Research and Development.* Boston: Little, Brown.

Neumann, John von (1903–1957)

One of the originators of quantum mechanics and the originator of game theory, which is based on mathematical strategies to minimize loss and maximize gain, John von Neumann is perhaps best remembered for his design for the first high-speed, stored-program computer. The Electronic Discrete

Variable Automatic Computer (EDVAC) was the first of what came to be known as "von Neumann computers." His giant computers, for which others have since claimed partial credit, helped make the calculations that led to the development of the hydrogen bomb.

Originally named Janos, von Neumann was born into a Jewish family on December 28, 1903, in Budapest, Hungary. His father was a banker. His parents knew their son was different almost immediately; even as a young child, he entertained guests by memorizing and reciting sections of the local phone book. He could also divide eight-digit numbers in his head, and with his photographic memory, he found it easy to learn several languages as a youngster.

Von Neumann attended private schools in Budapest at first but later went to one of the city's gymnasia, the equivalent of high schools in the United States. His math teachers were university professors, since his abilities were well beyond those of his regular teachers. By the time he graduated in 1921, he was already something of a phenomenon in the world of mathematics, having won a prize for the best math student in Hungary and published his first professional paper.

Von Neumann started college at the University of Budapest in the fall of 1921, but he also took classes at the University of Berlin. In 1923, he transferred to the Federal Institute of Technology in Switzerland, from which he received a degree in chemical engineering in 1925. It took him only another year to earn a doctorate in mathematics from the University of Budapest.

After working as a Rockefeller fellow at Germany's University of Göttingen, where he met and began a long friendship with physicist J. Robert Oppenheimer, in 1926 and 1927, von Neumann worked as an assistant professor at the University of Budapest from 1927 to 1930. It was during the latter period that he published a series of five papers that quickly made him famous in math circles. Those papers outlined his revolutionary ideas on quantum physics, introduced his theory of games, and explained his thoughts on the relationship between the limits of mathematics and formal logic systems.

Von Neumann left Budapest to accept an offer to work as a guest mathematical physics lecturer at Princeton University in New Jersey. He was appointed a full professor in 1931 at the unusually young age of 28, and in 1933, he left Princeton to become one of the first faculty members of the nearby Institute for Advanced Study (IAS).

During the 1930s, von Neumann did research in both pure and applied mathematics, but his most significant energies went to game theory. The result was his development of the minimax theorem, in which he showed that he could apply game theory mathematically to any field—whether business, social science, sports, biology, or war—in which two opponents compete, one winning and the other losing. In fact, his comparison in that manner of the computing ability of a machine and the human brain led him to develop his theory of automata, which scientists still use to study artificial computer intelligence.

Starting in 1940, the U.S. government began asking von Neumann to assist with various wartime tasks for the armed forces that required his mathematical expertise. In 1943, he began working as a consultant to the Los Alamos National Laboratory in New Mexico, where scientists were feverishly trying to build the first atomic bomb. He was especially helpful in the development of the bomb's "high-explosive lens," which increased its power. During the war, von Neumann became convinced of the need for machines that would automatically perform the thousands of complex calculations needed for the development of highly accurate and deadly new ballistics. In the meantime, he published his masterwork, *The Theory of Games and Economic Behavior,* in 1944.

In 1945, von Neumann published a report on the EDVAC in which he outlined his design for the first stored-program computer. (History indicates that John Mauchly and John Presper Eckert Jr., the inventors of the Electronic Numerical Integrator and Calculator [ENIAC] computer in 1946, should also have received some credit for the idea, but the press seems to have found it preferable to identify just one person as the author.) The basis of all modern computers, the stored-program computer had a memory in which to keep information and a control unit that could organize internal transfers of information in accordance with a program also stored in its memory. That is the major characteristic of a so-called von Neumann computer. Von Neumann also directed the IAS Electronic Computer Project after the war.

In the early 1950s, despite his continuing responsibilities as a professor at the IAS, von Neumann worked as a consultant for International Business Machines, evaluating ideas from new players in the rapidly evolving computer field. That may not have been his strongest suit, since he dismissed the FORTRAN (formula translator) computer language as useless when it was presented to him in 1954.

In about 1950, von Neumann became closely involved with the creation of the hydrogen bomb at Los Alamos. He greatly speeded up the weapon's development by making revolutionary contributions to the field of quantum theory, which governs the interaction between matter and radiation. Von Neumann's creation of high-speed ways to make the calculations necessary to construct the bomb made possible the weapon's first successful test in 1952. Those high-speed calculations also contributed significantly to the evolution of modern computing.

President Dwight D. Eisenhower appointed von Neumann in 1954 to the five-member Atomic Energy Commission (AEC), a high-level post with a five-year term that required von Neumann to take a leave of absence from the IAS. Also in 1954, he was appointed chairperson of the Atlas Scientific Advisory Committee, whose purpose was to expedite the development of what were later called intercontinental ballistic missiles (ICBMs). As such, von Neumann suggested that ICBMs be used to deliver nuclear weapons.

In 1955, von Neumann's health began to fail, and soon he discovered that he had cancer. He continued working, however, at the IAS and the AEC until shortly before his death on February 8, 1957.

Amanda de la Garza

See also: Los Alamos Laboratory; Oppenheimer, Julius Robert

References

Goldstein, Herman H. 1972. *The Computer from Pascal to von Neumann.* Princeton, NJ: Princeton University Press.

Ritchie, David. 1986. *The Computer Pioneers.* New York: Simon & Schuster.

Slater, Robert. 1987. *Portraits in Silicon.* Cambridge, MA: The MIT Press.

Nuclear Chain Reaction

A nuclear chain reaction begins when a single nuclear reaction causes one or more subsequent nuclear reactions. It is the basic concept allowing for development of the atomic bomb, as a nuclear chain reaction of a heavy isotope such as uranium-235 or plutonium-239 can release phenomenal amounts of energy.

On nuclear fission, a number of neutrons are rejected from the reaction. When more fissile material is present, these may be absorbed by those atoms, causing more fission. As long as more fuel is present, the process becomes self-sustaining. It can be controlled, as in a nuclear power plant. In a bomb, of course, the intent is a huge and immediate impact, so the concept is to create an uncontrolled and immediately expanding supercritical nuclear chain reaction.

On September 12, 1933, Leó Szilárd hypothesized the idea of a nuclear chain reaction, speculating that if a nuclear reaction produced neutrons, those neutrons would likely cause subsequent nuclear reactions and so on. His own subsequent experiments using indium and beryllium failed, but when fission was postulated by Otto Frisch and Lise Meitner on the heels of the Otto Hahn and Fritz Strassmann experiment, Szilárd (now in New York, having fled there from his native Hungary) and Enrico Fermi determined that there was neutron multiplication in uranium, showing that creation of a nuclear chain reaction with uranium was possible. At the same time, in France, Frédérick Joliet along with Hans von Halban and Lew Korwarski were reaching the same conclusion.

Knowing that others would be thinking along the same lines he was, Szilárd approached Albert Einstein, the world's most famous physicist and one person who could probably reach the world's top leaders, for assistance in alerting such leaders to the fact that Germany's scientists had most likely realized the same thing and arguing for urgent research into the development of an atomic bomb.

Enrico Fermi, working at the University of Chicago, led a team in further research, producing the first self-sustaining nuclear chain reaction on December 2, 1942, at Chicago Pile-1, a converted racquetball court at the university's Stagg Field. This is one of the dates with a real claim to being the start of the nuclear age.

Aaron Barlow

See also: Einstein, Albert; Fermi, Enrico; Hahn, Otto; Plutonium; Strassmann, Fritz; Szilárd, Léo; University of Chicago; Uranium-235

Reference

Sachs, Robert G., ed. 1984. *The Nuclear Chain Reaction—Forty Years Later.* Chicago: University of Chicago Press.

Nuclear Reactor

First called, rather facetiously by its creators, an atomic pile after the pile of graphite blocks interspersed with uranium and then named Pile-1 at the University of Chicago, the nuclear reactor has defined the current age for more than 75 years. Pile-1, that first successful nuclear reactor, was built by a team led by Enrico Fermi at the Metallurgical Laboratory. It achieved criticality, a self-sustained nuclear reaction, on December 2, 1942, ushering in the atomic age.

Within the next few years, nuclear reactors designed at the Met Lab were built at the Hanford Engineer Works in Washington for the production of the plutonium that would be used in the Fat Man–type bombs and at the Clinton Engineer Works at Oak Ridge, Tennessee, for the production of the uranium that would be used in the Little Boy–type bomb that would be dropped on Hiroshima, Japan. It wasn't until after the war that reactors were turned to peacetime use as producers of power, the first of these being successfully tested late in 1951.

Aaron Barlow

See also: Clinton Engineer Works; Fat Man; Fermi, Enrico; Hanford, Washington; Little Boy; Oak Ridge, Tennessee; Szilárd, Léo; University of Chicago

Reference

Kragh, Helge. 1999. *Quantum Generations: A History of Physics in the Twentieth Century.* Princeton, NJ: Princeton University Press.

O

Oak Ridge, Tennessee

Located about 25 miles from Knoxville, Oak Ridge is the site that was chosen in 1942 for the Clinton Engineer Works (CEW), the primary early and then East Coast base of the Manhattan Project. It was chosen by General Leslie Groves because it was accessible by both road and rail transport, had abundant water supplies, would be able to make use of the hydroelectric power of the nearby Norris Dam, was ridged (providing an element of safety between facilities), and was sparsely populated.

The 3,000 residents of the area were displaced and resettled (in a sometimes unfeeling and uncompromising swift process), and a new town, which grew to some 75,000 residents, was constructed to serve the Manhattan Project. Until 1949, the site was officially the Clinton Engineer Works, though the name "Oak Ridge" was in use from 1943.

The "secret" town began to take shape when the U.S. Army Corps of Engineers started to acquire what eventually amounted to more than 60,000 acres for the Clinton Engineer Works in October of 1942. Due to secrecy concerns, local authorities were told

A billboard in 1944 at Oak Ridge, Tennessee, reminding the people working there of the importance of secrecy. (Galerie Bilderwelt/Getty Images)

little of what was going on, fracturing relations between the representatives of the federal government (which was the project itself) and local governments and residents. To make matters worse, tax revenues lost by the removal of a large amount of land from the rolls was not compensated for. By March, when all of the residents had been removed, checkpoints and fences had been constructed, keeping everyone but authorized individuals out of the area. This further alienated local communities. Three plants were quickly begun for the separation of uranium-235 from uranium-238 and a fourth, a graphite reactor, for the production of plutonium.

To accommodate the workers needed at the CEW site, a new town was built at the eastern end of the site. The town and houses were designed by Skidmore, Owings and Merrill under the direction of John Merrill. The town eventually had 10 schools and 13 supermarkets, 17 eating establishments and the same number of church facilities. There were sports facilities, a library, and even an orchestra for the town, which soon had 70,000 residents served by 300 miles of new roads and 55 miles of railroad tracks. The homes were, for the most part, prefabricated modular houses. There were also apartments and dormitories quickly constructed for smaller families and single workers.

Aaron Barlow

See also: Clinton Engineer Works; Groves, Leslie Richard; Plutonium; Uranium-235; U.S. Army Corps of Engineers

References

Groves, Leslie. 1962. *Now It Can Be Told: The Story of the Manhattan Project.* New York: Harper & Brothers.

Johnson, Charles W., and Charles O. Jackson. 1981. *City Behind a Fence: Oak Ridge, Tennessee, 1942–1946.* Knoxville: University of Tennessee Press.

Nichols, Kenneth D. 1987. *The Road to Trinity: A Personal Account of How America's Nuclear Policies Were Made.* New York: William Morrow and Company.

Olwell, Russell. 2004 *At Work in the Atomic City: A Labor and Social History of Oak Ridge, Tennessee.* Knoxville: University of Tennessee Press.

Westcott, Ed. 2005. *Oak Ridge.* Charleston, SC: Arcadia Publishing.

Office of Scientific Research and Development

The Office of Scientific Research and Development (OSRD) was created by executive order by President Franklin Roosevelt on June 28, 1941. Its purpose was to bring all work toward advanced armament, by the military and by civilian entities, under one structure and with adequate (almost unlimited) funding. Its head was Vannevar Bush, who, to avoid bureaucratic infighting, was responsible only to Roosevelt himself. OSRD operated until 1947, more than a year after the end of World War II.

The OSRD took over from the National Defense Research Committee, which Bush had also chaired. Bush used the new authority he had acquired through OSRD to seek out and provide draft deferments for scientists he could recruit for OSRD projects, the most important of which would be the Manhattan Project. The OSRD was divided into five administrative units:

A. Sensory Devices Committee
B. Insect Control Committee
C. Office of Field Services
D. National Defense Research Committee (now headed by James Conant)
E. Committee on Medical Research

The OSRD, through combining military and civilian research operations, laid the groundwork for what President Dwight Eisenhower would warn about in his farewell address on leaving the presidency: the military-industrial complex.

Aaron Barlow

See also: Bush, Vannevar; National Defense Research Committee; Roosevelt, Franklin D.

References

Clark, Ronald W. 1961. *The Birth of the Bomb: The Untold Story of Britain's Part in the Weapon that Changed the World*. London: Phoenix House.

Conant, Jennet. 2002. *Tuxedo Park: A Wall Street Tycoon and the Secret Palace of Science that Changed the Course of World War II*. New York: Simon & Schuster.

Jewett, Frank Baldwin. 1978. "The Academy in World War II." In Rexmond C. Cochrane, ed. *The National Academy of Sciences: The First Hundred Years, 1863–1963*, 382–432. Washington, D.C.: National Academy of Sciences.

Zachary, G. Pascal. 1997. *Endless Frontier: Vannevar Bush, Engineer of the American Century*. New York: The Free Press.

Oliphant, Mark (1901–2000)

Born in Adelaide, Australia, on October 8, 1901, Mark Oliphant was a physicist at the University of Birmingham, England, when Otto Frisch and Rudolf Peierls wrote what has come to be called the "Frisch-Peierls Memorandum" there. He was the first person to read the memorandum and, in turn, shared it with Henry Tizard, a government scientist chairing the Committee for the Scientific Survey of Air Warfare. Tizard, realizing the importance of the memorandum's conclusion that it might be possible to unleash the explosive power of perhaps hundreds of tons of TNT through a mere kilogram of uranium-235, established a subcommittee soon known as the MAUD Committee.

Though Frisch and Peierls, as foreign nationals, had been kept away from the secret work on radar that Oliphant was directing, he was aware of their work and cognizant of their expertise, which is why he took their report so seriously and moved upon it so quickly. Once the British/Canadian Tube Alloys project was absorbed into the Manhattan Project, Oliphant spent time at the University of California working with Ernest Lawrence, focusing on electromagnetic uranium enrichment.

Aaron Barlow

See also: Electromagnetic Uranium Enrichment; Frisch, Otto; Frisch-Peierls Memorandum; Lawrence, Ernest Orlando; MAUD Committee; Peierls, Rudolf; Tube Alloys

References

Cockburn, Stewart, and David Ellyard. 1981. *Oliphant, the Life and Times of Sir Mark Oliphant*. Adelaide: Axiom Books.

Gowing, Margaret. 1964. *Britain and Atomic Energy, 1939–1945*. London: Macmillan Publishing.

Oliphant, Mark. 1949. *The Atomic Age*. London: G. Allen and Unwin.

Oliphant, Mark. 1972. *Rutherford: Recollections of the Cambridge Days*. Amsterdam: Elsevier Publishing Company.

Oppenheimer, Julius Robert (1904–1967)

A U.S. scientist who helped develop the atomic bomb and was born in New York City on April 22, 1904, Julius Robert Oppenheimer was gifted and precocious. Graduating *summa cum laude* in three years from Harvard University, he did his

The most important non-military participant in the Manhattan Project was J. Robert Oppenheimer (1904–1967). (Library of Congress)

graduate work at the Cavendish Laboratory (University of Cambridge) and at Göttingen under Max Born. A brilliant dissertation on quantum theory confirmed a vocation and his status as a leading theoretical physicist. In 1929, he accepted joint appointments in physics at the University of California, Berkeley, and at Caltech.

Ambitious and possessing an incredibly quick and agile mind, Oppenheimer attracted a coterie of stellar students at Berkeley. A chain smoker with a penchant for martinis, he stood six feet and weighed just 125 pounds. Economic depression and the rise of fascism piqued his interest in the Communist Party, and he later married a former party member. Yet his left-leaning political stance failed to deter Brigadier General Leslie R. Groves from recruiting Oppenheimer to lead a centralized laboratory for the construction of atomic bombs. Groves recognized Oppenheimer's genius for science, his extensive connections and ability to recruit talent, and, most important, his improvisational and organizational skills and his determination to prove his patriotism. Overriding objections from army counterintelligence, Groves appointed Oppenheimer in October 1942.

Oppenheimer assembled his initial team of approximately 30 scientists at Los Alamos in April 1943. Because Oppenheimer encouraged a sense of community and open communication, the team overcame seemingly intractable difficulties to produce a working nuclear device in just more than two years. Despite intellectual assertiveness that bordered on arrogance, Oppenheimer proved to be the indispensable man of the Manhattan Project. His unqualified success earned him the Presidential Medal of Merit in 1946.

In 1947, Oppenheimer became director of the Institute for Advanced Study at Princeton and chairman of the General Advisory Committee of the Atomic Energy Commission. Initially entranced by the "technically sweet" challenge of building atomic bombs, he later remarked that, with Hiroshima, physicists "have known sin." His opposition to the hydrogen bomb within the corrosive climate of McCarthyism in the early 1950s led to hearings in 1954 that stripped him of his security clearance. Rehabilitated by 1963, he received the Enrico Fermi Award. Oppenheimer died in Princeton, New Jersey, on February 18, 1967.

William J. Astore

See also: Alamogordo Bombing and Gunnery Range; Einstein, Albert; Fermi, Enrico; Groves, Leslie Richard; Hiroshima, Bombing of; Nagasaki, Bombing of. Documents: 9, 11, 13, 15, 16, 20, 27, 29, 31, 44, 46

References

Goodchild, Peter. 1985. *J. Robert Oppenheimer: Shatterer of Worlds*. New York: Fromm International.

Rummel, Jack. 1992. *Robert Oppenheimer: Dark Prince*. New York: Facts on File.

P

Pacific Theater: World War II

In the 1930s, Japanese desire for expansion conflicted with American interests to such an extent that Japan attacked the surprised U.S. fleet at Pearl Harbor on December 7, 1941. Surprise, speed, and experience allowed the Japanese to expand rapidly and secure resources. In 1942, however, the Allies stopped the Japanese at the Coral Sea, Guadalcanal, Midway, and New Guinea; both sides took serious losses during these battles. The United States forced the Japanese onto the strategic defensive after Midway, but the Japanese exacted a heavy price for each fortified island. While the United States secured sea and air superiority, ground forces—through brutal fighting—retook islands in the Gilberts, the Solomons, the Marianas, the Palaus, the Philippines, the Ryukyus, and the Volcanoes. After U.S. ground forces secured the Marianas, U.S. bombers began an offensive on Japan and U.S. submarines decimated Japanese shipping. Starting in 1944, Japanese military leaders demonstrated their resolve by employing suicide aerial attacks known as the kamikaze. The kamikaze, tenacity, and political factors led President Harry Truman to use atomic weapons on Hiroshima and Nagasaki in August 1945, which caused the Japanese emperor to surrender.

The origins of the Pacific War are complex, but the Imperial Japanese desire for expansion conflicting with the American national interests in the Pacific Rim and Asia is the overarching reason. The Japanese were a rising great power from the end of the nineteenth century, but European great powers blocked its ascent on several occasions, which the Japanese attributed to racism. Thus, Japan began expanding its empire onto mainland Asia by annexing Korea, turning Manchuria into a de facto colony, and going to war with China in 1937. American ire grew with Japanese aggression. Consequently, the United States began a series of diplomatic and economic maneuvers to stop Japan. When the United States embargoed scrap metal and oil, Japanese militant leaders felt they had to act. They felt they could defeat the Europeans and Americans in the initial offensive to gain resources, establish a strong defensive perimeter, force a peace from their weak-willed enemies, and hold onto their new empire.

1941–1943

The Japanese aerial attack on Pearl Harbor was the opening salvo of the Pacific War. On December 7, 1941, Japanese carrier-based planes attacked the U.S. Pacific Fleet, which was at anchor in Pearl Harbor on a sleepy Sunday morning. The Japanese had caught the Americans in Hawaii by surprise, and their ambassador arrived late with what was essentially a Japanese declaration of war. The Japanese mauled the American surface fleet, but the American carriers were away on maneuvers. Despite initial heavy damage, only two battleships were total losses—the *Oklahoma* and the *Arizona*. Japan had awoken the sleeping American giant.

This was a grim time for the United States, with only a temporary victory on December 8 at Wake, when its marine defenders held off an initial Japanese attack. While the United States recovered from the shock of the sneak attack, the Japanese took Wake, Guam, and the Dutch East Indies. The Japanese also invaded the American colony of the Philippines on December 22. They also attacked down the Malay Peninsula and forced the surrender of the vital British fortified port of Singapore on February 15, 1942. President Franklin D. Roosevelt and his senior advisers decided to launch a raid on the Japanese home islands. They named this raid after its colorful leader, James Doolittle. His B-25s flew off the navy's carrier *Hornet* on April 18 and dropped modest bombloads on Japan. Most of his men landed in China, but the Japanese captured eight others, three of whom they executed. To counter the negative impact the Doolittle raid had on Japanese morale, Admiral Isoroku Yamamoto would later push up an already planned attack on Midway Island. Part of this attack was a supporting attack on the Aleutians.

Due to the success of the Japanese invasion of the Philippines, President Roosevelt ordered Douglas MacArthur to leave his soldiers in the Philippines and command from Australia. MacArthur's forces in the Philippines surrendered on April 9, and during the infamous Bataan Death March, the Japanese killed roughly 10,000 American and Filipino prisoners of war, while the remainder faced slow starvation and brutal treatment in squalid prison camps. Meanwhile, the Japanese continued their expansion in the central, southern, and southwest Pacific islands.

The Japanese expansion included an attempt to seize all of New Guinea. If the Japanese took the island, it would be a natural springboard to cut off and conquer Australia. The Japanese sent a naval force with landing troops to take Port Moresby and, thus, all of New Guinea. The U.S. Navy interceded, which resulted in the Battle of the Coral Sea on May 8. This battle was a key engagement for several reasons. It was the first naval battle where the two surface fleets were never in visual range. Instead, U.S. and Japanese airplanes fought. The Japanese sunk the USS *Lexington* and damaged the *Yorktown* but abandoned their amphibious assault on Port Moresby, New Guinea. The Japanese instead attempted to take Port Moresby via the Kokoda Trail over the rugged, mountainous spine of New Guinea. However, Australian soldiers, steep mountains, and dense jungle slowed and then halted the advancing Japanese.

As the Japanese prepared to attack Midway, the change in schedule had several effects. First, not all of the Japanese carriers were able to participate in the attack. Second, the Japanese had to use a lot of radio traffic to coordinate the attack, which facilitated U.S. code-breaking efforts. This code-breaking intelligence—known as MAGIC—allowed the United States to know that the Japanese were going to attack Midway; thus, Admiral Chester Nimitz laid what he hoped was a trap with the *Hornet*, *Yorktown*, and *Enterprise*. Luck was with Nimitz and his forces on June 4 and 5—U.S. aircraft sunk four Japanese carriers and killed many of Japan's experienced aircrews. Despite the loss of the *Yorktown*, America had won the initiative in the Pacific.

While the Japanese, Australians, and Americans fought on New Guinea, U.S. Marines landed on the island of Guadalcanal in the Solomon Islands on August 7. The fighting for Guadalcanal raged for months. American airpower could only assist during daylight hours, which allowed the marines to take and hold an airstrip that they would later rename Henderson Field. At night, when the U.S. carriers withdrew, the Japanese surface fleet, with its outstanding night fighting capability, brought supplies, reinforcements, and naval gunfire. This seesaw dynamic continued until the United States could bring in additional airpower due to the victory at Midway. As additional air and sea power arrived, American marines and soldiers secured Guadalcanal in November.

1943–1944

On January 2, 1943, MacArthur's Australian and American forces took Buna on the east coast of New Guinea. The next American endeavor was MacArthur's Operation CARTWHEEL, which began on June 29. Forces under Admiral William "Bull" Halsey's command would attack through the Solomon Islands to Bougainville, while MacArthur's forces would attack along the north shore of New Guinea and then to the western end of New Britain. These were the first campaigns using the "island hopping" tactics of only taking areas necessary to stage the next "hop" and avoiding enemy strength. Island hopping also involved amphibious assaults, naval gunfire support, joint air support, and, on certain occasions, paratroopers and land assaults. By December 1943, CARTWHEEL had isolated the key Japanese base of Rabaul, and MacArthur decided to let Rabaul wither on the vine rather than risk immense casualties taking a neutralized base.

While CARTWHEEL was underway, Admiral Ernest King fought for a separate drive through the Central Pacific. With sealift the limiting factor, the joint chiefs of staff approved the navy's separate drive through the Central Pacific, which Admiral Chester Nimitz commanded. Thus, Nimitz's and MacArthur's drives became known as a twin axis or twin drive strategy. Nimitz's first target was the coral atoll of Tarawa in the Gilbert Islands. Tarawa was a bloody learning experience for the United States and amphibious warfare. The Japanese were well entrenched, and the United States did not have a sufficient or effective naval bombardment. The Japanese also demonstrated their will to fight and die for their country on November 20—only 17 of 5,000 defenders survived. The marines had 1,000 dead and 2,000 wounded. Meanwhile, the army took the island of Makin to complete U.S. control of the Gilbert Islands.

The next step in the Central Pacific drive was the Marshall Islands. The navy had debated how to take control of the Marshalls, but Nimitz decided on taking Kwajalein to avoid strong Japanese positions in the eastern Marshalls. After studying Tarawa carefully, marines and soldiers fought for Kwajalein from January 31 to February 4, 1944, with a fraction of the casualties of Tarawa. The success of Kwajalein led to Nimitz pushing up the timetable. Thus, U.S. forces attacked Eniwetok on February 18, rather than in May. After a carrier air raid neutralized the nearby Japanese base of Truk, marines and soldiers defeated the Japanese garrison on Eniwetok on February 21.

While American industry steadily increased the size of U.S. sea, air, and land power, U.S. forces wore down the quantitatively inferior Japanese forces. Additionally, U.S. submarines and airpower began decimating the Japanese Merchant Marine, which limited the raw materials reaching the Japanese factories in the home islands. This American *guerre de course* set the stage for MacArthur's seizure of Biak and Nimitz's attack on the Mariana Islands.

Nimitz targeted Saipan, Tinian, and Guam, and the landings brought out the

Japanese fleet for what the Japanese hoped would be a decisive, tide-turning victory. The Japanese got their decisive naval battle, but it did not turn the tide of the war. The Americans had roughly 500 fighters and 400 bombers to Japan's 200 fighters and 200 bombers. The Americans now had superior aircraft, and the U.S. pilots had gained experience as well. The resultant aerial Battle of the Philippine Sea is also known as the Marianas Turkey Shoot, as the Japanese lost roughly 300 planes to 30 American. Meanwhile, MacArthur's forces successfully seized Biak and its airfield on June 7; thus, U.S. aircraft could now reach the Philippines. Nimitz's forces also secured Saipan, Tinian, and Guam through heavy fighting from June 15 to late August. Like Biak, these islands were key air bases; Saipan and Tinian allowed the United States to begin attacking the Japanese home islands with the B-29 strategic bomber.

The United States was poised to begin cracking the inner circle of Japanese defenses in mid- to late 1944. In September, MacArthur took the island of Morotai to prepare to invade the Philippines. Another supporting attack for the Philippine operation called for the seizure of Peleliu in the Palau Islands by Nimitz's forces beginning on September 15 and ending in late November. Peleliu proved to be a bloody assault on heavily fortified ridges, and the marines suffered the highest casualty rate of the war: 40 percent. The heavy casualties on Peleliu were even more unfortunate as the island proved to be of little use to support the invasion of the Philippines.

While the marines fought for the bloody ridgelines of Peleliu, MacArthur planned the recapture of the Philippines. He would first take Leyte Island to prepare for subsequent operations to retake the main island of Luzon. The American assault on Leyte began on October 20, 1944, but the Japanese did not let this go unchallenged. The Japanese Navy launched its final effort, which resulted in the Battle of Leyte Gulf from October 24 to October 26. Like many previous Japanese naval operations, it was very complex. It involved forces converging on Leyte Gulf while a diversionary carrier force acted as bait to draw away the U.S. carriers from the invasion site. Despite losses, the Japanese carrier ruse drew away the aggressive Admiral William "Bull" Halsey, thus leaving the invasion force with little air support. Meanwhile, Japanese surface vessels attempted to reach the invasion site through Surigao Strait but were caught in narrow waters by a prepared U.S. force that included some of the repaired battleships damaged in Pearl Harbor; these U.S. forces devastated this group of Japanese vessels. Further north, another group of Japanese vessels moved through the San Bernardino Strait with only a few U.S. escort carriers barring their path. News of the defeat at Surigao Strait and Halsey attempting to return, as well as a fear of the unknown, made the Japanese commander withdraw. With the invasion site secure, the marines and soldiers fought a successful, grinding battle to liberate Leyte.

1945

In early 1945, MacArthur was ready to take the island of Luzon and the Philippine capital of Manila. General Yamashita Tomoyuki decided to cede the cities and defend the mountainous areas of northern Luzon, which he held until the Japanese surrender. Some of Yamashita's subordinates disobeyed him and fought for every inch of Manila, which is sometimes referred to as the Stalingrad of the Pacific, due to the ferocious house-to-house fighting. Additionally, the Japanese attacked the supporting U.S. vessels with suicide attacks—the kamikaze.

While the fighting raged in the Philippines, the U.S. strategic bombing campaign had picked up intensity. At the same time, the U.S. submarine efforts had all but wiped out the Japanese Merchant Marine, which never adopted the convoy system that served the Allies so well in the Battle of the Atlantic. Thus, Japanese industry was essentially crippled. The long B-29 flight from the Marianas to Japan showed the need for an emergency landing strip. An early warning radar on Iwo Jima in the Volcano Islands and the need for a landing strip made Iwo Jima the next U.S. target. Thus, U.S. Marines landed on Iwo Jima on February 19, 1945, resulting in one of the bloodiest battles in U.S. Marine Corps history—6,821 marines died, and few of the 21,000 Japanese defending the island survived.

One of the final steps before the invasion of the Japanese home islands was to secure a base of operations in the Ryukyu Islands. The United States chose Okinawa to seize for a base of operations and made an amphibious assault on April 1, 1945. The vicious land combat combined with massive, incessant kamikaze attacks made Okinawa costly for both sides. The Japanese lost roughly 70,000 soldiers and 80,000 civilians. The United States suffered over 65,000 casualties on land, at sea, and in the air.

The Japanese kamikaze tactics, tenacious defense, and other political factors led President Truman to decide to use atomic bombs on Japan. Thus, the United States dropped an atomic bomb on Hiroshima on August 6, 1945. The Soviets attacked Japanese forces in Manchuria on August 8, and the United States dropped another bomb on Nagasaki on August 9. Emperor Hirohito surrendered on August 15, 1945. The official surrender occurred on the decks of the U.S. battleship *Missouri* on September 2, 1945.

Jonathan P. Klug

See also: Churchill, Sir Winston L. S.; Hiroshima, Bombing of; Nagasaki, Bombing of; Roosevelt, Franklin D.; Truman, Harry

References

Costello, John. 1981. *The Pacific War 1941–1945: The First Comprehensive One-Volume Account of the Causes and Conduct of World War II in the Pacific.* New York: Atlantic Communications, Inc.

Murray, Williamson, and Allan R. Millet. 2000. *A War to Be Won: Fighting the Second World War.* Cambridge, U.K.: The Belknap Press of Harvard University Press.

Spector, Ronald H. 1987. *Eagle Against the Sun: The American War with Japan.* New York: Free Press.

Stokesbury, James L. 1980. *A Short History of World War II.* New York: William Morrow and Company, Inc.

Pegram, George Braxton (1876–1958)

George Braxton Pegram was a Columbia University physicist who was involved with what would become the Manhattan Project from its earliest days, helping fellow Columbia professor Enrico Fermi broach the possibility of an atomic bomb for the first time with the U.S. military (in this particular, with Navy Rear Admiral Stanford C. Hooper, who was technical assistant to the chief of naval operations) in March of 1939. Early in 1941, Pegram advised the Advisory Committee on Uranium that it was unlikely that a chain reaction (and, therefore, a viable atomic bomb) could be established without a process that could separate uranium-235 from uranium-238, a critical realization for

American research direction. In late 1941, in response to Mark Oliphant's visit to the United States on the heels of the MAUD Committee Report, Pegram and Harold Urey were sent to Great Britain to explore possibilities of Allied cooperation. While there, they attended the first meeting of what would become known as the Tube Alloys project, the British/Canadian predecessor to the Manhattan Project. On his return to the United States, Pegram was named to the S-1 Uranium Committee, soon renamed the S-1 Committee, and served until the committee was again reorganized, this time into the S-1 Executive Committee, in August of 1942.

It was at Columbia, where Pegram was then dean, that Fermi conducted the first American experiment in nuclear fission using water as the neutron moderator. This did not prove effective, so it was decided that graphite blocks be used instead. Fermi was in the process of collecting them when the National Defense Research Committee (of which Pegram was a member) decided that such research should be concentrated at the University of Chicago. Fermi soon moved his activities there.

Work in other areas pertinent to what was becoming the Manhattan Project continued at Columbia University even after administration of the Manhattan Engineer Works was moved to Oak Ridge, Tennessee, in late 1942.

A son of a professor at the predecessor of Duke University, where he did his own undergraduate work, he was also, through his mother, the grandson of the college's founder and first president. Pegram was born in Trinity, North Carolina, in 1876 and graduated from college in 1895, when he was but 19. After a short stint teaching high school, he moved to New York City and entered the physics program at Columbia University in 1900, completing his doctorate there three years later with a thesis on "Secondary Radioactivity in the Electrolysis of Thorium Solutions." He would later do postdoctoral study at Humboldt University in Germany, where he attended lectures by Max Planck, and in England.

On his return to New York, he obtained a position as an assistant professor at Columbia, where he progressed quickly through the ranks, achieving full professor status in 1918. He held that position until he retired in 1945. He served as a dean through most of the 1920s but returned to life as a research professor before assuming the role of dean again in 1937. In that capacity, he recruited refugee from Fascist Italy Enrico Fermi to Columbia in 1939 and arranged laboratory space for him, something he also did for Hungarian émigré Leó Szilárd. Under Pegram's leadership, the Columbia University Department of Physics became a top center for nuclear physics.

Aaron Barlow

See also: Advisory Committee on Uranium; Fermi, Enrico; MAUD Committee; National Defense Research Committee; Oliphant, Mark; Szilárd, Leó; Tube Alloys

References

Embrey, Lee Anna. 1970. *George Braxton Pegram, 1876–1958*. Washington, D.C.: National Academy of Sciences.

Hewlett, Richard G., and Oscar E. Anderson. 1962. *The New World, 1939–1946*. University Park: Pennsylvania State University Press.

Lanouette, William, and Bela Silard. 1992. *Genius in the Shadows: A Biography of Leo Szilard: The Man Behind the Bomb*. New York: Scribner.

Rhodes, Richard. 1986. *The Making of the Atomic Bomb*. New York: Simon & Schuster.

Segrè, Emilio. 1995. *Enrico Fermi, Physicist*. Chicago: University of Chicago Press.

Peierls, Rudolf (1907–1995)

Rudolf Peierls played a critical role in events leading up to the Tube Alloys project in Great Britain and Canada and the Manhattan Project in the United States. His work at the University of Birmingham was expanded upon by fellow German émigré Otto Frisch, who was also excluded from top-secret work on radar because of his immigrant status (after two years of trying, Peierls would finally be granted British citizenship in February 1940). Together, Frisch and Peierls created from their research the Frisch-Peierls Memorandum positing that an atomic bomb could be constructed around a small amount of fissile uranium-235. They were the first scientists to claim that an atomic bomb could be practical, for earlier calculations reached the conclusion that a huge amount of uranium would be necessary, the size of the resulting bomb essentially immovable.

The importance of the Frisch-Peierls Memorandum was quickly grasped by Mark Oliphant and Henry Tizard, whose recognition of its conclusion lead to the formation of the MAUD Committee, whose 1941 report, in turn, sparked formation of both the Tube Alloys and Manhattan projects. Though work toward an atomic bomb probably would have progressed even without the memorandum, it probably shortened the time span to development by a matter of months, if not a year—a critical amount of time, it would turn out.

Though the exclusion of Frisch and Peierls from top-secret work and information early on in the war may seem absurd from a later perspective, it should be remembered that one of the other German émigré scientists who Peierls brought onto his projects was Klaus Fuchs, who would prove to be one of the most successful Soviet spies of all time, passing critical work on Tube Alloys and, later, the Manhattan Project back to Moscow—even while contributing significantly to the development of the atomic bomb. Peierls, who had a Russian wife and left-wing political views, was himself often under suspicion of spying even to the extent of being denied a visa for returning to the United States to attend a conference in 1951. Even as late as the 1990s, questions were raised about him, though they were concluded to be baseless.

When Tube Alloys and the Manhattan Project were merged in August 1943 and the work concentrated in the United States, Peierls joined a group of British scientists (including Mark Oliphant) in relocating. Peierls first worked in New York City but, in February 1944, was reassigned to Los Alamos, New Mexico. He was present for the Trinity Test on July 16, 1945.

Peierls was born in the Berlin suburb of Oberschöneweide, Germany, in 1907, the third child of an electrical engineer. Though his family was of Jewish heritage, Peierls was raised Lutheran, though he practiced no religion as an adult. He studied first at the University of Berlin but transferred to the University of Munich in order to study with Arnold Sommerfeld, later moving to the University of Leipzig to study with Werner Heisenberg. In 1929, he left there for ETH Zurich to study with Wolfgang Pauli, though he successfully submitted his doctoral dissertation, "On the Kinetic Theory of Head Conduction in Crystals," to the University of Leipzig that same year.

Through a Rockefeller Fellowship, Peierls was able to study in Rome starting in 1932 with Enrico Fermi and then at the University of Cambridge in England. He chose to remain in England when Adolph Hitler became the German chancellor, working at the University of Manchester. In 1936, he moved to the University of Birmingham, where he worked on nuclear reactions. It was there that he began collaborating with Otto Frisch.

Aaron Barlow

See also: Frisch, Otto; Frisch-Peierls Memorandum; MAUD Committee. Document: 5

References

Gowing, Margaret. 1964. *Britain and Atomic Energy, 1935–1945*. London: Macmillan Publishing.

Hoddeson, Lillian, Paul W. Henriksen, Roger A. Meade, and Catherine L. Westfall. 1993. *Critical Assembly: A Technical History of Los Alamos During the Oppenheimer Years, 1943–1945*. New York: Cambridge University Press.

Peierls, Rudolf. 1985. *Bird of Passage: Recollections of a Physicist*. Princeton, NJ: Princeton University Press.

Szasz, Ferenc Morton. 1992. *British Scientists and the Manhattan Project: The Los Alamos Years*. New York: St. Martin's Press.

Plutonium

A generally artificially derived element with the atomic number 94, isotopes Pu-239 and Pu-241 of plutonium are fissile and so can be used in making nuclear bombs. This radioactive substance was used in the atomic bomb dropped on Nagasaki, Japan, by the United States in 1945, and its production is highly restricted worldwide. The element is quite dangerous and accumulates in human bones, making it impossible to counteract, and disposal of plutonium waste remains a concern.

Though Enrico Fermi at first believed he had identified atomic element number 94 in 1934, it wasn't until December 14, 1940, that Pu-238 was verifiably isolated for the first time by a team consisting of Joseph W. Kennedy, Edwin McMillan, Glenn T. Seaborg, and Arthur Wahl through deuteron bombardment of uranium using the University of California Berkeley Radiation Laboratory's cyclotron. They called the element "plutonium," which stuck, though Fermi had earlier suggested "hesperium." In England, working at the Cambridge University Cavendish Laboratory, Egon Bretscher and Norman Feather soon discovered that fissile Pu-239 could be produced as a by-product in a uranium-fueled slow neutron reactor.

With information supplied through Enrico Fermi's first self-sustaining chain reaction at the CP-1 Pile at the University of Chicago, an experimental reactor was built at the Clinton Engineer Works at Oak Ridge, Tennessee. Dubbed X-10 and working in tandem with a chemical separation plant, Seaborg began to remove plutonium from uranium. Soon, construction began on other reactors at Hanford Engineer Works in Washington. These were followed by construction of a facility at Los Alamos, New Mexico.

It was Pu-239 that most interested researchers on the atomic bomb, for it was likely to be much more powerful as an explosive than the uranium-235 also being extracted. However, the first batch of Pu-239 to arrive at Los Alamos from Oak Ridge was shown to contain too high a percentage of the much more volatile (and also fissile) Pu-240, making it unusable for the Thin Man bomb that had been designed around the assumption that it could be used. This led to a split in bomb-design objectives to long-term concentration on the Fat Man model, which could use the plutonium being produced and short-term focus on what would now be called "Little Boy," a bomb of similar design to Thin Man but using enriched U-235 rather than Pu-239.

Aaron Barlow

See also: Clinton Engineer Works; Fat Man; Fermi, Enrico; Hanford, Washington; Little Boy; Los Alamos Laboratory; Oak Ridge, Tennessee; Thin Man; Trinity Test; University of Chicago; Uranium-235

References

Asimov, Isaac. 1988. *Understanding Physics (Motion, Sound, and Heat/Light, Magnetism, and Electricity/The Electron, Proton, and Neutron)*. Dorchester, U.K.: Dorset.

Bernstein, Jeremy. 2007. *Plutonium: A History of the World's Most Dangerous Element*. Washington, D.C.: Joseph Henry Press.

Emsley, John. 2001. "Plutonium." In *Nature's Building Blocks: An A–Z Guide to the Elements*. Oxford: Oxford University Press.

Seaborg, Glenn, and Eric Seaborg. 2001. *Adventures in the Atomic Age: From Watts to Washington*. New York: Farrar, Straus and Giroux.

Welsome, Eileen. 2000. *The Plutonium Files: America's Secret Medical Experiments in the Cold War*. New York: Random House.

Potsdam Conference (July 17–August 2, 1945)

The final wartime conference involving the leaders of the major Allied powers, the conference was held in 1945 from July 17 to August 2 in the Cecilienhof Palace at Potsdam, near Berlin. Its code name, Terminal, signaled both the end of the war and the wartime alliance. U.S. President Franklin D. Roosevelt had died in April 1945; President Harry S. Truman represented the United States, assisted by Secretary of State James F. Byrnes and chairman of the Joint Chiefs of Staff Admiral William Leahy.

The results of British elections were announced in the midst of the conference, and in one of the most stunning upsets in British electoral history, the Conservatives were ousted. Prime Minister Winston L. S. Churchill resigned, replaced by leader of the British Labour Party Clement Attlee, with Foreign Secretary Ernest Bevin. No elections disturbed the Soviet delegation, headed by Joseph Stalin, assisted by Foreign Minister Vyacheslav Molotov. Despite French leader Charles de Gaulle's appeals to Washington, France was not represented at Potsdam. The day before the conference formally opened, Truman received word of the first successful explosion of an atomic bomb at Alamogordo, New Mexico.

Among issues discussed at the conference were the future of Germany and Eastern Europe and involving the Soviet Union in the war against Japan. On July 26, U.S. and British leaders issued a surrender ultimatum to Japan. Designed to weaken Japanese resistance to surrender, the Potsdam Declaration held out some hope to the Japanese for the future. Although their country would be disarmed, occupied, and shorn of its conquests, Japan would be allowed access to raw materials after the war and would have the opportunity for democratic development. If, however, Japanese leaders refused to surrender, the nation would be destroyed. The Soviet Union, several weeks away from a declaration of war against Japan, was not a party to this proclamation.

Stalin demanded heavy reparations from Germany for the vast damage suffered by the Soviet Union in the war. He held out for a firm figure, whereas Truman would agree only to the Soviet Union receiving a set percentage of a whole to be determined on the German capacity to pay. The U.S. delegation also disagreed with the Soviets over their loose interpretation of "war booty"—goods that could be confiscated without reference to reparations. Agreement was reached at Potsdam, however, that the Russians would receive 25 percent of plants and industrial equipment removed from the western zones. In return, the Soviets were to repay 15 of the total 25 percent in food and raw materials from their zone. The Soviets also received permission to seize German assets in Bulgaria, Hungary, Finland, Romania, and their zone of Austria. No agreement on reparations was ever reached, but it is estimated that the Russians probably took about $20 billion (the total sum discussed at the Yalta Conference) from their zone of Germany alone.

The Allies also reached agreement on the "three Ds"—democratization, denazification, and demilitarization. German leaders were also to be punished as war criminals, and Germany's resources were to be used to repair the damages that had been inflicted in the war on its neighbors. German industrial production was set at a level no higher than the average for Europe as a whole.

No peace treaty was signed between the Allies and Germany, and so further "temporary" arrangements sanctioned by Potsdam became permanent. Following the war, East Prussia was divided according to agreements made at the Tehran Conference. Königsberg, Memel, and northern East Prussia were appropriated by the Soviet Union, and the remainder of East Prussia went to Poland. The conferees at Potsdam agreed on an "orderly and humane" transfer of the German population from this region. This did not occur. Perhaps two million Germans lost their lives in the forced reparations and exodus that followed.

Agreement was reached over the surrender of Japanese forces in Korea and Indochina. In the case of Korea, the Soviets were to be responsible for their surrender north of the 38th parallel, and American forces were to be responsible south of that line. In Indochina, Chinese forces would take the Japanese surrender north of the 16th parallel and British forces south of it. Never intended as political boundaries, these too became part of the Cold War.

The leaders at Potsdam also established a Council of Foreign Ministers to plan the preparation of peace treaties. Their discussions produced increasingly bitter exchanges that reflected the start of the Cold War.

Spencer C. Tucker

See also: Churchill, Sir Winston L. S.; Roosevelt, Franklin D.; Truman, Harry. Document: 37

References

Byrnes, James F. 1947. *Speaking Frankly.* New York: Harper.

Gormly, James. 1990. *From Potsdam to the Cold War: Big Three Diplomacy, 1945–1947.* Wilmington, DE: Scholarly Resources Books.

Mastny, Vojtech. 1979. *Russia's Road to the Cold War: Diplomacy, Warfare, and the Politics of Communism, 1941–1945.* New York: Columbia University Press.

Mee, Charles L., Jr. 1975. *Meeting at Potsdam.* New York: Dell.

Thomas, Hugh. 1987. *Armed Truce: The Beginnings of the Cold War, 1945–1946.* New York: Atheneum.

Project Alberta

In March 1945, Project Alberta was formed and given the task of designing and putting together the nonnuclear parts of Fat Man and Little Boy bombs and transporting them to Tinian Island. It also worked at Wendover Army Air Field in Utah to help modify the Silverplate B-29 Superfortresses to hold and drop the bombs whose casings the project was responsible for. In addition, at North Field on Tinian, the project was responsible for assembling the bombs and loading them on the bombers.

Project Alberta was the responsibility of the Ordnance Division at the laboratory at Los Alamos, New Mexico, headed by navy captain William S. Parsons. In addition to its other responsibilities, it consisted of two bomb-assembly teams, one each for Fat Man and Little Boy.

In February 1945, Parsons sent navy commander Frederick Ashworth, his chief of operations, to Guam with a letter for Fleet Admiral Chester Nimitz to inform him of the Manhattan Project and the developing plans for dropping atomic bombs on Japan. Guam had been assumed to be the base from which planes of the 509th Composite Group would attack Japan, but based on what he saw there, Ashworth had reservations. For one thing, the island's harbor was already overcrowded. On the advice of the U.S. Army Air Force, he flew north into the Marianas for a look at Tinian, which had two usable airfields and was over a hundred miles closer to Japan. The island's commander, Brigadier General Frederick Kimble, recommended North Field, and Ashworth asked him to hold it.

General Leslie Groves assigned Colonel Elmer Kirkpatrick to oversee base development on Tinian, where the necessary buildings were quickly constructed. The bomb assembly and case pieces were shipped directly from San Francisco, California, to Tinian by boat. C-54 "Green Hornet" aircraft of the 509th transported Project Alberta personnel to Tinian, arriving on June 23, 1945. The members of the project who had stayed behind for the Trinity Test joined them on July 22, 1945, and bomb assemblage was completed.

Aaron Barlow

See also: Fat Man; 509th Composite Group; Groves, Leslie Richard; Little Boy; Los Alamos Laboratory; Trinity Test; Wendover Army Air Field

References

Bowen, Lee. 1959. *Project Silverplate 1943–1946*. Vol. 1 of *A History of the Air Force Atomic Energy Program*. The U.S. Air Force Historical Division.

Campbell, Richard H. 2005. *The Silverplate Bombers: A History and Registry of the Enola Gay and Other B-29s Configured to Carry Atomic Bombs*. Jefferson, NC: McFarland & Company.

Christman, Albert B. 1998. *Target Hiroshima: Deak Parsons and the Creation of the Atomic Bomb*. Annapolis, MD: Naval Institute Press.

Krauss, Robert, and Amelia Krauss, eds. 2005. *The 509th Remembered: A History of the 509th Composite Group as Told by the Veterans that Dropped the Bombs on Japan*. Wichita, KS: 509th Press.

Russ, Harlow W. 1990. *Project Alberta: The Preparation of Atomic Bombs for Use in World War II*. Los Alamos, NM: Exceptional Books.

Quebec Conference, 1st (August 14–24, 1943)

An Allied planning conference held in Quebec, Canada, from August 14 to 24, 1943 code-named Quadrant, this meeting included U.S. President Franklin D. Roosevelt, British Prime Minister Winston L. S. Churchill, Canadian Prime Minister William Lyon Mackenzie King, and Chinese Foreign Minister Tse-ven Soong, as well as their staffs and military advisers.

Regarding military strategy in Europe, Churchill continued to argue for concentration on the Balkans. The U.S. military chiefs were strongly opposed to this; they reminded their ally that the invasions of Sicily (July 9–August 22, 1943) and Italy (September 9) had been based on the premise that the next major objective would be the cross-channel invasion of France. The conferees then approved tentative plans for the cross-channel invasion, now code-named Operation Overlord, and fixed May 1, 1944, as the target date for its execution.

Churchill had argued that the commander of Overlord should be British, and he initially proposed General Sir Alan F. Brooke, chairman of the Imperial General Staff. By the time of the Quebec meeting, however, Churchill realized that the United States would have the preponderance of troops employed after the initial landing, and he had therefore concluded that the commander should be an American. At Quebec, therefore, he proposed and it was agreed that an American general would command Overlord and a British general would have charge of the Mediterranean Theater.

The Allies also agreed to accelerate the strategic bombing offensive against Germany from bases in the United Kingdom and Italy. The objectives of the bombing campaign would be to destroy German air combat strength; to dislocate the German military, industrial, and economic systems; and to prepare the way for a cross-channel invasion. The United States agreed to a large-scale buildup of its forces in the United Kingdom prior to the invasion of France. The Allies also agreed to press vigorously the war in the Mediterranean. The objective here was to drive Italy from the war and secure air bases for operations against Germany in Italy, Sardinia, and Corsica. The Allies discussed a second landing in France, code-named Operation Anvil, on the Mediterranean coast.

Allied operations in the Balkans would be limited to the supply of Balkan guerrillas by air and sea, minor commando raids, and strategic bombing. The Allies then agreed to intensify the war against German submarines and to make greater use of the Azores as an Allied naval and air base.

In the Pacific Theater, the Allies decided to establish a separate South-East Asia Command (SEAC) with Lord Louis Mountbatten as its commander. They also agreed to accelerate operations against Japan. The goals in the Pacific were to exhaust Japan's air, naval, and shipping resources; to cut its communications; and to secure bases from which to conduct strategic bombing of the Japanese home islands.

There was some disagreement on the last point about whether to set up air bases in China or on the Japanese barrier islands in the Central Pacific. This effort would be borne principally by expanding U.S. naval power, with large armies required only at the end to invade Japan. The British promised to participate fully in this effort once Germany was defeated. Finally, the United States, although it was opposed to formal "recognition" of General Charles de Gaulle's French Committee of National Liberation as the French government-in-exile, did issue a statement extending limited recognition to de Gaulle's government.

A second Quebec conference was held from September 12 to 16, 1944.

James Erik Vik

See also: Churchill, Sir Winston L. S.; Roosevelt, Franklin D. Document: 14

References

Kimball, Warren F. 1997. *Forged in War: Roosevelt, Churchill, and the Second World War*. New York: William Morrow and Company.

Sainsbury, Keith. 1994. *Churchill and Roosevelt at War: The War They Fought and the Peace They Hoped to Make*. New York: New York University Press.

U.S. Department of State. 1970. *Foreign Relations of the United States: The Conferences at Washington and Quebec (1943)*. Washington, DC: U.S. Government Printing Office.

R

Roosevelt, Franklin D. (1882–1945)

U.S. politician and president from 1933 to 1945, Franklin Delano Roosevelt was born on January 30, 1882, at his family's Hyde Park estate in Dutchess County, New York. Roosevelt was educated at home until age 14. He then attended Groton Preparatory School, Harvard University, and Columbia University Law School. In 1905, Roosevelt married his fifth cousin Eleanor Roosevelt, President Theodore Roosevelt's niece. First alerted to the possibility of an atomic bomb by the letter written by Léo Szilárd over Albert Einstein's signature in late 1939, Roosevelt's quick support for research in that direction led to the creation of the Manhattan Project less than three years later.

In November 1932, Roosevelt had been elected president of the United States on the Democratic ticket, triumphing over incumbent president Herbert Hoover. He promised the American people a "New Deal" and began regular radio broadcasts to the American people, the first U.S. president to do so. Known as "fireside chats," these addresses were designed to restore morale. Legislative products of his first frenzied hundred days in office included banking reform, the Agricultural Adjustment Act (AAA), and the National Industrial Recovery Act (NIRA). Congress allocated more than $3 billion under the NIRA for the Public Works Administration (PWA). The National Recovery Administration (NRA) set minimum wages and limited hours for employees. The Federal Emergency Relief Administration provided funds to relief agencies run by the state, and the new Civilian Conservation Corps (CCC) employed thousands of young men to replant forests, build parks, and work on flood-control projects. These massive governmental projects, and others, set the stage for the equally huge, though secret, Manhattan Project.

With the beginning of World War II in Europe in September 1939, Roosevelt increasingly turned his attention to foreign affairs and military preparedness, despite strong isolationist sentiments in Congress and among many American voters. On September 8, 1939, he proclaimed a limited national emergency, which allowed expansion of the army from 135,000 men to 227,000. Believing that the security of the United States demanded the defeat of the Axis powers and sensing that Adolf Hitler was a mortal threat to the world, Roosevelt gradually moved the United States from its isolationist stance. Later in September, he called on Congress to amend one of the Neutrality Acts, which it did the next month, allowing the Allies to purchase arms in the United States on a cash-and-carry basis. When, on October 11, Alexander Sachs, economist and friend of Roosevelt's, summarized the August letter to the president signed by Albert Einstein and composed by Léo Szilárd, Roosevelt moved quickly, asking Lyman Briggs, head of the National Bureau of Standards, to begin to look into the questions and possibilities of uranium, the first governmental action leading to the Manhattan Project.

Following the defeat of France in June 1940, Roosevelt pledged to support Britain in every manner short of declaring war. In September, he concluded an agreement with Britain whereby that country would receive 50 World War I–vintage destroyers in return for granting the United States rights to bases located in British territory in the Western Hemisphere, chiefly the Caribbean. He also initiated a major rearmament program in the United States and secured passage of the Selective Service Act, the first peacetime draft in the nation's history.

By early 1941, Roosevelt and British Prime Minister Winston L. S. Churchill were coordinating their nations' policies toward the Axis powers. In the spring of 1941, Roosevelt ordered U.S. destroyers to provide protection as far as Iceland for the North Atlantic convoys bound for Britain. In March 1941, on his urging, Congress passed the Lend-Lease Act, which extended U.S. aid to countries fighting the Axis powers. This type of cooperation extended to science, with the British beginning to share their own research into atomic possibilities that would result in the Tube Alloys project, which, in 1943, was enfolded into the Manhattan Project.

From 1941 to 1945, Roosevelt skillfully guided the United States through the war and worked to ensure a secure postwar world. During the course of the war, the United States fielded not only a navy larger than all the other navies of the world combined but also the largest air force and the most mobile, most heavily mechanized, and best-armed army in world history. It also provided the machines of war, raw materials, and food that enabled other nations to continue fighting the Axis powers. Amid these circumstances, full economic recovery was achieved in the United States.

In 1944, Roosevelt ran successfully for an unprecedented fourth presidential term against Republican candidate Thomas Dewey. In February 1945, he met Churchill and Soviet dictator Joseph Stalin at Yalta in the Crimea. The Yalta Conference built on decisions already reached at the prior Tehran Conference and was an effort to secure a stable postwar world. Roosevelt gambled that with his considerable charm, he could convince Stalin that he had nothing to fear from the United States and that Britain, the Soviet Union, China, and the United States could cooperate to secure a peaceful postwar world. Although accused of making unnecessary concessions to the Soviet Union at Yalta, Roosevelt really had little choice in these, as the Red Army already occupied much of Eastern Europe, and the U.S. military wished to induce the Soviets to enter the war against Japan.

At Yalta, Roosevelt was already gravely ill, and shortly afterward, he sought rest at his second home in Warm Springs, Georgia. He died there of a massive cerebral hemorrhage on April 12, 1945. Vice President Harry S. Truman succeeded him as president.

Kathleen G. Hitt and Spencer C. Tucker

See also: Briggs, Lyman; Churchill, Sir Winston L. S.; Einstein, Albert; Quebec Conference, 1st; Szilárd, Léo; Truman, Harry. Documents: 3, 4, 8, 14, 17, 18, 21

References

Cashman, Sean Dennis. 1989. *America, Roosevelt, and World War II*. New York: New York University Press.

Collier, Peter, and David Horowitz. 1995. *The Roosevelts: An American Saga*. New York: Touchstone.

Dallek, Robert. 1995. *Franklin D. Roosevelt and American Foreign Policy, 1932–1945.* New York: Oxford University Press.

Dawes, Kenneth S. 1993. *FDR: Into the Storm, 1937–1940—A History.* New York: Random House.

Dawes, Kenneth S. 2000. *FDR: The War President, 1940–1943—A History.* New York: Random House.

Freidel, Frank. 1990. *Roosevelt: A Rendezvous with Destiny.* New York: Little, Brown.

Goodwin, Doris Kearns. 1994. *No Ordinary Time: Franklin and Eleanor Roosevelt—The Home Front in World War II.* New York: Simon & Schuster.

Hamilton, Nigel. 2014. *The Mantle of Command: FDR at War, 1941–1943.* Boston, MA: Houghton Mifflin Harcourt.

Hanby, Alonzo L. 2004. *For the Survival of Democracy: Franklin Roosevelt and the World Crisis of the 1930s.* New York: Simon & Schuster.

Kaiser, David. 2014. *No End Save Victory: How FDR Led the Nation into War.* New York: Basic Books.

Larrabee, Eric. 1987. *Commander in Chief: Franklin Delano Roosevelt—His Lieutenants and Their War.* New York: Simon & Schuster.

S

Serber, Robert (1909–1997)

A set of three lectures by Robert Serber was put into a booklet, *The Los Alamos Primer*, which was distributed to new scientific staff at the Los Alamos Laboratory in New Mexico, making his one of the best-known names throughout the secretive Manhattan Project. He is also famous as the creator of the name of three bomb models (only two of which were produced)—Thin Man, Fat Man, and Little Boy. He was on Tinian Island for the Hiroshima and Nagasaki missions and was scheduled to be on the camera plane for the Nagasaki mission but did not go. He was part of the first team of Americans to enter the bombed cities of Hiroshima and Nagasaki after Japan's surrender to assess the damage of the atomic bomb from the ground.

Serber was born on March 14, 1909, in Philadelphia, Pennsylvania. He attended Lehigh University for his undergraduate degree before moving on to the University of Wisconsin at Madison, where he was awarded a PhD in physics in 1934. Soon after, he joined J. Robert Oppenheimer's team at the University of California at Berkeley and at the California Institute of Technology, remaining with Oppenheimer until accepting a position at the University of Illinois at Champaign Urbana in 1938, staying there until again joining Oppenheimer on the Manhattan Project in 1941. After the war, he found himself accused of disloyalty to the United States, though the charges were spurious.

Aaron Barlow

See also: Fat Man; Hiroshima, Bombing of; Little Boy; Los Alamos Laboratory; Nagasaki, Bombing of; Thin Man; Trinity Test. Documents: 10, 49a8

References

Hoddeson, Lillian, Paul W. Henriksen, Roger A. Meade, and Catherine L. Westfall. 2004. *Critical Assembly: A Technical History of Los Alamos During the Oppenheimer Years, 1943–1945*. New York: Cambridge University Press.

Serber, Robert. 1992. *The Los Alamos Primer: The First Lectures on How to Build an Atomic Bomb*. Berkeley: University of California Press.

Serber, Robert, and Robert Crease. 1998. *Peace & War: Reminiscences of a Life on the Frontiers of Science*. New York: Columbia University Press.

Stimson, Henry Lewis (1867–1950)

Serving as the U.S. secretary of war during World War II, Henry Lewis Stimson was born in New York City on September 21, 1867, into an old and distinguished family. He was educated at Yale University and Harvard Law School. In 1891, he entered the law firm of Root and Clarke. Its leading partner, Elihu Root, a future secretary of war and secretary of state, became one of Stimson's two lifelong role models, the other being future president Theodore Roosevelt.

Like Roosevelt, Stimson found public service more satisfying than practicing law, and he soon became active in New York

Secretary of War Henry Stimson (1867–1950) and Army Chief of Staff George Marshall (1880–1959). (Library of Congress)

Republican politics. Appointed secretary of war in 1911, Stimson attempted to modernize the army and improve troop training and the efficiency of the General Staff. He left office when Woodrow Wilson became president in 1913.

When World War I began in Europe in 1914, the staunchly interventionist and pro-Allied Stimson campaigned ardently for military preparedness. After Congress declared war on Germany in April 1917, Stimson volunteered, serving in France as a lieutenant colonel of artillery. He returned from the war convinced that the United States must assume a far greater international role.

As governor general of the Philippines in 1928, Stimson ruled in the spirit of benevolent paternalism. Appointed secretary of state in 1929 under President Herbert Hoover, he played a prominent role in negotiating the London Naval Treaty of 1930. He also attempted to strengthen the League of Nations by protesting Japan's establishment in 1931 of the puppet state of Manzhouguo (Manchukuo). He remained as secretary of state until 1933.

In the later 1930s, Stimson was among the strongest advocates of firm American opposition to the fascist states. When World War II began in 1939, Stimson, a convinced believer in an Anglo-American alliance, demanded extensive American assistance to the Allies and massive United States rearmament. Seeking bipartisan support for his foreign policies, in June 1940, Democratic President Franklin D. Roosevelt recruited Stimson as secretary of war, a position Stimson held throughout the war. With army chief of staff General George C. Marshall, Stimson and his able team oversaw the massive recruitment and industrial mobilization programs the war effort demanded.

Stimson oversaw the Manhattan Project, and in April 1945, he informed new president Harry S. Truman of this initiative's existence. In summer 1945, Stimson suggested that the Allies publicly warn the Japanese government that, unless Japan surrendered, it faced attack by devastating new weaponry. This advice led the United States, Britain, and the Soviet Union to issue the July 1945 Potsdam Declaration to this effect. Shortly afterward, Stimson urged Truman to share with the Soviets—with appropriate safeguards—the secrets of nuclear power. After retiring in 1945, Stimson endorsed a greatly enhanced American international role. He died in Huntington, New York, on October 20, 1950.

Priscilla Roberts

See also: Potsdam Conference; Roosevelt, Franklin D.; Truman, Harry. Documents: 12, 19, 22, 24, 25, 27, 28, 33, 40b, 42, 44

References

Hodgson, Godfrey. 1990. *The Colonel: The Life and Wars of Henry Stimson, 1867–1950*. New York: Alfred A. Knopf.

Schmitz, David F. 2000. *Henry L. Stimson: The First Wise Man*. Wilmington, DE: Scholarly Resources.

Strassmann, Fritz (1902–1980)

Analytical chemist Friedrich Strassmann, working with Otto Hahn, discovered a residue of barium after bombarding uranium with neutron particles in late 1938. Though there was no word for it at the time (Otto Frisch, working with Lise Meitner, would apply a term from biology to it the next year), this was the first demonstration of what we now know as nuclear fission.

Strassmann, who was born in Boppard, Germany, on February 22, 1902, was the son of a court clerk. He received a PhD in physical chemistry from the Technical University of Hannover in 1929 with a dissertation on the solubility of iodine in gaseous carbonic acid. His involvement with Hahn and with Lise Meitner, who (working with Frisch) would provide theoretical understanding for their discovery, started in 1934, with Strassmann replacing Meitner when she was forced to flee to Sweden to avoid the Nazis. His work with Hahn in 1938 discovering the presence of barium where, theoretically, it should not belong, let Meitner, working with Otto Frisch, to theorize the existence of nuclear fission the next year, setting the theoretical stage for development of the atomic bomb.

Strassmann did not leave Germany during World War II but was viewed with suspicion by the Nazis—with reason, for he and his wife even concealed a Jewish woman the Gestapo was seeking for two months during the war. Her name was Andrea Wolffenstein, and she hid in Strassmann's apartment with his wife and young son until she was able to find a more secure refuge. He was one of the scientists the Alsos Mission wanted to "secure" at the end of the war, though it was soon determined that he had had no connection with German efforts toward building an atomic bomb. Strassmann had withdrawn from the German Chemical Society in 1933 in protest to its dropping of Jewish members.

Strassmann died on April 22, 1980, in Mainz, West Germany.

Aaron Barlow

See also: Alsos Mission; Fissile Material; Frisch, Otto; Hahn, Otto; Meitner, Lise

References

Jungk, Robert, and James Cleugh, trans. 1958. *Brighter than a Thousand Suns: A Personal History of the Atomic Scientists.* New York: Harvest Books.

Simie, Ruth Lewin. 1997. *Lise Meitner: A Life in Physics.* Berkeley: The University of California Press.

Walker, Mark. 1993. *German National Socialism and the Quest for Nuclear Power 1939–1949.* Cambridge, U.K.: Cambridge University Press.

Sweeney, Charles (1919–2004)

Charles Sweeney flew the bombing mission that ended World War II, and from that point on, he ardently defended the use of atomic weapons against claims by revisionist historians that they were unnecessary. He is the only man to be present at the atomic bombings of both Hiroshima and Nagasaki.

Charles William Sweeney was born in Lowell, Massachusetts, on December 27, 1919. While a young man, he paid for an airplane ride and fell in love with flying. Sweeney then joined the army air corps as a cadet in April 1941 and received his wings shortly after the Japanese attack on Pearl Harbor. He sought a combat assignment but, much to his disappointment, was instead assigned as a test pilot at Eglin Field, Florida. Sweeney flew and tested virtually every aircraft in the American arsenal, but in September 1943, he glimpsed a new, gigantic aircraft coming in for a landing, one of the first Boeing B-29 Superfortresses, which was commanded by Colonel Paul Tibbets. Sweeney was so awed by the craft that he befriended Tibbets, secured a test hop in it, and expressed a desire to join the unit. Tibbets, impressed by Sweeney's skill as a pilot and his sincerity to fly, arranged a transfer. Sweeney did not realize it, but he had just joined the 509th Composite Group, a top-secret outfit destined to drop the first atomic bombs on Japan.

Soon after, Sweeney found himself at Wichita, Kansas, where the B-29s were being built, and he helped test and debug them. There, he had the delight of giving his childhood hero, Charles Lindbergh, a flight in the giant bomber. He also experienced stark terror while performing the same task for General Curtis E. LeMay, soon destined to lead B-29 formations on raids over Japan. The no-nonsense LeMay wanted to know everything about the airplane as soon as possible. Sweeney's knowledge of the aircraft impressed him, and the general handed him one of his rare compliments for a job well done. In the fall of 1944, Sweeney and Tibbets transferred again to desolate Wendover Field in Utah. There, the crews of the 509th honed their bombing skills by dropping huge, 10,000-pound concrete bombs, known as "pumpkins," whose weight and ballistics closely mimicked the atomic bombs they would carry. By May 1945, the men and equipment were considered proficient enough to deploy overseas, and Sweeney shipped from Seattle to the newly captured Pacific island of Tinian in the Marianas.

By that time, World War II had shifted in favor of the Allies; Germany had capitulated, and Japan had lost a succession of important island battles. The militaristic government of Japan, however, refused to concede defeat or even contemplate surrender. Moreover, its army and navy units resisted fanatically and fought to the death, and casualty rates for both sides made the prospects of invading the Japanese mainland appear prohibitive. The U.S. Department of War estimated that the 800,000-man force behind Operation Coronet, the projected attack on the home island of Honshu, would incur 300,000 casualties alone. The million-man force slated to undertake Operation Olympic, the invasion of the main island of Kyushu, would suffer similar casualties. For Japanese civilians caught in the cross fire, the toll was expected to be even higher, possibly in the millions. Nonetheless, the Japanese government mocked the July 1945 Potsdam Declaration calling for their unconditional surrender. Since the militarists were prepared to fight to the death, President Harry Truman felt he had little recourse but to employ atomic weapons. The only alternative, to subdue Japan by conventional means, might entail the loss of thousands of young American soldiers, sailors, and marines.

The first atomic strike was scheduled for August 6, 1945, and was commanded by Tibbets. Flying a B-29 called Enola Gay, he dropped a uranium device called Little Boy on Hiroshima, site of the Japanese Second Army headquarters. It was a textbook, flawless mission, but the Japanese government refused to surrender despite heavy devastation and loss of life. Truman, anxious to end the war and spare American lives, authorized a second atomic strike. Tibbets picked Sweeney to fly the mission. His target would be Kokura, a heavily industrialized city in southern Japan. On the morning of August 9, 1945, Sweeney gingerly eased his B-29, christened Bock's Car (now generally referred to as "Bockscar"), down the Tinian runway. Unlike the previous mission, he was carrying a plutonium-based weapon named Fat Man on account of its rotund shape. It was a third more powerful than the Hiroshima bomb, and because it had to be armed on the ground and not over the target, it was infinitely more dangerous to the crew.

In contrast to the previous mission, things immediately went awry. An internal pump failed and deprived Bock's Car of 600 gallons of fuel, which left the plane without adequate fuel reserves. Sweeney decided to press ahead rather than scrub the mission with a live weapon in his bomb bay. The ensuing approach to the target proved uneventful, but Kokura itself was obscured by thick smoke from a raid on nearby Yawata the day before. Sweeney made three passes over the city looking for a break in the cover, but none appeared. When antiaircraft fire began closing in, he aborted and made for his secondary target, Nagasaki, which was the site of three major Mitsubishi manufacturing plants that had helped Japan sustain the war effort. To Sweeney's disbelief, the city was also obscured by an impenetrable blanket of clouds. He was running low on fuel and preparing to drop the bomb on the sea when a small break suddenly appeared. Bock's Car then made an effective bomb run and took evasive action. When the device detonated, Sweeney noted in his autobiography how "the cloud was rising faster than at Hiroshima. It seemed more intense, more angry. It was a mesmerizing sight, at once breathtaking and ominous." However, his problems were scarcely over. As his B-29 raced for home, it became apparent that he lacked fuel to reach Tinian and had to make an emergency landing on Okinawa. After much confusion with air traffic control, the fuel gauges on Bock's Car were reading empty by the time he touched down.

The second strike on Nagasaki had the desired results. After intense deliberation, Japanese Emperor Hirohito ordered the war stopped, and the country announced its unconditional surrender on August 15, 1945. For his efforts, Sweeney was flown back to Tinian, where he received the Silver Star from General Nathan F. Twining. After the war, Tibbets and Sweeney visited Japan, where they witnessed the devastation wrought by atomic weapons. "There was no sense of joy among us as we walked the streets there," he confided. "We were relieved it was over, for us and for them."

Sweeney returned to the United States, where he went off active duty in July 1946 and joined the Massachusetts Air National Guard as operations officer of the 67th Fighter Wing. Sweeney rose to colonel in 1949 and brigadier general in 1957. He retired from the air force in May 1976 as a major general. He came out of retirement briefly in May 1995 to testify before a congressional subcommittee against the Smithsonian Institution's proposed *Enola Gay* exhibit, which was accused of being a piece of revisionist history intent on branding the United States as the aggressor in World War II. The ensuing uproar forced changes in the exhibit, which assumed a more objective, noncontroversial format.

Sweeney died on July 15, 2004, in Boston. His B-29, Bock's Car, remains on display at the Air Force Museum in Dayton, Ohio.

John C. Fredriksen

See also: Bockscar; Enola Gay; Fat Man; 509th Composite Group; Nagasaki, Bombing of; Tibbets, Paul

References

Burnham, Alexander. 1995. "Okinawa, Harry Truman, and the Atomic Bomb." *Virginia Quarterly Review* 71, no. 3 (Summer).

Chinnock, Frank W. 1969. *Nagasaki: The Forgotten Bomb*. New York: New American Library.

Ford, Daniel. 2016. *The Last Raid*. n.p.: Warbird Books.

Sweeney, Charles, James A. Antonucci, and Marion K. Antonucci. 1997. *War's End: An Eyewitness Account of America's Last Atomic Mission*. New York: Avon Books.

Szilárd, Leó (1898–1964)

Working with Enrico Fermi at Columbia University, Leó Szilárd created the first nuclear chain reaction in 1942. He was also among the scientists who urged the U.S. government to use the new technology to create an atomic weapon, if only to preempt Adolf Hitler from doing so. In his later years, Szilárd was an outspoken and tireless campaigner for peace and civilian control of atomic energy.

The son of a Jewish construction engineer and his wife, Szilárd was born in Budapest, Hungary, on February 11, 1898. He was a difficult, precocious child with obvious intellectual gifts and was known for his immodesty, moodiness, and wild imagination. He received his elementary and secondary education in Budapest and enrolled at the Budapest Institute of Technology for college in 1916, having decided to go into electrical engineering.

Aside from 1917–1918, which he spent in the Austro-Hungarian Army, Szilárd attended the institute until 1920, when he started studying at the Berlin Institute of Technology. There, his interest in engineering gradually gave way to a fascination with theoretical physics, partly because of the stimulating presence in the German city of such eminent physicists as Albert Einstein and Max Planck.

Leó Szilárd (1898–1964) was one of the first advocates of an American atomic bomb project and also one of the first to raise doubts about use of the bomb. (Esther Bubley/The LIFE Images Collection via Getty Images/Getty Images)

Szilárd switched schools again in 1921, enrolling at the University of Berlin to work in theoretical physics. In 1922, he finished his doctorate but stayed on at the school as an assistant at the Institute of Theoretical Physics. He held that post until 1925, when he was appointed a *privatdocent,* a special lecturer paid directly by the students. When he was not giving classes, Szilárd did research in thermodynamic statistics and X-rays at the university and at Berlin's famous Kaiser Wilhelm Institute, often working with Einstein on his theoretical problems.

Szilárd left Germany when Hitler came to power in 1933; he fled to Austria and from there to London. He spent some time deciding what to do next, but in the meantime, he helped other academics from Germany find places to stay as they arrived seeking asylum. In 1934, Szilárd found work as a physics instructor at St. Bartholomew's Hospital Medical College in London. In his spare time, he began experimenting with problems in nuclear physics and soon introduced a new method of separating isotopes in artificially radioactive elements.

Szilárd remained at St. Bartholomew's until 1935, when he moved to Oxford University and its famous Clarendon Laboratory to continue his experiments. The laboratory allowed him to spend six months of the year in the United States to do research, but in 1938, Szilárd moved there permanently after accepting a position as guest researcher at New York's Columbia University.

In 1939, Szilárd and his colleagues at Columbia confirmed, using special equipment he brought with him from England, that the emission of neutrons occurs when uranium releases its energy. He later recalled that when he saw the incontrovertible results of his experiment, as he would later write, he "knew the world was headed for sorrow" because it meant that "the liberation of atomic energy was possible in our lifetime." Szilárd was also terrified that the newspaper accounts of the new technology, so innocently published, would fall into the wrong hands, so he asked his scientific peers to stop publishing their results on nuclear fission.

Having quickly grasped the devastating amount of energy that "liberation" entailed, Szilárd applied for a patent so the information would not leak out. Next, he, Fermi, Einstein, Eugene Paul Wigner, and Edward Teller wrote to President Franklin D. Roosevelt. As World War II got underway in Europe, they urged him to authorize and support the speedy development of an atomic weapon. Their letter set in motion the program that would become known as the Manhattan Project.

Moving to the University of Chicago in 1942, which became one of the centers of the huge atomic bomb effort, Szilárd and many other scientists started the process of creating the first self-sustaining nuclear reactor. He survived an effort by a general to intern him because he was considered a security risk, and by late 1942, the scientists had obtained the first chain reaction from a plutonium pile, which they built on the squash court under the school's stadium. For the next three years, while Fermi and another team worked under J. Robert Oppenheimer on making the actual bomb at the Los Alamos National Laboratory in New Mexico, Szilárd and his team worked in Chicago to find a way to produce large amounts of plutonium cheaply and efficiently.

When the bomb was finally ready to use in 1945, Szilárd and some of his coworkers had an abrupt change of heart about their creation. Now they were just as afraid of what their government would do with the weapon as what Hitler might have done. They began a desperate campaign to convince President Harry Truman not to use the bomb or at most to drop it on an uninhabited piece of land somewhere just to demonstrate its awful power. However, the government and such scientists as Arthur Holly Compton ignored their pleas and dropped atomic bombs on two Japanese cities in August 1945.

Afterward, Szilárd launched a movement for civilian control of atomic energy and was the main personality behind physicist James Franck's 1945 letter to the secretary of war predicting a nuclear stalemate if governments failed to ban the bomb. He also organized and was a member of the Emergency Committee of Atomic Scientists, whose goal was to alert the public that "unparalleled catastrophe" was just around the corner because of the "unleashed power of the atom." Szilárd was also the scientist who managed to obtain Soviet Premier Nikita Khrushchev's personal permission to set up a dedicated "hotline" between Moscow and Washington, D.C., to prevent an accidental nuclear war.

After the war, Szilárd was so disgusted with his contribution to the conflict that he began taking classes in molecular biology at Cold Spring Harbor Laboratory. In 1946, he took a job as professor of biophysics at the University of Chicago and virtually gave birth to that new science. He went on to contribute significantly to the field by inventing the chemostat and developing new theories on the aging process and memory.

In 1962, Szilárd founded the Council for a Livable World to lobby politicians for civilian arms control. The following year, he became a resident fellow at the Salk Institute in La Jolla, California, which he helped Jonas Salk establish. The inventor of a radiotherapy treatment for cancer, Szilárd used the technique on himself when he contracted the disease. Unfortunately, it did not work, and he died in La Jolla on May 30, 1964.

Amanda de la Garza

See also: Compton, Arthur Holly; Einstein, Albert; Einstein-Szilárd Letter; Fermi, Enrico; Plutonium; Roosevelt, Franklin D.; Teller, Edward; Truman, Harry; University of Chicago; Wigner, Eugene Paul. Documents: 1, 2, 3, 4, 21, 30

References

Asimov, Isaac. 1982. *Asimov's Biographical Encyclopedia of Science & Technology.* New York: Doubleday.

Daintith, John. 1981. *The Biographical Encyclopedia of Scientists.* New York: Facts on File.

Wigner, Eugene P. 1969. "Leó Szilárd." *Biographical Memoirs: Vol 40.* Washington, D.C.: National Academies.

T

Teller, Edward (1908–2003)

U.S. physicist Edward Teller championed the design and construction of a successor to the atomic bomb and became known as the "father of the hydrogen bomb." He later championed the Strategic Defense Initiative (SDI) in the 1980s. Ede Teller was born on January 15, 1908, in Budapest, Hungary, then part of the Austro-Hungarian Empire. He changed his first name to Edward after moving to the United States. He died on September 9, 2003, in Stanford, California.

Teller obtained his doctorate in theoretical physics from the University of Leipzig in 1930, at the age of 22. When the Nazis came to power in Germany in 1933, Teller's Jewish heritage put him at risk, and he moved to the United States in 1935. He became a U.S. citizen in 1941 at the same time he became in involved in the secret atomic research that grew into the Manhattan Project. In late 1941, conversations between Teller and Enrico Fermi led to speculation that a more powerful type of bomb was possible, one based on fusion instead of fission. Teller advocated research into fusion bombs as well as fission bombs, but the Manhattan Project concentrated on the technically less challenging fission bomb.

Although disturbed by the destruction that the atomic bombs wrought on Hiroshima and Nagasaki, Teller did not question the morality of working on the bomb. Fascism was too great a threat. After three years at the University of Chicago, Teller returned to Los Alamos in 1949 as an assistant

Edward Teller, a Hungarian physicist who emigrated to the United States in 1935 to avoid persecution as a Jew, was a major contributor to the Manhattan Project and, later, to the development of the hydrogen bomb. (Library of Congress)

director. When the Soviets demonstrated their own atomic bomb in 1949, the U.S. government decided to pursue the hydrogen bomb based on fusion. Teller led this effort. Flawed calculations by Teller initially delayed the superbomb project, but eventually other scientists corrected the errors. In 1951, Stanislaw Ulam and Teller solved the chief technical problem by electing to use X-rays generated by an atomic bomb trigger to start the fusion reaction in the hydrogen bomb. The first hydrogen bomb was exploded in 1952 at Eniwetok Atoll in the Pacific, and Teller became known as the "father of the hydrogen bomb."

Teller convinced the Atomic Energy Commission (AEC), which set U.S. civilian and military nuclear policy, to establish the Lawrence Livermore Laboratory at the University of California at Berkeley. This laboratory combined important civilian work in nuclear physics with military contracts to design new generations of nuclear weapons. Teller was the associate director of the laboratory from 1954 to 1958 and from 1960 to 1975, with a brief two-year stint as director from 1958 to 1960.

A political conservative and ardent anticommunist, Teller encouraged the United States to build an ever-larger nuclear arsenal to counter the Soviet Union. He testified against J. Robert Oppenheimer, the "father of the atomic bomb," in the infamous 1954 AEC hearing that resulted in Oppenheimer losing his security clearance and being forced from government service. This testimony caused a rift in the physics community that made Teller something of a hero or a pariah, depending on one's point of view. In the 1980s, Teller became a vocal advocate of the Reagan administration's Strategic Defense Initiative (SDI), commonly referred to as "Star Wars." SDI was not popular with many physicists, an attitude that Teller blamed on fallout from the Oppenheimer decision rather than the technical difficulties inherent in the idea. Teller received the 1962 Enrico Fermi award from the AEC and the National Medal of Science in 1982.

Eric G. Swedin

See also: Einstein, Albert; Einstein-Szilárd Letter; Fermi, Enrico; Los Alamos Laboratory; Oppenheimer, Julius Robert; Szilárd, Léo; Wigner, Eugene Paul. Document: 3

References
Blumberg, Stanley A., and Louis G. Panos. 1990. *Edward Teller: Giant of the Golden Age of Physics*. New York: Scribner.
Teller, Edward. 1987. *Better a Shield than a Sword: Perspectives on Defense and Technology*. New York: The Free Press.
Teller, Edward, with Judith Shoolery. 2001. *Memoirs: A Twentieth-Century Journey in Science and Politics*. Cambridge, MA: Perseus.

Thermal Diffusion Uranium Enrichment

One of three methods for enriching uranium during the Manhattan Project, thermal diffusion uranium enrichment is a simple and relatively cheap way of separating uranium-235 gas molecules from uranium-238, though it was heavily dependent on an abundant source of water and not particularly effective. The S-50 plant at the Clinton Engineer Works at Oak Ridge, Tennessee, was not able to enrich enough uranium for the construction of a bomb, but it did feed its slightly enriched uranium to facilities using the other two methods, the Y-12 calutrons and the K-25 gaseous diffusion plant, speeding up production of useful enriched uranium slightly.

The process is based on the concept of thermophoresis, in which mobile particles of different types respond differently to temperature gradients. U-235 and U-238 in uranium hexafluoride respond slightly differently to heat and cold, allowing for them to be separated when one rises (the former) and the other drops (the latter).

The process was developed by physicist Philip H. Abelson, who was funded by the Uranium Committee established in 1939 under Lyman Briggs of the National Bureau of Standards and of the National Defense

Research Committee. The work was taken over by the U.S. Naval Research Laboratory (NRL) in 1941, with Abelson becoming an NRL employee.

At the urging of General Leslie Groves, the pilot project at Anacostia in Washington, D.C., was expanded, eventually leading to construction under Manhattan Project authorization at Clinton Engineer Works.

Aaron Barlow

See also: Advisory Committee on Uranium; Briggs, Lyman; Clinton Engineer Works; Groves, Leslie Richard; National Bureau of Standards; National Defense Research Committee; Uranium-235. Document: 40g

References

Brown, A. C., and C. B. MacDonald, eds. 1977. *Secret History of the Atomic Bomb.* New York: Dial Press.

Chapman, Sydney, and T. G. Cowling. 1970. *The Mathematical Theory of Non-Uniform Gases: An Account of the Kinetic Theory of Viscosity, Thermal Conduction and Diffusion in Gases.* Cambridge, U.K.: Cambridge University Press.

Groves, Leslie. 1962. *Now It Can Be Told: The Story of the Manhattan Project.* New York: Harper.

Smyth, Henry DeWolf. 1945. *Atomic Energy for Military Purposes: The Official Report on the Development of the Atomic Bomb under the Auspices of the United States Government, 1940–1945.* Princeton, NJ: Princeton University Press.

Thin Man

The Thin Man design for an atomic bomb was abandoned in favor of the Fat Man design and replaced by the Little Boy design. The fault lay in the volatility of plutonium-240 (its too-high rate of spontaneous fission), which would prompt the bomb to fizzle rather than explode. It was a gun-type design much like that of the Little Boy that would eventually be exploded over Hiroshima.

The gun-type design was proposed by a group led by J. Robert Oppenheimer in 1942. Two subcritical masses, one called a "bullet" and the other a "target," would be kept separate in the bomb until the time of detonation, when the bullet would be shot down the barrel at high speed toward the target. The collision would create a supercritical mass, and the speed of the impact would cause it to erupt in an atomic explosion.

At the Los Alamos Laboratory, where much of the design work for World War II atomic bombs was completed under the direction of Oppenheimer, both the gun-type and implosion-type atomic weapons were considered and designed, though priority was given to the gun-type. The two were named by physicist Robert Serber, who was either a movie buff or a fan of writer Dashiell Hammett—or both—for each name comes from a movie made from a Hammett Novel. *The Thin Man* became a series of films in the late 1930s and through the 1940s starring William Powell and Myrna Loy. The name Fat Man comes from a character from Hammett's novel *The Maltese Falcon* played in the 1941 film by rotund Sydney Greenstreet.

The question of necessary purity of the plutonium for a Thin Man–type bomb was not fully addressed (the bomb's creators believing it would be solved by new methods for the production of uranium) until it was realized that the level of impurities, especially Pu-240 could not be sufficiently reduced to allow for a stable bomb prior to detonation. At a Los Alamos meeting on July 17, 1944, this issue was addressed, and a decision was made to abandon design for a gun-type bomb using plutonium and change focus to a model on the same concept but using uranium-235 and named Little Boy. This would be the design of the bomb detonated over Hiroshima on August 6, 1945.

Aaron Barlow

See also: Enola Gay; Fat Man; 509th Composite Group; Gun-Type Fission Weapon; Hanford, Washington; Hiroshima, Bombing of; Little Boy; Plutonium; Project Alberta; Serber, Robert

References

Nichols, Kenneth D. 1987. *The Road to Trinity: A Personal Account of How America's Nuclear Policies Were Made.* New York: William Morrow and Company.

Serber, Robert, and Robert Crease. 1998. *Peace & War: Reminiscences of a Life on the Frontiers of Science.* New York: Columbia University Press.

Tibbets, Paul (1915–2007)

Paul Warfield Tibbets, a lowly lieutenant colonel at the time, flew the most important bombing mission in history. His strike against the Japanese city of Hiroshima ushered in the atomic age and led to the speedy conclusion of World War II. For this reason, he has consistently defended his actions as morally correct under the circumstances.

Tibbets was born in Quincy, Illinois, on February 23, 1915. He was raised in Florida, where, at the age of 12, he experienced his first airplane ride. The event changed his life, and from that point forward, he was determined to be a pilot. Tibbets attended both the University of Florida and the University of Cincinnati to study medicine, but in February 1937, he enlisted as a cadet with the army air corps. The following year, he won his wings at Kelly Field, Texas, and was commissioned a second lieutenant. In the early months of World War II, Tibbets flew anti-submarine patrols out of Pope Field, North Carolina, before becoming qualified in Boeing B-17 Flying Fortress bombers.

In February 1942, Tibbets became commander of the 340th Bomb Squadron and was dispatched to England as part of the newly organized Eighth Air Force. That August, he accompanied General Ira C. Eaker on the first bombing mission over Nazi-occupied Europe by hitting the rail yards at Rouen, France. After completing 25 missions in B-17s, Tibbets was selected to fly General Dwight D. Eisenhower and General Mark Clark for negotiations at Gibraltar and served as their personal pilot for many months. By November 1942, he was in Algeria leading the first bombardment mission in support of Operation Torch, the North Africa invasion. His reputation as an excellent officer culminated in his transfer back to the United States in March 1943, and he served as a test pilot in the Boeing B-29 Superfortress program at Wichita, Kansas. This gigantic bomber, a new and highly complicated weapon system, was undergoing its share of developmental problems. Tibbets soon accumulated over 400 hours in flight tests, more than any other pilot. Despite the dangers inherent in testing new technology, he performed well and was called to Washington, D.C., for an interview.

In September 1944, Tibbets was informed that, by dint of his superb military record, he had been chosen by army air force chief Hap Arnold for a special mission. This was the Manhattan Project, the four-year-old project to develop the atomic bomb. He was assigned to organize and train a handpicked unit to deliver this weapon, when available, over enemy sites yet selected. "It was bewildering," Tibbets confessed. "I was to train people in secret to drop a bomb that hadn't been built, on a target that hadn't been chosen." Using the code name Silverplate, he was authorized to command any resources he deemed necessary for the project. This was an enormous responsibility for a relatively low-ranking 29-year-old lieutenant colonel, but Tibbets threw himself into the project with his accustomed skill. He handpicked his crews from many individuals with whom he had flown over Europe. He next commandeered 15 new B-29s that were then specially modified for the mission. These craft were stripped of turrets and armor plating, had fuel injection systems installed for greater range and efficiency, and were fitted with the latest reversible pitch propellers to shorten runway rolls. Because secrecy was paramount, Tibbets assembled and trained his unit at remote Wendover Army Air Base in Utah. This bleak location became the site of the 509th Composite Group, which spent several months test-dropping 10,000-pound concrete bombs, or "pumpkins," in preparation for the actual raid. By May 1945, he considered his men proficient enough in their skills for deployment overseas, and they shipped from Seattle for the newly captured island of Tinian in the Marianas.

World War II at this time had entered its final phase. Once Germany had surrendered, the Japanese empire remained the sole obstacle to world peace, and it had recently suffered costly defeats in the Philippines, Okinawa, and elsewhere. Unfortunately, the militarists controlling the country were determined to fight to the end. They publicly scoffed at the July 1945 Potsdam Declaration, which called for unconditional surrender, and made clear their

Paul Tibbets, shown here in 1940, commanded the Enola Gay, a B-29 Superfortress that dropped an atomic bomb over Hiroshima on August 6, 1945. (Corbis via Getty Images)

determination to fight on. This posed a serious dilemma for President Harry Truman, who was anxious to end the war and the bloodshed. The recent victory at Okinawa was conclusive proof the Japanese military had lost none of its ferocity. Though losing 110,000 men, they managed to kill 12,000 Americans and wound another 38,000 before the battle ended. Knowing that an invasion of the Japanese home islands was inevitable, Truman began being briefed on the numbers of men required and the resultant casualties to be anticipated. It was projected that Operation Olympic, the forthcoming invasion of Kyushu, Japan, would require 800,000 soldiers alone and would likely suffer 30 percent casualties. Furthermore, Operation Coronet, the invasion of the main island of Honshu, would employ over one million men of all branches and sustain equally high losses. Moreover, in the face of such overwhelming firepower, Japanese military and civilian losses were calculated to be even greater. Faced with the prospect of half a million dead Americans, Truman felt he had no recourse but to employ atomic weapons to force Japan's capitulation and spare the lives of countless human beings. Otherwise, Japanese fanaticism rendered conventional methods too prohibitive to contemplate.

On August 6, 1945, Tibbets powered up his B-29, Enola Gay, which he christened after his mother. Onboard was a uranium nuclear device, the Little Boy, which weighed 10,000 pounds. Once released, it would explode with the force of 20,000 tons of dynamite. The Enola Gay lifted off at 2:30 a.m. and made for Hiroshima in southern Japan. That city had been selected by Tibbets for its pristine condition; despite the fact that Hiroshima was headquarters for the Japanese Second Army, it had never been bombed. The effects of the atomic weapons could therefore be studied without collateral damage from earlier raids. His approach to target was uneventful, weather was good, and at 9:15 a.m., Little Boy was released. Tibbets took immediate evasive action, but the resulting explosion was horrific and stunned the American crew. "A bright light filled the plane," he recalled. "We turned back to look at Hiroshima. The city was hidden by that awful cloud." The Enola Gay made an equally uneventful return trip to Tinian, where, after arrival, Tibbets received the Distinguished Service Cross from General Carl A. Spaatz. Rarely have the actions of a single individual wielded such profound impact on the course of human history.

The atomic age was born in horrific fashion, with an estimated 100,000 Japanese casualties resulting from the blast, heat, and—a new menace—radiation. Still, as grim as this tally was, it represented less than half the carnage of General Curtis E. LeMay's incendiary raid on Tokyo in February 1945, a fact the Japanese militarists seemed to appreciate. Despite Hiroshima, they summarily ignored Truman's second ultimatum to surrender. Following authorization for a second atomic strike, Tibbets chose Major Charles Sweeney to attack Kokura on August 9, 1945, but bad weather necessitated a run over the secondary target of Nagasaki. The second bomb was delivered and had the desired effect. After a week of wrangling in the Japanese cabinet, Emperor Hirohito announced that Japan was willing to abide by the Potsdam Declaration of August 15, 1945. Thus, World War II, the biggest bloodbath in human history, was brought to its sudden and triumphant conclusion.

After the war, Tibbets continued his association with atomic weapons. He witnessed the Bikini Atoll tests in 1946 as a technical adviser and went on to help develop the six-engine Boeing B-47 Stratojet bomber from 1947 to 1952. Thereafter, he commanded several units of the Strategic Air Command and helped establish the National Military Command Center at the Pentagon. Tibbets left the air force in 1966 with a rank of brigadier general and went on to direct an all-jet executive taxi service in Columbus, Ohio. He retired again in 1985 and resided in Chicago, Illinois, until his death on November 1, 2007. Although some have since questioned the use of atomic weapons on Japan, Tibbets never wavered in his belief that his actions were morally correct. "I did what I was told to do," he told a television documentary. "I have no regrets. I have never lost a night's sleep over it." In view of sterling service to the country, Tibbets was inducted into the National Aviation Hall of

Fame in Dayton, Ohio, in 1996. His plane, the Enola Gay, is on permanent display at the National Air and Space Museum in Washington, D.C.

John C. Fredriksen

See also: Enola Gay; 509th Composite Group; Hiroshima, Bombing of; Wendover Army Air Field

References

Cox, Alvin D. 1995. "The Enola Gay and Japan's Decision to Surrender." *Journal of East Asian Relations* 4: 161–167.

Lewis, Robert. 1995. "The Biggest Decision: Why We Had to Drop the Atomic Bomb." *American Heritage* 46: 70–77.

Oxford, Edward. 1985. "The Flight that Changed the World. Enola Gay." *American History Illustrated* 20: 12–19.

Thomas, Gordon, and Max M. Watts. 1977. *Enola Gay.* New York: Stein & Day.

Tibbets, Paul W. 1989. *Flight of the Enola Gay.* Reynoldsburg, OH: Buckeye Aviation Book Co.

Tibbets, Paul W. 1998. *Return of the Enola Gay.* New Hope, PA: Enola Gay Remembered, Inc.

Tibbets, Paul W., Clair C. Stebbins, and Harry Franken. 1978. *The Tibbets Story.* New York: Stein & Day.

Tinian Joint Chiefs

The three men responsible for the operations on Tinian Island that led to the bombings of Hiroshima and Nagasaki were known collectively and informally as the "Tinian Joint Chiefs." They were Brigadier General Thomas Farrell, who represented the Manhattan Project, Captain William S. Parsons, who commanded Project Alberta (which had been responsible for building and delivering the bombs to be used), and Rear Admiral William R. Purnell, representing the Military Policy Committee.

As informal executive officer to (now) Major General Leslie Groves, Farrell was cognizant of all aspects of Manhattan Project work. Born in 1891, he had served with distinction in the American Expeditionary Force in World War I. An engineer with a degree from Rensselaer Polytechnic Institute, he stayed in the army after the war, teaching at its Engineer School and then at West Point. From 1926 until the start of World War II, he was employed in New York State public works engineering projects and concerns. Though he worked with Groves early in the war, he was not involved in the Manhattan Project until the start of 1945. From that point on, he was intimately involved with almost all Manhattan Project activities, including witnessing the Trinity Test on July 16, 1945. After the surrender of Japan, he oversaw the teams that went into Hiroshima and Nagasaki to explore the effects of the bombs.

Captain Parsons, known as "Deak," would fly as the weaponeer on the Enola Gay on its mission to drop an atomic bomb over Hiroshima. Worried about the dangers of takeoff, he armed the bomb during the flight, inserting into place the nonnuclear explosive that would propel the "bullet" of uranium-235 into the "target" of the same substance at high speed to create a supercritical mass and explosion. At that point, he had been with the Manhattan Project for more than two years as an associate director at the laboratory at Los Alamos, New Mexico. His direct responsibility was ordnance and the design, construction and testing of the nonnuclear parts of the Little Boy bomb in particular. He also managed Project Alberta, which was responsible for getting the bomb (and the Fat Boy bomb) to Tinian Island in preparation for the attacks.

Like Farrell, Purnell was a World War I veteran (Parsons was too young to serve). A graduate of the U.S. Naval Academy at Annapolis, he commanded the destroyer USS *Lamson* during the earlier conflict, staying with the navy during the peacetime years and being promoted to rear admiral in November 1941, a month before the United States entered World War II. From September 1942, he served as the representative of the navy on the Military Policy Committee that oversaw military contributions to the Manhattan Project.

Aaron Barlow

See also: Groves, Leslie Richard; Los Alamos Laboratory; Project Alberta

References

Christman, Albert B. 1998. *Target Hiroshima: Deak Parsons and the Creation of the Atomic Bomb.* Annapolis, MD: Naval Institute Press.

Furer, Julius Augustus. 1959. *Administration of the Navy Department in World War II.* Washington, D.C.: U.S. Government Printing Office.

Lewis, Robert A., and Eliot Tolzer. 1957. "How We Dropped the A-Bomb." *Popular Science* (August): 71–75, 209–210.

Tizard Mission

The British Technical and Scientific Mission, generally known as the "Tizard Mission" after its head, Henry Tizard, was an August and September 1940 outreach by the United Kingdom to the United States to begin coordination in areas of military research and development. The idea was to present British research developments, including Tube Alloys, as a first step in maintaining a close and open cooperation.

Tizard himself was a chemist at Oxford University for a short time after World War I before becoming assistant secretary to the Department of Scientific and Industrial Research of the British government in 1920. In 1929, he left government to become president and rector of Imperial College London. He stayed in that position until 1942.

At the time, the United States was still officially uninvolved in the war, though it had begun to support Great Britain as much as it could without overstepping its neutral status. Wanting to establish a quid pro quo with the Americans, the British decided to start by offering their own information, hoping they would then be allowed use of American resources. Among what was initially shared was the Frisch-Peierls Memorandum, which showed the feasibility of an atomic bomb.

During a meeting with National Defense Research Committee (NDRC) Chairman Vannevar Bush on August 31, 1940, the two agreed on a series of meetings between British representatives and relevant NDRC divisions. Included among these was Enrico Fermi at Columbia University, who was informed of the conclusions of the Frisch-Peierls Memorandum. Like most of the British delegation, Fermi was skeptical that a bomb could be built, given limitations on the possibilities of uranium isotope separation as they were known at the time.

The great success of the mission lay in the opening of channels of communication and personal connection between scientists on both sides of the Atlantic. This would prove particularly important on production of the MAUD Committee Report and the events it sparked leading to the American Manhattan Project.

Aaron Barlow

See also: Bush, Vannevar; Fermi, Enrico; Frisch-Peierls Memorandum; MAUD Committee; National Defense Research Committee

References

Celinscak, Mark. 2013. "Henry T. Tizard." In *Philosophers of War: The Evolution of History's Greatest Military Thinkers*, 487. Santa Barbara, CA: ABC-CLIO.

Clark, Ronald W. 1965. *Tizard*. Cambridge, MA: MIT Press.

Conant, Jennet. 2002. *Tuxedo Park: A Wall Street Tycoon and the Secret Palace of Science that Changed the Course of World War II*. New York: Simon & Schuster.

Phelps, Stephen. 2010. *The Tizard Mission: The Top-Secret Operation that Changed the Course of World War II*. Yardley, PA: Westholme.

Zimmerman, David. 1996. *Top Secret Exchange: The Tizard Mission and the Scientific War*. Montreal: McGill-Queen's University Press.

Transmutation of Uranium into Plutonium

Quickly after it was first identified, plutonium isotope plutonium-239 became the preferred fissile matter for use in construction of nuclear weapons. Initially, uranium-235 was also used, but from the beginning, plutonium was preferred due to its greater power and its higher probability for fission.

It requires nuclear chain reaction followed by chemical separation for plutonium to be produced from uranium-238, a nonfissile uranium isotope. The resulting plutonium, however, contains both plutonium-239 and the more unstable plutonium-240, which is prone to spontaneous fission. It was on discovery of this that the Thin Man plutonium bomb was abandoned, for its gun-type design made such spontaneous fission more likely than in bombs of the implosion-type design (Fat Man). Developing effective and efficient processes of transmutation of uranium into plutonium was a major goal of the Manhattan Project, for one of the main fears was that enough fuel for the bombs could not be produced in time for the atomic bomb to have an impact on the war.

The first transmutations of uranium into plutonium took place at the Berkeley Radiation Laboratory of the University of California at Berkeley and at the University of Cambridge's Cavendish Laboratory. On August 20, 1942, a measurable amount of plutonium was produced and isolated at the University of Chicago's Metallurgical Laboratory just months before the even more significant self-sustaining chain reaction achieved by Enrico Fermi and his team at Staff Field of the same university. From these events, an experimental air-cooled production reactor (named X-10) was able to be developed and built at the Clinton Engineer Works at Oak Ridge, Tennessee, soon followed by the reactors at the Hanford, Washington, site.

Plutonium metal was first produced from the new processes when plutonium trifluoride was reduced. For the first time, plutonium could be seen by the unaided human eye.

Aaron Barlow

See also: Clinton Engineer Works; Fat Man; Fermi, Enrico; Metallurgical Laboratory; Oak Ridge, Tennessee; Plutonium; Thin Man; Uranium-235

References

Bernstein, Jeremy. 2007. *Plutonium: A History of the World's Most Dangerous*

Element. Washington, D.C.: Joseph Henry Press.

Clark, Ronald W. 1961. *The Birth of the Bomb: The Untold Story of Britain's Part in the Weapon that Changed the World*. London: Phoenix House.

Rhodes, Richard. 1986. *The Making of the Atomic Bomb*. New York: Simon & Schuster.

Trinity Test

On July 16, 1945, in the Jornada del Muerto (Dead Man's Trail) desert, the first ever atomic bomb was detonated. The event was code-named "Trinity," and the site, 35 miles southeast of Sorcorro, New Mexico, was part of the U.S. Army Air Force's Alamogordo Bombing and Gunnery Range. Like December 2, 1942, the date of Enrico Fermi's first nuclear chain reaction at the University of Chicago, the date of Trinity can be argued as that of the start of the nuclear age. It is not clear where the name "Trinity" comes from, but J. Robert Oppenheimer wrote to Manhattan Project head General Leslie Groves in response to a query in 1962 that he had been thinking a lot at the time of a poem written by John Donne. However, neither the word "trinity" nor the concept seems apparent in the poem.

The bomb tested was of the same type as that which would be dropped over Nagasaki less than a month later, though it lacked the shell casing necessary for dropping the bomb from a great height. This first exploded atomic bomb was nicknamed "Gadget." The test was overseen by Kenneth Bainbridge, a Harvard University physicist who had joined the Manhattan Project in 1943.

Recognition that a test would be necessary before attempting to drop an atomic bomb in actual hostilities led to discussions at the laboratories at Los Alamos, New Mexico, beginning in January 1944. At first, there was concern that a test would further limit the amount of plutonium that could be used for an actual bombing. A smaller bomb was suggested, one that would take place in a containment vessel, thereby allowing for the recovery of the uranium. Oppenheimer argued for a test of a full-sized bomb but still in a containment vessel and won support from Groves. In the event, however, the prepared vessel, nicknamed "Jumbo," was not used and, as the blast showed, would not have been effective.

The Fat Man–type Gadget implosion-type weapon was put together in a trial run on July 3, 1945, when it was driven to the Trinity site and then back to Los Alamos. Final assembly of the bomb began on July 13 at the one building in the area that had predated the Trinity project, the abandoned McDonald Ranch House, which had been modified for this express purpose, with a bedroom turned into a "clean room." A 100-foot steel tower had been constructed at the Trinity site, and the bomb was raised to the top. As it was planned to detonate the actual bombs while still in the air, this would allow the test explosion to approximate more closely the sort of damage that could be expected than if Gadget were exploded while lying on the ground. The bomb was armed at about 10 p.m. on July 15.

Planning for the test had been exhaustive, for no one knew what to expect. Bainbridge's group, known as E-9, had been subdivided to seven sections whose work was now nearing completion.

Seven Sections of E-9

TR-1.   Services
TR-2.   Shock and Blast
TR-3.   Measurements

The Trinity explosion on July 16, 1945, the first atomic bomb test, made clear both the power of the bomb and the feasibility of a successful atomic attack on Japan. (National Archives)

TR-4. Meteorology
TR-5. Spectrographic and Photographic
TR-6. Airborne Measurements
TR-7. Medical

The site for the test had been chosen both because of its proximity to the Los Alamos Laboratory and because it was far removed from human population and activities. That it was flat and generally windless was also important, for nothing would impede the blast and radioactive fallout would not likely blow onto inhabited areas. The fact that it was part of an established air force bombing range was also of importance, for no new land would need to be acquired.

Security for the site had begun back at the beginning of 1945 through both patrols on horseback (at first) and security checkpoints. Soon the security staff replaced the horses with jeeps. Basic facilities were constructed on the site, and personnel were moved there, the number growing from 160 to over 400 on the eve of the test. Almost everything needed had to have been trucked in on new roads laid down for just that purpose.

A rehearsal explosion had been set off on May 7, 1945, when a quantity of standard Composition B explosives with the power of 108 tons of TNT was placed on a two-foot tower and, after a quantity of radioactive material had been laced in, was ignited. Though the amount of radioactivity had been deliberately kept low, a specially altered M4 Sherman tank with lead shielding had practiced retrieving samples after the blast. The main lesson from the test was that available equipment would not be enough for the real thing. Roads and facilities needed to be improved, and more radios were needed, along with a teletype and buried telephone lines for better communications. This was done quickly in the days before the actual test.

Though weather conditions were expected to be better after July 18, 1945, political considerations would not be. President Harry Truman mandated that the test take place at or before the beginning of the Potsdam Conference in Germany between the three main victors in the war in Europe: Great Britain, the Union of Soviet Socialist Republics, and the United States. Truman wanted to be able to use the success of the test as a background bargaining chip.

At 5:30 in the morning, Gadget was detonated, the energy of the blast equivalent to about 20 kilotons of TNT. The test was observed on the ground and from a pair of B-29s above. Unfortunately, overcast skies limited what they could see from the planes. Observers on the ground saw the surrounding mountains illuminated greater than at day and felt heat hotter than an oven strike them.

Expecting that at least a few civilians would notice a blast of the magnitude expected, Groves had ordered William L. Laurence of *The New York Times* to prepare four press releases, each for a different possible outcome of the test. The one used, written for the most successful outcome, claimed that a remote munitions dump had accidentally blown up but without loss of life.

As quickly as possible, news of the positive result of the test was sent in a coded message to Secretary of War Henry Stimson, who was accompanying President Truman in Germany. The coded message, sent by Stimson's assistant, George Harrison, read, "Operated on this morning. Diagnosis not yet complete but results seem satisfactory and already exceed expectations. Local press release necessary as interest extends great distance. Dr. Groves pleased. He returns tomorrow. I will keep you posted." Stimson had the news taken to Truman immediately.

Aaron Barlow

See also: Alamogordo Bombing and Gunnery Range; Fat Man; Fermi, Enrico; Groves, Leslie Richard; Laurence, William Leonard; Los Alamos Laboratory; Oppenheimer, Julius Robert; Potsdam Conference; Stimson, Henry Lewis; Truman, Harry; University of Chicago. Documents: 32, 33, 34, 49a

References

Alperovitz, Gar, and Sanho Tree. 1996. *The Decision to Use the Atomic Bomb.* New York: Vintage.

Angelo, Joseph A. 2004. *Nuclear Technology.* Westport, CT: Greenwood Press.

Groves, Leslie. 1962. *Now It Can Be Told: The Story of the Manhattan Project.* New York: Harper.

Hawkins, David, Edith C. Truslow, and Ralph C. Smith. 1961. *Manhattan District History, Project Y, the Los Alamos Story.* Los Angeles: Tomash Publishers.

Hoddeson, Lillian, Paul W. Henriksen, Roger A. Meade, and Catherine L. Westfall. 1993. *Critical Assembly: A Technical History of Los Alamos During the Oppenheimer Years, 1943–1945.* New York: Cambridge University Press.

Laurence, William Leonard. 1946. *Dawn Over Zero: The Story of the Atomic Bomb.* New York: Knopf.

Monk, Ray. 2012. *Robert Oppenheimer: A Life Inside the Center.* New York: Doubleday.

Norris, Robert S. 2002. *Racing for the Bomb: General Leslie R. Groves, the Manhattan Project's Indispensable Man*. South Royalton, VT: Steerforth Press.

Szasz, Ferenc Morton. 1984. *The Day the Sun Rose Twice: The Story of the Trinity Site Nuclear Explosion, July 16, 1945*. Albuquerque: University of New Mexico Press.

Truman, Harry (1894–1972)

The 33rd president of the United States, Harry S. Truman came into office with little knowledge of the Manhattan Project, the culminating activities of which he would have to approve within four months. When President Franklin Roosevelt died on April 12, 1945, World War II was about to end in Europe and the United States was gearing up for what would likely be a long and costly invasion of Japan—and Truman had been vice president for less than three months, hardly enough time to master that job, let alone prepare to take over a presidency that had been held by one man for 12 years.

Truman's experience in federal government and international affairs had begun in 1935, after his 1934 election to the U.S. Senate by the State of Missouri. A county judge and part of the corrupt Pendergast political machine (T. J. Pendergast himself would be convicted of tax evasion in 1939 and would spend 15 months in prison), Truman showed little of what one would expect from a politician about to step onto a national and, indeed, international stage.

In his second term in the Senate, he began to learn something about international affairs, though he sometimes seemed hopelessly naïve and even ill-informed. However, he began to take an interest in the military and in waste in military procurement. Going against expectations rising from his own beginnings, he became an active proponent of honest government and an enemy of big business. He chaired a special investigating committee, the Senate Special Committee to Investigate the National Defense Program, to look into graft and war profiteering, and for his efforts, he began to establish a national reputation as a reformer.

Truman, who had not actively sought the 1944 vice presidential nomination, won it for the simple reason that he was not sitting vice president Henry Wallace, who, many leaders of the Democratic Party felt, should not be the one to step into Roosevelt's shoes in the likely event of the president's death (those who knew him could see clearly the decline in Roosevelt's health). Wallace had made clear that he would advocate worldwide changes in keeping with New Deal ideology after the war, including the abolishment of colonialism and the establishment of powerful labor unions. This, in the eyes of many powerful Democrats, would be a step too far.

On the other hand, Truman, for all of his work toward honest government, was seen as nonideological and non-manipulatable. Wallace, though, was popular, and Truman was not—at least not with the convention delegates. It took a great deal of bargaining and backroom manipulation to turn the tide against Wallace and in favor of Truman, but it was done.

As vice president, Truman was not invited into the inner circle of the Roosevelt administration but was left to his own devices, meeting alone with the president only twice during his tenure. He knew virtually nothing about the role he would take on when the president died on April 12, 1944. Eleanor Roosevelt informed him of her husband's death. When he asked if he could do anything for her, she famously responded, "Is there anything we can do for you? For you are the one in trouble now."

Surrounding himself with old cronies and Roosevelt holdovers, Truman began his presidency on an inauspicious note. Secretary of War Henry Stimson informed him of the Manhattan Project within days of his swearing in, but it was not until almost two weeks had passed that he began to get any detailed information. It was only continued war success that kept Truman popular at that time. The war in Europe was declared over on May 8, 1945, coincidentally, the new president's 61st birthday. Truman wanted to see the war against Japan ended as soon after that as possible.

Though Truman had hoped to use the success of the Trinity Test as added weight to perceived American strength during the Potsdam Conference in Germany, he was not aware that Soviet spies had already informed Joseph Stalin of the Manhattan Project and the upcoming test, which took place the day the conference started. In fact, it is probable that Stalin knew about the Manhattan Project long before Truman himself was made aware of it.

One of the outcomes of the Potsdam Conference was a Proclamation Defining Terms for Japanese Surrender issued on July 26, 1945, by Truman, British Prime Minister Winston Churchill, and Chinese Nationalist Chairman Chiang Kai-shek. If there was a threat of atomic bombing if the terms were not accepted, it was so veiled that it is still not clear if the use of "utter destruction" in the declaration had anything to do with the power now unleashed by the Manhattan Project.

When the Japanese government refused to surrender, Truman authorized the use of the two available bombs, Little Boy and Fat Man, as an alternative to invasion. Within days of the dropping of the second bomb on August 9, 1945, Japan announced its surrender. Ever since, there have been arguments about the decision covering everything from Truman's ability to make such a decision in such a short time to the balance between lives lost in bombing and lives lost in invasion, with some arguing that Japan was so weak by that time that an invasion would not even have been necessary. Such arguments, however, are all speculative. The fact of the matter is that the bombs were dropped, over 100,000 were killed, and Japan surrendered, ending the war.

Aaron Barlow

See also: Churchill, Sir Winston L. S.; Fat Man; Hiroshima, Bombing of; Little Boy; Nagasaki, Bombing of; Potsdam Conference; Roosevelt, Franklin D.; Stimson, Henry Lewis; Trinity Test. Documents: 12, 22, 24, 35, 40a, 41, 45, 48

References

Boyer, Paul. 1994. *By the Bomb's Early Light: American Thought and Culture at the Dawn of the Atomic Age*. Chapel Hill: University of North Carolina Press.

Donovan, Robert J. 1996. *Conflict and Crisis: The Presidency of Harry Truman, 1945–1948*. Columbia: University of Missouri Press.

Ferrell, Robert H. 1994. *Harry S. Truman: A Life*. Columbia: University of Missouri Press.

Gosnell, Harold Foote. 1980. *Truman's Crises: A Political Biography of Harry S. Truman*. Westport, CT: Greenwood Press.

Holloway, David. 1994. *Stalin and the Bomb: The Soviet Union and Atomic Energy, 1939–1956*. New Haven, CT: Yale University Press.

McCullough, David. 1992. *Truman*. New York: Simon & Schuster.

Walker, J. Samuel. 1997. *Prompt and Utter Destruction: Truman and the Use of Atomic Bombs Against Japan*. Chapel Hill: University of North Carolina Press.

Tube Alloys

The first dedicated atomic bomb development program, Tube Alloys was a British/Canadian response to the challenge posed by the MAUD Committee Report of 1940. The Tube Alloys Directorate was overseen by the British Department of Scientific and Industrial Research (DSIR) and was led by Wallace Akers, who chose the name for the project because it meant nothing yet sounded like it must mean something.

Trained as a chemist, Akers had been an executive at Imperial Chemical Industries before the war and was quite involved with munitions production. He was asked to direct the Tube Alloys project when it was formed in 1941, bringing, as had been hoped, a combination of scientific knowledge and industrial acumen to the project.

When the Defence Services Panel of the Scientific Advisory Committee considered the MAUD Committee Report, the biggest fear was that German scientists would develop an atomic bomb before the English. On August 30, 1941, Prime Minister Winston Churchill authorized what would become Tube Alloys with facilities both in the United Kingdom and in Canada (where they would be safe from German bombings).

Though the United States knew of the MAUD Committee Report, it was not yet in the war and did not view the matter with the same urgency as Great Britain. Thus it was that the initiation of research into development of an atomic bomb first fell to the English.

Aaron Barlow

See also: Churchill, Sir Winston L. S.; MAUD Committee; National Defense Research Committee; Office of Scientific Research and Development; Roosevelt, Franklin D. Documents: 5, 7, 14

References

Bernstein, Barton J. 1976. "The Uneasy Alliance: Roosevelt, Churchill, and the Atomic Bomb, 1940–1945." *The Western Political Quarterly* 29, no. 2: 202–230.

Cathcart, Brian. 1995. *Test of Greatness: Britain's Struggle for the Atom Bomb*. London: John Murray.

Clark, Ronald W. 1961. *The Birth of the Bomb: The Untold Story of Britain's Part in the Weapon that Changed the World*. London: Phoenix House.

Ehrman, John. 1953. *The Atomic Bomb: An Account of British Policy in the Second World War*. London: Cabinet Office.

Farmelo, Graham. 2013. *Churchill's Bomb: How the United States Overtook Britain in the First Nuclear Arms Race*. New York: Basic Books.

Gowing, Margaret. 1964. *Britain and Atomic Energy 1939–1945*. London: Macmillan Publishing.

Szasz, Ferenc Morton. 1992. *British Scientists and the Manhattan Project: The Los Alamos Years*. New York: St. Martin's Press.

U

University of Chicago

The University of Chicago is arguably the birthplace of the atomic age. The specific place was a squash court under the bleachers on the west side of Stagg Field. It was there that Enrico Fermi and a team of scientists piled graphite blocks and laced the structure with uranium. This first atomic "pile" allowed for the engineering of a controlled and self-sustaining nuclear chain reaction.

The scientists of the Metallurgical Laboratory, or "Met Lab," stacked 40,000 of the graphite blocks enclosing 19,000 pieces of uranium in metallic form as well as uranium oxide powder within a wooden frame that was a 24-foot square to create this first atomic pile, or reactor.

Met Lab had been founded at the University of Chicago specifically for the study of plutonium in February 1942. It became part of the Metallurgical Project that created the X-10 Reactor at the Clinton Engineer Works at Oak Ridge, Tennessee, as part of the broader Manhattan Project. By the middle of 1944, it had a staff of about 2,000.

The current University of Chicago (there had been an older one at the same location, closing after a fire in 1886) itself had been founded in 1890 on land donated by retail magnate Marshall Field and funded in part by oil tycoon John D. Rockefeller. During World War II, the college was led (and had been, since 1929) by Robert Maynard Hutchins, who had renovated the university's undergraduate and graduate curricula, creating one of the most intellectually powerful institutions in the United States.

Aaron Barlow

See also: Clinton Engineer Works; Fermi, Enrico; Metallurgical Laboratory; Oak Ridge, Tennessee; Szilárd, Léo

References

Boyer, John. 2015. *The University of Chicago: A History*. Chicago: University of Chicago Press.

Compton, Arthur. 1956. *Atomic Quest*. New York: Oxford University Press.

Goodspeed, Thomas Wakefield. 1972. *A History of the University of Chicago, Founded by John D. Rockefeller: The First Quarter-Century*. Chicago: University of Chicago Press.

Hacker, Barton C. 1987. *The Dragon's Tail: Radiation Safety in the Manhattan Project, 1942–1946*. Berkeley: University of California Press.

Szanton, Andrew. 1992. *The Recollections of Eugene P. Wigner*. New York: Plenum.

Uranium Enrichment

If uranium could not be enriched, that is, the fissile U-235 separated from the bulk of U-238, the projects toward development of an atomic bomb would have taken much longer, if they would have been possible at all. Early calculations had shown that an atomic bomb, though feasible to build, would be so large as to be immobile due to the necessary amount of uranium. Through enrichment, as postulated in the Frisch-Peierls Memorandum, the amount of uranium needed could be reduced to an amount that could fuel a bomb that could be transported and dropped by an airplane such as the American Boeing B-29 Superfortress or even the British Avro Lancaster bomber. The bulk of the work of the Manhattan Project revolved around producing sufficient U-235 (and the derivative plutonium Pu-239) for fueling the three bombs that would be exploded at Trinity and over Hiroshima and Nagasaki in July and August 1945. The enrichment process is repeated in order to produce what is called Highly Enriched Uranium, or weapons-grade uranium.

Natural uranium consists primarily of U-238 and less than 1 percent of U-235. During the Manhattan Project, three methods were selected for separating out the U-235. These processes of isotope separation were diffusion, electromagnetic, and chemical. Ultimately, they produced enough enriched U-235 for the Little Boy bomb exploded over Hiroshima and for production of the Pu-239 used in the Trinity Test and over Nagasaki.

Aaron Barlow

See also: Hiroshima, Bombing of; Little Boy; Nagasaki, Bombing of; Trinity Test; Uranium-235. Document: 40d

References

Beams, J. W., and F. B. Haynes. 1936. "The Separation of Isotopes by Centrifuging." *Physics Review* 50: 491–492.

Lindemann, F. A., and F. W. Aston. 1919. "The Possibility of Separating Isotopes." *Philosophical Magazine* 6: 523–534.

Uranium-235

A small part of natural uranium (about 0.7 percent), uranium-235 is a fissile material—that is, it is an isotope of uranium that can sustain a nuclear chain reaction. It was first identified by Arthur Jeffrey Dempster, a physicist working at the University of Chicago, in 1935. It was the first weapons-grade uranium produced and became the primary active component of the Little Boy bomb that was exploded over Hiroshima, Japan, on August 6, 1945.

Aaron Barlow

See also: Fissile Material; Hiroshima, Bombing of; Little Boy. Documents: 6, 40d

References

Atomic Energy Commission. 2017. *The New World: A History of the United States Atomic Energy Commission (AEC), Volume 1, 1939 to 1946, The Race for the Atomic Bomb, Uranium 235, Plutonium, Controlling the Bomb after World War II.* Washington, D.C.: U.S. Department of Energy.

Muller, John E. 1967. *Uranium 235.* London: John Spencer & Co.

U.S. Army Corps of Engineers

The U.S. Army created the Corps of Engineers on March 16, 1802, and charged the USACE with founding and operating the U.S. Military Academy at West Point, New York. The military academy was under the direction of USACE until 1866. The USACE is now headquartered in Washington, D.C., but it is organized geographically with eight divisions within the United States that are defined by watershed boundaries, not by state lines.

In addition to water-related and hydroelectric projects, the USACE has achieved other notable accomplishments, including the construction of the Washington Monument and the Pentagon and participation in the Manhattan Project. It was the Corps of Engineers that was responsible for the massive construction projects at Oak Ridge, Tennessee, and Hanford, Washington, which provided the facilities for the Manhattan Project. In fact, the Manhattan Project was named following Corps of Engineers protocols. The project, first based on Manhattan Island in New York City, was renamed Manhattan District (from Development of Substitute Materials) when the army got involved.

Grenetta Thomassey

See also: Clinton Engineer Works; Development of Substitute Materials; Hanford, Washington; Oak Ridge, Tennessee

References

Office of History, U.S. Army Corps of Engineers. 2004. *The History of the U.S. Army Corps of Engineers.* n.p.: University Press of the Pacific.

Pilkey, Orrin H., and Katharine L. Dixon. 1998. *The Corps and the Shore.* Reprint ed. Washington, D.C.: Island Press.

Torres, Louis. 2001. *The United States Army Corps of Engineers and the Construction of the Washington Monument.* n.p.: University Press of the Pacific.

W

Wendover Army Air Field

Located near Wendover in northwestern Utah, the Wendover Army Air Field was taken over by the 509th Composite Group on December 17, 1944, for training in reconfigured Silverplate Boeing B-29 Superfortress bombers in preparation for a move to the Pacific (the base chosen would be North Field on Tinian Island in the North Marianas) and an attack on Japan. The site was chosen for training by Lieutenant Colonel Paul Tibbets, who had been assigned command of the group.

Training at Wendover continued into May, with the entire group arriving on Tinian by the beginning of July. Training was carried out using inert bombs of the shape and weight of Little Boy and Fat Man and with "pumpkin bombs" also configured to the size and shape of the developing Fat Man atomic bombs but loaded with conventional explosives.

Aaron Barlow

See also: Fat Man; 509th Composite Group; Little Boy; Project Alberta; Tibbets, Paul

References

Campbell, Richard H. 2005. *The Silverplate Bombers: A History and Registry of the Enola Gay and Other B-29s Configured to Carry Atomic Bombs.* Jefferson, NC: McFarland & Company.

Craven, Wesley F., and James L. Cate, eds. 1955. *Men and Planes.* Vol. 7 in *The Army Air Forces in World War II.* Chicago: University of Chicago Press.

Wigner, Eugene Paul (1902–1995)

Widely considered one of the finest theoretical physicists of the twentieth century, Eugene Paul Wigner shared the 1963 Nobel Prize in Physics with Maria Goeppert-Mayer. His work in the field of quantum mechanics, a mathematical theory for physics that has largely replaced classical physics and concerns measurable quantities in atomic systems, included his discovery of the important conservation of parity (CP) law. Although physicists later found exceptions to the law, it guided an entire generation of scientists in their research on nuclear reactions. Wigner was also closely involved in the construction of the first nuclear weapon in the 1940s.

The son of a businessman, Wigner was born in Budapest, Hungary, on November 17, 1902. He spent his childhood in Hungary and Germany, attending a Lutheran high school in Budapest and graduating in 1920 with classmate John Von Neumann. In the fall, Wigner began classes at Berlin's Technical Institute, from which he earned a degree in chemical engineering in 1924. He finished his doctorate in the subject the following year.

In 1926, Wigner started working as an assistant in the Berlin Technical Institute's physics department, but after a year, he moved to the University of Göttingen to perform the same job. While he was at Göttingen, in 1927, he introduced the mathematical concept of parity as a conserved characteristic of nuclear reactions. In other words, he proposed that the mirror image of a nuclear reaction is identical to the reaction itself. In 1928, Wigner returned to his alma mater, working as a private lecturer to pay for his continuing studies. Wigner stayed there until 1930, when he left to live in the United States, partly because the Nazis had eliminated his position.

Wigner settled in New Jersey after finding work as a physics lecturer at Princeton University. When the school saw how talented he was, he received a promotion to half-time professor of mathematical physics. He remained in that position at Princeton until 1937. During that period, he delivered a paper at Harvard University on his theories about nuclear symmetry that helped make his name known in physics circles. In addition, in 1936, he and a colleague came up with a formula to describe how neutrons interact with a stationary nucleus that became known as the Breit-Wigner formula.

In 1937, Wigner accepted a new job as full professor of physics at the University of Wisconsin, but he stayed for only a year before going back to Princeton to work as a full-time professor of mathematical physics and chairperson of the physics department at the school's Palmer Physical Laboratories. It was that summer that he, Albert Einstein, Leó Szilárd, and Enrico Fermi, afraid that Nazi Germany was on the trail of an atomic weapon, banded together to convince the U.S. government to start funding a program to research nuclear fission.

After Japan's Pearl Harbor attack in 1941, the government began gathering all the nation's best nuclear scientists together to try to make an atomic bomb. Wigner was one of those scientists, and he was present at the University of Chicago Metallurgical Laboratories when the group achieved the first self-sustaining nuclear reaction. (The Breit-Wigner formula was integral in the accomplishment.) By then, he had long since realized that nuclear fission was about to be used as "the basis of a horrible military weapon."

Wigner spent from 1942 to 1945 at the University of Chicago, after which he worked for two years as director of research and development at the Clinton Laboratories for the Oak Ridge Project in Tennessee. That project was a program, run by the War Department and carried out by the Monsanto Chemical Company, to manufacture radioisotopes for outside research. He finally returned to Princeton University in 1947.

In the 1950s, Wigner worked on the government's hydrogen bomb project, which explored fusion as a source of explosive energy. He was as shocked as most other scientists in 1956, when two nuclear researchers, Tsung-Dao Lee and C. N. Yang, showed that CP violation can and does occur in weak nuclear interactions. In 1963, Wigner won a share of the Nobel Prize in Physics.

Wigner remained a physics professor at Princeton until 1971, when he retired as an emeritus professor. He kept that honorary status until his death at his home in Princeton on January 1, 1995. Wigner's first wife died soon after their marriage in 1936. He married again in 1941 and had two children with his second wife.

Amanda de la Garza

See also: Einstein, Albert; Metallurgical Laboratory; Szilárd, Léo; Teller, Edward; University of Chicago. Document: 3

References

Asimov, Isaac. 1982. *Asimov's Biographical Encyclopedia of Science & Technology.* New York: Doubleday.

Daintith, John. 1981. *The Biographical Encyclopedia of Scientists.* New York: Facts on File.

Millar, David, ed. 1996. *The Cambridge Dictionary of Scientists.* Cambridge, U.K.: Cambridge University Press.

World War II

World War II was the most destructive enterprise in human history. It is sobering to consider that more resources, material, and human lives (approximately 50 million) were expended on the war than on any other human activity. Indeed, this conflict was so all-encompassing that very few "side" wars took place simultaneously, the 1939–1940 Finnish-Soviet War (Winter War) being one of the few exceptions.

The Early Phases of the War

The traditional and widely accepted date for the start of World War II is September 1, 1939, with the quick but not quite blitzkrieg-speed German invasion of Poland. This action brought France and Great Britain into the conflict two days later, in accordance with their guarantees to Poland. (The Soviet Union's invasion of eastern Poland on September 17 provoked no such reaction.)

The Germans learned from their Polish Campaign and mounted a true blitzkrieg offensive against the Low Countries and France that commenced on May 10, 1940. The Allies were simply outmaneuvered, losing France in six weeks. The Germans found that the French Routes Nationales (National Routes), designed to enable French forces to reach the frontiers, could also be used in the opposite direction by an invader. The Germans themselves would relearn this military truth on their autobahns in 1945.

Germany suffered its first defeat of the war when its air offensive against Great Britain, the world's first great air campaign, was thwarted in the Battle of Britain. The main advantages of the Royal Air Force (RAF) in this battle were radar and the geographic fact that its pilots and their warplanes were shot down over home territory. German pilots and aircraft in a similar predicament were out of action for the duration of the war, and they also had farther to fly from their bases. But Britain's greatest advantage throughout this stage of the war was its prime minister, Winston L. S. Churchill, who gave stirring voice and substance to the Allied defiance of Adolf Hitler.

Nonetheless, by spring 1941, Nazi Germany had conquered or dominated all of the European continent, with the exception of Switzerland, Sweden, and Vatican City. Greece, which had held off and beaten back an inept Italian offensive, finally capitulated to the German Balkan blitzkrieg in spring 1941.

Nazi Germany then turned on its erstwhile ally, the Soviet Union, on June 22, 1941, in Operation Barbarossa. Joseph Stalin's own inept generalship played a major role in the early Soviet defeats, and German forces drove almost to within sight of the Kremlin's towers in December 1941 before being beaten back.

The United States Enters the War

Early that same month, war erupted in the Pacific with Japan's coordinated combined attacks on the U.S. naval base at Pearl Harbor and on British, Dutch, and American imperial possessions. With the Soviet Union holding out precariously and the United

States now a belligerent, the Axis had lost the war, even though few recognized that fact at the time. The United States' "great debate" as to whether and to what extent to aid Britain was silenced in a national outpouring of collective wrath against the new enemy.

Japanese forces surprised and outfought their opponents by land, sea, and air. British and Dutch forces in Asia, superior only in numbers, had been routed in one of the most successful combined-arms campaigns in history. Singapore, the linchpin of imperial European power in Asia, surrendered ignominiously on February 16, 1942. Only the Americans managed to delay the Japanese seriously, holding out on the Bataan Peninsula and then at the Corregidor fortifications until May. The end of imperialism, at least in Asia, can be dated to the capitulation of Singapore, as Asians witnessed other Asians with superior technology and professionalism completely defeat European and American forces.

And yet, on Pearl Harbor's very "day of infamy," Japan actually lost the war. Its forces missed the American aircraft carriers there, as well as the oil tank farms and the machine shop complex. On that day, the Japanese killed many U.S. personnel, and they destroyed mostly obsolete aircraft and sank a handful of elderly battleships. But, above all, they outraged Americans, who determined to avenge the attack. Japan would receive no mercy in the relentless land, sea, and air war that the United States was now about to wage against it. More significantly, American industrial and manpower resources vastly surpassed those Japan could bring to bear in a protracted conflict.

The tide would not begin to turn until the drawn-out naval-air clash in the Coral Sea (May 1942), the first naval battle in which neither side's surface ships ever came within sight of the opponent. The following month, the U.S. Navy avenged Pearl Harbor in the Battle of Midway, sinking no fewer than four Japanese carriers, again without those surface ships involved ever sighting each other. The loss of hundreds of superbly trained, combat-experienced naval aviators and their expert maintenance crews was as great a blow to Japan as the actual sinking of its invaluable carriers. The Americans could make up their own losses far more easily than the Japanese.

By this time, U.S. production was supplying not only American military needs but also those of most of the Allies. Everything from aluminum ingots and the canned-meat product Spam to Sherman tanks and finished aircraft crossed the oceans to the British Isles, the Soviet Union, the Free French, the Nationalist Chinese, the Fighting Poles, and others. Moreover, quantity was not produced at the expense of quality. Although some of the Allies might have had reservations in regard to Spam, the army trucks, the boots, the small arms, and the uniforms provided by the United States were unsurpassed. The very ships that transported the bulk of this war material—the famous mass-produced Liberty ships ("rolled out by the mile, chopped off by the yard")—could still be found on the world's oceanic trade routes decades after they were originally scheduled to be scrapped.

The War in Europe

Although considered a sideshow by the Soviets, Operation Torch was of the utmost strategic importance, and until mid-1943, it was the only continental land campaign that the Western Allies were strong enough to mount. Had North Africa, including Egypt, fallen to the Axis, the Suez Canal could not have been held and German forces could have gone through the Middle East, mobilizing Arab nationalism, threatening the area's vast oil fields, and even menacing the embattled Soviet Union. Not until the British commander in North Africa, General Bernard Montgomery, amassed a massive superiority in armor was Germany's General Erwin Rommel defeated at El Alamein in October 1942 and slowly pushed back toward Tunisia. U.S. and British landings in Algeria and Morocco to the rear of Rommel's forces were successful, but the American troops received a bloody nose at Kasserine Pass. The vastly outnumbered North African Axis forces did not capitulate until May 1943.

After the North African Campaign ended in 1943, the Allies drove the Axis forces from Sicily, and then, in September 1943, they began the interminable Italian Campaign. It is perhaps indicative of the frustrating nature of the war in Italy that the lethargic Allies allowed the campaign to begin with the escape of most Axis forces from Sicily to the Italian peninsula. The Germans conducted well-organized retreats from one mountainous fortified line to the next. The Italian Campaign was occasionally justified for tying down many German troops, but the truth is that it tied down far more Allied forces—British, Americans, Free French, Free Poles, Brazilians, Canadians, Indians, and British and French African colonials among them. German forces in Italy ultimately surrendered in late April 1945, only about a week before Germany itself capitulated.

The aftermath of World War II proved considerably different from that of World War I, with its prevailing spirit of disillusionment. Amazingly, all of World War II's belligerents, winners and losers alike, could soon look back and realize that the destruction of the murderous, archaic, racialist Axis regimes had genuinely cleared the way to a better world. All enjoyed peace and the absence of major war. Even for the Soviets, the postwar decades were infinitely better than the prewar years, although much of this measure of good fortune might be attributed simply to the death of Stalin. The United States and much of the British Commonwealth emerged from the war far stronger than when they entered it. By the 1950s, both war-shattered Western Europe and Japan were well on their way to becoming major economic competitors with the United States. The uniquely sagacious and foresighted Western Allied military occupations of Germany, Japan, and Austria in many ways laid the foundations for the postwar prosperity of these former enemy nations. (For the most part, however, similar good fortune bypassed the less developed nations.) Within a few years, former belligerents on both sides could agree that, despite its appalling casualties and destruction, World War II had been if not perhaps "the Good War," then at least something in the nature of a worthwhile war.

Hedley P. Willmott and
Michael B. Barrett

See also: Churchill, Sir Winston L. S.; Pacific Theater: World War II; Roosevelt, Franklin D.; Stimson, Henry Lewis; Truman, Harry

References
Baldwin, Hanson W. 2000. *Battles Lost and Won: Great Campaigns of World War II.* New York: Harper & Row.

d'Albas, Andrieu, and M. A. Emmanuel. 1957. *Death of a Navy: Japanese Naval Action of World War II.* New York: Devin-Adair.

Primary Documents

Due, in part, to the care of a military-influenced bureaucracy (which put a premium on documentation), much of what we know, or at least believe, about the Manhattan Project comes from the series of documents carefully created and released in the days following the bombing of Hiroshima in Japan on August 6, 1945. The flow of information was carefully controlled—and has been ever since, with declassification of secret documents in an orchestrated process.

One of the more interesting aspects of public knowledge of the Manhattan Project is just how much of our knowledge of it comes directly from governmental and military publicists of 1945. Whether or not one is comfortable with information deliberately constructed to provide a single and unified view of the project, it is impossible not to admire the skill with which this was handled, especially in light of the bungling we so often associate with government operations, especially when secrecy was involved.

These documents don't only show the history of the Manhattan Project but demonstrate how information distribution works. The amount of work, just in the preparation of press releases, is evident here, as is the care to present the Manhattan Project in a way that would allow Americans to accept the secrecy now torn away as well as to support the actions, the bombings of Hiroshima and Nagasaki, as necessary actions for ending the war. As the documents show, not everyone involved agreed that they were, and there were furious attempts to convince others—attempts that, obviously, failed. However, the documents and other orchestrated support for the project created almost a consensus view in the United States, at least, that the droppings of the bombs were necessary.

These documents can help one decide where one comes down on this ongoing debate.

I. Leó Szilárd's Letter to Hugo Hirst, March 17, 1934

The possibility of atomic power and atomic bombs had been posited for some time before the advent of Tube Alloys and then the Manhattan Project. Leó Szilárd, one of the fathers of atomic power for quite a number of reasons, was one of the first to understand that the speculation of writers like H. G. Wells contained more than idle thought. Wells wrote, in the passage from The World

Set Free chapter "The New Source of Energy" referred to in this letter:

The problem which was already being mooted by such scientific men as Ramsay, Rutherford, and Soddy, in the very beginning of the twentieth century, the problem of inducing radio-activity in the heavier elements and so tapping the internal energy of atoms, was solved by a wonderful combination of induction, intuition, and luck by Holsten so soon as the year 1933. From the first detection of radio-activity to its first subjugation to human purpose measured little more than a quarter of a century. For twenty years after that, indeed, minor difficulties prevented any striking practical application of his success, but the essential thing was done, this new boundary in the march of human progress was crossed, in that year. He set up atomic disintegration in a minute particle of bismuth; it exploded with great violence into a heavy gas of extreme radio-activity, which disintegrated in its turn in the course of seven days, and it was only after another year's work that he was able to show practically that the last result of this rapid release of energy was gold. But the thing was done—at the cost of a blistered chest and an injured finger, and from the moment when the invisible speck of bismuth flashed into riving and rending energy, Holsten knew that he had opened a way for mankind, however narrow and dark it might still be, to worlds of limitless power. He recorded as much in the strange diary biography he left the world, a diary that was up to that particular moment a mass of speculations and calculations, and which suddenly became for a space an amazingly minute and human record of sensations and emotions that all humanity might understand.

Szilárd was one of the first scientists to recognize the reality underlying the fiction of Wells.

From: Leó Szilárd
To: Sir Hugo Hirst
Date: March 17, 1934

6, Halliwick Road
London, N. 10.
17th March, 1934
Dear Sir Hugo,

As you are on holiday you might find pleasure in reading a few pages out of a book by H. G. Wells which I am sending you. I am certain you will find the first three paragraphs of Chapter The First (The New Source of Energy, page 42) interesting and amusing, whereas the other parts of the book are rather boring. It is remarkable that Wells should have written those pages in 1914.

Of course, all this is moonshine, but I have reason to believe that in so far as the industrial applications of the present discoveries in physics are concerned, the forecast of the writers may prove to be more accurate than the forecast of the scientists. The physicists have conclusive arguments as to why we cannot create at present new sources of energy for industrial purposes; I am not so sure whether they do not miss the point.

It is perhaps possible to be more definite some time after your return, and in the meantime I hope you will in any case enjoy glancing through these few pages.

With best wishes for a pleasant stay,

Yours very truly,
Leó Szilárd

Source: Leo Szilard Papers. MSS 32, Box 8, Folder 28. "Correspondence." Special Collections & Archives, UC San Diego Library. https://library.ucsd.edu/dc/object/bb84998959. Accessed April 26, 2019. Courtesy of Leo Szilard Papers, Special Collections & Archives, UC San Diego.

2. Leó Szilárd Letter to Lewis Strauss on Discoveries Relating to Fission of Uranium, January 25, 1939

As World War II loomed, Szilárd, who had left his native Hungary to study in Germany and, with the rise of Hitler, had fled to Germany, moved further on, to the United States. There, he secured research funding from investment banker Lewis Strauss, who had become interested in radiation treatment for cancer after the deaths of both parents to the disease. Strauss, though he would have no role in the Manhattan Project, would become an important figure in governmental oversight of atomic power. In this letter, Szilárd informs Strauss of the Otto Hahn, Fritz Strassmann experiment that led to first recognition of nuclear fission.

Hotel King's Crown
Opposite Columbia University
420 West 116th Street
New York City
January 25th, 1939

Mr. Lewis L. Strauss
c/o Kuhn, Loeb & Co.
52 William Street
New York City

Dear Mr. Strauss:

I feel that I ought to let you know of a very sensational new development in nuclear physics. In a paper in the "Naturwissenschaften" Hahn reports that he finds when bombarding uranium with neutrons the uranium breaking up into two halves giving elements of about half the atomic weight of uranium. This is entirely unexpected and exciting news for the average physicist. The Department of Physics at Princeton, where I spent the last few days, was like a stirred-up ant heap.

Apart from the purely scientific interest there may be another aspect of this discovery, which so far does not seem to have caught the attention of those to whom I spoke. First of all it is obvious that the energy released in this new reaction must be very much higher than in all previously known cases. It may be 200 million [electron-] volt instead of the usual 3–10 million volts. This in itself might make it possible to produce power by means of nuclear energy, but I do not think that this possibility is very exciting, for if the energy output is only two or three times the energy input, the cost of investment would probably be too high to make the process worthwhile.

Unfortunately, most of the energy is released in the form of heat and not in the form of radioactivity.

I see, however, in connection with this new discovery potential possibilities in another direction. These might lead to a large-scale production of energy and radioactive elements, unfortunately also perhaps to atomic bombs. This new discovery revives all the hopes and fears in this respect which I had in 1934 and 1935, and which I have as good as abandoned in the course of the last two years. At present I am running a high temperature and am therefore confined to my four walls, but perhaps I can tell you more about these new developments some other time. Meanwhile you may look out for a paper in "Nature" by Frisch and Meitner which will soon appear and which might give you some information about this new discovery.

With best wishes,
Yours sincerely,
Leó Szilárd

Source: Leo Szilard Papers. MSS 32, Box 18, Folder 21. "Correspondence." Special Collections & Archives, UC San Diego Library. https://library.ucsd.edu/dc/object/bb8295126z. Accessed April 26, 2019. Courtesy of Leo Szilard Papers, Special Collections & Archives, UC San Diego.

3. Albert Einstein Letter to President Franklin Roosevelt, August 2, 1939 (Received October 11, 1939)

Even before Germany was formally at war with the Allies, anti-Nazi scientists were well aware of the possibility that Germany might develop an atomic bomb. Albert Einstein, the renowned German physicist who had developed the theory of relativity, a man whose Jewish origins had forced him to flee to the United States, sent to President Franklin D. Roosevelt a letter on the subject composed by Leó Szilárd, who had turned to Einstein because his fame would likely gather more attention to the letter, with input from Edward Teller and Eugene Wigner. He urged that the United States should attempt to buy up international uranium stocks and encourage its scientists to develop atomic weapons before the Nazi regime succeeded in doing so. Once he was made aware of the letter in October, Roosevelt responded positively and quickly to Einstein's exhortations.

Albert Einstein
Old Grove Road
Peconic, Long Island
August 2nd, 1939

F.D. Roosevelt
President of the United States
White House
Washington, D.C.

Sir:

Some recent work by E. Fermi and L. Szilárd, which has been communicated to me in manuscript, leads me to expect that the element uranium may be turned into a new and important source of energy in the immediate future. Certain aspects of the situation which has arisen seem to call for watchfulness and if necessary, quick action on the part of the Administration. I believe therefore that it is my duty to bring to your attention the following facts and recommendations.

In the course of the last four months it has been made probable—through the work of Joliot in France as well as Fermi and Szilárd in America—that it may be possible to set up a nuclear chain reaction in a large mass of uranium, by which vast amounts of power and large quantities of new radium-like elements would be generated. Now it appears almost certain that this could be achieved in the immediate future.

This new phenomenon would also lead to the construction of bombs, and it is conceivable—though much less certain—that extremely powerful bombs of this type may thus be constructed. A single bomb of this type, carried by boat and exploded in a port, might very well destroy the whole port together with some of the surrounding territory. However, such bombs might very well prove too heavy for transportation by air.

The United States has only very poor ores of uranium in moderate quantities. There is some good ore in Canada and former Czechoslovakia, while the most important source of uranium is in the Belgian Congo.

In view of this situation you may think it desirable to have some permanent contact maintained between the Administration and the group of physicists working on chain reactions in America. One possible way of achieving this might be for you to entrust the task with a person who has your confidence and who could perhaps serve in an unofficial capacity. His task might comprise the following:

a) to approach Government Departments, keep them informed of the further development, and put forward recommendations for Government action, giving particular attention to the problem of securing a supply of uranium ore for the United States.
b) to speed up the experimental work, which is at present being carried on within the limits of the budgets of University laboratories, by providing funds, if such funds be required, through his contacts with private persons who are willing to make contributions for this cause, and perhaps also by obtaining co-operation of industrial laboratories which have necessary equipment.

I understand that Germany has actually stopped the sale of uranium from the Czechoslovakian mines which she has taken over. That she should have taken such early action might perhaps be understood on the ground that the son of the German Under-Secretary of State, von Weizsacker, is attached to the Kaiser-Wilhelm Institute in Berlin, where some of the American work on uranium is now being repeated.

Yours very truly,
Albert Einstein

Source: Smyth, Henry DeWolf. 1954. *A General Account of the Development of Methods of Using Atomic Energy for Military Purposes Under the Auspices of the United States Government, 1940–1945.* Washington, D.C.: U.S. Government Printing Office.

4. President Franklin Roosevelt's Response to Albert Einstein, October 19, 1939

Banker Alexander Sachs, who knew both Leó Szilárd and President Franklin Roosevelt, agreed to act as a go-between, delivering the Szilárd-composed letter over Einstein's signature to Roosevelt. Though he had had the letter in hand since the second week of August, it wasn't until October 11 that he was able to meet with the president and convey the contents of the letter. The delay resulted from the commencement of World War II with the German invasion of Poland on September 1, 1939, pushing back just about all governmental business even though the United States would not be directly involved in the conflict for more than another two years.

THE WHITE HOUSE
WASHINGTON

October 19, 1939

My dear Professor:

I want to thank you for your recent letter and the most interesting and important enclosure.

I found this data of such import that I have convened a Board consisting of the head of the Bureau of Standards and a chosen representative of the Army and Navy to thoroughly investigate the possibilities of your suggestion regarding the element of uranium.

I am glad to say that Dr. Sachs will cooperate and work with this Committee and I feel this is the most practical and effective method of dealing with the subject.

Please accept my sincere thanks.

Frankin Roosevelt

Dr. Albert Einstein,
Old Grove Road,
Nassau Point,
Peconic, Long Island,
New York.

Source: Franklin D. Roosevelt Presidential Library. Atomic Bomb File, 1935–1976. Available online at http://www.fdrlibrary.marist.edu/_resources/images/atomic/atomic_02.pdf. Accessed April 26, 2019.

5. The Frisch-Peierls Memorandum

Otto Frisch and Rudolf Peierls, working at the University of Birmingham but outside of the main security-conscious (they were, as yet, foreign nationals, not citizens) radar project of their boss, Mark Oliphant, sent him this memo with two parts—one for a general audience, and the other for scientists and technicians. In it, they refute the conclusion that an atomic bomb would be undeliverable due to the sheer weight of the uranium needed. They posited that enriched uranium of a much smaller mass would be sufficient to create a bomb that could conceivably be carried and dropped by bombers such as the extant English bomber Avro Manchester and its replacement, the Avro Lancaster, then under development. These memos were critical sparks for what became the Tube Alloys project in Great Britain and Canada and the Manhattan Project in the United States.

5a. O. R. Frisch and R. Peierls "Memorandum on the Properties of a Radioactive 'Super-bomb,'" March 1940. Part 1

The attached detailed report concerns the possibility of constructing a "super-bomb" which tilizes the energy stored in atomic nuclei as a source of energy. The energy liberated in the explosion of such a super-bomb is about the same as that produced by the explosion of 1,000 tons of dynamite. This energy is liberated in a small volume, in which it will, for an instant, produce a temperature comparable to that in the interior of the sun. The blast from such an explosion would destroy life in a wide area. The size of this area is difficult to estimate, but it will probably cover the center of a big city.

In addition, some part of the energy set free by the bomb goes to produce radioactive substances, and these will emit very powerful and dangerous radiations. The effects of these radiations is greatest immediately after the explosion, but it decays only gradually and even for days after the explosion any person entering the affected area will be killed.

Some of this radioactivity will be carried along with the wind and will spread the contamination; several miles downwind this may kill people.

In order to produce such a bomb it is necessary to treat a substantial amount of uranium by a process which will separate from the uranium its light isotope (U235) of which it contains about 0.7 percent. Methods for the separation of such isotopes have recently been developed. They are slow and they have not until now been applied to uranium, whose chemical properties give rise to technical difficulties. But these difficulties are by no means insuperable. We have not sufficient experience with large-scale chemical plant to give a reliable estimate of the cost, but it is certainly not prohibitive.

It is a property of these super-bombs that there exists a "critical size" of about one pound. A quantity of the separated uranium isotope that exceeds the critical amount is explosive; yet a quantity less than the critical amount is absolutely safe. The bomb would therefore be manufactured in two (or more) parts, each being less than the critical size, and in transport all danger of a premature explosion would be avoided if these parts were kept at a distance of a few inches from each other. The bomb would be provided with a mechanism that brings the two parts together when the bomb is intended to go off. Once the parts are joined to form a block which exceeds the critical amount, the effect of the penetrating radiation always present in the atmosphere will initiate the explosion within a second or so.

The mechanism which brings the parts of the bomb together must be arranged to work fairly rapidly because of the possibility of the bomb exploding when the critical conditions have just only been reached. In this case the explosion will be far less powerful. It is never possible to exclude this altogether, but one can easily ensure that only, say, one bomb out of 100 will fail in this way, and since in any case the explosion is strong enough to destroy the bomb itself, this point is not serious.

We do not feel competent to discuss the strategic value of such a bomb, but the following conclusions seem certain:

1. As a weapon, the super-bomb would be practically irresistible. There is no material or structure that could be expected to resist the force of the explosion. If one thinks of using the bomb for breaking through a line of fortifications, it should be kept in mind that the radioactive radiations will prevent anyone from approaching the affected territory for several days; they will equally prevent defenders from reoccupying the affected positions. The advantage would lie with the side which can determine most accurately just when it is safe to re-enter the area; this is likely to be the aggressor, who knows the location of the bomb in advance.

2. Owing to the spread of radioactive substances with the wind, the bomb could probably not be used without killing large numbers of civilians, and this may make it unsuitable as a weapon for use by this country. (Use as a depth charge near a naval base suggests itself, but even there it is likely that it would cause great loss of civilian life by flooding and by the radioactive radiations.)

3. We have no information that the same idea has also occurred to other scientists but since all the theoretical data bearing on this problem are published, it is quite conceivable that Germany is, in fact, developing this weapon. Whether this is the case is difficult to find out, since the plant for the separation of isotopes need not be of such a size as to attract attention. Information that could be helpful in this respect would be data about the exploitation of the uranium mines under German control (mainly in Czechoslovakia) and about any recent German purchases of uranium abroad. It is likely that the plant would be controlled by Dr. K. Clusius (Professor of Physical Chemistry in Munich University), the inventor of the best method for separating isotopes, and therefore information as to his whereabouts and status might also give an important clue.

   At the same time it is quite possible that nobody in Germany has yet realized that the separation of the uranium isotopes would make the construction of a super-bomb possible. Hence it is of extreme importance to keep this report secret since any rumour about the connection between uranium separation and a super-bomb may set a German scientist thinking along the right lines.

4. If one works on the assumption that Germany is, or will be, in the possession of this weapon, it must be realized that no shelters are available that would be effective and that could be used on a large scale. The most effective reply would be a counter-threat with a similar bomb. Therefore it seems to us important to start production as soon and as rapidly as possible, even if it is not intended to use the bomb as a means of attack. Since the separation of the necessary amount

of uranium is, in the most favourable circumstances, a matter of several months, it would obviously be too late to start production when such a bomb is known to be in the hands of Germany, and the matter seems, therefore, very urgent.

5. As a measure of precaution, it is important to have detection squads available in order to deal with the radioactive effects of such a bomb. Their task would be to approach the danger zone with measuring instruments, to determine the extent and probable duration of the danger and to prevent people from entering the danger zone. This is vital since the radiations kill instantly only in very strong doses whereas weaker doses produce delayed effects and hence near the edges of the danger zone people would have no warning until it was too late.

For their own protection, the detection squads would enter the danger zone in motor-cars or airplanes which would be armoured with lead plates, which absorb most of the dangerous radiation. The cabin would have to be hermetically sealed and oxygen carried in cylinders because of the danger from contaminated air.

The detection staff would have to know exactly the greatest dose of radiation to which a human being can safely be exposed for a short time. This safety limit is not at present known with sufficient accuracy and further biological research for this purpose is urgently required.

As regards the reliability of the conclusions outlined above, it may be said that they are not based on direct experiments, since nobody has ever built a super-bomb yet, but they are mostly based on facts which, by recent research in nuclear physics, have been very safely established. The only uncertainty concerns the critical size for the bomb. We are fairly confident that the critical size is roughly a pound or so, but for this estimate we have to rely on certain theoretical ideas which have not been positively confirmed. If the critical size were appreciably larger than we believe it to be, the technical difficulties in the way of constructing the bomb would be enhanced. The point can be definitely settled as soon as a small amount of uranium has been separated, and we think that in view of the importance of the matter immediate steps should be taken to reach at least this stage; meanwhile it is also possible to carry out certain experiments which, while they cannot settle the question with absolute finality, could, if their result were positive, give strong support to our conclusions.

Source: The original of the memorandum is in the Bodleian Museum at Oxford University in the United Kingdom. Transcriptions, which differ slightly, can be found in Robert Serber, et al.'s 1992 *The Los Alamos Primer* (Berkeley: University of California Press); Philip L. Cantelon, et al.'s 1984 *The American Atom* (Philadelphia: The University of Pennsylvania Press) for part 2; Ferenc Morton Stasz's 1992 *British Scientists and the Manhattan Project: The Los Alamos Years* (New York: St. Martin's Press) with parts 1 and 2 reversed; Ronald Clark's 1965 *Tizard* (London: Methuen), also with the parts reversed, and in numerous other places. This version is based on Serber's.

5b. O. R. Frisch and R. Peierls, "On the Construction of a 'Super-bomb' based on a Nuclear Chain Reaction in Uranium," March 1940. Part 2 of the Frisch-Peierls Memorandum

The possible construction of "super-bombs" based on a nuclear chain reaction in uranium has been discussed a great deal and arguments have been brought forward which seemed to exclude this possibility. We wish here to point out and discuss a possibility which seems to have been overlooked in these earlier discussions.

Uranium consists essentially of two isotopes, 238U (99.3%) and ^{235}U (0.7%). If a uranium nucleus is hit by a neutron, three processes are possible: (1) scattering, whereby the neutron changes directions and if its energy is above 0.1 MeV, loses energy; (2) capture, when the neutron is taken up by the nucleus; and (3) fission, i.e. the nucleus breaks up into two nuclei of comparable size, with the liberation of an energy of about 200 MeV.

The possibility of chain reaction is given by the fact that neutrons are emitted in the fission and that the number of these neutrons per fission is greater than 1. The most probable value for this figure seems to be 2.3, from two independent determinations.

However, it has been shown that even in a large block of ordinary uranium no chain reaction would take place since too many neutrons would be slowed down by inelastic scattering into the energy region where they are strongly absorbed by 238U.

Several people have tried to make chain reactions possible by mixing the uranium with water, which reduces the energy of the neutrons still further and thereby increases their efficiency again. It seems fairly certain however that even then it is impossible to sustain a chain reaction.

In any case, no arrangement containing hydrogen and based on the action of slow neutrons could act as an effective superbomb, because the reaction would be too slow. The time required to slow down a neutron is about 10^{-5} sec and the average time loss before a neutron hits a uranium nucleus is even 10^{-4}. In the reaction, the number of neutrons would increase exponentially, like $e^{t/\tau}$ where τ would be at least 10^{-4} sec. When the temperature reaches several thousand degrees the container of the bomb will break and within 10^{-4} sec the uranium would have expanded sufficiently to let the neutrons escape and so to stop the reaction. The energy liberated would, therefore, be only a few times the energy required to break the container, i.e. of the same order of magnitude as with ordinary high explosives.

Bohr has put forward strong arguments for the suggestion that the fission observed with slow neutrons is to be ascribed to the rare isotope ^{235}U, and that this isotope has, on the whole, a much greater fission probability than the common isotope 238U. Effective methods for the separation of isotopes have been developed recently, of which the method of thermal diffusion is simple enough to permit separation on a fairly large scale.

This permits, in principle, the use of nearly pure ^{235}U in such a bomb, a possibility which apparently has not so far been seriously considered. We have discussed this possibility and come to the conclusion that a moderate amount of ^{235}U would indeed constitute an extremely efficient explosive.

The behavior of ^{235}U under bombardment with fast neutrons is not experimentally, but from rather simple theoretical arguments it can be concluded that almost every collision produces fission and that neutrons of any energy are effective. Therefore it is not necessary to add hydrogen, and the reaction, depending on the action of fast neutrons, develops with very great rapidity so that a considerable part of the total energy is liberated before the reaction gets stopped on account of the expansion of the material.

The critical radius γ_o - i.e. the radius of sphere in which the surplus of neutrons created by the fission is just equal to the loss of neutrons by escape through the surface-is, for a material with a given composition, in a fixed ration to the mean free path of neutrons, and this in turn is inversely proportional to the density . It therefore pays to bring the material into the densest possible form, i.e. the metallic state, probably sintered or hammered. If we assume for 235, no appreciable scattering, and 2.3 neutrons emitted per fission, then the critical radius is found to be 0.8 time the mean free path. In the metallic state (density 15), and assuming a fission cross-section of 10^{-23} cm^2, the mean free path would be 2.6 cm and would be 2.1 cm, corresponding to a mass of 600 grams. A sphere of metallic ^{235}U of a radius greater than would be explosive, and one might think of about 1 kg as suitable size for a bomb.

The speed of the reaction is easy to estimate. The neutrons emitted in the fission have velocities of about 10^{-9} cm/sec and they have to travel 2.6 cm before hitting a uranium nucleus. For a sphere well above the critical size the loss through neutron escape would be small, so we may assume that each neutron after a life of 2.6 x 10^{-9} sec, produces fission, giving birth to two neutrons. In the expression $e^{t/\tau}$ for the increase of neutron density with time, it would be about 4 x 10^{-9} sec, very much shorter than in the case of a chain reaction depending on slow neutrons.

If the reaction proceeds until most of the uranium is used up, temperatures of the order of 10^{10} degrees and pressure of about 10^{13} atmospheres are produced. It is difficult to predict accurately the behavior of matter under these extreme conditions, and the mathematical difficulties of the problem are considerable. By a rough calculation we get the following expression for the energy liberated before the mass expands so much that the reaction is interrupted:

$E = 0.2M(r^2/\tau^2)\sqrt{((r/r_0)-1)}$

(M, total mass of uranium; r, radius of sphere; r_0, critical radius; τ, time required for neutron density to multiply by a factor e). For a sphere of radius 4.2 cm (r_0 = 2.1 cm), M = 4700 grams, τ = 4 x 10^{-9} sec, we find E = 4 x 10^{20} ergs, which is about one-tenth of the total fission energy. For a radius of about 8 cm (m = 32 kg) the whole fission energy is liberated, according to the formula (1). For small radii the efficiency falls off even faster than indicated by formula (1) because τ goes up as r approaches r_0. The energy liberated by a 5 kg bomb would be equivalent to that of several thousand tons of dynamite, while that of a 1 kg bomb, though about 500 times less, would still be formidable.

It is necessary that such a sphere should be made in two (or more) parts which are brought together first when the explosion is wanted. Once assembled, the bomb would explode within a second or less, since one neutron is sufficient to start the reaction and there are several neutrons passing through the bomb every second, from the cosmic radiation. (Neutrons originating from the action of uranium alpha rays on light-element impurities would be negligible provided the uranium is reasonably pure.) A sphere with a radius of less than about 3 cm could be made up in two hemispheres, which are pulled together by springs and kept separated by a suitable structure which is removed at the desired moment. A larger sphere would have to be composed of more than two parts, if the parts, taken separately, are to be stable.

It is important that the assembling of the parts should be done as rapidly as possible, in order to minimize the chance of a reaction getting started at a moment when the critical conditions have only just been reached. If this happened, the reaction rate would be much slower and the energy liberation would be considerably reduced; it would, however, always be sufficient to destroy the bomb.

For the separation of the ^{235}U, the method of thermal diffusion, developed by Clusius and others, seems to be the only one which can cope with the large amounts required. A gaseous uranium compound, for example uranium hexafluoride, is placed between two vertical surfaces which are kept at a different temperature. The light isotope tends to get more concentrated near the hot surface, where it is carried upwards by the convection current. Exchange with the current moving downwards along the cold surface produces a fractionating effect, and after some time a state of equilibrium is reached when the gas near the upper end contains markedly more of the light isotope than near the lower end.

For example, a system of two concentric tubes, of 2mm separation and 3 cm diameter, 150 cm long, would produce a difference of about 40% in the concentration of the rare isotope between its end without unduly upsetting the equilibrium.

In order to produce large amounts of highly concentrated ^{235}U, a great number of these separating units will have to be used, being arranged in parallel as well as in series. For a daily production of 100 grams of ^{235}U of 90% purity, we estimate that about 100,000 of these tubes would be required. This seems a large number, but it would undoubtedly be possible to design some kind of a system which would have the same effective area in a more compact and less expensive form.

In addition to the destructive effect of the explosion itself, the whole material of the bomb would be transformed into a highly radioactive stage. The energy radiated by these active substances will amount to about 20% of the energy liberated in the explosion, and the radiations would be fatal to living beings even a long time after the explosion.

The fission of uranium results in the formation of a great number of active bodies with periods between, roughly speaking, a second and a year. The resulting radiation is found to decay in such a way that the intensity is about inversely proportional to the time. Even one day after the explosion the radiation will correspond to a power expenditure of the order 1,000 kW, or to the radiation of a hundred tons of radium.

Any estimates of the effects of this radiation on human beings must be rather uncertain because it is difficult to tell what will happen to the radioactive material after the explosion. Most of it will probably be blown into the air and carried away by the wind. This cloud of radioactive material will kill everybody within a strip estimated to be several miles long. If it rained the danger would be even worse because the active material would be carried down to the ground and stick to it, and persons entering the contaminated area would be subjected to dangerous radiations even after days. If 1% of the active material sticks to the debris in the vicinity of the explosion and if the debris is spread over an area of, say, a square mile, any person entering this area would be in serious danger, even several days after the explosion.

In estimates, the lethal dose penetrating radiation was assumed to be 1,000 Roentgen; consultation of a medical specialist on X-ray treatment and perhaps further biological research may enable one to fix the danger limit more accurately. The main source of uncertainty is our lack of knowledge as to the behavior of materials in such a super-explosion, an expert on high explosives may be able to clarify some of these problems.

Effective protection is hardly possible. Houses would offer protection only at the margins of the danger zone. Deep cellar or tunnels may be comparatively safe from the effects of radiation, provided air can be supplied from an uncontaminated area (some of the active substance would be noble gases which are not stop by ordinary filters)

The irradiation is not felt until hours later when it may become too late. Therefore it would be very important to have an organization which determines the exact extent of the danger area, by means of ionization measurements, so that people can be warned from entering it.

O. R. Frisch

R. Peierls

Source: The original of the memorandum is in the Bodleian Museum at Oxford University in the United Kingdom. Transcriptions, which differ slightly, can be found in Robert Serber, et al.'s 1992 *The Los Alamos Primer* (Berkeley: University of California Press); Philip L. Cantelon, et al.'s 1984 *The American Atom* (Philadelphia: The University of Pennsylvania Press) for part 2; Ferenc Morton Stasz's 1992 *British Scientists and the Manhattan Project: The Los Alamos Years* (New York: St. Martin's Press) with parts 1 and 2 reversed; Ronald Clark's 1965 *Tizard* (London: Methuen), also with the parts reversed, and in numerous other places. This version is based on Serber's.

6. Arthur Compton Report of the National Academy of Sciences Committee on Atomic Fission, May 17, 1941

This Compton report, the first of two he would submit (the second the following November), forcefully urged that the United States engage in a stepped-up program for, essentially, the development of an atomic bomb. The report, however, was much broader than that in scope, even speculating on uses of nuclear power far beyond the tools of war. The report warns that it would be unlikely that a usable atomic bomb could be developed before 1945 but hints that, after that, it could become "a determining factor in warfare." It covers, also, the needs for producing sufficient fissile material of mass low enough for an effective and deliverable bomb. This detailed report laid out a plan that would eventually develop into the Manhattan Project.

REPORT OF
NATITONAL ACADEMY OF SCIENCES
COMMITTEE ON ATOMIC FISSION

Frank B. Jewett, President
National Academy of Sciences
2101 Constitution Avenue
Washington, D.C.

Dear President Jewett:

The committee of the National Academy of Sciences to which you have referred the matter of possible military aspects of atomic fission, held a meeting in Washington, April 30, with Dr. Briggs' "Uranium Committee", and a second meeting in Cambridge, May 5. Further conferences were held by mail and wire.

We have been concerned primarily with question "b" of your letter of appointment, "as-to whether, all things considered, larger funds and facilities and more pressure are indicated in the light of our present scientific knowledge and the probability of applications useful in connection with national defense problems."

Our primary recommendation is that <u>during the next 6 months a strongly intensified effort should be spent on this problem</u>. This is in accord with the view urged by Dr. Briggs on behalf of his committee, and with the unanimous opinion of the other qualified persons with whom we have consulted.

It now appears probable that the results obtained by that time will show the need for a large scale program with regard to atomic fission. It remains possible that on the contrary the results will then indicate that vigorous effort will no longer be justified in view of other urgent military demands on the attention of physicists. The possibilities associated with a successful outcome of the work are however of such importance and are so imminent that, in our opinion, we must not risk giving an enemy nation the advantage of first putting atomic fission to military use.

Intensive immediate effort will involve sharply increased appropriations in support of present work, and means for facilitating the efficient use of the men qualified to work in this field.

For accomplishing these objectives specific recommendations are presented in the final section of this report.

It would seem to us unlikely that the use of nuclear fission can become of military importance within less than two yews, though it would appear that some of the British experts anticipate applications more prompt than this. If, however, the chain reaction can be produced and controlled, it may rapidly become a determining factor in warfare. Looking, therefore, to a struggle which may continue for a decade or more, it is important that we gain the lead in this development. That nation which first produces and controls the process will have an advantage which will grow as its applications multiply.

Possible Military Applications

Applications of military importance in connection with atomic fission are based upon the expectation of producing a nuclear chain reaction. In this reaction, when a U235 atom combines with a slow neutron, it divides with great energy (the process of "fission"), emitting rays among which are fast neutrons. When these neutrons are slowed down by collision with other atoms, such as deuterium, beryllium or carbon, they may be captured by other U235 atoms, which in turn divide. This is the chain reaction, continuing as long as a sufficient number of U235 atoms and atoms of the slowing agent are present. The energy thus liberated per atom of U235 is about 130,000,000 times that developed per atom from such a chemical reaction as combustion of carbon in oxygen or about 2,000,000 times as much per pound of U235 as per pound of carbon burning in oxygen. It is anticipated that under suitable conditions the reaction will be under control with respect to speed of development, but that under other conditions it may proceed with explosive violence.

Proposed military applications of a uranium fission reaction include:

(a) Production of violently radioactive materials to be used as missiles destructive to life in virtue of their ionizing radiations. For this purpose the function of the central installation for producing the chain fission reaction would be to produce the artificially active materials. These might then be carried by airplanes to be scattered as bombs over enemy territory. While this might be the most promptly applicable military use of the method, because of the hazards that will necessarily be involved, it could hardly be applied within less than twelve months from the first successful production of a chain reaction. This would mean not earlier than 1943.

(b) As a power source on submarines and other ships. This is perhaps the most straightforward use of atomic power, but because of the engineering difficulties involved, and the necessary protection against hazards, it can hardly have important application within less than three years from the time of production of the first chain reaction.

(c) Violently explosive bombs. It would now appear that a strong concentration of uranium 235, or of some other element which is subject to fission on capturing thermal neutrons, will be required in order to produce an explosive atomic reaction. The destructive power of such an explosion should be enormous as compared with that from chemical explosives. Optimistic estimates of the time required for separation of adequate amounts of uranium isotopes would be from three to five years. It is possible that element 94, usable for this purpose, may be produced abundantly by the chain fission reaction. If this is true, such atomic bombs might become available within twelve months from the time of the first fission chain reaction. Because of the hazard in its use, however, some years will be required for development. This means that atomic bombs can hardly be anticipated before 1945.

In making these time estimates, we have been guided by normal, high pressure development of scientific and engineering processes. It is possible that with luck the times would in certain cases be appreciably reduced. It seems to us more likely, however, that the effectiveness of the methods concerned will become most evident at later dates than those here indicated.

On the other hand, it should be kept in mind that the outcome of a new process such as this will certainly open new possibilities now unthought of. Some of these may be of prompt application, but most of them will only gradually be realized.

Progress toward Securing a Chain Reaction

The calculations seem to make it clear that a chain reaction of atomic fission should easily be produced with a sufficiently, large quantity of the 235 isotope of uranium. The separation of this isotope is possible, but according to present indications, can be achieved in quantity only by the installation of large, expensive plants whose suitable design has not yet been determined. In time, this may become a most important aspect of the problem, and work now under way in studying the methods of isotope separation must, therefore, be continued.

Those working on the fission problem are, however, agreed that the probability of obtaining a chain reaction with the normal mixture of uranium isotopes is good. To make this process a success involves the use of an agent to slow down the fast neutrons liberated at the time of fission to a speed so low that they will not readily be captured by uranium 238. The best estimates indicate better than even chances that continued work along the lines now being followed will effect this reaction. If given sufficient support, adequate tests of these methods should be completed and the reaction perhaps obtained within 18 months.

The time and cost required to complete the tests needed to produce the chain reaction, if the method. is practicable, is now estimated as follows:

a. <u>Mixtures of uranium and carbon.</u>

1. <u>Intermediate experiment now in hand at Columbia University.</u> Details are given in the attached report by George B. Pegram.

Cost - materials $ 117,000
Salaries   33,000
Incidentals   24,000 $174,000

Time of completion: about July 1, 1942

Anticipated results: Definite evidence whether uranium-carbon mixture can give chain reaction, and reliable data from which to determine amount of material required to produce such reaction.

Present status: about $60,000 worth of material on order.

2. <u>Production of chain reaction with carbon and uranium.</u> This cannot be intelligently explained until experiment (1) is complete. As now anticipated, it will require at least 120 tons of graph and the erection of suitable

housing. The cost of this stage will probably be between $500,000 and $1,000,000.

The uranium-carbon experiment is the most immediately applicable of the proposed methods. This is because the materials required are immediately available. It is estimated by Fermi to have an even chance of success. It does not appear as hopeful as methods b. and c. mentioned below. Because of its immediate applicability, however, and the importance of learning what the chain reaction will do, it is important to go ahead now with the intermediate stage (1) of this experiment.

b. <u>Mixtures of uranium with beryllium or beryllium oxide.</u>

Be and BeO seem to have advantages, over C as slowing agents, because (1) the path required to bring the neutrons to rest is shorter, and (2) additional neutrons are released within the beryllium. BeO is available in suitable quantity. Time will be required to produce metallic Be.

1. <u>Intermediate experiment on relative effectiveness of Be, BeO, and C as slowing agents.</u> Experiments now in hand at University of Chicago. (See attached report by S. K. Allison)

   Cost- materials, including 2 tons
   BeO and 250 $35,000
      pounds Be
   Salaries, $15,000 +   22,500+
      50 percent
   Incidentals   7,500 $65,000
   Completion date of experiment: December 1, 1941 Result: Knowledge of comparative value of beryllium and carbon as slowing agent for neutrons, and an estimate of relative amount of beryllium, beryllium oxide, or carbon, required to produce a chain reaction.

[Note added 5/17/41]
Allison suggests that plans should be made now for an experiment using about 1 cubic meter of BeO (3 to 4 tons), some 200 lbs. of Be metal, and 2 to 3 tons of uranium oxide or metal. Arranging the uranium in 2 concentric shells filled with beryllium, he believes a definite answer to the possibility of a chain reaction by this method can be given, and the amounts required definitely determined. There would be perhaps some chance of securing at once the chain reaction.

If the uranium and the metallic beryllium is borrowed from the carbon experiment, the material cost would be confined to that of the beryllium oxide, roughly 50,000. This would replace experiments b1 and b2 here indicated.

                    A.H.C.

2. <u>Determinative uranium-beryllium experiment.</u> This will involve use of larger quantities of the materials. The design of the experiment will depend upon the state of the problem at the time. It should give definite information regard to amount of materials required to produce the reaction. Its completion will probably be limited by the rate at which the materials can be supplied, but should not be later than July 1, 1942. Probable cost, about $130,000 additional.

3. <u>Chain reaction with beryllium oxide and uranium.</u> On the basis of present rough estimates comparable with those used for experiment a-2 above, this experiment will require some 20 tons of uranium oxide and 30 tons of beryllium oxide. Total cost should be roughly somewhat less than that of the corresponding uranium carbon experiment. This, however, is based upon uncertain data.

By July 1942, it should be possible to choose reliably whether the carbon or the beryllium slowing agent is preferable and, thus, to select either experiment a-2 or b-3. It will probably not be desirable to carry through both at that time.

c. <u>Mixtures of uranium with pure, heavy water.</u> (See attached report by H. C. Urey). The use of heavy water as a slowing agent is the most promising method now on the horizon. Its effective use, however, awaits the separation of the necessary quantities of heavy hydrogen. Eventually it may be less expensive than the other methods, even though the other methods may be the first to give results and at lower initial cost. The most promising method of separating deuterium (heavy hydrogen) is, according to Urey, the chemical exchange reaction between water and hydrogen, in which the water is fed through a countercurrent system containing a catalyst, then converting this to hydrogen and feeding the hydrogen back through the catalyst system.

Studies of the appropriate catalyst and of the construction of a pilot fractionation system are now in progress.

2. <u>Large scale production of heavy water.</u> "The plant may cost a half million or a million dollars". The heavy water should cost between $10,000 and $25,000 per ton. As a rough estimate, several tons will be required for effecting the fission chain reaction.

3. <u>Tests of uranium and heavy water mixtures.</u> Preliminary tests of this type have been performed by Halban in England, using 120 kilograms of heavy water. The result was very encouraging, and has apparently convinced the British physicists that the chain reaction can be produced by this method. The experiment is not however clear cut, and needs repetition with perhaps a ton of heavy water before the conditions for the chain reaction experiment itself can be definitely formulated. Materials available for making this test may be available by July 1942.

4. <u>Chain reaction with uranium and heavy water.</u> This experiment should be possible not later than 1943 at a cost, in addition to that for the building of the deuterium separation plant, of from $200,000 to $400,000.

<u>Recommendations</u>
<u>Budget</u>

We understand that the intermediate experiment on uranium and graphite is already partially financed, as is also a pilot plant for the production of pure heavy water. In addition to giving these two projects full support, we would urge emphasis on the beryllium project to the extent of approximately the $65,000 for the next six months indicated above. The other work on the separation of uranium isotopes should also be kept active, although it does not need the urgent emphasis that should be placed upon the use of normal uranium. There should thus be made available for the next six months a total of about $350,000. This is as far as the committee believes the present information justifies definite plans.

Toward the end of this 6 month period, i. e. about November, 1941, the results should however be reconsidered by a committee similar to the present one. If the indications are favorable, one or both of the following projects should then be carried through: (a) The next stage of the beryllium experiment, at a cost of about $130,000, and (b) the construction of the separation plant for producing heavy water, at a cost of perhaps $800,000.

It would now seem that a comparable expenditure during the following year may be required in order actually to produce the atomic chain reaction in usable form. It is doubtful whether the cost can be reduced much below a total of two million dollars without so prolonging the experiments that we should be trailing the work done in other countries.

We recognize that this is a heavy demand on the funds available for national defense research. We believe, however, that the military possibilities of atomic fission are so vast, and the dangers of its neglect until some other nation has outdistanced us are so serious, that if necessary a request should be made for a special appropriation to cover this work. Within a half dozen years the consequences of such investigations may be crucial in determining the nation's military position.

It is noteworthy that our emphasis on its high importance reflects the seemingly unanimous judgment of those in this country and England who have studied intimately the possibilities of atomic fission. This includes all of the individual members of the Uranium Committee, as well as the investigators with whom we have conferred. (See especially the minutes of the May 5 meeting of our committee)

<u>Personnel</u>

The question of employing on this problem scientific men who might be more useful at other national defense problems has been considered. This difficulty is not as serious as would at first appear, for two reasons: (1) The greater part of the expense does not go into the employment of physicists, but rather into the supplying of the expensive materials required. (2) The physicists to be used on this project are and will continue to be, for the most part, those whose qualifications do not fit them for important positions in other national defense projects. This applies to most of the physicists and chemists now employed at Columbia and Chicago, with the exception of Mr. Pegram and Mr. Allison.

In order to insure the rapid and efficient progress of these studies we would recommend:

1. <u>The formation of a sub-committee called perhaps the Research Committee of the Uranium Committee consisting of S. K. Allison, G. Breit, E. Fermi, G. Pegram, and H. C. Urey</u>. As its chairman, Coolidge, Slater and Compton favor Allison; Van Vleck favors Urey, and Lawrence favors either Urey or Allison. It would be the function of this sub-committee (1) to plan and carry through the research program, (2) to confer continuously on the developments as they occur, (3) to see that newly obtained information is promptly available to those investigators that need it, and (4) to report as may be desired to the central uranium committee.

2. We consider it vital that every effort be made to insure that those working on the uranium problem at the request of the uranium committee be kept acquainted with the advances made by other investigators and be encouraged to confer upon their mutual problems. Experience indicates that only thus can rapid progress be made; and rapid progress is in the present instance of first importance.

3. In order to progress most rapidly, it will be of value to bring immediately by air to the United States Mr. Halban, now at work on this problem in Cambridge, England. He has information that will greatly aid our investigations, and can take back to England such information as we may have obtained that may be of value in their study of the same problem.

We wish to congratulate the Uranium Committee on the excellent progress that has thus far been made. We would encourage the National Defense Research Committee to give even more complete support to the capable men now engaged upon this research. This we believe can best be done by giving prompt and adequate financial support along the lines indicated above.

Respectfully submitted,
Arthur H. Compton

With the expressed approval of the following members of the committee: W. D. Coolidge, E. O. Lawrence, J. C. Slater, J. H. Van Vleck. Because of illness, Mr. Bancroft Gherardi has taken no part in the committee's discussions.

A.H.C.

Source: National Archives, Records of the Office of Scientific Research and Development, Record Group 227, Bush-Conant papers microfilm collection, Roll 1, Target 2, Folder 1, "S-1 Historical File, Section A (1940–1941)."

7. MAUD Committee Report, July 1941

The MAUD Committee Report was the direct result of 15 months of work by British scientists on the heels of the Frisch-Peierls Memorandum. It posited the feasibility of a deliverable atomic bomb, proposing in some detail a path to development. The report was composed primarily by George Thomson, who had been awarded the Nobel Prize in Physics in 1937, with extensive editing by James Chadwick, who had also won the Nobel Prize in Physics (1935). The report was based on coordinated work carried out at four universities: Birmingham, Cambridge, Liverpool, and Oxford. It led directly to the Tube Alloys project for development of an atomic bomb in Great Britain and Canada and, once it was shared with the United States, the Manhattan Project.

S E C R E T
Report by M.A.U.D. Committee
On the Use of Uranium for a Bomb
Part I

1. General Statement

Work to investigate the possibilities of utilising the atomic energy of uranium for military purposes has been in progress since 1939, and a stage has now been reached when it seems desirable to report progress.

We should like to emphasize at the beginning of this report that we entered the project with more skepticism than belief, though we felt it was a matter which had to be investigated. As we proceeded we became more and more convinced that release of atomic energy on a large scale is possible and that conditions can be chosen which would make it a very powerful weapon of war. We have now reached the conclusion that it will be possible to make an effective uranium bomb which, containing some 25 lbs. of active material, would be equivalent as regards destructive effect to 1,800 tons of T.N.T. and would also release large quantities of radioactive substances, which would make places near to where the bomb exploded dangerous to human life for a long period. The bomb would be composed of an active constituent (referred to in what follows as U.235) present to the extent of about 1 part in 140 in ordinary Uranium. Owning to the very small difference in properties (other than explosive) between this substance and the rest of the Uranium, its extraction is a matter of great difficulty and a plant to produce 2¼ lbs (1 kilogram) per day (or 3 bombs per month) is estimated to cost approximately £5,000,000 of which sum a considerable proportion would be spend on engineering requiring labour of the same highly skilled character as is needed for making turbines.

In spite of this very large expenditure we consider that the destructive effect both material and moral is so great that every effort should be made to produce bombs of this kind. As regards the time required, Imperial Chemical Industries after consultation with Dr. Guy of Metropolitan Vickers, estimate that the material for the first bomb could be ready by the end of 1943. This of course assumes that no major difficulty of an entirely unforeseen character arises. Dr. Ferguson of Woolwich estimates that the time required to work out the method of producing high velocities required for fusing (see para. 3) is 1 – 2 months. As this could be done concurrently with the production of the material no further delay is to be anticipated on this score. Even if the war should end before the bombs are ready the effect would not be wasted, except in the unlikely event of complete disarmament, since no nation would risk being caught without a weapon of such destructive possibilities.

We know that Germany has taken a great deal of trouble to secure supplies of the substance known as heavy water. In the earlier stages we thought that this substance might be of great importance for our work. It appears in fact that its usefulness in the release of atomic energy is limited to processes which are not likely to be of immediate war value

By far the largest supplies of Uranium are in Canada and the Belgian Congo, and since it has been actively looked for because of the radium which accompanies it, it is unlikely that any considerable quantities exist which are unknown expect possibly in unexplored regions.

2. Principle Involved

This type of bomb is possible because of the enormous store of energy resident in atoms and because of the special properties of the active constituent of uranium. The explosion is very different in its mechanism from the ordinary chemical explosion, for it can occur only if the quantity of U.235 is greater than a certain critical amount. Quantities of the material less than the critical amount are quite stable. Such quantities are therefore perfectly safe and this is a point which we wish to emphasize. On the other hand, if the amount of material exceeds the critical value it is unstable and a reaction will develop and multiply itself with enormous rapidity, resulting in an explosion of unprecedented violence. Thus all that is necessary to detonate the bomb is to bring together two pieces of the active material each less than the critical size but which when in contact form a mass exceeding it.

3. Method of Fusing

In order to achieve the greatest efficiency in an explosion of this type, it is necessary to bring the 2 halves together at high velocity and it is proposed to do this by firing them together with charges of ordinary explosive in the form of a double gun.

The weight of this gun will of course greatly exceed the weight of the bomb itself, but should not be more than 1 ton, and it would certainly be within the carrying capacity of a modern bomber. It is suggested that the bomb (contained in the gun) should be dropped by parachute and that the gun should be fired by means of a percussion device when it hits the ground. The time of drop can be made long enough to allow the aeroplane to escape from the danger zone, and as this is very large, great accuracy of aim is not required.

4. Probable Effect

The best estimate of the kind of damage likely to be produced by the explosion of 1,800 tons of TNT is afforded by the great explosion at Halifax N.S. in 1917. The following account is from the "History of Explosives". "The ship contained 450,000 lb. of TNT, 122,960 lb. of guncotton, and 4,661,794 lb. of picric acid wet and dry, making a total of 5,234,754 lib. The zone of the explosion extended for about ¾ mile in every direction and in this zone the destruction was almost complete. Severe structural damage extended generally for a radius of 1$\frac{1}{8}$ to 1¼ miles, and in one direction up to 1¾ miles from the origin. Missiles were projected to 3 - 4 miles, window glass broken up to 10 miles generally, and in one instance up to 61miles."

In considering this description it is to be remembered that part of the explosives cargo was situated below water level and part above.

5. <u>Preparation of Material and Cost</u>

We have considered in great detail the possible methods of extracting the U.235 from ordinary Uranium and have made a number of experiments. The scheme which we recommend is described in Part II of this report and in greater detail in Appendix IV. It involves essentially the gaseous diffusion of a compound of Uranium through gauzes of very fine mesh.

In the estimates of size and cost which accompany this report, we have only assumed types of gauze which are at present in existence. It is probable that a comparatively small amount of development would enable gauzes of smaller mesh to be made and this would allow the construction of a somewhat smaller and consequently cheaper separation plant for the same output.

Although the cost per lb. of this explosive is go great it compares very favourably with ordinary explosives when reckoned in terms of energy released and damage done. It is, in fact, considerably cheaper, but the points which we regard as of overwhelming importance are the concentrated destruction which it would produce, the large moral effect, and the saving in air effort the use of this substance would allow, as compared with bombing with ordinary explosives.

6. <u>Discussion</u>

One outstanding difficulty of the scheme is that the main principle cannot be tested on a small scale. Even to produce a bomb of the minimum critical size would involve a great expenditure of time and money. We are however convinced that the principle is correct, and whilst there is still some uncertainty as to the critical size it is most unlikely that the best estimate we can make is so far in error as to invalidate the general conclusions. We feel that the present evidence is sufficient to justify the scheme being strongly pressed.

As regards the manufacture of the U.235 we have gone nearly as far as we can on a laboratory scale. The principle of the method is certain, and application does not appear unduly difficult as a piece of chemical engineering. The need to work on a larger scale is now very apparent and we are beginning to have difficulty in finding the necessary scientific personnel. Further, if the weapon is to be available in say two years from now, it is necessary to start plans for the erection of a factory, though no really large expenditure will be needed till the 20 stage model has been tested. It is also important to begin training men who can ultimately act as supervisors of the manufacture. There are a number of auxiliary pieces of apparatus to be developed, such as those for measuring the concentration of the U.235. In addition, work on a fairly large scale is needed to develop the chemical side for the production in bulk of uranium hexafluoride, the gaseous compound we propose to use.

It will be seen from the foregoing that a stage in the work has now been reached at which it is important that a decision should be made as to whether the work is to be continued on the increasing scale which would be necessary if we are to hope for it as an effective weapon for this war. Any considerable delay would now retard by an equivalent amount the date by which the weapon could come into effect.

7. <u>Action in the U.S.</u>

We are informed that while the Americans are working on the uranium problem the bulk of their effort has been directed to the production of energy, as discussed in our report on Uranium as a source of power, rather than to the production of a bomb. We are in fact co-operating with the United States to the extent of exchanging information, and they have undertaken one or two pieces of laboratory work for us. We feel that it is important and desirable that development work should proceed on both sides of the Atlantic irrespective of where it may be finally decided to locate the plant for separating the U.235, and for this purpose it seems desirable that certain members of the committee should visit the United States. We are informed that such a visit would be welcomed by members of the United States committees which are dealing with this matter.

8. <u>Conclusions and Recommendations</u>
   (i) The committee considers that the scheme for a Uranium bomb is practicable and likely to lead to decisive results in the war.
   (ii) It recommends that this work be continued on the highest priority and on the increasing scale necessary to obtain the weapon in the shortest possible time, and
   (iii) That the present collaboration with America should be continued and extended especially in the region of experimental work.

Source: National Archives microfilm collection M1392, *Bush-Conant File Relating to the Development of the Atomic Bomb, 1940–1945* (Washington: National Archives and Records Administration, 1990), reel 1/14.

8. Vannevar Bush Letter to Franklin Roosevelt, March 9, 1942

The consummate scientist-politician, Vannevar Bush was the linchpin of U.S. governmental efforts leading to the establishment of the Manhattan Project. As can be seen in this letter, which emphasizes his alliance with Vice President Henry Wallace and name-drops U.S. Army Chief of Staff George Marshall and his chemist colleague James Conant, who he had made his replacement as head of the National Defense Research Committee when he moved up to head the new Office of Scientific Research and Development, Bush was a careful political strategist, leaving nothing to chance even in his reporting to a supportive president.

OFFICE FOR EMERGENCY MANAGEMENT
OFFICE OF SCIENTIFIC RESEARCH AND DEVELOPMENT
1530 P STREET NW.
WASHINGTON, D.C.
Vannevar Bush
Director
March 9, 1942

The President,
The White House,
Washington, D.C.
Dear Mr. President:

On October 9, 1941, Mr. Wallace and I presented to you the status of research in this country and Great Britain on a possible powerful explosive.

In accordance with your instructions, I have since expedited this work in every way possible. I now attach a brief summary report of the status of the matter.

Considerations of general policy and of international relations have been limited for the present to a group consisting of Mr. Wallace, Secretary Stimson, General Marshall, Dr. Conant, and myself. Mr. Wallace has called a conference of this group, to which he invited also Mr. Harold D. Smith as the matter of funds was there considered.

The technical aspects are in the hands of a group of notable physicists, chemists, and engineers, as noted in the report. The corresponding British organization is also indicated. The work is under way at full speed.

Recent developments indicate, briefly, that the subject is more important than I believed when I last spoke to you about it. The stuff will apparently be more powerful than we then thought, the amount necessary appears to be less, the possibilities of actual production appear more certain. The way to full accomplishment is still exceedingly difficult, and the time schedule on this remains unchanged. We may be engaged in a race toward realization; but, if so, I have no indication of the status of the enemy program, and have taken no definite steps toward finding out.

The subject is rapidly approaching the pilot plant stage. I believe that, by next summer, the most promising methods can be selected, and production plants started. At that time I believe the whole matter should be turned over to the War Department.

You returned to me the previous reports, in order that I might hold them subject to you call. I shall be glad to guard this report also if you wish.
Respectfully yours,

V. Bush,
Director.

Source: National Archives, Record Group 227, Records of the Office of Scientific Research and Development, 1939–1947.

9. J. Robert Oppenheimer Letter to James Conant on the Properties of Uranium, November 30, 1942

This two-part letter from Oppenheimer, who had been recruited by National Defense Research Committee head James Conant and then by General Leslie Groves to head the secret weapons laboratory of the new Manhattan Engineer District (the Manhattan Project), shows the importance of leadership that could understand both the intricacies of the science and technology of the project and the nuances of management. Oppenheimer could assume that Conant would read between the lines as Oppenheimer commented delicately on directives from Groves, whose background, after all, was in engineering, not the physics and chemistry essential to the theoretical work behind what would be, of course, the engineering of the atomic bomb. Questions of personnel, addressed later in the letter, are also handled deftly and carefully. "S-1," after the S-1 Advisory Committee, was a convenient euphemism for the Manhattan Project and the atomic bomb itself.

To James B. Conant

Berkeley
November 30, 1942

Dear Dr. Conant:
Your letter reached me with some delay since I returned to Berkeley only a day or so ago. I should like to answer first your P.S. You are quite right that the purities listed in

Groves' compulsory memo are a little misleading. The reason for this is that Groves defined a satisfactory bomb as one that had a 50 per cent chance of exceeding a 1,000-ton TNT equivalent. The absolute requirements are figured on this basis. It is, of course, my opinion that we should be wanton to strive for such a low goal, but I believe that some good was in fact done by indicating at that time that the purity requirements are not fantastic. The desirable requirements are equally undefined since the purer the material (up to a purity of about 100-fold that given) the less must we be worried about getting the maximum speed for the firing mechanism of the detonator; and this will make for simplicity and reliability in operation. In the Washington memo all impurities were listed on the assumption that not more than five elements would reach the tabulated values. I have, in the meantime, given a much more careful account of what the actual situation is to the committee. I met with them one day in Chicago, came out with them on the train, and have spent two days with them here in Berkeley, and we have had ample opportunity to discuss the purity question and many other aspects of our problem. The information which I have given them now is contained in a Chicago report on the feasibility of the 49 project and is as follows: If the concentrations by weight are as given in the accompanying table, then the chance of pre-detonation is 5 per cent, if only one element is present in the listed amount. If n elements are present in the listed amount the chance of pre-detonation is 5n per cent. The chance of a pre-detonation in which the energy release is less than 10,000 tons TNT equivalent is 0.5n per cent. In this range the effects of impurities are additive, and from the actual concentrations and figures listed one can figure out the probability of any given energy release. In any case, unless the firing mechanism fails completely the energy release will be more than sufficient to destroy the material and to make its recovery impossible. The figures given in the table are in part based on experimental values. In the case of 0 and C the figures represent highly conservative estimates based on the assumption that those isotopes which are dangerous will be as dangerous as the worst element, namely, Be.

Element Concentration by Weight

Be	10^{-7}	F	5×10^{-6}
Li	5×10^{-7}	Na	2×10^{-5}
B	2×10^{-7}	Mg	10^{-4}
C	2×10^{-5}	Al	2×10^{-5}
O	10^{-4}	Si	5×10^{-4}
		P	10^{-4}

(Some purity requirements on elements between P and Fe, none beyond Cu)

The only essential changes since the Washington memo are that we have sufficiently examined the experiments somewhat; and that we have studied the case of N carefully enough to be positive that there are no purity requirements on that element. The committee was of the opinion that the purity requirements as they now stand could, with a very high probability, be met. In fact, the Chicago uranium is good enough except for C and O, and they have made no effort at all to solve this problem. If it were necessary it would be possible to work with depleted C and O and so considerably relax the chemical conditions on these elements. In fact, the committee was of the opinion that the major extraction processes which have to be handled automatically and the removal of traces of active material, coupled with the necessity for working in lots of less than 100 grams or of introducing suitable neutron absorbers as "safers," would present greater technical difficulties than the purification. Nevertheless, in our last discussions they seemed convinced that the helium-cooled graphite pile was a good bet.

Now to the second point, the main subject of your letter, where I feel myself on less secure ground. It is, of course, natural that the men we are after will leave a big hole. I may though, in this connection, remind you that when McMillan himself left the Radiation Laboratory for San Diego there were the same dire predictions of disastrous disruption. Nevertheless, the Radiation Laboratory has not only survived but has, as you know, flourished and expanded. In view of this and of the very large number of men of the first rank who are now working on that project, I am inclined not to take too seriously the absolute no's with which we shall be greeted. I believe that it is important to emphasize that we should in any case be willing to let these men have time enough in their old positions to try to minimize the disruption of their leaving. I also agree that a fundamental clarification on this personnel problem, which can hardly be complete without Dr. Bush's participation, will be necessary. The job we have to do will not be possible without personnel substantially greater than that which we now have available, and I should only be misleading you and all others concerned with the S-1 project if I were to promise to get the work done without this help.

The suggestion of Eckhardt as a substitute for Kurie is a welcome one and we shall arrange to talk with him on our next trip east. There are, however, two reasons more substantial than prejudice why the limitation to men who are known to us is sound: 1) that the technical details of this work will in large part have to do with atomic physics so that any man whose experience has been in another field will necessarily be of more limited usefulness; Kurie, for instance, would have had as one of his responsibilities the installation and servicing of the cyclotron. The second reason is that in a tight isolated group such as we are now planning, some warmth and trust in personal relations is an indispensable prerequisite, and we are, of course, able to insure this only in the case of men whom we have known in the past. You will have had from me a note on possible alternatives to Kurie. If none of our suggestions seem practicable we shall see whether Dr. Eckhardt could fill the bill.

With good wishes,

Very sincerely yours,
Robert Oppenheimer

Source: James B. Conant, November 30, 1942, Records of the Office of Scientific Research and Development (OSRD), Record Group 227. National Archives.

10. Leslie Groves and James Conant Letter to J. Robert Oppenheimer, February 25, 1943

Without careful management of the necessary bureaucracy, the Manhattan Project would have had no chance of success. Coordinating work that, by 1943, spread across the country from Washington, D.C., to the Clinton Engineer Works at Oak Ridge, Tennessee, to the Hanford Engineer Works in Hanford, Washington, to the laboratories at Los Alamos, New Mexico, (not to mention the network of universities where work was also taking place) was a massive undertaking, particularly given the paramount need for extreme secrecy throughout. This letter, on the stationary of Vannevar Bush's Office of Scientific Research and Development, connects three of the men most responsible for keeping the Manhattan Project running smoothly: recipient J. Robert Oppenheimer and authors

James Conant and General Leslie Groves. This letter clarifies the roles of each in the project. "S-1" refers on the atomic bomb and is taken from the S-1 Executive Committee.

Office for Emergency Management
Office of Scientific Research and
Development
1530 P Street NW.
Washington, D. C.

Vannevar Bush
Director

February 25, 1943
Dr. J. R. Oppenheimer
University of California
Berkeley, California
Dear Dr. Oppenheimer:
We are addressing this letter to you as the Scientific Director of the special laboratory in New Mexico in order to confirm our many conversations on the matters of organization and responsibility. You are at liberty to show this letter to those with whom you are discussing the desirability of their joining the project with you; they of course realizing their responsibility as to secrecy, including the details of organization and personnel.

I. The laboratory will be concerned with the development and final manufacture of an instrument of war, which we may designate as Projectile S-1-T. To this end, the laboratory will be concerned with:
A. Certain experimental studies in science, engineering and ordnance; and
B. At a later date large-scale experiments involving difficult ordnance procedures and the handling of highly dangerous material.

The work of the laboratory will be divided into two periods in time: one, corresponding to the work mentioned in section A; the other, that mentioned in section B. During the first period, the laboratory will be on a strictly civilian basis, the personnel, procurement and other arrangements being carried on under a contract arranged between the War Department and the University of California. The conditions of this contract will be essentially similar to that of the usual OSRD contract. In such matters as draft deferment, the policy of the War Department and OSRD in regard to the personnel working under this contract will be practically identical. When the second division of the work is entered upon (mentioned in B), which will not be earlier than January 1, 1944, the scientific and engineering staff will be composed of commissioned officers. This is necessary because of the dangerous nature of the work and the need for special conditions of security. It is expected that many of those employed as civilians during the first period (A) will be offered commissions and become members of the commissioned staff during the second period (B), but there is no obligation on the part of anyone employed during period A to accept a commission at the end of that time.

II. The laboratory is part of a larger project which has been placed in a special category and assigned the highest priority by the President of the United States. By his order, the Secretary of War and certain other high officials have arranged that the control of this project shall be in the hands of a Military Policy Committee, composed of Dr. Vannevar Bush, Director of OSRD, as Chairman, Major General W. D. Styer, Chief of Staff, SOS, Rear Admiral W. R. Purnell, Assistant Chief of Staff to Admiral King; Dr. James B. Conant serves as Dr. Bush's deputy and alternate on this Committee, but attends all meetings and enters into all discussions. Brigadier General L. R. Groves of the Corps of Engineers has been given over-all executive responsibility for this project, working under the direction of the Military Policy Committee. He works in close cooperation with Dr. Conant, who is Chairman of the group of scientists who were in charge of the earlier phases of some aspects of the investigation.

III. Responsibilities of the Scientific Director.
1. He will be responsible for:
   A. The conduct of the scientific work so that the desired goals as outlined by the Military Policy Committee are achieved at the earliest possible dates.
   B. The maintenance of secrecy by the civilian personnel under his control as well as their families.
2. He will of course be guided in his determination of policies and courses of action by the advice of his scientific staff.
3. He will keep Dr. James B. Conant and General Groves informed to such an extent as is necessary for them to carry on the work which falls in their respective spheres. Dr. Conant will be available at any time for consultation on general scientific problems as well as to assist in the determination of definite scientific policies and research programs. Through Dr. Conant complete access to the scientific world is guaranteed.

IV. Responsibilities of the Commanding Officer.
1. The Commanding Officer will report directly to General Groves.
2. He will be responsible for:
   A. The work and conduct of all military personnel.
   B. The maintenance of suitable living conditions for civilian personnel.
   C. The prevention of trespassing on the site.
   D. The performance of duty by such guards as may be established within the reservation for the purpose of maintaining the secrecy precautions deemed necessary by the Scientific Director.

V. Cooperation.
The closest cooperation is of course necessary between the Commanding Officer and the Scientific Director if each is to perform his function to the maximum benefit of the work. Such a cooperative attitude now exists on the part of Dr. Conant and General Groves and has so existed since General Groves first entered the project.
Very sincerely yours,
James B. Conant
Leslie R. Groves

Source: Hadden, Gavin, ed. 1947. *Manhattan District History.* Book VIII Los Alamos Project (Y), Volume 2 Technical, Appendices, No. 1. Letter. Washington, D.C.: Department of Energy, Office of History and Heritage Resources, 460. Available online at https://www.osti.gov/opennet/manhattan_district. Accessed April 27, 2019.

II. Robert Serber's "Los Alamos Primer" from Lectures Delivered in April 1943

This primer, excerpted here, was distributed to all new technical and scientific staff at the laboratories at Los Alamos, New Mexico, starting soon after the lectures were delivered to the scientists there. It is one of the most concise and clear synopses of the goals of the Manhattan Project written at the time or, for that matter, since (though the science presented was quickly superseded, as it was expected would happen, even at the time). Serber, who had already been working with J. Robert Oppenheimer, who was heading the labs, was tasked with providing his new colleagues at the Los Alamos labs a comprehensive understanding of a project that was too easily compartmentalized, especially given the concerns for secrecy.

THE LOS ALAMOS PRIMER

The following notes are based on a set of five lectures given by R. Serber during the first two weeks of April 1943, as an "indoctrination course" in connection with the starting of the Los Alamos Project. The notes were written up by E. U. Condon.

1. Object

The object of the project is to produce a practical military weapon in the form of a bomb in which the energy is released by a fast neutron chain reaction in one or more of the materials known to show nuclear fission.

2. Energy of Fission Process

The direct energy release in the fission process is of the order of 170 MEV per atom. This is considerably more than 10⁷ times the heat of reaction per atom in ordinary combustion processes....

3. Fast Neutron Chain Reaction

Release of this energy in a large scale way is a possibility because of the fact that in each fission process, which requires a neutron to produce it, two neutrons are released. Consider a very great mass of active material, so great that no neutrons are lost through the surface and assume the material so pure that no neutrons are lost in other ways than by fission. One neutron released in the mass would become 2 after the first fission, each of these would produce 2 after they each had produced fission so in the nth generation of neutrons there would be 2^n neutrons available....

While this is going on the energy release is making the material very hot, developing great pressure and hence tending to cause an explosion.

In an actual finite setup some neutrons are lost by diffusion out through the surface. There will be therefore a certain size of say a sphere for which the surface losses of neutrons are just sufficient to stop the chain reaction. This radius depends on the density. As the reaction proceeds the material tends to expand, increasing the required minimum size faster than the actual size increases.

The whole question of whether an effective explosion is made depends on whether the reaction is stopped by this tendency before an appreciable fraction of the active material has fissiled....

4. Fission Cross-sections

The materials in question are U 235/92 = 25, U 238/92 = 28 and element 94^{239} = 49 and some others of lesser interest.

Ordinary uranium as it occurs in nature contains about 1/140 of 25, the rest being 28 except for a very small amount of 24....

8. Why ordinary U is safe

Ordinary U, containing only 1/140 of 25, is safe against a fast neutron chain because, (a) only 3/4 of the neutrons from a fission have energies above the threshold of 28, (b) only ¼ of the neutrons escape being slowed below 1 MEV, the 28 threshold before they make a fission.... Evidently a value greater than 1 is needed for a chain reaction. Hence a contribution of at least 0.6 is needed from the fissionability of the 25 constituent. One can estimate that the fraction of 25 must be increased at least 10-fold to make an explosive reaction possible.

9. Material 49

As mentioned above this material is prepared from the neutron capture reaction in 28. So far only microgram quantities have been produced so bulk physical properties of this element are not known. Also its ν value has not been measured. Its σ_f has been measured and found to be about twice that of 25 over the whole energy range. It is strongly α-radioactive with a half-life of about 20000 years.

Since there is every reason to expect its ν to be close to that for U and since it is fissionable with slow neutrons it is expected to be suitable for our problem and another project is going forward with plans to produce it for us in kilogram quantities.

Further study of all its properties has an important place on our program as rapidly as suitable quantities become available. . . .

11. Effect of Tamper

If we surround the core of active material by a shell of inactive material the shell will reflect some neutrons which would otherwise escape. Therefore a smaller quantity of active material will be enough to give rise to an explosion. The surrounding case is called a tamper.

The tamper material serves not only to retard the escape of neutrons but also by its inertia to retard the expansion of the active material. (The retardation provided by the tensile strength of the case is negligible.) For the latter purpose it is desirable to use the densest available materials (Au, W, Re, U). Present evidence indicates that for neutron reflecting properties also, one cannot do better than use these heavy elements. Needless to say, a great deal of work will have to be done on the properties of tamper materials. . . .

12. Damage

Several kinds of damage will be caused by the bomb.

A very large number of neutrons is released in the explosion. One can estimate a radius of about 1000 yards around the site of explosion as the size of the region in which the neutron concentration is great enough to produce severe pathological effects.

Enough radioactive material is produced that the total activity will be of the order of 10^6 curies even after 10 days. Just what effect this will have in rendering the locality uninhabitable depends greatly on very uncertain factors about the way in which this is dispersed by the explosion. However the total amount of radioactivity produced, as well as the total number of neutrons, is evidently proportional just to the number of fission processes, or to the total energy released.

The mechanical explosion damage is caused by the blast or shock wave. The explosion starts acoustic waves in the air which travel with the acoustic velocity, c, superposed on the velocity u of the mass motion with which material is convected out from the center. Since $c \sim \sqrt{T}$ where T is the absolute temperature and since both u and c are greater farther back in the wave disturbance it follows that the back of the wave overtakes the front and thus builds up a sharp front. This is essentially discontinuous in both pressure and density. . . .

If destructive action may be regarded as measured by the maximum pressure amplitude, it follows that the radius of destructive action produced by an explosion varies as $\sqrt[3]{E}$. Now in a ½ ton bomb, containing ¼ ton of TNT the destructive radius is of the order of 150 feet. Hence in a bomb equivalent to 100000 tons of TNT (or 5 kg of active material totally converted) one would expect a destructive radius of the order of [the cube root of 400000]×150=1.1×10^4 feet or about 2 miles.

This points roughly to the kind of results which may be expected from a device of the kind we hope to make. Since the one factor that determines the damage is the energy release, our aim is simply to get as much energy from the explosion as we can. And since the materials we use are very precious, we are constrained to do this with as high an efficiency as is possible.

13. Efficiency

As remarked in Sec. 3, the material tends to blow apart as the reaction proceeds, and this tends to stop the reaction. In general then the reaction will not go to completion in an actual gadget. The fraction of energy released relative to that which would be released if all active material were transformed is called the efficiency. . . .

14. Effect of Tamper on Efficiency

For a given mass of active material, tamper always increases efficiency. It acts both to reflect neutrons back into the active material and by its inertia to slow the expansion thus giving opportunity for the reaction to proceed farther before it is stopped by the expansion.

However the increase in efficiency given by a good tamper is not as large as one might judge simply from the reduction in the critical mass produced by the tamper. This is due to the fact that the neutrons which are returned by diffusion into and back out of the tamper take a long time to return, particularly since they are slowed down by inelastic impacts in the tamper material.

The time scale, for masses near critical where one has to rely on the slowest neutrons to keep the chain going, now becomes effectively the lifetime of neutrons in the tamper, rather than the lifetime in the bomb. The lifetime of neutrons in a U tamper is ~ 10^{-7} sec, ten times that in the bomb. The efficiency is consequently very small just above the critical mass, so to some extent the reduction in critical mass is of no use to us. . . .

In addition to reflecting neutrons, the tamper also inhibits the tendency of the edge of the bomb to blow off. The edge expands into the tamper material, starting a shock wave which compresses the tamper material sixteenfold. These edge effects as remarked in Sec. 13 always act to reduce the factor K in the formula, $f = K \Delta 3$, but not by as great an amount in the case of tamped bomb as in the case of the untamped bomb.

15. Detonation

Before firing, the active material must be disposed in such a way that the effective neutron number ν' is less than unity. The act of firing consists in producing a rearrangement such that after the rearrangement ν' is greater than unity.

This problem is complicated by the fact that, as we have seen, we need to deal with a total mass of active material considerably greater than the critical in order to get appreciable efficiency.

For any proposed type of rearrangement we may introduce a coordinate χ which changes from 0 to 1 as the rearrangement of parts proceeds from its initial to its final value. . . .

[I]f neutron multiplication happens to start before the pieces reach their final configuration an explosion will occur that is of lower efficiency corresponding to the lower value of ν' at the instant of explosion. To avoid predetonation it is therefore necessary to keep the neutron background as low as possible and to effect the rearrangement as rapidly as possible.

16. Probability of predetonation

Since it will be clearly impossible to reduce the neutron background rigorously to zero, there will always be some chance of predetonation. In this section we try to see how great this chance is in order to see how this affects the firing problem.

The chance of predetonation is dependent on the likelihood of a neutron appearing in the active mass while ν' is still small and on the likelihood that such a neutron will really set off a chain reaction. With just a single neutron released when v' > 0 it is by no means certain that a chain reaction will start, since any particular neutron may escape from the active material without causing a chain reaction. . . .

[It is important to take] great pains to get the least possible neutron background, and of shooting the firing rearrangement with the maximum possible velocity. It seems one should strive for a neutron background of 10000 neutron/sec or less and firing velocities of 3000 ft/sec or more. Both of these are difficulty of attainment.

17. Fizzles

The question now arises: what if by bad luck or because the neutron background is very high, the bomb goes off when v' is very close to zero? It is important to know whether the enemy will have an opportunity to inspect the remains and recover the material. We shall see that this is not a worry; in any event the bomb will generate enough energy to completely destroy itself.

It has been remarked in the last section that for very small v' (v' < 0.1), the explosion takes so long that the pieces do have time to move an appreciable distance before the reaction ends. Thus even if a neutron enters and starts a chain just when v' = 0 there will be time for v' to rise to a positive value, and give an efficiency small, but greater than zero. . . .

The mass of 25 in the bomb is about 40 kg. The mass used up is thus $40 \times 8 \times 10^{-3}$ = .003 kg, and the energy release is $.003 \times 20000$ = 60 tons of TNT equivalent, ample to destroy the bomb.

18. Detonating Source

To avoid predetonation we must make sure that there is only a small probability of a neutron appearing while the pieces of the bomb are being put together. On the other hand, when the pieces reach their best position we want to be very sure that a neutron starts the reaction before the pieces have a chance to separate or break. It may be possible to make the projectile seat and stay in the desired position. Failing in this, or in any event as extra insurance, another possibility is to provide a strong neutron source which becomes active as soon as the pieces come into position. For example one might use a Ra + Be source in which the Ra is on one piece and the Be on the other so neutrons are only produced when the pieces are close to the proper relative position. . . .

[I]t might be necessary to rise several grams of radium since it will probably not be used efficiently in this type of source. Some other substance such as polonium that is not so γ-active as radium will probably prove more satisfactory. Evidently a source of this strength that can be activated within about 10^{-5} sec and is mechanically rugged enough to stand the shocks associated with firing presents a difficult problem.

19. Neutron Background

There are three recognized sources of neutrons which provide the background which gives rise to danger of predetonation: (a) cosmic ray neutrons, (b) spontaneous fission, (c) nuclear reactions which produce neutrons.

(a) Cosmic Rays. The number of cosmic ray neutrons is about 1 per cm^2 per minute which is too few to be of any importance.

(b) Spontaneous fission. The spontaneous fission rate is known only for 28 which is responsible for the fission activity of ordinary U. At present we have only upper limits for 25 and 49 since the activity of these has not been detected. . . .

It is considered probable that the rates for 25 and 49 are much smaller than these upper limits. Even if 25 and 49 were the same as 28, a 40 kg bomb would have a background from this source of 600 neutron/sec. This does not seem difficult to beat.

But if U is used as tamper this will weigh about a ton which gives 15000 neutron/sec. Of course not all of these will get into the active material but one may expect a background of several thousand per second from this source.

Thus with a U tamper one is faced with the problem of high velocity firing. In the range of moderately high efficiencies, say 4Mc of active material, it might for this reason not be worth while to use a U tamper, since as we have seen, an inactive tamper will cost only about 15% more active material. Or one might use a compromise in which the tamper was an inner layer of U, backed up by inactive material; for masses this large the time scale is so short that neutrons do not have time to penetrate more than about 5 cm into the tamper anyway.

(c) Nuclear reactions. The only important reactions are the (α, n) reactions of light elements which might be present as impurities. The (γ, n) reactions have a negligible yield. Let us examine what sort of limit on light element impurities in the active material is set by the need of holding down the neutron background from this source. . . .

It is thus recognized that the preparation and handling of the 49 in such a way as to attain and maintain such high standards of purity is an extremely difficult problem. And it seems very probable that the neutron background will be high and therefore high velocity firing will be desirable. With 25 the situation is much more favorable. The α's come from 24 present in normal U to about 1/10000. If all 24 goes with 25 in the separation from 28 we shall have 1/100 of 24 in the 25. The lifetime of 24 is 100 times that of 49 so the concentration of impurities in 25 may be 10^4 times that in 49 for the same background, which is not at all difficult of attainment. To summarize: 49 will be extremely difficult to work with from the stand-point of neutron background whereas 25 without U tamper will be not very difficult.

20. Shooting

We now consider briefly the problem of the actual mechanics of shooting so that the pieces are brought together with a relative velocity of the order of 10^5 cm/sec or more. This is the part of the job about which we know least at present.

One way is to use a sphere and to shoot into it a cylindrical plug made of some active material and some tamper, as in the sketch. This avoids fancy shapes and gives the most favorable shape for shooting; to the projected piece whose mass would be of the order of 100 lbs.

The highest muzzle velocity available in U.S. Army guns is one whose bore is 4.7 inches and whose barrel is 21 feet long This gives a 50 lb. projectile a muzzle velocity of 3150 ft/sec. The gun weighs 5 tons. It appears that the ratio of projectile mass to gun mass is about constant for different guns so a 100 lb. projectile would require a gun weighing about 10 tons.

The weight of the gun varies very roughly as the cube of the muzzle velocity hence there is a high premium on using lower velocities of fire.

Another possibility is to use two guns, and to fire two projectiles at each other. For the same relative velocity this arrangement requires about 1/8 as much total gun weight. Here the worst difficulty lies in timing the two guns. This can be partly overcome by using an elongated tamper mass and putting all the active material in the projectiles so it does not matter exactly where they meet. We have been told that at present it would be possible to synchronize so the spread in places of impact on various shots would be 2 or 3 feet. One serious restriction imposed by these shooting methods is that the mass of active material that can be gotten together is limited by the fact that each piece separately must be non-explosive. Since the separate pieces are not of the best shape, nor surrounded by the best tamper material, one is not limited to two critical masses for the completed bomb, but might perhaps get as high as four critical masses. However in the two gun scheme, if the final mass is to be ~ 4Mc, each piece separately would probably be explosive as soon as it entered the tamper, and better synchronization would be required. It seems worthwhile to investigate whether present performance might not be improved by a factor ten.

Severe restrictions on the mass of the bomb can be circumvented by using pieces of shape more difficult to shoot. For example a flat plate of actual material tamped on only one side, has a minimum thickness below which it can no longer support a chain reaction, no matter how large its area, because of neutron leakage across the untamped surface. If two such plates were slid together, untamped surfaces in contact, the resulting arrangement could be well over the critical thickness for a plate tamped on both sides, and the mass would depend only on the area of the plates.

Calculations show that the critical mass of a well tamped spheroid, whose major axis is five times its minor axis, is only 35% larger than the critical mass of a sphere. If such a spheroid 10 cm thick and 50 cm in diameter were sliced in half, each piece would be sub-critical though the total mass, 250 Kg, is 12 times the critical mass. The efficiency of such an arrangement would be quite good, since the expansion tends to bring the material more and more nearly into a spherical shape.

Thus there are many ordnance questions we would like to have answered. We would like to know how well guns can be synchronized. We shall need information about the possibilities of firing other than cylindrical shapes at lower velocities. Also we shall need to know the mechanical effects of the blast wave proceeding the projectile in the gun barrel. Also whether the projectile can be made to seat itself properly and whether a piston of inactive material may be used to drive the active material into place, this being desirable because thus the active material might be kept out of the gun barrel which to some extent acts as a tamper.

Various other sheeting arrangements have been suggested as yet not carefully analyzed.

For example it has been suggested that the pieces might be mounted to on a ring. . . . If explosive material were distributed around the ring and fired the pieces would be blown inward to form a sphere.

Another more likely possibility is to have the sphere assembled but with a wedge of neutron-absorbing material built into it, which on firing would be blown out by an explosive charge causing ν' to go from less than unity to more than unity. Here the difficulty lies in the fact that no material is known whose absorption coefficient for fast neutrons is much larger than the emission coefficient of the bomb material. Hence the absorbing plug will need to have a volume comparable to that of the absorber and when removed will leave the active material in an unfavorable configuration, equivalent to a low mean density.

21. Autocatalytic Methods

The term "autocatalytic method" is being used to describe any arrangement in which the motions of material produced by the reaction will act, at least for a time, to increase ν' rather than to decrease it. Evidently if arrangements having this property can be developed they would be very valuable, especially if the tendency toward increasing ν' was possessed to any marked degree.

Suppose we had an arrangement in which for example v' would increase of its own accord from a low value like 0.01 up to a value 10 to 50 times greater. The firing problem would be simplified by the low initial value of v' and the efficiency would be maintained by the tendency to develop a high value of v' as the reaction proceeds. It may be that a method of this kind will be absolutely essential for utilization of 49 owing to the difficulties of high neutron background from (α, n) reactions with the impurities as already discussed.

The simplest scheme which might be autocatalytic is … where the active material is disposed in a hollow shell. Suppose that when the firing plug is in place one has just the critical mass for this configuration. If as the reaction proceeds the expansion were to proceed only inward it is easy to see from diffusion theory that v' would increase. Of course in actual fact it will proceed outward (tending to decrease v') as well as inward and the outward expansion would in reality give the dominant effect. However, even if the outward expansion were very small compared to the inward expansion it has been calculated that this method gives very low efficiency: with 12 Mc an efficiency of only about 10^{-9} was calculated.

A better arrangement is the "boron bubble" scheme. B^{10} has the largest known absorption cross-section for fast neutrons, $1152 \cdot 10^{-24}$ cm^2. Suppose we take a large mass of active material and put in enough boron to make the mass just critical. The device is then fired by adding some more active material or tamper. As the reaction proceeds the boron is compressed and is less effective at absorbing neutrons than when not compressed. This can be seen most readily if one considers the case in which the bubbles are large compared to the mean depth in which a neutron goes in boron before being absorbed. Then their effectiveness in removing neutrons will be proportional to their total area and so will drop on compression. Hence v' will increase as the bubbles are compressed. If the bomb is sufficiently large this tendency is bound to overweigh the opposing one due to the general expansion of the bomb material, since the edge of the bomb must move to produce a given decrease in v' increases with the radius of the bomb, whereas for a larger bomb the distance the edge of a bubble must move is unchanged, since it is not necessary to increase the radius of the bubbles but only to use more of them.

The density of particles (electrons plus nuclei) in boron is 8.3×10^{23} particle/cm3 while in uranium it is more than 5 times greater. Therefore as soon as the reaction has proceeded to the point where there is a high degree of ionization and the material behaves as a gas there will be a great action to compress the boron. An opposing tendency to the one desired will be the stirring or turbulence acting to mix the boron uniformly with the uniform, but the time scale is too short for this to be effective.

It can be shown that if initially v' = 0, allowing for the boron absorption, and if no expansion of the outer edge occurs then v' will rise to v' ~ 1/C (v−1) by compression of the boron. This scheme requires at least five times the critical mass for no boron, and the efficiency is low unless considerably more is used.

If one uses just that amount of boron which makes twice the no-boron critical mass be just critical, then the efficiency is lower by a factor at least 30.

All autocatalytic schemes that have been thought of so far require large amounts of active material, are low in efficiency unless very large amounts are used, and are dangerous to handle. Some bright ideas are needed.

22. Conclusion

From the preceding outline we see that the immediate experimental program is largely concerned with measuring the neutron properties of various materials, and with the ordnance problem. It is also necessary to start now studies on techniques for direct experimental determination of critical size and time scale, working with large but sub-critical amounts of active material.

12. J. Robert Oppenheimer Memorandum to Leslie Groves on Los Alamos, April 30, 1943

The problem of secrecy for a project so large and in so many locations deviled the Manhattan Project's leaders throughout the period from its establishment until the dropping of the first bomb on Hiroshima, Japan, on August 5, 1945—and after (with reason: Klaus Fuchs, who worked at the labs at Los Alamos, New Mexico, would later be convicted of spying for the Soviet Union even during the war). Part of necessary considerations was keeping populations adjacent to project sites incurious so that as little attention as possible was drawn to them. The measures for secrecy such as those described in this letter would never work today, but Americans in 1943 were much more trusting of their national government. One of the unintended consequences of the necessary abuse of that trust by the project, in fact, may be our contemporary suspicion of so many government statements and willingness to seriously consider the conspiracy theories that swirl about us.

From: J R Oppenheimer
To: Leslie R Groves, Brigadier General
Date: April 30, 1943

Los Alamos
April 30, 1943

In accordance with our discussion of last week, I have given some thought to the question of a story about the Los Alamos Project which, if disseminated in the proper way, might serve somewhat to reduce the curiosity of the local population, and at least to delay the dissemination of the truth.

We propose that it be let known that the Los Alamos Project is working on a new type of rocket and that the detail be added that this is a largely electrical device. We feel that the story will have a certain credibility; that the loud noises which we will soon be making here will fit in with the subject; and that the fact, unfortunately not kept completely secret, that we are installing a good deal of electrical equipment, and the further fact that we have a large group of civilian specialists would fit in quite well. We further believe that the remoteness of the site for such a development and the secrecy which has surrounded the project would both be appropriate, and that the circumstance that a good deal of work is in fact being done on rockets, together with the appeal of the word, makes this story one which is both exciting and credible.

This question has been discussed with the governing board of the laboratory who approve it and who further recommend that the technical staff of the laboratory be specially warned neither to contradict nor to support a story of this kind if they should run into it.

J. R. Oppenheimer

Source: Leslie R. Groves, Memorandum, April 30, 1943. J. Robert Oppenheimer papers, 1799–1980, Manuscript Division, Library of Congress.

13. Harry Truman Telephone Conversation with Henry Stimson, June 17, 1943

In 1943, Harry Truman was still a senator from Missouri with no expressed ambition to the vice presidency, an office he would assume after the 1944 election. He would know nothing about the Manhattan Project, as this conversation with Secretary of War Henry Stimson shows, before becoming president on April 12, 1945. Stimson would soon fully brief him, and Truman would find himself faced with one of the most monumental decisions ever: whether or not to use the most powerful bomb human beings had ever imagined, a bomb he had not even dreamed existed even while vice president. This conversation also provides a remarkable contrast to the lack of trust today between the branches of government.

Sec: The other matter is a very different matter. It's connected with—I think I've had a letter from Mr. Hally, I think, who is an assistant of Mr. Fulton of your office.
Truman: That's right.
Sec: In connection with the plant at Pasco, Washington.
Truman: That's right.
Sec: Now that's a matter which I know all about personally, and I am one of the group of two or three men in the whole world who know about it.
Truman: I see.
Sec: It's part of a very important secret development.
Truman: Well, all right then—
Sec: And I—
Truman: I herewith see the situation, Mr. Secretary, and you won't have to say another word to me. Whenever you say that to me, that's all I want to hear.
Sec: All right.
Truman: Here is what caused that letter. There is a plant in Minneapolis that was constructed for a similar purpose and it had not been used, and we had been informed that they were taking the machinery out of that plant and using it at this other one for the same purpose, and we just couldn't understand that and that's the reason for the letter.
Sec: No, no, something—
Truman: You assure that this is for a specific purpose and you think it's all right; that's all I need to know.
Sec: Not only for a specific purpose, but a unique purpose.
Truman: All right, then.
Sec: Thank you very much.
Truman: You don't need to tell me anything else.
Sec: Well, I'm very much obliged.
Truman: Thank you very much.
Sec: Goodby.
Truman: Goodby.

Source: Henry Lewis Stimson Papers, microfilm roll 127, Yale University Library.

14. Leslie Groves Letter to J. Robert Oppenheimer on Personal Safety, July 29, 1943

Sometimes concern for secrecy and safety can seem to become obsessive. As overall head of the Manhattan Project, J. Robert Oppenheimer, at least in the view of General Leslie Groves, had to be protected at all cost, so important had he become to the progress of the project. As a scientist, Oppenheimer had probably grown used to coming and going as he pleased and without notice. Now, as the key person in the most secret project the United States had ever engaged in, he was obliged to limit his movements and submit to armed escort.

July 29, 1943.
Dr. J. R.Oppenheimer
P. O. BOX 1663
Santa Fe. New Mexico

Dear Dr. Oppenheimer:
In view of the nature of the work on which you are engaged, the knowledge of it which is possessed by you and the dependence which rests upon you for its successful accomplishment, it seems necessary to ask you to take certain special precautions with respect to your personal safety.

It is requested that:

(a) You refrain from flying in airplanes of any description; the time saved is not worth the risk. (If emergency demands their use my prior consent should be requested.)
(b) You refrain from driving an automobile for any appreciable distance (above a few miles) and from being without suitable protection on any lonely road, such as the road from Los Alamos to Santa Fe. On such trips you should be accompanied by a competent, able bodied, armed guard. There is no objection to the guard serving as chauffeur.
(c) Your cars be driven with due regard to safety and that in driving about town a guard of some kind should be used, particularly during hours of darkness. The cost of such guard is a proper charge against the United States.

I realize that these precautions may be personally burdensome and that they may appear to you to be unduly restrictive but I am asking you to bear with them until our work is successfully completed.

Sincerely,
L. R. Groves
Brigadier General, C. E.

Source: Robert Oppenheimer (from Leslie R. Groves), July 29, 1943. J. Robert Oppenheimer papers, 1799–1980, Manuscript Division, Library of Congress.

15. Quebec Agreement, August 19, 1943

Recognizing that Great Britain and Canada lacked the financial resources to continue Tube Alloys to its conclusion (construction of a deliverable atomic bomb), an agreement on coordinated nuclear projects was negotiated between the United States and Great Britain (with Canadian concurrence) over the summer of 1943. The agreement brought Tube Alloys under the Manhattan Project umbrella while establishing joint English-American oversight of the whole through a Combined Policy Committee that included Canadian participation. The First Quebec Conference, where the agreement was signed, covered a great deal more than the two nuclear projects and had even been envisioned to include Soviet Union leader Joseph Stalin (though not host Canadian Prime Minister Mackenzie King) in addition to U.S. President Franklin Roosevelt and British Prime Minister Winston Churchill.

Quebec Agreement
August 19, 1943
The Citadel, Quebec.

Articles of Agreement Governing Collaboration Between The Authorities of the U.S.A. and the U.K. in the Matter of Tube Alloys

Whereas it is vital to our common safety in the present War to bring the Tube Alloys project to fruition at the earliest moments; and

Whereas this maybe more speedily achieved if all available British and American brains and resources are pooled; and

Whereas owing to war conditions it would be an improvident use of war resources to duplicate plants on a large scale on both sides of the Atlantic and therefore a far greater expense has fallen upon the United States;

It is agreed between us

First, that we will never use this agency against each other.

Secondly, that we will not use it against third parties without each other's consent.

Thirdly, that we will not either of us communicate any information about Tube Alloys to third parties except by mutual consent.

Fourthly, that in view of the heavy burden of production falling upon the United States as the result of a wise division of war effort, the British Government recognize that any post-war advantages of an industrial or commercial character shall be dealt with as between the United States and Great Britain on terms to be specified by the President of the United States to the Prime Minister of Great Britain. The Prime Minister expressly disclaims any interest in these industrial and commercial aspects beyond what may be considered by the President of the United States to be fair and just and in harmony with the economic welfare of the world.

And Fifthly, that the following arrangements shall be made to ensure full and effective collaboration between the two countries in bringing the project to fruition:

(a) There shall be set up in Washington a Combined Policy Committee composed of:
The Secretary of War. (United States)
Dr. Vannevar Bush. (United States)
Dr. James B. Conant. (United States)
Field-Marshal Sir John Dill, G.C.B., C.M.G., D.S.O. (United Kingdom)
Colonel the Right Hon. J. J. Llewellin, C.B.E., M.C., M.P. (United Kingdom)
The Honourable C. D. Howe. (Canada)

The functions of this Committee, subject to the control of the respective Governments, will be:
(1) To agree from time to time upon the programme of work to be carried out in the two countries.
(2) To keep all sections of the project under constant review.
(3) To allocate materials, apparatus and plant, in limited supply, in accordance with the requirements of the programme agreed by the Committee.
(4) To settle any questions which may arise on the interpretation or application of this Agreement.

(b) There shall be complete interchange of information and ideas on all sections of the project between members of the Policy Committee and their immediate technical advisers.

(c) In the field of scientific research and development there shall be full and effective interchange of information and ideas between those in the two countries engaged in the same sections of the field.

(d) In the field of design, construction and operation of large-scale plants, interchange of information and ideas shall be regulated by such ad hoc arrangements as may, in each section of the field, appear to be necessary or desirable if the project is to be brought to fruition at the earliest moment. Such ad hoc arrangements shall be subject to the approval of the Policy Committee.

Aug. 19th 1943

Approved
Franklin D. Roosevelt
Winston S. Churchill

Source: Treaties and Other International Acts Series No. 2993, U.S. Treaties and Other International Agreements, vol. 5, pt. 1, p. 1114.

16. J. Robert Oppenheimer Letter to Leslie Groves on Aliases, November 2, 1943

Questions of security plagued Oppenheimer as much as they did his superiors back in Washington, D.C. After the Quebec Agreement, famous scientists from Great Britain would be joining the staff at Los Alamos, New Mexico. This led to new concerns on top of existing ones relating to the well-known physicists and chemists already there. The expansion of known names would make it just all that more likely that someone might begin to put the pieces together and begin to speculate as to what these scientists were up to. As a result, Niels Bohr would be referred to as "Nicholas Baker."

Letter on Aliases
From: J R Oppenheimer
To: Leslie R Groves, Brigadier General
Date: November 2, 1943

Los Alamos
November 2, 1943

Dear General Groves:

After you gave me the list during your last visit of the men whom we may expect from the United Kingdom, it occurred to me that it might be wise before they arrive here to give them new names. This refers especially to Niels Bohr. I am thinking of the fact that mail will be addressed to them, that they may on occasion originate or receive long-distance calls, that they will be making some local purchases, and that for all these routine matters it would be preferable if such well known names were not put in circulation.

It has, in fact, troubled us some that we are forced to place calls for Dr. Conant, Fermi, Lawrence, etc. This does not happen very often, but in view of the fact that we try not to use these names over the telephone, the placing of the calls themselves seems to us rather unwise. I doubt whether at this late date it would be practicable to assign new names to those who have been associated with the project in the past. In the case of Bohr and Chadwick I think it would be advisable to do so before they get here.

Sincerely yours,
J. R. Oppenheimer

Source: Leslie R. Groves, November 2, 1943. J. Robert Oppenheimer papers, 1799–1980, Manuscript Division, Library of Congress.

17. J. Robert Oppenheimer Memorandum on the Test of an Implosion Gadget, February 16, 1944

"Gadget" was what the bomb that would be exploded as the Trinity Test on July 16, 1945, was often called, an easy code that would keep the uninitiated wondering but that also implies something small and insignificant. In fact, though, this would be the defining device of the entire Manhattan Project; if it worked, if the explosion proved as powerful as expected, an entirely new era of warfare might be introduced—and, in fact, would be. In this memo, J. Robert Oppenheimer rejects a series of suggestions for limited tests though does say that the test bomb could be somewhat smaller than the final version. He recognized that a viable test could only be of the full product, sparking the process that would lead to the Trinity Test at Alamogordo a year and a half later.

February 16, 1944

1. The implosion gadget must be tested in a range where the energy release is comparable with that contemplated for final use. . . . This test is required because of the incompleteness of our knowledge. Thus the reaction will proceed at a temperature unobtainable in the laboratory, which corresponds to energies at which nuclear properties are, and will probably remain, rather imperfectly known. Further, pressures under which the gadget will operate are likewise unobtainable in the laboratory and the information which we may obtain on the spaciotemporal distribution of the pressures will in all probability be not only imperfectly known to us, but somewhat erratic from case to case.

Various attempts have been made to propose an experimental situation which would enable a test of the kind mentioned above to be carried out under conditions so controlled that the energy release was small. . . . All present proposals seem to me unsatisfactory, at least in the sense that they cannot replace more realistic tests. The proposals which have been made are the following:

a. That the amount of active material used be so limited that the nuclear reaction proceeds over a matter of some 30 ± 15 [neutron] generations to give a readily detectable radio-activity or neutron burst, but no appreciable energy liberation.
b. That the reaction be limited by the thermal stability and increased time scale of excess hydrogenation.
c. That the reaction be limited with normal or excess hydrogenation by the addition of appropriate resonance absorbers which will quench the reaction at temperatures of the order of tens of volts.

As for the first of these proposals, . . . we do not now have, and probably will never have, information precise enough to predict an appropriate mass with any degree of probability. . . . This would involve, among other things, knowing the radius of the compressed core to within 5 per cent. Furthermore, it is doubtful whether one could approach this limited explosion by gradual stages with any certainty and without very numerous subcritical trials since there is no a priori assurance, and some a prior doubt, that the implosions will be reproducible to the extent required.

As for the second and third proposals, which have been advocated with eloquence by Dr. Teller, it appears at the present time extremely doubtful whether a sufficiently complete knowledge of the hydrodynamics and nuclear physics involved will be available to make these tests either completely safe or essentially significant. We should like to leave open at the present time the possibility that either these experiments or others not yet proposed may, some months from now, be capable of essentially unambiguous interpretation. . . .

4 . . . . It is my decision that we should plan . . . an implosion . . . so designed that the energy release be comparable with that of the final gadget, but possibly smaller by as much as a factor of 10; . . . that no definite decision against more controlled experiments be made at the present time . . . ; and that in the light of the above considerations, all methods which hold promise of giving reliable information about the hydrodynamics and nuclear physics of the implosion be pursued with greatest urgency. . . . It would appear to be very much less difficult to predict and interpret the dimensions and construction of a gadget releasing some thousands of tons of TNT equivalent in nuclear energy than to make the corresponding predictions for nuclear explosions whose energy release, though finite, is negligible.

J.R.O

Source: Los Alamos National Library Archives, A-84-019, 22-7.

18. Niels Bohr's Memorandum to President Roosevelt, July 1944

Danish physicist Niels Bohr had arrived in the United States in December of 1943, visiting the Los Alamos Laboratory soon thereafter. He had left Denmark on warning that he risked arrest by the occupying Nazis because of Jewish heritage through his mother, heading first to Sweden then England before going to Washington, D.C. He understood quite well both the civilian and military possibilities of nuclear power, as his opening to this memorandum indicates. He also had a strong belief in the community of scholars and their commitment to the common good of humanity and hoped that the world's statesmen could develop a framework that could protect atomic power from nefarious use, channeling it toward the good.

It certainly surpasses the imagination of anyone to survey the consequences of the project in years to come, where, in the long run, the enormous energy sources which will be available may be expected to revolutionize industry and transport. The fact of immediate preponderance is, however, that a weapon of an unparalleled power is being created which will completely change all future conditions of warfare.

Quite apart from the question of how soon the weapon will be ready for use and what role it may play in the present war, this situation raises a number of problems which call for the most urgent attention. Unless, indeed, some agreement about the control of the use of the new active materials can be obtained in due time, any temporary advantage, however great, may be outweighed by a perpetual menace to human security.

Ever since the possibilities of releasing atomic energy on a vast scale came in sight, much thought has naturally been given to the question of control, but the further the exploration of the scientific problems concerned is proceeding, the clearer it becomes that no kind of customary measures will suffice for this purpose, and that the terrifying prospect of a future competition between nations about a weapon of such formidable character can only be avoided through a universal agreement in true confidence.

In this connection it is particularly significant that the enterprise, immense as it is, has still proved far smaller than might have been anticipated, and that the progress of the work has continually revealed new possibilities for facilitating the production of the active materials and of intensifying their efforts.

The prevention of a competition prepared in secrecy will therefore demand such concessions regarding exchange of information and openness about industrial efforts, including military preparations, as would hardly be conceivable unless all partners were assured of a compensating guarantee of common security against dangers of unprecedented acuteness.

The establishment of effective control measures will of course involve intricate technical and administrative problems, but the main point of the argument is that the accomplishment of the project would not only seem to necessitate but should also, due to the urgency of mutual confidence, facilitate a new approach to the problems of international relationship.

The present moment where almost all nations are entangled in a deadly struggle for freedom and humanity might, at first sight, seem most unsuited for any committing arrangement concerning the project. Not only have the aggressive powers still great military strength, although their original plans of world domination have been frustrated and it seems certain that they must ultimately surrender, but even when this happens, the nations united against aggression may face grave causes of disagreement due to conflicting attitudes toward social and economic problems.

A closer consideration, however, would indicate that the potentialities of the project as a means of inspiring confidence under these very circumstances acquire real importance. Moreover, the present situation affords unique possibilities which might be forfeited by a postponement awaiting the further development of the war situation and the final completion of the new weapon.

In view of these eventualities the present situation appears to offer a most favorable opportunity for an early initiative from the side which by good fortune has achieved a lead in the efforts of mastering mighty forces of nature hitherto beyond human reach.

Without impeding the immediate military objectives, an initiative, aiming at forestalling a fateful competition, should serve to uproot any cause of distrust between the powers on whose harmonious collaboration the fate of coming generations will depend.

Indeed, it would appear that only when the question is raised among the united nations as to what concessions the various powers are prepared to make as their contribution to an adequate control arrangement, will it be possible for any one of the partners to assure himself of the sincerity of the intentions of the others.

Of course, the responsible statesmen alone can have insight as to the actual political possibilities. It would, however, seem most fortunate that the expectations for a future harmonious international co-operation, which have found unanimous expressions from all sides within the united nations, so remarkably correspond to the unique opportunities which, unknown to the public, have been created by the advancement of science.

Many reasons, indeed, would seem to justify the conviction that an approach with the object of establishing common security from ominous menaces, without excluding any nation from participating in the promising industrial development which the accomplishment of the project entails, will be welcomed, and be met with loyal cooperation in the enforcement of the necessary far-reaching control measures.

It is in such respects that helpful support may perhaps be afforded by the world-wide scientific collaboration which for years has embodied such bright promises for common human striving. Personal connections between scientists of different nations might even offer means of establishing preliminary and unofficial contact.

It need hardly be added that any such remark or suggestion implies no underrating of the difficulty and delicacy of the steps to be taken by the statesmen in order to obtain an arrangement satisfactory to all concerned, but aims only at pointing to some aspects of the situation which might facilitate endeavors to turn the project to the lasting benefit of the common cause.

Source: Bohr, Niels. 1950. "For an Open World." *Bulletin of the Atomic Scientists* 6, no. 7 (July): 214. Used by permission of Taylor & Francis.

19. Franklin Roosevelt and Winston Churchill, "Aide Memoire," September 18, 1944

At the Second Quebec Conference between U.S. President Franklin Roosevelt and British Prime Minister Winston Churchill, an agreement was made to use the atomic bomb, which was now becoming a real possibility, against Japan—but that knowledge of the bomb should be held closely by the two countries. In addition, knowing the internationalist tendencies of Niels Bohr, Roosevelt and Churchill agreed that he needed to be monitored as a possible agent for the Soviet Union, which, though still a wartime ally, was already seen as a postwar rival to both countries.

Top Secret   [Hyde Park, September 19, 1944]
              Tube Alloys

Aide-Mémoire of Conversation Between the President and the Prime Minister at Hyde Park, September 18, 1944

1. The suggestion that the world should be informed regarding Tube Alloys, with a view to an international agreement regarding its control and use, is not accepted. The matter should continue to be regarded as of the utmost secrecy; but when a "bomb" is finally available, it might perhaps, after mature consideration, be used against the Japanese, who should be warned that this bombardment will be repeated until they surrender.
2. Full collaboration between the United States and the British Government in developing Tube Alloys for military and commercial purposes should continue after the defeat of Japan unless and until terminated by joint agreement.
3. Enquiries should be made regarding the activities of Professor Bohr and steps taken to ensure that he is responsible for no leakage of information, particularly to the Russians.

F[ranklin] D R[oosevelt]
W[inston] S C[hurchill]

Source: "Aide-Memoire Initialed by President Roosevelt and Prime Minister Churchill." 1972. Document 299. *Foreign Relations of the United States, Conference at Quebec, 1944.* Washington, D.C.: Government Printing Office.

20. Vannevar Bush and James Conant Memoranda to Henry Stimson, September 30, 1944

There was quite a bit of concerned idealism about the future atomic age among the scientists involved in the Manhattan Project, tempered with a great deal of realism and concern for what could devolve into an arms race. They knew their success could be consigning tens of thousands, even hundreds of thousands, to death. Perhaps if only to make that palatable, they also imagined a future where atomic power could be a savior of humankind. The two memoranda follow a similar structure but were intended for slightly different audiences (the reason for the cover letter, also included here) to be forwarded at the discretion of the secretary of war, who, however, set them aside.

OFFICE OF SCIENTIFIC RESEARCH
AND DEVELOPMENT
1530 P Street, N.W.
Washington, D.C.
September 30, 1944.

The Secretary of War,
Washington, D.C.

Dear Mr. Secretary:

In response to your suggestion we outline in the two attached memoranda our thoughts on the international post-war aspects of the special projects. We believe that the following points are correct, and of great importance to the future peace of the world.

1. By next summer this will become a matter of great military importance.
2. The art will expand rapidly after the war, and the military aspects may become overwhelming.
3. This country has a temporary advantage which may disappear, or even reverse, if there is a secret arms race on this subject.
4. Basic knowledge of the matter is widespread and it would be foolhardy to attempt to maintain our security by preserving secrecy.
5. Controlling supplies of materials cannot be depended upon to control use, especially in forms which the subject may take in the future.
6. There is hope that an arms race on this basis can be prevented, and even that the future peace of the world may be furthered, by complete international scientific and technical interchange on this subject, backed up by an international commission acting under an association of nations and having the authority to inspect.

Very sincerely yours,
V. BUSH
J. B. CONANT

September 30, 1944.
MEMORANDUM
To: The Secretary of War
From: V. Bush and J. B. Conant
Subject Salient Points Concerning Future International Handling of Subject of Atomic Bombs.

1. Present Military Potentialities. There is every reason to believe that before August 1, 1945, atomic bombs will have been demonstrated and that the type then in production would be the equivalent of 1,000 to 10,000 tons of high explosive in so far as general blast damage is concerned. This means that one B-29 bomber could accomplish with such a bomb the same damage against weak industrial and civilian targets as 100 to 1,000 B-29 bombers.

2. Future Military Potentialities. We are dealing with an expanding art and it is difficult to predict the future. At present we are planning atomic bombs utilizing the energy involved in the fission of the uranium atom.

It is believed that such energy can be used as a detonator for setting off the energy which would be involved in the transformation of heavy hydrogen atoms into helium. If this can be done a factor of a thousand or more would be introduced into the amount of energy released. This means that one such super-super bomb would be equivalent in blast damage to 1,000 raids of 1,000 B-29 Fortresses delivering their load of high explosive on one target. One must consider the possibility of delivering either the bombs at present contemplated or the super-super bomb on an enemy target by means of a robot plane or guided missile. When one considers these possibilities we see that very great devastation could be caused immediately after the outbreak of hostilities to civilian and industrial centers by an enemy prepared with relatively few such bombs. That such a situation presents a new challenge to the world is evident.

3. Present Advantage of United States and Great Britain Temporary. Unless it develops that Germany is much further along than is now believed it is probable that the present developments in the United States undertaken in cooperation with Great Britain put us in a temporary position of great ascendency. It would be possible, however, for any nation with good technical and scientific resources to reach our present position in three or four years. Therefore it would be the height of folly for the United States and Great Britain to assume that they will always continue to be superior in this new weapon. Once the distance between ourselves and those who have not yet developed this art is eliminated the accidents of research could give another country a temporary advantage as great as the one we now enjoy.

4. Impossibility of maintaining complete secrecy after the war is over. In order to accomplish our present gigantic technical and scientific task it has been necessary to bring a vast number of technical men into the project. Information in regard to various aspects of it is therefore widespread. Furthermore, all the basic facts were known to physicists before the development began. Some outside the project have undoubtedly guessed a great deal of what is going on. Considerable information is already in the hands of various newspaper men who are refraining from writing our stories only because of voluntary censorship. In view of this situation it is our strong recommendation that plans be laid for complete disclosure of the history of the development and all but the manufacturing and military details of the bombs as soon as the first bomb has been demonstrated. This demonstration might be for enemy territory, or in our own country, with subsequent notice to Japan that the materials would be used against the Japanese mainland unless surrender was forthcoming.

5. Dangers of partial secrecy and international armament race. It is our contention that it would be extremely dangerous for the United States and Great Britain to attempt to carry on in complete secrecy further developments of the military applications of this art. If this were done Russia would undoubtedly proceed in secret along the same lines and so too might certain other countries, including our defeated enemies. We do not believe that over a period of a decade the control of the supply could be counted on to prevent such secret developments in other countries. This is particularly true if the super-super bomb were developed for the supply of heavy hydrogen is essentially unlimited and the rarer materials such as uranium and thorium would be used only as detonators. If a country other than Great Britain and the United States developed the

super-super bomb first we should be in a terrifying situation if hostilities should occur. The effect on public reaction of the uncertainties in regard to an unknown threat of this new nature would be very great.

6. Proposed international exchange of information. In order to meet the unique situation created by the development of this new art we would propose that free interchange of all scientific information on this subject be established under the auspices of an international office deriving its power from whatever association of nations is developed at the close of the present war. We would propose further that as soon as practical the technical staff of this office be given free access in all countries not only to the scientific laboratories where such work is contained, but to the military establishments as well. We recognize that there will be great resistance to this measure, but believe the hazards to the future of the world are sufficiently great to warrant this attempt. If accurate information were available as to the development of these atomic bombs in each country, public opinion would have true information about the status of the armament situation. Under these conditions there is reason to hope that the weapons would never be employed and indeed that the existence of these weapons might decrease the chance of another major war.

J. B. CONANT
V. BUSH

September 30, 1944.
MEMORANDUM

To: The Secretary of War
From: V. Bush and J. B. Conant
Subject: Supplementary memorandum giving further details concerning military potentialities of atomic bombs and the need for international exchange of information.

1. <u>Present military potentialities</u>. The present schedule of production should yield sufficient materials during the spring and summer of 1945 to provide either several bombs each having the equivalent effect of 10,000 tons of high explosives, or a correspondingly large number of bombs each having the equivalent of 1,000 tons of high explosive. When it is recalled that each B-29 bomber was designed to carry about 8 tons of high explosive, it is clear that the military effect of these atomic bombs is to reduce enormously the number of bombers required to produce damage to the type of target found in civilian and industrial centers. For example, one 10,000 ton HE equivalent bomb would produce the same order of effect as 1,000 B-29 bombers carrying full load. If, as seems probably at the outset, the smaller atomic bombs would be developed, then one B-29 bomber carrying such a bomb (1,000 ton equivalent HE) would produce the same damage as 100 B-29 bombers fully equipped. Which of these two types of bombs comes into use first depends upon certain technical developments now in progress. It is probably that the most efficient use of the material from the point of view of causing the maximum damage for every pound expended would through the smaller bombs accurately placed on an industrial target, which, to repeat, would be the equivalent of 100 B-29 normal loads.

It should be pointed out that these bombs, like all high explosive bombs, give a maximum of damage when used against weak targets, that is industrial installations and large collections of buildings. The protection against them would be underground installations and heavy concrete structures. Just as in the case of ordinary high explosive bombs such structures would be relatively safe even against super bombs unless a direct hit were made, although in the case of an atomic bomb the definition of a direct hit would probably include bombs which landed within a few hundred yards.

Although these memoranda are directed to the international situation, we would like to point out again at this time that the manufacture of these atomic bombs and any further experimentation in the whole field of atomic power presents very great hazards to the health of a country unless the experiments are carefully controlled. It is now relatively easy to construct a device which develops atomic energy in the form of heat using relatively small quantities of separated uranium. Such atomic energy machines, which can produce heat but not explosive energy, are known as "water boilers". These small water boilers also produce intense neutron radiation which is fatal to anyone coming within 100 feet or so unless adequate shielding is provided. Furthermore, in the operation of these water boilers radioactive poisons are produced. Clearly such establishments should be allowed only under careful regulation by the government, yet such installations will be of prime importance to the further development of the sciences of physics, chemistry, and biology. It would be unthinkable to prohibit developments of this sort in private laboratories, yet clearly all such experimentation must be carefully supervised and controlled.

A great many industrial companies will want to work in this whole field because there are many applications of the byproducts of this new science. Quite apart from the major development of atomic energy as a source of industrial power industrial concerns will wish to experiment with water boilers and their products, radioactive poisons. Clearly all such developments should be licensed and all patent right should come to the government. No one can tell what may be the new developments in this field of science, or what will come out of the experiments performed in many different places with these new materials and these new techniques. Results of all such experiments should be made available to the United States Government and, as proposed later, through an international arrangement to the world. As suggested in our earlier memorandum to you, the legislation to control this whole field of experimentation and development, as well as to provide for a national agency for furtherance of the art, might derive its power from an international treaty.

2. <u>Future military potentialities</u>. Two materials are at present in production for use in atomic bombs. One is an isotope of uranium commonly called "25", the other a product of a fission reaction of uranium, a new element known as "49". Both these substances produce energy under certain conditions by the fission of the nuclei into fragments.

Some of our theoretical physicists believe that it is extremely probable that the energy generated by the fission of the nuclei of "25" and "49" could under certain circumstances produce such a high temperature as to initiate a reaction which has never taken place on this earth, but is closely analogous to the sources of energy of the sun. This reaction involves the transformation of heavy hydrogen into helium. Enormous amounts of energy are released in this reaction. A super bomb using heavy hydrogen (in the form of heavy water) and detonated by an atomic bomb using "25" or "49" would be of a different order of magnitude in its destructive power from an atomic bomb itself. We may therefore designate it as a super-super bomb. While such a possibility lies in the future, it could even happen that a bomb of this type would prove feasible within six months or a year after the first atomic bomb is constructed.

When one considers that such a super-super bomb might be delivered on an enemy target by the principle of a robot bomb or guided missile, or even without this possibility from a bomber coming at night or in overcast guided by modern radar devices, we see how vulnerable would be centers of population in a future war. Unless one proposed to put all one's cities and industrial factories under ground, or one believes that the antiaircraft defenses could guarantee literally that no enemy plane or flying bomb could be over a vulnerable area, every center of the population in the world in the future is at the mercy of the enemy that strikes first.

In painting this lurid picture of the future it is hardly necessary to add, however, that it seems extremely unlikely that any nation would thus destroy large industrial centers or civilian centers unless it was prepared to follow up with air, naval, or land forces. Therefore it seems unnecessary to be disturbed about the possibilities of small countries, particularly countries with little industrial potential, disturbing the peace of the world by secret development of such weapons. The possibility of any major power or former major power undertaking this development, however, seems great indeed.

3 <u>Present advantage of United States and Great Britain temporary</u>. The probabilities are great that Germany is not far advanced along the road of development of atomic bombs. It is also extremely unlikely that Russia has as yet had opportunity to carry this subject far. On the other hand, once the war is over Russia, at least, and possibly Germany and other countries, could quite easily make up the advantage which we now possess in technical knowledge and scientific information. Much that we have found out in the way of basic facts were just over the horizon when the war came on and secrecy prevailed. Quite apart from any leakage of information which would be bound to occur if we foolishly attempted to maintain a secrecy order on our present scientific information, foreign scientists would soon come to the same scientific point of view as we now hold. Our present advantage lies entirely in the construction of plants for the manufacture of materials. Even this could be much more quickly overcome and at much less cost that at first sight would seem to be the case. It is an old story in the advance of technology that after the first person has shown how something can be done there are soon developed cheaper and easier ways of accomplishing the same end. Lest we be deluded on this point by the large sums of money expended by the United States, we must recall that in order to save time and to arrive with assurance at our goal, we proceeded to ride three horses at the same time. We now know that probably any one of four or five methods could produce materials from which an atomic bomb could be constructed. The erection of a plant to operate any one of these methods would not be nearly as costly an undertaking and certainly could be accomplished in a few years. We also believe now that the fundamental basis for the construction of an atomic bomb from the material presents no great difficulty and the way that anyone could naturally try to accomplish this end will succeed. Our present difficulties in this area and our large expenditures of money and manpower on the ordnance aspects of the problem are only because we wish to produce as rapidly as possible bombs using small amounts of material. This requires difficult experimentation which is not yet complete. The way through on a more orthodox procedure is not clear and would not be difficult for anyone to undertake. In

short, it now seems that it is by no means a prohibitively difficult, expensive, or laborious undertaking to construct a plant to produce atomic bombs. There is the further point that the basic scientific information would be essentially rediscovered, if necessary, by another group of scientists starting in the field when the war is over. The advantage, therefore, that the United States and Great Britain possess in this area is very temporary indeed. We cannot overemphasize this point.

4. <u>Impossibility of maintaining complete secrecy after the war is over</u>. This point is so obvious that it needs very little further expansion of what was said in our summary memorandum. Only strict censorship of the press or a continuation of the present voluntary arrangement would prevent free discussion of this subject. Furthermore, to attempt to impose complete secrecy would be to interfere seriously with scientific advance in many related fields. It seems to us from every point of view of the greatest importance to have this whole subject out in the open as soon as military conditions allow, so that (a) there may be a public understanding of the dangers, (b) we may have open control by a newly-authorized agency set up by Congress, (c) we may regulate whatever experiments may now be going on without our knowledge in private places, and (d) we may use this new field to advance the sciences of physics, chemistry, and biology including medicine.

5. <u>Dangers of partial secrecy and international armament race</u>. As has already been pointed out in this memorandum, certainly the Russian scientists and perhaps the Germans and others may be before long hard in the race of developing this new type of weapon. They could catch up with our present position in the course of three or four years. The danger is that we would never know, if secrecy prevails as between countries, whether indeed this were the case. Hence our own thoughts about using this weapon in a future war might be based on the false premise that our enemies could not retaliate in kind. But more dangerous still are the possibilities of the super atomic bomb referred to in Section 2. The devastating effects of this bomb would be of another order of magnitude from the atomic bomb itself and it would require materials that are readily available. One cannot say with certainty that such a bomb can be constructed, but it seems as probable as was the atomic bomb development when this research was first undertaken by the government. But whether or not this particular line should prove profitable from a military point of view one can be certain that there will be unexpected developments which would increase enormously the effectiveness of atomic energy for destructive purposes.

If we are in a situation in which several powerful countries are proceeding in secret to develop these potentialities we shall be living in a most dangerous world. One need not elaborate on the repercussions of such a situation on public opinion or on any attempts to develop an association of nations to keep the peace. We should like to emphasize, however, how closely all these developments are tied up with advances in physics and chemistry; any attempt to shroud developments in this country with secrecy for military reasons would run into innumerable problems involving various branches of science. By the same token, however, this subject is by its very nature ideal for free international exchange of scientific information. And if there be such free interchange of information anyone will know fairly clearly what is the status of the armament situation in so far as this weapon is concerned.

6. Proposed international exchange of information. For the reasons already outlined we come to the conclusion that the safety of the United States and the prospects of world peace will be furthered by providing for free interchange of scientific information with all countries in the field of atomic energy. We believe this should not be left to the usual haphazard methods of scientific publication, but should be centered in an international office responsible to an association of nations. The signatories of the treaty would guarantee that all their scientists would make their results freely available to the agents of this international office, who in turn would see that they were given worldwide publication as fast as they are obtained. The nations in the association would further agree to allow the agents of the international office to visit freely within their countries and discuss all matters of atomic energy with all the scientists, including the government employees in the country in question. It appears to us that Russia would be the one most reluctant to enter into this combination, but since we hold the advantage, if only temporary, in this art it would seem that the quid pro quo was evident.

While we believe that arrangements for free interchange of scientific information would be a great step forward in removing some of the dangers to civilization inherent in this new development, we believe that arrangements should proceed further, if not at once, as the second step. The same international office should provide not only for the free circulation of its agents among the scientific laboratories of all countries and the free publication of all the scientific aspects of the subject of atomic energy, but should also provide for inspection of all technical installations. This presents still greater difficulties and would presumably be violently opposed in this country as well as Russia since it would mean in the last analysis the opening of all industrial plants to officials of an international organization. We believe, however, that if people in this country and in other countries are convinced of the terrific potentialities of the new weapons which now lie just over the horizon they will be willing to provide for such an arrangement with due safeguards to commercial secrets. Since the inspecting agents would be scientific and technical men with the traditions of the professions, we believe there could be developed before long in such an international corps of experts a tradition of integrity and responsibility that would insure that their inspectorial powers would not be abused. That is to say, they would resist the temptation to divulge secret information not in the field in question which they obtained in the course of their duties to their own government or to some commercial concern.

We recognize that even at the scientific level there is some chance for evasion and that at the technical and industrial level there are very great chances for evasion. Nevertheless, we believe that along the path we outline it would be possible to proceed toward a definite goal, and that even if the achievements were far less than ideal the attempt would be worth while. We have been unable to devise any other plan which holds greater possibilities than these new developments can be utilized to promote peace rather than to insure devastating destruction in another war.

J. B. CONANT
V. BUSH

Source: National Archives, RG 77, Harrison-Bundy Files (H-B Files), Folder 69 (copy from microfilm).

21. J. Robert Oppenheimer Letter to Leslie Groves, October 6, 1944

The William Parsons mentioned in this letter, in addition to his duties at Los Alamos, would be the weaponeer on the Enola Gay on its bombing mission over Hiroshima, Japan. He was the officer responsible for the final arming of the Little Boy bomb. Oppenheimer, of course, was a scientist while Groves was an engineer, a distinction of increasing importance as the Manhattan Project neared its goal of creating a deliverable nuclear weapon, for once the science was understood and laid out, engineers and technicians had to take over or, at least, become involved to a degree that would not have been practical before.

October 6, 1944

Dear General Groves:

I am glad to transmit the enclosed report of Captain Parsons, with the general intent and spirit of which I am in full sympathy. There are a few points on which my evaluation differs somewhat from that expressed in the report and it seems appropriate to mention them at this time.

1. I believe that Captain Parsons somewhat misjudges the temper of the responsible members of the laboratory. It is true that there are a few people here whose interests are exclusively "scientific" in the sense that they will abandon any problem that appears to be soluble. I believe that these men are now in appropriate positions in the organization. For the most part the men actually responsible for the prosecution of the work have proven records of carrying developments through the scientific and into the engineering stage. For the most part these men regard their work here not as a scientific adventure, but as a responsible mission which will have failed if it is let drop at the laboratory phase. I therefore do not expect to have to take heroic measures to insure something which I know to be the common desire of the overwhelming majority of our personnel.

2. I agree completely with all the comments of Captain Parsons' memorandum on the fallacy of regarding a controlled test as the culmination of the work of this laboratory. The laboratory is operating under a directive to produce weapons; this directive has been and will be rigorously adhered to. The only reason why we contemplate making a test, and why I have in the past advocated this, is because with the present time scales and the present radical assembly design this appears to be a necessary step in the production of a weapon. I do not wish to prejudge the issue: it is possible that information available to us within the next months may make such a test unnecessary. I believe, however, that the probability of this is extremely small.

3. The developmental program of the laboratory, whether or not it has been prosecuted with intelligence and responsibility, is still far behind the minimal requirements set by our directive. This fact, which rests on no perfectionist ideals for long-range development, means that there must inevitably be some duplication of effort and personnel if the various phases of our program - scientific, engineering and military - are to be carried out without too great mutual interference. It is for this reason that I should like to stress Captain Parsons' remark that a very great strengthening in engineering is required. The organizational experience which the

last year has given us is no substitute for competent engineers.

Sincerely yours,

J. R. Oppenheimer

Source: Leslie R. Groves, October 6, 1944. J. Robert Oppenheimer papers, 1799–1980, Manuscript Division, Library of Congress.

22. Albert Einstein's Fourth Letter to President Franklin Roosevelt, March 25, 1945

Much had changed in the five and a half years since Albert Einstein's first letter to U.S. President Franklin Roosevelt. Once again, though, Leó Szilárd managed to convince his fellow physicist to write the president, this time explicitly on his behalf. Szilárd, like a number of the scientists working on the Manhattan Project, had become extremely concerned with the handling of decisions regarding the use of atomic bombs by politicians who did not, perhaps, understand the gravity of such use. Szilárd couldn't share with Einstein much of his own thinking, for Einstein had been denied security clearance due to his political beliefs as a pacifist, but felt that Einstein might be able to arrange for him to meet with the president. Roosevelt, however, never saw the letter, dying before it could be delivered.

112 Mercer Street
Princeton, New Jersey
March 25, 1945

The Honorable Franklin D. Roosevelt
The President of the United States
The White House
Washington, D.C.

Sir:

I am writing you to introduce Dr. L. Szilárd who proposes to submit to you certain considerations and recommendations. Unusual circumstances which I shall describe further below induce me to take this action in spite of the fact that I do not know the substance of the considerations and recommendations which Dr. Szilárd proposes to submit to you.

In the summer of 1939 Dr. Szilárd put before me his views concerning the potential importance of uranium for national defense. He was greatly disturbed by the potentialities involved and anxious that the United States Government be advised of them as soon as possible. Dr. Szilárd, who is one of the discovers of the neutron emission of uranium on which all present work on uranium is based, described to me a specific system which he devised and which he thought would make it possible to set up a chain reaction in unseparated uranium in the immediate future. Having known him for over twenty years both for his scientific work and personally, I have much confidence in his judgment and it was on the basis of his judgment as well as my own that I took the liberty to approach you in connection with this subject. You responded to my letter dated August 2, 1939 by the appointment of a committee under the chairmanship of Dr. Briggs and thus started the Government's activity in this field.

The terms of secrecy under which Dr. Szilárd is working at present do not permit him to give me information about his work; however, I understand that he now is greatly concerned about the lack of adequate contact between scientists who are doing this work and those members of your Cabinet who are responsible for formulating policy. In the circumstances I consider it my duty to give Dr. Szilárd this introduction and I wish to express the hope that you will be able to give his presentation of the case your personal attention.

Yours very truly,
A. Einstein

Source: Albert Einstein to Franklin D. Roosevelt, March 25, 1945. Miscellaneous Historical Documents Collection, 345. Harry S. Truman Presidential Library and Museum.

23. Henry Stimson Letter to Harry Truman on the Manhattan Project, April 24, 1945

U.S. Secretary of War Henry Stimson knew that the new U.S. president, Harry Truman, who had been in office less than two weeks after not even three months as vice president, had no knowledge at all of the Manhattan Project that was just a few months away from its major test at Alamogordo, New Mexico. The secrecy of the project had been so tight and so successful that even the vice president knew nothing of it—and Stimson wanted to keep it that way. So, he did not mention anything in his letter asking for a meeting that could remotely be connected to the project.

WAR DEPARTMENT
WASHINGTON

April 24, 1945.

Dear Mr. President:

I think it is very important that I should have a talk with you as soon as possible on a highly secret matter.

I mentioned it to you shortly after you took office but have not urged it since on account of the pressure you have been under. It, however, has such a bearing on our present foreign relations and has such an important effect upon all my thinking in this field that I think you ought to know about it without much further delay.

Faithfully yours,
Henry L. Stimson
Secretary of War.

The President,
The White House.

Source: Henry Stimson to Harry S. Truman, April 24, 1945. Truman Papers, Confidential File. War Department. Harry S. Truman Presidential Library and Museum.

24. Memorandum to Leslie Groves on the Second Meeting of the Target Committee, May 12, 1945

As preparations continued for the Trinity Test at Alamogordo, New Mexico, the decision was being made on targets in Japan should the test be successful and President Truman order an attack. This memorandum, chilling in its dispassionate outlining of the concerns and decisions relating to target choice with absolutely no concern for the lives that would be lost and the destruction created (though, frankly, these could not be considered once the decision to drop the bomb had been made and the committee was operating on the assumption that it might be), is a triumph of bureaucratic language and thinking, completely removed from human aspects of the situation.

12 May 1945

Memorandum For: Major General L. R. Groves

Subject: Summary of Target Committee Meetings on 10 and 11 May 1945

1. The second meeting of the Target Committee convened at 9:00 AM 10 May in Dr. Oppenheimer's office at Site Y with the following present:

General Farrell Dr. C. Lauritsen
Colonel Seeman Dr. Ramsey
Captain Parsons Dr. Dennison
Major Derry Dr. von Neumann
Dr. Stearns Dr. Wilson
Dr. Tolman Dr. Penney
Dr. Oppenheimer

Dr. Bethe and Dr. Brode were brought into the meeting for discussion of Item A of the agenda. During the course of the meeting panels were formed from the committee members and others to meet in the afternoon and develop conclusions to items discussed in the agenda. The concluding meeting was held at 10:00 AM 11 May in Dr. Oppenheimer's office with the following present:

Colonel Seeman Dr. Stearns
Captain Parsons Dr. Von Neumann
Major Derry Dr. Dennison
Dr. Tolman Dr. Penney
Dr. Oppenheimer Dr. Ramsey
Dr. Wilson

2. The agenda for the meetings presented by Dr. Oppenheimer consisted of the following:
A. Height of Detonation
B: Report on Weather and Operations
C: Gadget Jettisoning and Landing
D: Status of Targets
E: Psychological Factors in Target Selection
F: Use Against Military Objectives
G: Radiological Effects
H: Coordinated Air Operations
I: Rehearsals
J: Operating Requirements for Safety of Airplanes
K: Coordination with 21st Program

3. Height of Detonation
A. The criteria for determining height selection were discussed. It was agreed that conservative figures should be used in determining the height since it is not possible to predict accurately the magnitude of the explosion and since the bomb can be detonated as much as 40% below the optimum with a reduction of 25% in area of damage whereas a detonation 14% above the optimum will cause the same loss in area. It was agreed that fuses should be prepared to meet the following possibilities:

(1) For the Little Boy the detonation heights should correspond to a pressure of 5 psi, a height of the Mach-stem of 100 feet and a magnitude of detonation of either 5,000 or 15,000 tons of H.E. equivalent. With present knowledge the fuse setting corresponding to 5,000 tons equivalent would be used but fusing for the other should be available in case more is known at the time of delivery. The height of detonation corresponding to 5,000 and 15,000 tons are 1550 feet and 2400 feet, respectively.

(2) For the Fat Man the detonation heights should correspond to a pressure of 5 psi, a height of the Mach-stem of 100 feet, and a magnitude of explosion of 700, 2,000, or 5,000 tons of H.E. equivalent. With the present information the fuse should be set at 2,000 tons equivalent but fusing for the other values should be available at the time of final delivery. The heights of detonation corresponding to 700, 2,000, and 5,000 tons are 580 feet, 1,000 feet and 1,550 feet, respectively. Trinity data will be used for this gadget.

B. In the case of the Fat Man delay circuits are introduced into the unit for purposes which make the detonation of the bomb 400 feet below the height at which the fuse is set. For this reason as far as the Fat Man is concerned the fuse settings should be 980 feet, 1,400 feet, or 1,950 feet.

C. In view of the above it was agreed by all present that fuses should be available at four

(4) different height settings. These heights are 1,000 feet, 1,400 feet, 2,000 feet and 2,400 feet. With present information the 1,400 feet fuse would be most likely to be used for both the Fat Man and the Little Boy. (Later data presented by Dr. Brode modify the above conclusions on fusing and detonating heights; the differential height for the Little Boy is 210 feet and for the Fat Man 500 feet. For this reason some of the above figures must be revised).

4. Report on Weather and Operations

A. Dr. Dennison reported on the above subject. His report essentially covered the materials in his Top Secret memo of 9 May - Subject: "Preliminary report on Operational Procedures." For this reason his report will not be repeated here but is attached as an appendix. It was agreed by those present that the mission if at all possible should be a visual bombing mission. For this we should be prepared to wait until there is a good weather forecast in one or more of three alternative targets. There is only a 2% chance in this case that we will have to wait over two weeks. When the mission does take place there should be weather spotter aircraft over each of three alternative targets in order that an alternative target may be selected in the last hour of the flight if the weather is unpromising over the highest priority target.

B. In case the aircraft reaches the target and finds, despite these precautions that visual bombing is impossible, it should return to its base provided that it is in good operating condition. Only if the aircraft is in sufficiently bad shape that it is unlikely that it can return to base and make a safe landing or if it is essential that the drop be made that day should the drop be made with radar equipment. For this purpose it may be desirable to have an Eagle radar equipped plane accompany the mission in order that formation bombing with the Eagle plane in the lead can be made to obtain the increased accuracy from Eagle. A final decision as to the desirability of this emergency procedure can only be made after further combat experience is obtained with Eagle aircraft. In any case every effort should be made to have the mission such that blind bombing will be unnecessary.

C. It was agreed that Dr. Stearns and Dr. Dennison should keep themselves continuously informed as to radar developments. If at any time new developments are available which show in combat a marked improvement of accuracy the basic plan may be altered.

D. It was agreed that Shoran was a very promising development for the 21st Bomber Command but that we should make no plans to use Shoran until its success is fully confirmed in normal bombing missions in that area.

E. The plan to use the gadget with visual bombing even though this may require a one day to three weeks delay requires that the gadget be such that for a period of at least three weeks it can be held in readiness in such a state that on twelve hours notice it can be prepared for a combat mission. No difficulty in this regard was foreseen by those present.

5. Gadget Jettisoning and Landing

A. It was agreed that if the aircraft has to return to its base with the gadget and if it is in good condition when it has reached there, it should make a normal landing with the greatest possible care and with such precautions as stand-by fire equipment being held in readiness on the ground. This operation will inevitably involve some risks to the base and to the other aircraft parked on the field. However, the chance of a crash when the aircraft is in good condition and the chances of a crash initiating a high order explosion are both sufficiently small that it was the view of those present that the landing operation with the unit under these circumstances was a justifiable risk. Frequent landings with inert and H.E. filled units have been made in the past. Training in landing with the unit should be given to all crews who carry an active unit.

B. In case the aircraft returns to its base and then finds that it cannot make a normal landing it may be necessary to jettison the bomb. In the case of the Fat Man this can probably best be accomplished by dropping the bomb into shallow water from a low altitude. Tests on this will be carried out with both inert and live units. In the case of the Little Boy the situation is considerably more complicated since water leaking into the Little Boy will set off a nuclear reaction, and since the American held territory in the vicinity of the base is so densely filled that no suitable jettisoning ground for the Little Boy has been found which is sufficiently devoid of moisture, which is sufficiently soft that the projectile is sure not to seat from the impact, and which is sufficiently remote from extremely important American installations whose damage by a nuclear explosion would seriously affect the American war effort. The best emergency procedure that has so far been proposed is considered to be the removal of the gunpowder from the gun and the execution of a crash landing. In this case there is no danger of fire setting off the gun and the accelerations should be sufficiently small to prevent seating of the projectile by the impact. Tests on the feasibility of unloading the gun powder in flight will be conducted.

C. It was agreed that prior to actual delivery some form of instructions should be prepared as a guide to the senior man on the aircraft as to procedures to be followed in cases of different types of disasters.

6. Status of Targets

A. Dr. Stearns described the work he had done on target selection. He has surveyed possible targets possessing the following qualification: (1) they be important targets in a large urban area of more than three miles in diameter, (2) they be capable of being damaged effectively by a blast, and (3) they are unlikely to be attacked by next August. Dr. Stearns had a list of five targets which the Air Force would be willing to reserve for our use unless unforeseen circumstances arise. These targets are:

(1) Kyoto - This target is an urban industrial area with a population of 1,000,000. It is the former capital of Japan and many people and industries are now being moved there as other areas are being destroyed. From the psychological point of view there is the advantage that Kyoto is an intellectual center for Japan and the people there are more apt to appreciate the significance of such a weapon as the gadget. (Classified as an AA Target)

(2) Hiroshima - This is an important army depot and port of embarkation in the middle of an urban industrial area. It is a good radar target and it is such a size that a large part of the city could be extensively damaged. There are adjacent hills which are likely to produce a focusing effect which would considerably increase the blast damage. Due to rivers it is not a good incendiary target. (Classified as an AA Target)

(3) Yokohama - This target is an important urban industrial area which has so far been untouched. Industrial activities include aircraft manufacture, machine tools, docks, electrical equipment and oil refineries. As the damage to Tokyo has increased additional industries have moved to Yokohama. It has the disadvantage of the most important target areas being separated by a large body of water and of being in the heaviest

anti-aircraft concentration in Japan. For us it has the advantage as an alternate target for use in case of bad weather of being rather far removed from the other targets considered. (Classified as an A Target)

(4) Kokura Arsenal - This is one of the largest arsenals in Japan and is surrounded by urban industrial structures. The arsenal is important for light ordnance, anti-aircraft and beach head defense materials. The dimensions of the arsenal are 4100' x 2000'. The dimensions are such that if the bomb were properly placed full advantage could be taken of the higher pressures immediately underneath the bomb for destroying the more solid structures and at the same time considerable blast damage could be done to more feeble structures further away. (Classified as an A Target)

(5) Niigata - This is a port of embarkation on the N.W. coast of Honshu. Its importance is increasing as other ports are damaged. Machine tool industries are located there and it is a potential center for industrial dispersion. It has oil refineries and storage. (Classified as a B Target)

(6) The possibility of bombing the Emperor's palace was discussed. It was agreed that we should not recommend it but that any action for this bombing should come from authorities on military policy. It was agreed that we should obtain information from which we could determine the effectiveness of our weapon against this target.

B. It was the recommendation of those present at the meeting that the first four choices of targets for our weapon should be the following:
  a. Kyoto
  b. Hiroshima
  c. Yokohama
  d. Kokura Arsenal

C. Dr. Stearns agreed to do the following:
(1) brief Colonel Fisher thoroughly on these matters, (2) request reservations for these targets, (3) find out more about the target area including exact locations of the strategic industries there, (4) obtain further photo information on the targets, and (5) to determine the nature of the construction, the area, heights, contents and roof coverage of buildings. He also agreed to keep in touch with the target data as it develops and to keep the committee advised of other possible target areas. He will also check on locations of small military targets and obtain further details on the Emperor's palace.

7. Psychological Factors in Target Selection
A. It was agreed that psychological factors in the target selection were of great importance. Two aspects of this are (1) obtaining the greatest psychological effect against Japan and (2) making the initial use sufficiently spectacular for the importance of the weapon to be internationally recognized when publicity on it is released.

B. In this respect Kyoto has the advantage of the people being more highly intelligent and hence better able to appreciate the significance of the weapon. Hiroshima has the advantage of being such a size and with possible focusing from nearby mountains that a large fraction of the city may be destroyed. The Emperor's palace in Tokyo has a greater fame than any other target but is of least strategic value.

8. Use Against "Military" Objectives
A. It was agreed that for the initial use of the weapon any small and strictly military objective should be located in a much larger area subject to blast damage in order to avoid undue risks of the weapon being lost due to bad placing of the bomb.

9. Radiological Effect
A. Dr. Oppenheimer presented a memo he had prepared on the radiological effects of the gadget. This memo will not be repeated in this summary but it is being sent to

General Groves as a separate exhibit. The basic recommendations of this memo are (1) for radiological reasons no aircraft should be closer than 2-1/2 miles to the point of detonation (for blast reasons the distance should be greater) and (2) aircraft must avoid the cloud of radio-active materials. If other aircraft are to conduct missions shortly after the detonation a monitoring plane should determine the areas to be avoided.

10. Coordinated Air Operations

A. The feasibility of following the raid by an incendiary mission was discussed. This has the great advantage that the enemies' fire fighting ability will probably be paralyzed by the gadget so that a very serious conflagration should be capable of being started. However, until more is learned about the phenomena associated with a detonation of the gadget, such as the extent to which there will be radio-active clouds, an incendiary mission immediately after the delivery of the gadget should be avoided. A coordinated incendiary raid should be feasible on the following day at which time the fire raid should still be quite effective. By delaying the coordinated raid to the following day, the scheduling of our already contemplated operations will not be made even more difficult, photo reconnaissance of the actual damage directly caused by our device can be obtained without confusion from the subsequent fire raid, and dangers from radio-active clouds can be avoided.

B. Fighter cover should be used for the operation as directed by the 21st Bomber Command.

11. Rehearsals

A. It was agreed by all that very complete rehearsals of the entire operation are essential to its success. It is possible for thirty (30) pumpkin units for this purpose to be shipped from this country in June with perhaps sixty (60) being shipped in July. These rehearsals overseas should take place beginning in July. At least some of the rehearsals should be very complete including the placing of spotter aircraft over the alternative targets, use of fighter cover, etc. Even though it is hoped that radar will not be used some rehearsals of radar operations are required in order that the operations may be carried out successfully if emergency arises for which they are required.

12. Operating Requirements for Safety of Aircraft

A. Dr. Penney reported some very encouraging information he had just received from England in this respect. His previous information was that no one could guarantee the safety of a large aircraft at blast pressures greater than 1/2 lb. per square inch. However, in some recent experiments in England large aircraft have been flown over detonations of 2,000 lbs. of TNT and pilots have not objected to going as low as 900 feet. On this basis with a 100,000 ton total equivalent energy release or a 64,000 ton equivalent blast energy 23,000 feet would be a safe altitude on the basis of these experiments if allowance is made for the rarefaction of the atmosphere at high altitudes. However, due to the greater duration of the blast in our case, the safe height will probably be somewhat greater.

13. Coordination with 21st Program

A. This matter was included as part of the other discussion and is included in previous paragraphs of this summary.

14. It was agreed that the next meeting of the Target Committee should take place at 9:00 AM EWT on 28 May in Room 4E200 of the Pentagon Building in Washington. Dr. Oppenheimer recommended and others agreed that either Captain Parsons and/or Dr. Ramsey should attend this meeting.

15. In view of the high classification of the minutes of this meeting it was agreed that copies should not be sent to those present

but that instead one copy should be kept on file in General Groves' office, one copy in Dr. Oppenheimer's office, and one copy in Captain Parson's office.

[signature]
[signature]
Major J. A. Derry
Dr. N. F. Ramsey
dc
Distribution:
Copy 1: Maj Gen L. R. Groves
Copy 2: Capt. Parsons
Copies 3 & 4: J. R. Oppenheimer

Source: J. A. Darry to Leslie R. Groves, May 12, 1945. Vertical File. Atomic Bomb-Yale University Documents. Harry S. Truman Presidential Library and Museum.

25. Henry Stimson Memorandum to Harry Truman on the Campaign Against Japan, May 16, 1945

The process of getting U.S. President Harry Truman up to speed on the war effort was extremely complicated amid the fast-moving events of the spring of 1945. This memorandum, for example, was sent to Truman just eight days after the end of the war in Europe, which itself raised an entirely new crop of issues that the president had to address with speed. There is no mention or allusion to the Manhattan Project here, though discussion of deployment of U.S. troops was, as both Stimson and Truman knew, central to any decision on dropping the atomic bomb.

Dear Mr. President:

Here is a skeleton outline of the views which I presented to you this morning:

I.
The campaign against Japan

1. There should be no attempt to engage the masses of the Japanese Army in China by our own ground forces. It is neither the best strategic way to beat Japan nor in my opinion would it be acceptable to the American people, and it would be a hard strain upon the morale of our Army which has fought so well thus far. If those Jap [sic] troops have to be beaten in that location, China should do it.

2. The plans for the campaign are now being worked out by the Joint Chiefs of Staff. I believe they will be adequate for the defeat of Japan without such a sacrifice of American lives as would be involved in such an engagement in China.

3. The work of redeploying our forces from Europe to the Pacific will necessarily take so long that there will be more time for your necessary diplomacy with the other large allies than some of our hasty friends realize. Therefore I believe that good and not harm would be done by the policy towards your coming meeting which you mentioned to me. We shall probably hold more cards in our hands later than now.

4. For reasons I mentioned to you, I am anxious to hold our Air Force, so far as possible, to the 'precision' bombing which it has done so well in Europe. I am told that it is possible and adequate. The reputation of the United States for fair play and humanitarianism is the world's biggest asset for peace in the coming decades. I believe the same rule of sparing the civilian population should be applied as far as possible to the use of any new weapons....

All of this is a tough problem requiring coordination between the Anglo-American allies and Russia. Russia will occupy most of the good food lands of central Europe while we have the industrial portions. We must find some way of persuading Russia to play ball.

Source: Folder 22A, Box WD3, Series 8: War Department, John J. McCloy Papers, Amherst College Archives and Special Collections, Amherst College Libraries.

26. John McCloy's Memorandum on Meeting with George Marshall and Henry Stimson Regarding Objectives toward Japan, May 29, 1945

Two of the most important decision-makers in the U.S. government concerning the war in its last years were U.S. Army Chief of Staff George Marshall and Assistant Secretary of War John McCloy, both of whom reported directly to Secretary of War Henry Stimson. Mentioned in the memorandum is the "acting secretary of state," Edward Stettinius Jr., who would have been a carryover from the Roosevelt administration. "Forrestal" was U.S. Secretary of the Navy James Forrestal. Even in this private memorandum to himself, Stimson was clearly reluctant to name the atomic weapon that he (and the president) were now considering using. "S-1," in the memorandum, refers to the atomic bomb.

Present:
Secretary of War
General Marshall
Mr. McCloy

Subject:
Objectives toward Japan and methods of concluding war with minimum casualties.

The Secretary of War referred to the earlier meeting with the Acting Secretary of State and Mr. Forrestal on the matter of the President's speech and the reference to Japan. He felt the decision to postpone action now was a sound one. This only postponed consideration of the matter for a time, however, for we should have to consider it again preparatory to the employment of S-1.

The Secretary referred to the burning of Tokyo and the possible ways and means of employing the larger bombs. The Secretary referred to the letter from Dr. Bush and Dr. Conant on the matter of disclosing the nature of the process to other nations as well as to Dr. Bush's memorandum on the same general subject. General Marshall took their letters and stated he would read them and give his views on their recommendations as soon as possible.

General Marshall said he thought these weapons might first be used against straight military objectives such as a large naval installation and then if no complete result was derived from the effect of that, he thought we ought to designate a number of large manufacturing areas from which the people would be warned to leave—telling the Japanese that we intended to destroy such centers. There would be no individual designations so that the Japs would not know exactly where we were to hit—a number [of possible targets] should be named and the hit should follow shortly after. Every effort should be made to keep our record of warning clear [although no warning was given to Hiroshima before it was hit with the atomic bomb]. We must offset by such warning methods the opprobrium which might follow from an ill considered employment of such force.

The General then spoke of his stimulation of the new weapons and operations people to the development of new weapons and tactics to cope with the care and last ditch defense tactics of the suicidal Japanese. He sought to avoid the attrition we were now suffering from such fanatical but hopeless defense methods—it requires new tactics. He also spoke of gas and the possibility of using it in a limited degree, say on the outlying islands where operations were now going on or were about to take place. He spoke of the type of gas that might be employed. It did not need to be our newest and most potent—just drench them and sicken them so that the fight would be taken out of them—saturate an area, possibly with mustard, and just stand off.

He said he had asked the operations people to find out what we could do quickly—where the dumps were and how much time and effort would be required to bring the gas to bear. There would be the matter of public opinion which we had to consider, but that was something which might also be dealt with. The character of the weapon was no less humane than phosphorus and flame throwers and need not be used against dense populations or civilians—merely against these last pockets of resistance which had to be wiped out but had no other military significance.

The General stated that he was having these studies made and in due course would have some recommendations to make.

The Secretary stated that he was meeting with scientists and industrialists this week on S-1 and that he would talk with the Chief of Staff again after these meetings and the General repeated that he would shortly give the Secretary his views on the suggestions contained in the letter above referred to.

Source: Record Group 107, Office of the Secretary of War, Formerly Top Secret Correspondence of Secretary of War Stimson ("Safe File"), July 1940–September 1945, Box 12, S-1. National Archives.

27. James Franck, Report of the Committee on Political and Social Problems: Manhattan Project "Metallurgical Laboratory," University of Chicago, June 11, 1945

By the middle of 1945, scientists other than Szilárd (but under his influence, for he was a member of this committee) had also become concerned with the political ramifications raised by the Manhattan Project and had started to express their reservations and cautious speculations. This report is blunt in its conclusion: "We urge that the use of nuclear bombs in this war be considered as a problem of long-range national policy rather than military expediency, and that this policy be directed primarily to the achievement of an agreement permitting an effective international control of the means of nuclear warfare." There might be a desire to use the atomic bomb to wrap up the war against Japan quickly, but, Franck and his coauthors ask, what will the consequences be? The group worried that this question was not being considered carefully enough.

Report of the Committee on Political and Social Problems
Manhattan Project "Metallurgical Laboratory" University of Chicago
June 11, 1945
Political and Social Problems

I. Preamble
II. Prospectives of Armament Race
III. Prospectives of Agreement
IV. Methods of Control
V. Summary

I. Preamble
The only reason to treat nuclear power differently from all the other developments in

the field of physics is its staggering possibilities as a means of political pressure in peace and sudden destruction in war. All present plans for the organization of research, scientific and industrial development, and publication in the field of nucleonics are conditioned by the political and military climate in which one expects those plans to be carried out. Therefore, in making suggestions for the postwar organization of nucleonics, a discussion of political problems cannot be avoided. The scientists on this Project do not presume to speak authoritatively on problems of national and international policy. However, we found ourselves, by the force of events, the last five years in the position of a small group of citizens cognizant of a grave danger for the safety of this country as well as for the future of all the other nations, of which the rest of mankind is unaware. We therefore felt it our duty to urge that the political problems, arising from the mastering of atomic power, be recognized in all their gravity, and that appropriate steps be taken for their study and the preparation of necessary decisions. We hope that the creation of the Committee by the Secretary of War to deal with all aspects of nucleonics, indicates that these implications have been recognized by the government. We feel that our acquaintance with the scientific elements of the situation and prolonged preoccupation with its world-wide political implications, imposes on us the obligation to offer to the Committee some suggestions as to the possible solution of these grave problems.

Scientists have often before been accused of providing new weapons for the mutual destruction of nations, instead of improving their well-being. It is undoubtedly true that the discovery of flying, for example, has so far brought much more misery than enjoyment or profit to humanity. However, in the past, scientists could disclaim direct responsibility for the use to which mankind had put their disinterested discoveries. We cannot take the same attitude now because the success which we have achieved in the development of nuclear power is fraught with infinitely greater dangers than were all the inventions of the past. All of us, familiar with the present state of nucleonics, live with the vision before our eyes of sudden destruction visited on our own country, of Pearl Harbor disaster, repeated in thousand-fold magnification, in every one of our major cities.

In the past, science has often been able to provide adequate protection against new weapons it has given into the hands of an aggressor, but it cannot promise such efficient protection against the destructive use of nuclear power. This protection can only come from the political organization of the world. Among all arguments calling for an efficient international organization for peace, the existence of nuclear weapons is the most compelling one. In the absence of an international authority which would make all resort to force in international conflicts impossible, nations could still be diverted from a path which must lead to total mutual destruction, by a specific international agreement barring a nuclear armaments race.

II. Prospectives of Armaments Race
It could be suggested that the danger of destruction by nuclear weapons can be prevented—at least as far as this country is concerned—by keeping our discoveries secret for an indefinite time, or by developing our nucleonic armaments at such a pace that no other nations would think of attacking us from fear of overwhelming retaliation.

The answer to the first suggestion is that although we undoubtedly are at present ahead of the rest of the world in this field, the fundamental facts of nuclear power are a subject of common knowledge. British scientists know as much as we do about the basic wartime progress of nucleonics—with the exception of specific processes used in our engineering developments—and the background of French nuclear physicists plus their occasional contact with our Projects, will enable them to catch up rapidly, at least as far as basic scientific facts are concerned. German scientists, in whose discoveries the whole development of this field has originated, apparently did not develop it during the war to the same extent to which this has been done in America; but to the last day of the European war, we have been living in constant apprehension as to their possible achievements. The knowledge that German scientists were working on this weapon and that their government certainly had no scruples against using it when available, was the main motivation of the initiative which American scientists have taken in developing nuclear power on such a large scale for military use in this country. In Russia, too, the basic facts and implications of nuclear power were well understood in 1940, and the experiences of Russian scientists in nuclear research is entirely sufficient to enable them to retrace our steps within a few years, even if we would make all attempts to conceal them. Furthermore, we should not expect too much success from attempts to keep basic information secret in peacetime, when scientists acquainted with the work on this and associated Projects will be scattered to many colleges and research institutions and many of them will continue to work on problems closely related to those on which our developments are based. In other words, even if we can retain our leadership in basic knowledge of nucleonics for a certain time by maintaining the secrecy of all results achieved on this and associated Projects, it would be foolish to hope that this can protect us for more than a few years.

It may be asked whether we cannot achieve a monopoly on the raw materials of nuclear power. The answer is that even though the largest now known deposits of uranium ores are under the control of powers which belong to the "western" group (Canada, Belgium and British Indies); the old deposits in Czechoslovakia are outside this sphere. Russia is known to be mining radium on its own territory; and even if we do not know the size of the deposits discovered so far in the USSR, the probability that no large reserves of uranium will be found in a country which covers 1/5 of the land area of the earth (and whose sphere of influence takes in additional territory), is too small to serve as a basis for security. Thus, we cannot hope to avoid a nuclear armament race, either by keeping secret from the competing nations the basic scientific facts of nuclear power, or by cornering the raw materials required for such a race.

One could further ask whether we cannot feel ourselves safe in a race of nuclear armaments by virtue of our greater industrial potential, including greater diffusion of scientific and technical knowledge, greater volume and efficiency of our skilled labor corps, and greater experience of our management—all the factors whose importance has been so strikingly demonstrated in the conversion of this country into an arsenal of the Allied Nations in the present war. The answer is that all that these advantages can give us, is the accumulation of a larger number of bigger and better atomic bombs—and this only if we produce those bombs at the maximum of our capacity in peace time, and do not rely on conversion of a peace time nucleonics industry to military production after the beginning of hostilities.

However, such a quantitative advantage in reserves of bottled destructive power will not make us safe from sudden attack. Just because a potential enemy will be afraid of being "outnumbered and outgunned," the temptation for him may be overwhelming to attempt a sudden unprovoked blow—particularly if he would suspect us of harboring aggressive intentions against his security or "sphere of influence." In no other type of warfare does the advantage lie so heavily with the aggressor. He can place his "infernal machines" in advance in all our major cities and explode them simultaneously, thus destroying a major part of our industry and killing a large proportion of our population, aggregated in densely populated metropolitan districts. Our possibilities of retaliation—even if retaliation would be considered compensation for the loss of tens of millions of lives and destruction of our largest cities—will be greatly handicapped because we must rely on aerial transportation of the bombs, particularly if we would have to deal with an enemy whose industry and population are dispersed over a large territory.

In fact, if the race of nuclear armaments is allowed to develop, the only apparent way in which our country could be protected from the paralyzing effects of a sudden attack is by dispersal of industries which are essential for our war effort and dispersal of the population of our major metropolitan cities. As long as nuclear bombs remain scarce (this will be the case until uranium and thorium cease to be the only basic materials for their fabrication) efficient dispersal of our industry and the scattering of our metropolitan population will considerably decrease the temptation of attacking us by nuclear weapons.

Ten years hence, an atomic bomb containing perhaps 20 kg of active material, may be detonated at 6% efficiency, and thus have an effect equal to that of 20,000 tons of TNT. One of these may be used to destroy something like 3 square miles of an urban area. Atomic bombs containing a larger quantity of active material but still weighing less than one ton may be expected to be obtainable within ten years which could destroy over ten square miles of a city. A nation which is able to assign 10 tons of atomic explosives for the preparation of a sneak attack on this country, can then hope to achieve the destruction of all industry and most of the population in an area from 500 square miles upwards. If no choice of targets, in any area of five hundred square miles of American territory, will contain a large enough fraction of the nation's industry and population to make their destruction a crippling blow to the nation's war potential and its ability to defend itself, then the attack will not pay, and will probably not be undertaken. At present, one could easily select in this country a hundred blocks of five square miles each whose simultaneous destruction would be a staggering blow to the nation. (A possible total destruction of all the nation's naval forces would be only a small detail of such a catastrophe.) Since the area of the United States is about six million square miles, it should be possible to scatter its industrial and human resources in such a way as to leave no 500 square miles important enough to serve as a target for nuclear attack.

We are fully aware of the staggering difficulties of such a radical change in the social and economic structure of our nation. We felt, however, that the dilemma had to be stated, to show what kind of alternative methods of protection will have to be considered if no successful international agreement is reached. It must be pointed out that in this field we are in a less favorable position than nations which are either now more diffusely populated and whose industries are more scattered, or whose governments have unlimited power over the movement of population and the location of industrial plants.

If no efficient international agreement is achieved, the race of nuclear armaments will be on in earnest not later than the morning after our first demonstration of the existence of nuclear weapons. After this, it might take other nations three or four years to overcome our present head start, and 8 or 10 years to draw even with us if we continue to do intensive work in this field. This might be all the time we have to bring about the regroupment of our population and industry. Obviously, no time should be lost in inaugurating a study of this problem by experts.

III. Prospectives of Agreement

The prospect of nuclear warfare and the type of measures which have to be taken to protect a country from total destruction by nuclear bombing, must be as abhorrent to other nations as to the United States. England, France, and the smaller nations of the European continent, with their congeries of people and industries, are in an entirely hopeless situation in the face of such a threat. Russia, and China are the only great nations which could survive a nuclear attack. However, even though these countries value human life less than the peoples of Western Europe and America, and even though Russia, in particular, has an immense space over which its vital industries could be dispersed and a government which can order this dispersion, the day it is convinced that such a measure is necessary—there is no doubt that Russia, too, will shudder at the possibility of a sudden disintegration of Moscow and Leningrad, almost miraculously preserved in the present war, and of its new industrial sites in the Urals and Siberia. Therefore, only lack of mutual trust, and not lack of desire for agreement, can stand in the path of an efficient agreement for the prevention of nuclear warfare.

From this point of view, the way in which nuclear weapons, now secretly developed in this country, will first be revealed to the world appears of great, perhaps fateful importance.

One possible way—which may particularly appeal to those who consider the nuclear bombs primarily as a secret weapon developed to help win the present war—is to use it without warning on an appropriately selected object in Japan. It is doubtful whether the first available bombs, of comparatively low efficiency and small size, will be sufficient to break the will or ability of Japan to resist, especially given the fact that the major cities like Tokyo, Nagoya, Osaka, and Kobe already will largely be reduced to ashes by the slower process of ordinary aerial bombing. Certain and perhaps important tactical results undoubtedly can be achieved, but we nevertheless think that the question of the use of the very first available atomic bombs in the Japanese war should be weighed very carefully, not only by military authority, but by the highest political leadership of this country. If we consider international agreement on total prevention of nuclear warfare as the paramount objective, and believe that it can be achieved, this kind of introduction of atomic weapons to the world may easily destroy all our chances of success. Russia, and even allied countries which bear less mistrust of our ways and intentions, as well as neutral countries, will be deeply shocked. It will be very difficult to persuade the world that a nation which was capable of secretly preparing and suddenly releasing a weapon, as indiscriminate as the rocket bomb and a thousand times more destructive, is to be trusted in its proclaimed desire of having such weapons abolished by international agreement. We have large accumulations of poison gas, but do not use them, and recent polls have shown that public opinion in this country would disapprove of such a use even if it would accelerate the winning of the Far Eastern war. It is true, that some irrational element in mass psychology makes gas poisoning more revolting that blasting by explosive, even though gas warfare is in no way more "inhuman" than the war of bombs and bullets. Nevertheless, it is not at all certain that the American public opinion, if it could be enlightened as to the effect of atomic explosives, would support the first introduction by our own country of such an indiscriminate method of wholesale destruction of civilian life.

Thus, from the "optimistic" point of view—looking forward to an international agreement on prevention of nuclear warfare—the military advantages and the saving of American lives, achieved by the sudden use of atomic bombs against Japan, may be outweighed by the ensuing loss of confidence and wave of horror and repulsion, sweeping over the rest of the world, and perhaps dividing even the public opinion at home.

<u>From this point of view a demonstration of the new weapon may best be made before the eyes of representatives of all United Nations, on the desert or a barren island.</u> The best possible atmosphere for the achievement of an international agreement could be achieved if America would be able to say to the world, "You see what weapon we had but did not use. We are ready to renounce its use in the future and to join other nations in working out adequate supervision of the use of this nuclear weapon."

This may sound fantastic, but then in nuclear weapons we have something entirely new in the order of magnitude of destructive power, and if we want to capitalize fully on the advantage which its possession gives us, we must use new and imaginative methods. After such a demonstration the weapon could be used against Japan if a sanction of the United Nations (and of the public opinion at home) could be obtained, perhaps after a preliminary ultimatum to Japan to surrender or at least to evacuate a certain region as an alternative to the total destruction of this target.

It must be stressed that if one takes a pessimistic point of view and discounts the possibilities of an effective international control of nuclear weapons, then the advisability of an early use of nuclear bombs against Japan becomes even more doubtful—quite independently of any humanitarian considerations. If no international agreement is concluded immediately after the first demonstration, this will mean a flying start of an unlimited armaments race. If this race is inevitable, we have all reason to delay its beginning as long as possible in order to increase our headstart still further. It took us three years, roughly, under forced draft of wartime urgency, to complete the first stage of production of nuclear explosives—that based on the separation of the rare fissionable isotope U-235, or its utilization for the production of an equivalent quantity of another fissionable element. This stage required large-scale, expensive constructions and laborious procedures. We are now on the threshold of the second stage—that of converting into fissionable material the comparatively abundant common isotopes of thorium and uranium. This stage requires no elaborate plans and can provide us in about 5–6 years with a really substantial stockpile of atomic bombs. Thus it is to our interest to delay the beginning of the armaments race at least until the successful termination of this second stage. The benefit to the nation, and the saving of American lives in the future, achieved by renouncing an early demonstration of nuclear bombs and letting the other nations come into the race only reluctantly, on the basis of guesswork and without definite knowledge that the "thing does work," may far outweigh the advantages to be gained by the immediate use of the first and comparatively inefficient bombs in the war against Japan. At the least, pros and cons of this use must be carefully weighed by the supreme political and military leadership of the country, and the decision should not be left to considerations, merely, of military tactics.

One may point out that the scientists themselves have initiated the development of this "secret weapon" and it is therefore strange that they should be reluctant to try it out on the enemy as soon as it is available. The answer to this question was given above—the compelling reason for creating this weapon with such speed was our fear that Germany had the technical skill necessary to develop such a weapon without any moral constraints regarding its use.

Another argument which could be quoted in favor of using atomic bombs as soon as they are available is that so much taxpayers' money has been invested in these Projects that the Congress and the American public will require a return for their money. The above-mentioned attitude of the American public opinion in the question of the use of poison gas against Japan shows that one can expect it to understand that a weapon can sometimes be made ready only for use in extreme emergency; and as soon as the potentialities of nuclear weapons will be revealed to the American people, one can be certain that it will support all attempts to make the use of such weapons impossible.

Once this is achieved, the large installations and the accumulation of explosive materials at present earmarked for potential military use, will become available for important peace time developments, including power production, large engineering undertakings, and mass production of radioactive materials. In this way, the money spent on war time development of nucleonics may become a boon for the peace time development of national economy.

IV. Methods of International Control

We now consider the question of how an effective international control of nuclear armaments can be achieved. This is a difficult problem, but we think it to be soluble. It requires study by statesmen and international lawyers, and we can offer only some preliminary suggestions for such a study.

Given mutual trust and willingness on all sides to give up a certain part of their sovereign rights, by admitting international control of certain phases of national economy, the control could be exercised (alternatively or simultaneously) on two different levels.

The first and perhaps simplest way is to ration the raw materials—primarily, the uranium ores. Production of nuclear explosives begins with processing of large quantities of uranium in large isotope separation plants or huge production piles. The amounts of ore taken out of the ground at different locations could be controlled by resident agents of the international Control Board, and each nation could be allotted only an amount which would make large scale separation of fissionable isotopes impossible.

Such a limitation would have the drawback of making impossible also the development of nuclear power production for peace time purposes. However, it does not need to prevent the production of radioactive elements on a scale which will revolutionize the industrial, scientific and technical use of these materials, and will thus not eliminate the main benefits which nucleonics promises to bring to mankind.

An agreement on a higher level, involving more mutual trust and understanding, would be to allow unlimited production, but keep exact bookkeeping on the fate of each pound of uranium mined. Certain difficulty with this method of control will arise in the second stage of production, when one pound of pure fissionable isotope will be used again and again to produce additional fissionable material from thorium. These could perhaps be overcome by extending control to the mining and use of thorium, even though the commercial use of this metal may cause complications.

If check is kept on the conversion of uranium and thorium ore into pure fissionable materials, the question arises how to prevent accumulation of large quantities of such material in the hands of one or several nations. Accumulations of this kind could be rapidly converted into atomic bombs if a nation would break away from international control. It has been suggested that a compulsory denaturation of pure fissionable isotopes may be agreed upon—they should be diluted after production by suitable isotopes to make them useless for military purposes (except if purified by a process whose development must take two or three years), while retaining their usefulness for power engines.

One thing is clear: any international agreement on prevention of nuclear armaments must be backed by actual and efficient controls. No paper agreement can be sufficient since neither this or any other nation can stake its whole existence on trust into other nations' signatures. Every attempt to impede the international control agencies must be considered equivalent to denunciation of the agreement.

It hardly needs stressing that we as scientists believe that any systems of controls envisaged should leave as much freedom for the peace development of nucleonics as is consistent with the safety of the world.

V. Summary

The development of nuclear power not only constitutes an important addition to the technological and military power of the United States, but also creates grave political and economic problems for the future of this country.

Nuclear bombs cannot possibly remain a "secret weapon" at the exclusive disposal of this country, for more than a few years. The scientific facts on which their construction is based are well known to scientists of other countries. Unless an effective international control of nuclear explosives is instituted, a race of nuclear armaments is certain to ensue following the first revelation of our possession of nuclear weapons to the world. Within ten years other countries may have nuclear bombs, each of which, weighing less than a ton, could destroy an urban area of more than five square miles. In the war to which such an armaments race is likely to lead, the United States, with its agglomeration of population and industry in comparatively few metropolitan districts, will be at a disadvantage compared to the nations whose population and industry are scattered over large areas.

We believe that these considerations make the use of nuclear bombs for an early, unannounced attack against Japan inadvisable. If the United States would be the first to release this new means of indiscriminate destruction upon mankind, she would sacrifice public support throughout the world, precipitate the race of armaments, and prejudice the possibility of reaching an international agreement on the future control of such weapons.

Much more favorable conditions for the eventual achievement of such an agreement could be created if nuclear bombs were first revealed to the world by a demonstration in an appropriately selected uninhabited area.

If chances for the establishment of an effective international control of nuclear weapons will have to be considered slight at the present time, then not only the use of these weapons against Japan, but even their early demonstration may be contrary to the interests of this country. A postponement of such a demonstration will have in this case the advantage of delaying the beginning of the nuclear armaments race as long as possible. If, during the time gained, ample support could be made available for further development of the field in this country, the postponement would substantially increase the lead which we have established during the present war, and our position in an armament race or in any later attempt at international agreement will thus be strengthened.

On the other hand, if no adequate public support for the development of nucleonics will be available without a demonstration, the postponement of the latter may be deemed inadvisable, because enough information might leak out to cause other nations to start the armament race, in which we will then be at a disadvantage. At the same time, the distrust of other nations may be aroused by a confirmed development under cover of secrecy, making it more difficult eventually to reach an agreement with them.

If the government should decide in favor of an early demonstration of nuclear weapons it will then have the possibility to take into account the public opinion of this country and of the other nations before deciding whether these weapons should be used in the war against Japan. In this way, other nations may assume a share of the responsibility for such a fateful decision.

To sum up, we urge that the use of nuclear bombs in this war be considered as a problem of long-range national policy rather than military expediency, and that this policy be directed primarily to the achievement of an agreement permitting an effective international control of the means of nuclear warfare.

The vital importance of such a control for our country is obvious from the fact that the only effective alternative method of protecting this country, of which we are aware, would be a dispersal of our major cities and essential industries.

Members of the Committee:
James Franck (Chairman)
Donald J. Hughes
J. J. Nickson
Eugene Rabinowitch
Glenn T. Seaborg
J. C. Stearns
Leó Szilárd

Source: Record Group 77, MED Records, H-B files, Folder 76 (copy from microfilm). National Archives.

28. Arthur Compton, Enrico Fermi, Ernest Lawrence, and J. Robert Oppenheimer, Report on the Use of the Atomic Bomb in Wartime, June 16, 1945

The U.S. Secretary of War instituted an Interim Committee in May 1945 to recommend possible wartime uses of the atomic bomb. Within it was a Science Committee composed of Arthur Compton, Enrico Fermi, Ernest Lawrence, and J. Robert Oppenheimer. These four, aware of the growing concern many Manhattan Project scientists were expressing about possible uses of the bomb, concluded that, given the particulars of the situation in mid-1945, they saw "no acceptable alternative" to the use of the bomb. The recommendation that the other Allies be appraised of progress on the bomb, however, was ignored.

Science Panel's Report to the Interim Committee
June 16, 1945
TOP SECRET
RECOMMENDATIONS ON THE IMMEDIATE USE OF NUCLEAR WEAPONS

You have asked us to comment on the initial use of the new weapon. This use, in our opinion, should be such as to promote a satisfactory adjustment of our international relations. At the same time, we recognize our obligation to our nation to use the weapons to help save American lives in the Japanese war.

(1) To accomplish these ends we recommend that before the weapons are used not only Britain, but also Russia, France, and China be advised that we have made considerable progress in our work on atomic weapons, that these may be ready to use during the present war, and that we would welcome suggestions as to how we can cooperate in making this development contribute to improved international relations.

(2) The opinions of our scientific colleagues on the initial use of these weapons are not unanimous; they range from the proposal of a purely technical demonstration to that of the military application best designed to induce surrender. Those who advocate a purely technical demonstration would wish to outlaw the use of atomic weapons, and have feared that if we use the weapons now our position in future negotiations will be prejudiced. Others emphasize the opportunity of saving American lives by immediate military use, and believe that such use will improve the international prospects, in that they are more concerned with the prevention of war than with the elimination of this specific weapon. We find ourselves closer to these latter views; we can propose no technical demonstration likely to bring an end to the war; we see no acceptable alternative to direct military use.

(3) With regard to these general aspects of the use of atomic energy, it is clear that we, as scientific men, have no proprietary rights. It is true that we are among the few citizens who have had occasion to give thoughtful consideration to these problems during the past few years. We have, however, no claim to special competence in solving the political, social, and military problems which are presented by the advent of atomic power.

A. H. Compton
E. O. Lawrence
J. R. Oppenheimer
E. Fermi

Signed
J.R. Oppenheimer
For the Panel

Source: Record Group 77, Records of the Office of the Chief of Engineers, Manhattan Engineer District, Harrison-Bundy File, Folder 76. National Archives.

29. Undersecretary of the Navy Ralph Bard's Memorandum to Secretary of War Henry Stimson, June 27, 1945

"S-1" is one of the monikers for the atomic bomb used out of concern for secrecy. U.S. Undersecretary of the Navy Ralph Bard, like many others with some knowledge of

the progress and possibilities of the Manhattan Project, had become concerned about the damage use of the bomb could cause. Though he surely recognized that movement toward using the bomb on a target in Japan was probably unstoppable, Bard wrote this memorandum to U.S. Secretary of War Henry Stimson in the vain hope of convincing him to seriously consider the alternative of allowing Japan enough knowledge of the atomic bomb to recognize the devastation its use would engender. The "three powers conference" referred to was the upcoming (in August) Potsdam Conference with the United States, Great Britain, and the Soviet Union.

MEMORANDUM ON THE USE OF S-1 BOMB:

Ever since I have been in touch with this program I have had a feeling that before the bomb is actually used against Japan that Japan should have some preliminary warning for say two or three days in advance of use. The position of the United States as a great humanitarian nation and the fair play attitude of our people generally is responsible in the main for this feeling.

During recent weeks I have also had the feeling very definitely that the Japanese government may be searching for some opportunity which they could use as a medium of surrender. Following the three-power conference emissaries from this country could contact representatives from Japan somewhere on the China Coast and make representations with regard to Russia's position and at the same time give them some information regarding the proposed use of atomic power, together with whatever assurances the President might care to make with regard to the Emperor of Japan and the treatment of the Japanese nation following unconditional surrender. It seems quite possible to me that this presents the opportunity which the Japanese are looking for.

I don't see that we have anything in particular to lose in following such a program. The stakes are so tremendous that it is my opinion very real consideration should be given to some plan of this kind. I do not believe under present circumstances existing that there is anyone in this country whose evaluation of the chances of the success of such a program is worth a great deal. The only way to find out is to try it out.

RALPH A. BARD
27 June 1945

Source: Record Group 77, Records of the Chief of Engineers, Manhattan Engineer District, Harrison-Bundy File, Folder 77, "Interim Committee, International Control," National Archives.

30. Office Diary of Leslie Groves on the Setting of the Test Date, July 2, 1945

Major General Leslie Groves had the ultimate responsibility for the use of the atomic bomb in terms of timing, place, and method. The diary for this day concerns, among other things, establishing the date for the Trinity Test at Alamogordo, New Mexico, and transporting the Little Boy and Fat Man bombs to Tinian Island. Captain "Deak" Parsons, mentioned in the diary, was the ordnance officer involved in both activities and would be part of the crew of the Enola Gay when it dropped the Little Boy bomb on August 6, 1945. The cryptic nature of the diary reflects both the frenetic pace of activity as well as the continuing need for a degree of secrecy even in internal documents.

           Monday, July 2, 1945

VISITS

8:30 am	Maj Satterfield
1:45 pm	Dr. Bain
2:35 pm	Mr. Archer

CALLS

11:45 am   Gen Groves returned Mr. Makins call. Mr. M. advised that he had a paper for Gen G. Gen G. advised that he is very interested in seeing it and will send a messenger over for it. Makin advised that he will give one copy to Gen. G. for his information. Gen G advised that he would have them move on it rapidly and would like to see it and later talk to Makin about it.

12:35 pm   Gen Groves called Cong. Jennings and spoke to his secretary re insurance matters in which Jennings is interested. Gen. G. said that Jennings might like to talk with Maj. Satterfield who could answer the questions that Jennings might like to ask. His Secretary said that Jennings was expected in about 2:00 pm and would call LRG upon his return

12:50 pm   Gen Groves called Dr. Oppenheimer, Santa Fe. Oppy said they discussed Mr. CT for the 19, 20, and 21, and therefore scheduled it for the 17th. Dr. O said that the 14th was possible but was not sure. Dr. O thought the wisest thing was to schedule it for the 17th in which case they would be fairly sure of getting the thing done within a few days of that day. GG asked what the prospects were on that and Dr. O said that they were very high and ought to be able to go fishing on the morning of the 18th. Dr. O said that by that time there would be no delay nor would the material be sitting around which would be a distinct disadvantage. The 3 days involved is 3 days in which everyone could take advantage of. This would cause what would have been a frantic one to a reasonable one. GG said that he did not like the idea of a later date because of the various things that were involved. GG also said that it was extremely important that it be completed by the earlier date because of the various things that were involved. Dr. O. said that Hissell (?) and Sheal (?) got word of our intentions and did not know whether or not they had talked to anyone. Dr. O is getting them down to talk to them. GG also talked to Mr. Rowe. GG said that he was going to ask Farrell to get after it and see what he could do. Gen Farrell had already put Johnson to work on it. Mr. Rowe said that he was going to stay out there until Thursday and then going back to Boston, and will be there until next week and then going back to the site. GG said that Farrell would call to report on just how far he had gotten. Capt Parsons then came on the line. Parsons said that he had talked to Farrell re the joint letter. Parsons asked the Gen. whether or not it looked reasonable. GG said the first date in

Par. 4 is the day it is to leave where Parsons is now. GG said that precautions should be taken to protect it especially over water. Parsons asked whether or not Purnell had the date and the Gen said no but that it could be given to him very easily. Parsons said that he would call Purnell and give him his schedule when it becomes pretty exact, so that Purnell can meet Parsons in the event he gets out west. GG then talked with Dr. O. Dr. O said that he had talked with the rest of the men involved and they believed that the later date would be better. GG then told Dr. O the reason why the earlier date had to be. Dr. O said that they would meet the earlier date but it went against his own feeling but if the Gen wanted it that way they would do it. GG then talked with Col. Tyler re the telephone situation out there. GG requested Col T to check into the matter. Capt. Bradshaw was with the Signal Corps and is a good traffic man. GG said he did not think they needed a traffic man.

3:30 pm Gen Groves called Dr. Conant, Ipswich, Mass re conversation with JRO. Dr. Conant said that the Gen had done right to stay along with the earlier date. Dr C suggested that GG get in touch with Tolman and request him to exert his efforts in getting Oppy and the men persuaded to the earlier date. Dr. C said that the Gen could tell Tolman that he agreed to the earlier date and did not see how they could predict weather so far in advance. Dr C said that they did not give one good reason why they could not meet the earlier date.

4:30 pm Gen Groves called Mr. Harrison with respect to the first date. Gen Groves said that he had a very strong urging from the people in charge at the site to postpone the date four days. Gen Groves said that he had told Oppy that they had to have the first date because of things beyond his control. Mr. Harrison said that was a sound decision. GG said that he had told Dr. O that he would review the situation some more. Mr. H then told Mr. Bundy of the situation and Mr. B said that other things were involved and the earlier date was the one.

5:45 pm Dr. Tolman called Gen Groves from Y re: GG told Tolman that he wanted to talk to him about what he had told director in previous telephone conversation. GG said that since he had talked to Y the upper crust wanted it as soon as possible. So to stress the urgency of having it done the 14th. GG said he was not in agreement with the upper crust. GG said he wanted Tolman to stress to the people out there that he was not needling them but there was nothing he could do about it. Tolman transferred GG to Oppie. GG told Oppie since his talk with him earlier he talked with a number of people, also called Uncle Jim. GG told Oppie this afternoon he talked with alternate chairman and associate and also again with Uncle Jim. They wanted earlier date - 14th. Oppie told GG that material has not been coming in from Nichols as should and considerable poorer quality. Oppie said he didn't believe it was anybody's fault. GG stressed on Oppie the importance of trying to arrange for the 14th and he also told Oppie to tell his people that it wasn't his fault but came from higher authority.

Source: Record Group 200, National Archives Gift Collection, "Diary of Lt. Gen. Leslie R. Groves," Microfilm roll 2. National Archives.

31. Leó Szilárd's Petition to Harry Truman

Apparently, neither this petition (in any of its manifestations) nor word of the discussion reached Harry Truman before the decision was made to bomb Japanese cities with nuclear weapons. The group of scientists led by Leó Szilárd had great concerns about the damage atomic bombs could do and hoped the United States would take every possible step short of actual use before dropping the bombs—including a warning to Japan of the damage use of the bombs would incur. They also argued that, after the war, nuclear power should come under international control. Once Manhattan Project director General Leslie Groves got wind of the petitions, he ordered investigations of Szilárd. The scientists who had worked with Szilárd on the petition or had simply signed it soon found themselves frozen out of work on development of nuclear weapons.

31a. Leó Szilárd's First Version of His Petition to Harry Truman, July 3, 1945

July 3, 1945

A PETITION TO THE PRESIDENT OF THE UNITED STATES

Discoveries of which the people of the United States are not aware may affect the welfare of this nation in the near future. The liberation of atomic power which has been achieved places atomic bombs in the hands of the Army. It places in your hands, as Commander-in-Chief, the fateful decision whether or not to sanction the use of such bombs in the present phase of the war against Japan.

We, the undersigned scientists, have been working in the field of atomic power for a number of years. Until recently we have had to reckon with the possibility that the United States might be attacked by atomic bombs during this war and that her only defense might lie in a counterattack by the same means. Today with this danger averted we feel impelled to say what follows:

The war has to be brought speedily to a successful conclusion and the destruction of Japanese cities by means of atomic bombs may very well be an effective method of warfare. We feel, however, that such an attack on Japan could not be justified in the present circumstances. We believe that the United States ought not to resort to the use of atomic bombs in the present phase of the war, at least not unless the terms which will be imposed upon Japan after the war are publicly announced and subsequently Japan is given an opportunity to surrender.

If such public announcement gave assurance to the Japanese that they could look forward to a life devoted to peaceful pursuits in their homeland and if Japan still refused to surrender, our nation would then be faced with a situation which might require a re-examination of her position with respect to the use of atomic bombs in the war.

Atomic bombs are primarily a means for the ruthless annihilation of cities. Once they were introduced as an instrument of war it would be difficult to resist for long the temptation of putting them to such use.

The last few years show a marked tendency toward increasing ruthlessness. At present our Air Forces, striking at the Japanese cities, are using the same methods of warfare which were condemned by American public opinion only a few years ago when applied by the Germans to the cities of England. Our use of atomic bombs in this war would carry the world a long way further on this path of ruthlessness.

Atomic power will provide the nations with new means of destruction. The atomic bombs at our disposal represent only the first step in this direction and there is almost no limit to the destructive power which will become available in the course of this development. Thus a nation which sets the precedent of using these newly liberated forces of nature for purposes of destruction may have to bear the responsibility of opening the door to an era of devastation on an unimaginable scale.

In view of the foregoing, we, the undersigned, respectfully petition that you exercise your power as Commander-in-Chief to rule that the United States shall not, in the present phase of the war, resort to the use of atomic bombs.

Source: Record Group 77, Records of the Chief of Engineers, Manhattan Engineer District, Harrison-Bundy File, Folder 76. National Archives.

31b. Leó Szilárd's Cover Letter for His Petition to Harry Truman, July 4, 1945

Dear

Inclosed is the text of a petition which will be submitted to the President of the United States. As you will see, this petition is based on purely moral considerations.

It may very well be that the decision of the President whether or not to use atomic bombs in the war against Japan will largely be based on considerations of expediency. On the basis of expediency, many arguments could be put forward both for and against our use of atomic bombs against Japan. Such arguments could be considered only within the framework of a thorough analysis of the situation which will face the United States after this war and it was felt that no useful purpose would be served by considering arguments of expediency in a short petition.

However small the chance might be that our petition may influence the course of events, I personally feel that it would be a matter of importance if a large number of scientists who have worked in this field went clearly and unmistakably on record as to their opposition on moral grounds to the use of these bombs in the present phase of the war.

Many of us are inclined to say that individual Germans share the guilt for the acts which Germany committed during this war because they did not raise their voices in protest against those acts, Their defense that their protest would have been of no avail hardly seems acceptable even though these Germans could not have protested without running risks to life and liberty. We are in a position to raise our voices without incurring any such risks even though we might incur the displeasure of some of those who are at present in charge of controlling the work on "atomic power."

The fact that the people of the United States are unaware of the choice which faces us increases our responsibility in this matter since those who have worked on "atomic power" represent a sample of the population and they alone are in a position to form an opinion and declare their stand.

Anyone who might wish to go on record by signing the petition ought to have an opportunity to do so and, therefore, it would be appreciated if you could give every member of your group an opportunity for signing.

Leó Szilárd

Source: Record Group 77, Records of the Chief of Engineers, Manhattan Engineer District, Harrison-Bundy File, Folder 76. National Archives.

31c. Edward Teller's Reply to Leó Szilárd's Petition Letter, July 4, 1945

July 4, 1945

Dr. Leó Szilárd
P. O. Box 5207
Chicago 80, Illinois

Dear Szilárd:
Since our discussion I have spent some time thinking about your objections to an immediate military use of the weapon we may produce. I decided to do nothing; I should like to tell you my reasons.

First of all let me say that I have no hope of clearing my conscience. The things we are working on are so terrible that no amount of protesting or fiddling with politics will save our souls.

This much is true: I have not worked on the project for a very selfish reason and I have gotten mucsh (sic) more trouble than pleasure out of it. I worked because the problems interested me and I should have felt it a great restraint not to go ahead. I can not claim that I simply worked to do my duty. A sense of duty could keep me out of such work. It could not get me into the present kind of activity against my inclinations. If you should succeed in convincing me that your moral objections are valid, I should quit working. I hardly think that I should start protesting.

But I am not really convinced of your objections. I do not feel that there is any chance to outlaw any one weapon. If we have a slim chance of survival, it lies in the possibility to get rid of wars. The more decisive a weapon is the more surely it will be used in any real conflict and no agreements will help.

Our only hope is in getting the facts of our results before the people. This might help to convince everybody that the next war would be fatal. For this purpose actual combat use might even be the best thing.

And this brings me to the main point. The accident that we worked out this dreadful thing should not give us the responsibility of having a voice in how it is to be used. This responsibility must in the end be shifted to the people as a whole and that can be done only by making the facts known. This is the only cause for which I feel entitled in doing something: the necessity of lifting the secrecy at least as far as the broad issues of our work are concerned. My understanding is that this will be done as soon as the military situation permits it.

All this may seem to you quite wrong. I should be glad if you showed this letter to Eugene and to Franck who seem to agree with you rather than with me. I should like to have the advice of all of you whether you think it is a crime to continue to work. But I feel that I should do the wrong thing if I tried to say how to tie the little toe of the ghost to the bottle from which we just helped it to escape.
With best regards.

Yours,
E. Teller

Source: Edward Teller to Leo Szilard (2 July 1945), copy in the J. Robert Oppenheimer papers (MS35188), Box 71 "Teller, Edward, 1942–1963." Library of Congress.

31d. Leslie Groves Response to the Szilárd Petition

Leslie Groves Letter to Frederick Lindemann, Lord Cherwell, July 4, 1945

4 July 1945

The Right Honorable
The Lord Cherwell
War Cabinet Offices
London, England

Dear Lord Cherwell,

I wonder if it would be taxing your memory unduly if I were to ask you to write me briefly the subjects of your discussion in your meeting with Dr. Leó Szilárd in May of 1943, when you were in this country.

Dr. Szilárd, as you will recall, worked in the Clarendon Laboratory during the years 1935 to 1938.

Frankly, Dr. Szilárd has not, in our opinion, evidenced wholehearted cooperation in the maintenance of security.

In order to prevent any unjustified action, I am examining all of the facts which can be collected on Dr. Szilárd and I am therefore seeking your assistance.

I am looking forward to the day when I will be able to see you again.

Sincerely yours,
L. R. GROVES
Major General, USA

Frederick Lindemann, Lord Cherwell's Response to Leslie Groves, July 12, 1945

PAYMASTER GENERAL
GREAT GEORGE STREET,
S.W.1.
12th July 1945

My Dear General,

Thank you for your letter. I was very glad to hear from you again and to have a talk with Major Traynor who looked after me so well last autumn.

I am sorry to hear that Szilárd has been indiscreet. As you may wish to attach it to your file I have put my recollections of our conversation on a separate sheet. As you know he worked in my laboratory at Oxford and always had rather a bee in his bonnet about the awful implications of these matters. I cannot say that I really took his conversation very seriously, but I think the attached statement gives a fair account of its general tenour.

I think from all accounts that success in your great project is on the verge of being achieved. I hope I may add my congratulations on the unequalled effort in which you have played such a remarkable part. If I could manage it, I should very much like to come over to America again before the year is out and if so I should look forward to seeing you again. But perhaps you will be able to get away yourself and come over here for your long promised visit before then.

With kindest regards believe me
yours very sincerely
Cherwell

P.S. I hope your daughter's tennis is making good progress.

PAYMASTER GENERAL
GREAT GEORGE STREET,
S.W.1.
CONVERSATION WITH DR. SZILARD, MAY 1943, WASHINGTON D.C.

When I spoke to Szilárd in Washington in 1943, he was, so far as I can remember, mainly concerned with a topic which has inflamed so many scientists' minds, namely what sort of arrangements could be made to prevent an arms race with all the disastrous consequences to which this would lead. I do not recall that he offered any solution, although when we had discussed the same matter in Oxford before the war he had advocated some agreement between scientists not to lend themselves to any application of nuclear chain reactions to lethal purposes.

My impression is that his security was good to the point of brusqueness. He did, I believe, complain that compartmentalism was carried to undue lengths in America, but on the other hand, when I asked him about some point—I forget what—deriving from our work in Oxford he replied that he was not at liberty to discuss it as he had passed into the employment of the American Government. We did not, so far as I can recollect, have any further conversation on technical processes, but he kept harking back to his general anxiety about the future of the world.

Cherwell

Source: Record Group 77, Records of the Office of the Chief of Engineers, Manhattan Engineer District, decimal files, "201 (Szilard, Leo)," National Archives.

31e. Oak Ridge Addendum to the Szilárd Petition, July 13, 1945

July 13, 1945.

We, the undersigned, agree in essence with the attached petition, but feel that our attitude is more clearly expressed if its last paragraph is replaced by the following:

We respectfully petition that the use of atomic bombs, particularly against cities, be sanctioned by you as the Chief Executive only under the following conditions:

1. Opportunity has been given to the Japanese to surrender on terms ensuring them the possibility of peaceful development in their homeland.
2. Convincing warnings have been given that a refusal to surrender will be followed by the use of a new weapon.
3. Responsibility for use of atomic bombs is shared with our allies.

1. Garland M. Branch, Jr.
2. Edmond D. Cashwell
3. Frank C. Hoyt
4. Edwin P. Meiners, Jr.
5. Forrest H. Murray
6. Lothar W. Nordheim
7. Lionel D. Norris, Jr.
8. Louis A. Pardue
9. J. H. Rush
10. Raymond B. Sawyer
11. David Saxon
12. Richard Scalettar
13. Frederic Schuler
14. Harold Schweinler
15. Arthur H. Snell
16. Harry Soodak
17. Alvin M. Weinberg
18. E. O. Wollan

Source: Record Group 77, Records of the Chief of Engineers, Manhattan Engineer District, Harrison-Bundy File, Folder 76. National Archives.

31f. Leó Szilárd's Final Petition Regarding the Atom Bomb, July 17, 1945

July 17, 1945

<u>A Petition to the President of the United States</u>

Discoveries of which the people of the United States are not aware may affect the welfare of this nation in the near future. The liberation of atomic power which has been achieved places atomic bombs in the hands of the Army. It places in your hands, as Commander-in-Chief, the fateful decision whether or not to sanction the use of such bombs in the present phase of the war against Japan.

We, the undersigned scientists, have been working in the field of atomic power. Until recently, we have had to fear that the United States might be attacked by atomic bombs during this war and that her only defense might lie in a counterattack by the same means. Today, with the defeat of Germany, this danger is averted and we feel impelled to say what follows:

The war has to be brought speedily to a successful conclusion and attacks by atomic bombs may very well be an effective method of warfare. We feel, however, that such attacks on Japan could not be justified, at least not unless the terms which will be imposed after the war on Japan were made public in detail and Japan were given an opportunity to surrender.

If such public announcement gave assurance to the Japanese that they could look forward to a life devoted to peaceful pursuits in their homeland and if Japan still refused to surrender our nation might then, in certain circumstances, find itself forced to resort to the use of atomic bombs. Such a step, however, ought not to be made at any time without seriously considering the moral responsibilities which are involved.

The development of atomic power will provide the nations with new means of destruction. The atomic bombs at our disposal represent only the first step in this direction, and there is almost no limit to the destructive power which will become available in the course of their future development. Thus a nation which sets the precedent of using these newly liberated forces of nature for purposes of destruction may have to bear the responsibility of opening the door to an era of devastation on an unimaginable scale.

If after this war a situation is allowed to develop in the world which permits rival powers to be in uncontrolled possession of these new means of destruction, the cities of the United States as well as the cities of other nations will be in continuous danger of sudden annihilation. All the resources of the United States, moral and material, may have to be mobilized to prevent the advent of such a world situation. Its prevention is at present the solemn responsibility of the United States—singled out by virtue of her lead in the field of atomic power.

The added material strength which this lead gives to the United States brings with it the obligation of restraint and if we were to violate this obligation our moral position would be weakened in the eyes of the world and in our own eyes. It would then be more difficult for us to live up to our responsibility of bringing the unloosened forces of destruction under control.

In view of the foregoing, we, the undersigned, respectfully petition: first, that you exercise your power as Commander-in-Chief, to rule that the United States shall not resort to the use of atomic bombs in this war unless the terms which will be imposed upon Japan have been made public in detail and Japan knowing these terms has refused to surrender; second, that in such an event the question whether or not to use atomic bombs be decided by you in light of the considerations presented in this petition as well as all the other moral responsibilities which are involved.

1. DAVID S. ANTHONY
2. LARNED B. ASPREY

3. WALTER BARTKY
4. AUSTIN M. BRUES
5. MARY BURKE
6. ALBERT CAHN, JR.
7. GEORGE R. CARLSON
8. KENNETH STEWART COLE
9. ETHALINE HARTGE CORTELYOU
10. JOHN CRAWFORD
11. MARY M. DAILEY
12. MIRIAM P. FINKEL
13. FRANK G. FOOTE
14. HORACE OWEN FRANCE
15. MARK S. FRED
16. SHERMAN FRIED
17. FRANCIS LEE FRIEDMAN
18. MELVIN S. FRIEDMAN
19. MILDRED C. GINSBERG
20. NORMAN GOLDSTEIN
21. SHEFFIELD GORDON
22. WALTER J. GRUNDHAUSER
23. CHARLES W. HAGEN
24. DAVID B. HALL
25. DAVID L. HILL
26. JOHN PERRY HOWE, JR.
27. EARL K. HYDE
28. JASPER B. JEFFRIES
29. WILLIAM KARUSH
30. TRUMAN P. KOHMAN
31. HERBERT E. KUBITSCHEK
32. ALEXANDER LANGSDORF, JR.
33. RALPH E. LAPP
34. LAWRENCE B. MAGNUSSON
35. ROBERT JOSEPH MAURER
36. NORMAN FREDERICK MODINE
37. GEORGE S. MONK
38. ROBERT JAMES MOON
39. MARIETTA CATHERINE MOORE
40. ROBERT SANDERSON MULLIKEN
41. J. J. NICKSON
42. WILLIAM PENROD NORRIS
43. PAUL RADELL O'CONNOR
44. LEO ARTHUR OHLINGER
45. ALFRED PFANSTIEHL
46. ROBERT LEROY PLATZMAN
47. C. LADD PROSSER
48. ROBERT LAMBURN PURBRICK
49. WILFRED RALL
50. MARGARET H. RAND
51. WILLIAM RUBINSON
52. B. ROSWELL RUSSELL
53. GEORGE ALAN SACHER
54. FRANCIS R. SHONKA
54. ERIC L. SIMMONS
56. JOHN A. SIMPSON, JR.
57. ELLIS P. STEINBERG
58. D. C. STEWART
59. GEORGE SVIHLA
60. MARGUERITE N. SWIFT
61. LEO SZILARD
62. RALPH E. TELFORD
63. JOSEPH D. TERESI
64. ALBERT WATTENBERG
65. KATHERINE WAY
66. EDGAR FRANCIS WESTRUM, JR
67. EUGENE PAUL WIGNER
68. ERNEST J. WILKINS, JR.
69. HOYLANDE YOUNG
70. WILLIAM F. H. ZACHARIASEN

Source: Record Group 77, Records of the Chief of Engineers, Manhattan Engineer District, Harrison-Bundy File, Folder 76. National Archives.

31g. Second Oak Ridge Petition, July 1945

To the President of the United States:

We, the undersigned scientific personnel of the Clinton Laboratories, believe that the world-wide social and political consequences of the power of the weapon now being developed on this Project impose a special moral obligation on the government and people of the United States in introducing the weapon in warfare.

It is further believed that the power of this weapon should be made known by demonstration to the peoples of the world, irrespective of the course of the present conflict, for in this way the body of world opinion may be made the determining factor in the absolute preservation of peace.

Therefore we recommend that before this weapon be used without restriction in the present conflict, its powers should be adequately described and demonstrated, and the Japanese nation should be given the opportunity to consider the consequences of further refusal to surrender. We feel that this course of action will heighten the effectiveness of the weapon in this war and will be of tremendous effect in the prevention of future wars.

1. A. W. Adamson
2. Nathan E. Ballou
3. James G. Barrick
4. J. O. Blomeke
5. Edward G. Bohlmann
6. F. Boldridge
7. C. J. Borkowski
8. Melvin G. Bowman
9. Edward L. Brady
10. A. R. Brosi
11. Harrison S. Brown
12. W. H. Burgus
13. Robert L. Butenhoff
14. Waldo E. Cohn
15. Charles D. Coryell
16. Elwin H. Covey
17. M. Creek
18. John R. Dam
19. Jack K. East
20. Raymond R. Edwards
21. Norman Elliot
22. S. G. English
23. Bernard J. Finkle
24. Howard Gest
25. L. H. Gevantman
26. John A. Ghormley
27. L. E. Glendenin
28. Lionel S. Goldring
29. Joseph Halperin
30. D. N. Hume
31. John P. Hunt
32. Alan Jarrett
33. Glenn H. Jenks
34. Gordon Johnson
35. B. H. Ketelle
36. Joseph Khym
37. William J. Knox
38. D. E. Koshland, Jr.
39. Kurt A. Kraus
40. Jim Kroner
41. R. F. Leininger
42. William B. Leslie
43. Dwight C. Lincoln
44. Ralph Livingston
45. John P. McBride
46. L. T. McClinton
47. A. J. Miller
48. R. K. Money
49. Cecil M. Nelson
50. Theodore B. Novey
51. John B. Otto
52. Robert A. Penneman
53. Earl R. Purchase
54. Stanley Rasmussen
55. Walton A. Rodger
56. J. E. Sattizahn
57. Donald S. Schover
58. Robert B. Scott
59. Edward Shapiro
60. Jack Siegel
61. Charles W. Stanley
62. R. W. Stoughton
63. Paul C. Tompkins
64. Elton H. Turk
65. Clinton R. Vanneman
66. Louis B. Werner
67. Russell R. Williams, Jr.

Source: Record Group 77, Records of the Chief of Engineers, Manhattan Engineer District, Harrison-Bundy File, Folder 76. National Archives.

32. Norman Ramsey to J. Robert Oppenheimer, Memorandum on Dangers from Accidental Detonations, July 9, 1945

Norman Foster Ramsey Jr. was a Harvard physicist seconded to the Manhattan Project from the office of the U.S. secretary of war. An integral figure at the Los Alamos Laboratory, Ramsey was principally involved in development of delivery methods for atomic bombs, particularly the choice of the modified B-29 Superfortress that would come to be called "Silverplate." His concern regarding accidental detonation evolved naturally from his work in this area. The Francis Birch mentioned in the memorandum was another Harvard physicist. It was their concern that would lead Captain Deak Parsons to arm the Little Boy bomb in flight to Hiroshima, Japan, on August 6, 1945, rather than before takeoff.

9 July, 1945
To: J. R. Oppenheimer
From: N. F. Ramsey
Subject: Dangers from Accidental Detonations of Active Gadgets

1. The seriousness of accidental detonations of active gadgets has been discussed at some length by the Weapons Committee. Consistent with the tight time schedules and newness of our device every effort has been made to reduce the chances of such an accidental detonation to the lowest possible value. Nevertheless, the chances of such a catastrophe although small are nevertheless finite. Such a catastrophe would be very serious if a large nuclear explosion resulted, in that it could neutralize a considerable fraction of an important Army advance base. For this reason it is the view of the members of the Weapons Committee that the existence of such a hazard should be called to the attention of General Groves in order that it is certain that the decision to use the gadget in its present form is made with the knowledge of the existence of these risks.

2. It was the unanimous feeling of the weapons Committee that one of the more serious dangers for a high order nuclear explosion was the firing of the gun gadget by a possible fire caused by crashing in take off. The Weapons Committee therefore agreed with Birch's recommendation that the gun be loaded in flight subsequent to take off. Birch assured the committee that this operation can be sufficiently simple that the gain in safety more than compensates for the small loss in reliability.

N.F. Ramsey

cc: Birch, Brode, Bradbury, Morrison, Warner, Fussell

Source: Atomic Heritage Foundation. Available online at https://www.atomicheritage.org/key-documents/dangers-accidental-detonations. Accessed April 29, 2019.

33. War Department Press Release on Trinity, "First Test Conducted in New Mexico," July 16, 1945

More than the subsequent bombings of Hiroshima and Nagasaki in Japan, it was the Trinity Test that signaled the success of the Manhattan Project. The first ever explosion of an atomic weapon, it was, though unknown to the public at the time, the most momentous event of the year if not of this decade already filled with significant turning points. At the time, however, very few people were aware that this test was taking place; this press release was not distributed until after the August 6, 1945, bombing of Hiroshima, Japan.

WAR DEPARTMENT
WASHINGTON, D.C.
IMMEDIATE RELEASE
First Test Conducted
In New Mexico
(This Release Issued
Locally in New Mexico)

Mankind's successful transition to a new age, the Atomic Age, was ushered in July 16, 1945, before the eyes of a tense group of renowned scientists and military men gathered in the desertlands of New Mexico to witness the first end results of their $2,000,000,000 effort. Here in a remote section of the Alamogordo Air Base 120 miles southeast of Albuquerque, the first man-made atomic explosion, the outstanding achievement of nuclear science, was achieved at 5:30 A.M. of that day. Darkening heavens pouring forth rain and lightning immediately up to the zero hour heightened the drama.

Mounted on a steel tower, a revolutionary weapon destined to change war as we know it, or which may even be the instrumentality to end all major wars was set off with an impact which signalized man's entrance into a new physical world. Success was greater than the most ambitious estimates. A small amount of matter, the product of a chain of huge specially constructed industrial plants, was made to release the energy of the universe locked up within the atom from the beginning of time. A fabulous achievement had been reached. Speculative theory, barely established in pre-war laboratories, had been projected into practicality.

This phase of the Atomic Bomb Project, which is headed by Major General Leslie R. Groves, was under the direction of Dr. J. R. Oppenheimer, theoretical physicist of the University of California. He is to be credited with achieving the implementation of atomic energy for military purposes.

Tension before the actual detonation was at a tremendous pitch. Failure was an ever-present possibility. Too great a success, envisioned by some of those present, might have meant an uncontrollable unusable weapon.

Final assembly of the atomic bomb began on the night of July 12 in an old ranch house. As various component assemblies arrived from distant points, tension among the scientists mounted apace. Coolest of all was the man charged with the actual assembly of the vital core, Dr. R. F. Bacher in normal times a Professor at Cornell University.

The entire cost of the project, representing the erection of whole cities and radically new plants spread over many miles of countryside, plus unprecedented experimentation, was represented in the pilot bomb and its parts. Here was the focal point of the venture. No other country in the world had been capable of such an outlay in brains and technical effort.

The full significance of these closing moments before the final factual test was <u>not</u> lost on these men of science. They fully knew their position as pioneers into another Age. They also knew that one false move would blast them and their entire effort into eternity. Before the assembly started a receipt for the vital matter was signed by Brigadier General Thomas F. Farrell, General Groves' deputy. This signalized the formal transfer of the irreplaceable material from the scientists back to the Army, which had originally produced it at one of its great separation plants.

During final preliminary assembly, a bad few minutes developed when the assembly of an important section of the bomb was delayed. The entire unit was machine-tooled to the finest measurement. The insertion was partially completed when it apparently wedged tightly and would go no farther. Dr. Bacher, however, was undismayed and reassured the group that time would solve the problem. In three minutes time, Dr. Bacher's statement was verified and basic assembly was completed without further incident.

Specialty teams, comprised of the top men on specific phases of science, all of which were bound up in the whole, took over their specialized parts of the assembly.

On Saturday, July 14, the unit which was to determine the success or failure of the entire project was elevated to the top of the steel tower. All that day and the next, the job of preparation went on. In addition to the apparatus necessary to cause the detonation, complete instrumentation to determine all the reactions of the bomb was rigged on the tower.

The ominous weather which had dogged the assembly of the bomb had a very sobering affect on the assembled experts whose work was accomplished amid lightning flashes and peals of thunder. The weather, unusual and upsetting, blocked aerial observation of the test. It even held up the actual explosion scheduled at 4 A.M. for an hour and a half. For many months the approximate date and time had been set and had been one of the high level secrets of the best kept secret of the entire war.

Nearest observation point was set up 10,000 yards south of the tower where in a timber and earth shelter the controls for the test were located. At a point 17,000 yards from the tower at a point which would give the best observation the key figures in the atomic bomb project took their posts. These included General Groves, Dr. Vannevar Bush, head of the Office of Scientific Research and Development and Dr. James B. Conant, president of Harvard University.

Actual detonation was in charge of Dr. K. T. Bainbridge of Massachusetts Institute of Technology. He and Lieutenant Bush, in charge of the Military Police Detachment, were the last men to inspect the tower with its cosmic bomb.

At three o'clock in the morning the party moved forward to the control station. General Groves and Dr. Oppenheimer consulted with the weathermen. The decision was made to go ahead with the test despite the lack of assurance of favorable weather. The time was set for 5:30 A.M.

General Groves rejoined Dr. Conant and Dr. Bush and just before the test time, they joined the many scientists gathered at the Base Camp. Here all present were ordered to lie on the ground, face downward, heads away from the blast direction.

Tension reached a tremendous pitch in the control room as the deadline approached. The several observation points in the area were tied in to the control room by radio and with 20 minutes to go, Dr. S. K. Allison of Chicago University took over the radio net and made periodic time announcements.

The time Signals, "minus 20 minutes, minus fifteen minutes", and on and on increased the tension to the breaking point as the group in the control room, which included Dr. Oppenheimer and General Farrell, held their breaths, all praying with the intensity of the moment which will live forever with each man who was there. At "minus 45 seconds", robot mechanism took over and from that point on the whole great complicated mass of intricate mechanism was in operation without human control. Stationed at a reserve switch, however, was a soldier scientist ready to attempt to stop the explosion should the order be issued. The order never came.

At the appointed time, there was a blinding flash lighting up the whole area brighter than the brightest daylight. A mountain range three miles from the observation point stood out in bold relief. Then came a tremendous sustained roar and a heavy pressure wave which knocked down two men outside the control center. Immediately thereafter, a huge multi-colored surging cloud boiled to an altitude of over 40,000 feet. Clouds in its path disappeared. Soon the shifting substratosphere winds dispersed the now grey mass.

The test was over, the project a success.

The steel tower had been entirely vaporized. Where the tower had stood, there was a huge sloping crater. Dazed but relieved at the success of their tests, the scientists promptly marshalled their forces to estimate the strength of America's new weapon. To examine the nature of the crater, specially equipped tanks were wheeled into the area, one of which carried Dr. Enrico Fermi, noted nuclear scientist. Answer to their findings rest in the destruction effected in Japan today in the first military use of the atomic bomb.

Had it not been for the desolated area where the test was held and for the cooperation of the press in the area, it is certain that the test itself would have attracted far-reaching attention. As it was, many people in that area are still discussing the effect of the smash. A significant aspect, recorded by the press, was the experience of a blind girl near Albuquerque many miles from the scene, who, when the flash of the test lighted the sky before the explosion could be heard, exclaimed, "What was that?"

Interviews of General Groves and General Farrell give the following on-the-scene versions of the test. General Groves said: "My impressions of the night's high points follow: After about an hour's sleep I got up at 0100 and from that time on until about 0500 I was with Dr. Oppenheimer constantly. Naturally he was tense, although his mind was working at its usual extraordinary efficiency. I attempted to shield him from the evident concern of many of his assistants who were disturbed by the uncertain weather conditions. By 0400 we decided that we could probably fire at 0530. By 0400 the rain had stopped but the sky was heavily overcast. Our decision became firmer as time went on.

"During most of these hours the two of us journeyed from the control house out into the darkness to look at the stars and to assure each other that the one or two visible stars were becoming brighter. At 0510 I left Dr. Oppenheimer and returned to the main observation point which was 17,000 yards from the point of explosion. In accordance with our orders I found all personnel not otherwise occupied massed on a bit of high ground.

"Two minutes before the scheduled firing time all persons lay face down with their feet pointing towards the explosion. As the remaining time was called over the loud speaker from the 10,000-yard control station there was complete awesome silence. Dr. Conant said he had never imagined seconds could be so long. Most of the individuals in accordance with orders shielded their eyes in one way or another.

"First came the burst of light of a brilliance beyond any comparison. We all rolled over and looked through dark glasses at the ball of fire. About forty seconds later came the shock wave, followed by the sound, neither of which seemed startling after our complete astonishment at the extraordinary lighting intensity.

"A massive cloud was formed which surged and billowed upward with tremendous power, reaching the substratosphere in about five minutes.

"Two supplementary explosions of minor effect other than the lighting occurred in the cloud shortly after the main explosion.

"The cloud traveled to a great height first in the form of a ball, then mushroomed, then changed into a long trailing chimney-shaped column and finally was sent in several directions by the variable winds at the different elevations.

"Dr. Conant reached over and we shook hands in mutual congratulations. Dr. Bush, who was on the other side of me, did likewise. The feeling of the entire assembly, even the uninitiated, was one of profound awe. Drs. Conant and Bush and myself were struck by an even stronger feeling that the faith of those who had been responsible for the initiation and the carrying on of this Herculean project had been justified."

General Farrell's impressions are: "The scene inside the shelter was dramatic beyond words. In and around the shelter were some twenty odd people concerned with last minute arrangements. Included were Dr. Oppenheimer, the Director, who had borne the great scientific burden of developing the weapon from the raw materials processed in Tennessee and the State of Washington, and a dozen of his key assistants, Dr. Kistiakowsky, Dr. Bainbridge, who supervised all the detailed arrangements for the test; the weather expert, and several others. Besides these, there were a handful of soldiers, two or three Army officers and one Naval officer. The shelter was filled with a great variety of instruments and radios.

"For some hectic two hours preceding the blast, General Groves stayed with the Director. Twenty minutes before zero hour, General Groves left for his station at the base camp, because it provided a better observation point.

"Just after General Groves left, announcements began to be broadcast of the interval remaining before the blast to the other groups participating in and observing the test. As the time interval grew smaller and changed from minutes to seconds, the tension increased by leaps and bounds. Everyone in that room knew the awful potentialities of the thing that they thought was about to happen. The scientists felt that their figuring must be right and that the bomb had to go off but there was in everyone's mind a strong measure of doubt.

"We were reaching into the unknown and we did not know what might come of it. If the shot were successful, it was a justification of the several years of intensive effort of tens of thousands of people—statesmen, scientists, engineers, manufacturers, soldiers, and many others in every walk of life.

"In that brief instant in the remote New Mexico desert, the tremendous effort of the brains and brawn of all these people came suddenly and startlingly to the fullest fruition. Dr. Oppenheimer, on whom had rested a very heavy burden, grew tenser as the last seconds ticked off. He scarcely breathed. He held on to a post to steady himself. For the last few seconds, he stared directly ahead and then when the announcer shouted "Now!" and there came this tremendous burst of light followed shortly thereafter by the deep growling roar of the explosion, his face relaxed into an expression of tremendous relief. Several of the observers standing back of the shelter to watch the lighting effects were knocked flat by the blast.

"The tension in the room let up and all started congratulating each other. Everyone sensed "This is it!" No matter what might happen now all knew that the impossible scientific job had been done. Atomic fission would no longer be hidden in the cloisters of the theoretical physicists' dreams. It was almost full grown at birth. It was a great new force to be used for good or for evil. There was a feeling in that shelter that those concerned with its nativity should dedicate their lives to the mission that it would always be used for good and never for evil.

"Dr. Kistiakowsky threw his arms around Dr. Oppenheimer and embraced him with shouts of glee. Others were equally enthusiastic. All the pent-up emotions were released in those few minutes and all seemed to sense immediately that the explosion had far exceeded the most optimistic expectations and wildest hopes of the scientists. All seemed to feel that they had been present at the birth of a new age—The Age of Atomic Energy—and felt their profound responsibility to help in guiding into right channels the tremendous forces which had been unlocked for the first time in history.

"As to the present war, there was a feeling that no matter what else might happen, we now had the means to insure its speedy conclusion and save thousands of American lives. As to the future, there had been brought into being something big and something new that would prove to be immeasurably more important than the discovery of electricity or any of the other great discoveries which have so affected our existence.

"The effects could well be called unprecedented, magnificent, beautiful, stupendous and terrifying. No man-made phenomenon of such tremendous power had ever occurred before. The lighting effects beggared description. The whole country was lighted by a searing light with the intensity many times that of the midday sun. It was golden, purple, violet, gray and blue. It lighted every peak, crevasse and ridge of the nearby mountain range with a clarity and beauty that cannot be described but must be seen to be imagined. It was that beauty the great poets dream about but describe most poorly and inadequately. Thirty seconds after the explosion came first, the air blast pressing hard against the people and things, to be followed almost immediately by the strong, sustained, awesome roar. Words are inadequate tools for the job of acquainting those not present with the physical, mental and psychological effects. It had to be witnessed to be realized."

END

DISTRIBUTION: Aa, Af, B, Da, Dd, Dm, N.

Source: Smyth, Henry De Wolf. 1945. *Atomic Energy for Military Purposes*, 247–254.

Princeton, NJ: Princeton University Press.

34. Leslie Groves Memorandum to Henry Stimson on the July 16 Trinity Test, July 18, 1945

This report was probably the first detailed information that U.S. Secretary of War Henry Stimson (and, by extension, President Harry Truman) received on the Trinity Test. Over the signature of Manhattan Project director Major General Leslie Groves, it details the events at Alamogordo, New Mexico, on July 16, 1945, events Groves himself had been on hand to observe. The scientists and staff of the Manhattan Project, especially those at the nearby Los Alamos Laboratory, knew of the momentous nature of the test, and many took careful notes of what they were seeing as well as the events directly leading up to the test. Not even Groves, an experienced army engineer used to writing in the distancing bureaucratize of military communication, could not contain his amazement at the test, writing in this memorandum, "And what an explosion!"

     Washington, 18 July 1945.
Top secret
  MEMORANDUM FOR THE
   SECETARY OF WAR
SUBJECT: The Test.

1. This is not a concise, formal military report but an attempt to recite what I would have told you if you had been here on my return from New Mexico.
2. At 0530, 16 July 1945, in a remote section of the Alamogordo Air Base, New Mexico, the first full scale test was made of the implosion type atomic fission bomb. For the first time in history there was a nuclear explosion.

<u>And what an explosion!</u>
 The bomb was dropped from an airplane but was exploded on a platform on top of a 100-foot high steel tower.
3. The test was successful beyond the most optimistic expectations of anyone. Based on the data which it has been possible to work up to date, I estimate the energy generated to be in excess of the equivalent of 15,000 to 20,000 tons of TNT; and this is a conservative estimate. Data based on measurements which we have not yet been able to reconcile would make the energy release several times the conservative figure. There were tremendous blast effects. For a brief period there was a lighting effect within a radius of 20 miles equal to several suns in midday; a huge ball of fire was formed which lasted for several seconds. This ball mushroomed and rose to a height of over ten thousand feet before it dimmed. The light from the explosion was seen clearly at Albuquerque, Santa Fe, Silver City, El Paso and other points generally to about 180 miles away. The sound was heard to the same distance in a few instances but generally to about 100 miles. Only a few windows were broken although one was some 125 miles away. A massive cloud was formed which surged and billowed upward with tremendous power, reaching the substratosphere at an elevation of 41,000 feet, 36,000 feet above the ground, in about five minutes, breaking without interruption through a temperature inversion at 17,000 feet which most of the scientists thought would stop it. Two supplementary explosions occurred in the cloud shortly after the main explosion. The cloud contained several thousand tons of dust picked up from the ground and a considerable amount of iron in the gaseous form. Our present thought is that this iron ignited when it mixed with the oxygen in the air to cause these supplementary explosions. Huge concentrations of highly radioactive materials resulted from the fission and were contained in this cloud.
4. A crater from which all vegetation had vanished, with a diameter of 1200 feet and a slight slope toward the center, was formed. In the center was a shallow bowl 130 feet in diameter and 6 feet in depth. The material within the crater was deeply pulverized dirt. The material within the outer circle is greenish

and can be distinctly seen from as much as 5 miles away. The steel from the tower was evaporated. 1500 feet away there was a four-inch iron pipe 16 feet high set in concrete and strongly guyed. It disappeared completely.

5. One-half mile from the explosion there was a massive steel test cylinder weighing 220 tons. The base of the cylinder was solidly encased in concrete. Surrounding the cylinder was a strong steel tower 70 feet high, firmly anchored to concrete foundations. This tower is comparable to a steel building bay that would be found in typical 15 or 20 story skyscraper or in warehouse construction. Forty tons of steel were used to fabricate the tower which was 70 feet high, the height of a six story building. The cross bracing was much stronger than that normally used in ordinary steel construction. The absence of the solid walls of a building gave the blast a much less effective surface to push against. The blast tore the tower from its foundation, twisted it, ripped it apart and left it flat on the ground. The effects on the tower indicate that, at that distance, unshielded permanent steel and masonry buildings would have been destroyed. I no longer consider the Pentagon a safe shelter from such a bomb. Enclosed are a sketch showing the tower before the explosion and a telephotograph showing what it looked like afterwards. None of us had expected it to be damaged.

6. The cloud traveled to a great height first in the form of a ball, then mushroomed, then changed into a long trailing chimney-shaped column and finally was sent in several directions by the variable winds at the different elevations. It deposited its dust and radioactive materials over a wide area. It was followed and monitored by medical doctors and scientists with instruments to check its radioactive effects. While here and there the activity on the ground was fairly high, at no place did it reach a concentration which required evacuation of the population. Radioactive material in small quantities was located as much as 120 miles away. The measurements are being continued in order to have adequate data with which to protect the Government's interests in case of future claims. For a few hours I was none too comfortable about the situation.

7. For distances as much as 200 miles away, observers were stationed to check on blast effects, property damage, radioactivity and reactions of the population. While complete reports have not yet been received, I now know that no persons were injured nor was there any real property damage outside our Government area. As soon as all the voluminous data can be checked and correlated, full technical studies will be possible.

8. Our long range weather predictions had indicated that we could expect weather favorable for our test beginning on the morning of the 17th and continuing for four days. This was almost a certainty if we were to believe our long range forecasters. The prediction for the morning of the 16th was not so certain but there was about an 80% chance of the conditions being suitable. During the night there were thunder storms with lightning flashes all over the area. The test had been originally set for 0400 hours and all the night through, because of the bad weather, there were urgings from many of the scientists to postpone the

test. Such a delay might well have crippling results due to mechanical difficulties in our complicated test set-up. Fortunately, we disregarded the urgings. We held firm and waited the night through hoping for suitable weather. We had to delay an hour and a half, to 0530, before we could fire. This was 30 minutes before sunrise.

9. Because of bad weather, our two B-29 observation airplanes were unable to take off as scheduled from Kirtland Field at Albuquerque and when they finally did get off, they found it impossible to get over the target because of the heavy clouds and the thunder storms. Certain desired observations could not be made and while the people in the airplanes saw the explosion from a distance, they were not as close as they will be in action. We still have no reason to anticipate the loss of our plans in an actual operation although we cannot guarantee safety.

10. Just before 1100 the news stories from all over the state started to flow into the Albuquerque Associated Press. I then directed the issuance by the Commanding Officer, Alamogordo Air Base of a news release as shown on the inclosure. With the assistance of the Office of Censorship we were able to limit the news stories to the approved release supplemented in the local papers by brief stories from the many eyewitnesses not connected with our project. One of these was a blind woman who saw the light.

11. Brigadier General Thomas F. Farrell was at the control shelter located 10,000 yards south of the point of explosion. His impressions are given below:

"The scene inside the shelter was dramatic beyond words. In and around the shelter were some twenty-odd people concerned with last minute arrangements prior to firing the shot. Included were: Dr. Oppenheimer, the Director who had borne the great scientific burden of developing the weapon from the raw materials made in Tennessee and Washington and a dozen of his key assistants—Dr. Kistiakowsky, who developed the highly special explosive; Dr. Bainbridge, who supervised all the detailed arrangements for the test; Dr. Hubbard, the weather expert, and several others. Besides these, there were a handful of soldiers, two or three Army officers and one Naval officer. The shelter was cluttered with a great variety of instruments and radios.

"For some hectic two hours preceding the blast, General Groves stayed with the Director, walking with him and steadying his tense excitement. Every time the director would be about to explode because of some untoward happening, General Groves would take him off and walk with him in the rain, counselling with him and reassuring him that everything would be all right. At twenty minutes before zero hour, General Groves left for his station at the base camp, first because it provided a better observation point and second, because of our rule that he and I must not be together in situations where there is an element of danger, which existed at both points.

"Just after General Groves left, announcements began to be broadcast of the interval remaining before the blast. They were sent by radio to the other groups participating in and observing the test. As the time interval grew smaller and changed from minutes to seconds, the tension increased by leaps and bounds. Everyone in that room knew the awful potentialities of the thing that they thought was about to happen. The scientists felt that their figuring must be right and that the bomb had to go off but there was in everyone's mind a strong measure of doubt. The feeling of many could be expressed by "Lord, I believe; help Thou mine unbelief." We were reaching into the unknown and we did not know what might come of it. It can be safely said that most of those present—Christian, Jew and Athiest—were praying and praying harder than they had ever prayed before. If the shot were successful, it was a justification of the several years of intensive effort of tens of thousands of people—statesmen, scientists, engineers, manufacturers, soldiers, and many others in every walk of life.

"In that brief instant in the remote New Mexico desert the tremendous effort of the brains and brawn of all these people came suddenly and startlingly to the fullest fruition. Dr. Oppenheimer, on whom had rested a very heavy burden, grew tenser as the last seconds ticked off. He scarcely breathed. He held on to a post to steady himself. For the last few seconds, he started directly ahead and then when the announcer shouted "Now!" and there came this tremendous burst of light followed shortly thereafter by the deep growing roar of the explosion, his face relaxed into an expression of tremendous relief. Several of the observers standing back of the shelter to watch the lighting effects were knocked flat by the blast.

"The tension in the room let up and all started congratulating each other. Everyone sensed "This is it!" No matter what might happen now all knew that the impossible scientific job had been done. Atomic fission would no longer be hidden in the cloisters of the theoretical physicists' dreams. It was almost full grown at birth. It was a great new force to be used for good or for evil. There was a feeling in that shelter that those concerned with its nativity should dedicate their lives to the mission that it would always be used for good and never for evil.

"Dr. Kistiakowsky, the impulsive Russian, threw his arms around Dr. Oppenheimer and embraced him with shouts of glee. Others were equally enthusiastic. All the pent-up emotions were released in those few minutes and all seemed to sense immediately that the explosion had far exceeded the most optimistic expectations and wildest hopes of the scientists. All seemed to feel that they had been present at the birth of a new age—The Age of Atomic Energy—and felt their profound responsibility to help in guiding into right channels the tremendous forces which had been unlocked for the first time in history.

"As to the present war, there was a feeling that no matter what else might happen, we now had the means to insure its speedy conclusion and save thousands of American lives. As to the future, there had been brought into being something big and something new that would prove to be immeasurably more important than the discovery of electricity or any of the other great discoveries which have so affected our existence.

"The effects could well be called unprecedented, magnificent, beautiful, stupendous and terrifying. No man-made phenomenon of such tremendous power had ever occurred before. The lighting effects beggared description. The whole country was lighted by a searing light with the intensity many times that of the midday sun. It was golden, purple, violet, gray and blue. It lighted every peak, crevasse and ridge of the nearby mountain range with a clarity and beauty that cannot be described but must be seen to be imagined. It was that beauty the great poets dream about but describe most poorly and inadequately. Thirty seconds after the explosion came first, the air blast pressing hard against the people and things, to be followed almost immediately by the strong, sustained, awesome roar which warned of doomsday and made us feel that we puny things were blasphemous to dare tamper with the forces heretofore reserved to The Almighty. Words are inadequate tools for the job of acquainting those not present with the physical, mental and psychological effects. It had to be witnessed to be realized."

12. My impressions of the night's high points follow:

After about an hour's sleep I got up at 0100 and from that time on until about five I was with Dr. Oppenheimer constantly. Naturally he was nervous, although his mind was working at its usual extraordinary efficiency. I devoted my entire attention to shielding him from the excited and generally faulty advice of his assistants who were more than disturbed by their excitement and the uncertain weather conditions. By 0330 we decided that we could probably fire at 0530. By 0400 the rain had stopped but the sky was heavily overcast. Our decision became firmer as time went on. During most of these hours the two of us journeyed from the control house out into the darkness to look at the stars and to assure each other that the one or two visible stars were becoming brighter. At 0510 I left Dr. Oppenheimer and returned to the main observation point which was 17,000 yards from the point of explosion. In accordance with our orders I found all personnel not otherwise occupied massed on a bit of high ground.

At about two minutes of the scheduled firing time all persons lay face down with their feet pointing towards the explosion. As the remaining time was called from the loud speaker from the 10,000 yard control station there was complete silence. Dr. Conant said he had never imagined seconds could be so long. Most of the individuals in accordance with orders shielded their eyes in one way or another. There was then this burst of light of a brilliance beyond any comparison. We all rolled over and looked through dark glasses at the ball of fire. About forty seconds later came the shock wave followed by the sound, neither of which seemed startling after our complete astonishment at the extraordinary lighting intensity. Dr. Conant reached over and we shook hands in mutual congratulations. Dr. Bush, who was on the other side of me, did likewise. The feeling of the entire assembly was similar to that described by General Farrell, with even the uninitiated feeling profound awe. Drs. Conant and Bush and myself were struck by an even stronger feeling that the faith of those who had been responsible for the initiation and the carrying on of this Herculean project had been justified. I personally thought of Blondin crossing Niagara Falls on his tight rope, only to me this tight rope had lasted for almost three years and of my repeated confident-appearing assurances that such a thing was possible and that we would do it.

13. A large group of observers were stationed at a point about 27 miles north of the point of explosion. Attached is a memorandum written shortly after the explosion by Dr. E. O. Lawrence which may be of interest.

14. While General Farrell was waiting about midnight for a commercial airplane to Washington at Albuquerque—120 miles away from the site—he overheard several airport employees discussing their reaction to the blast. One said that he was out on the parking apron; it was quite dark; then the whole southern sky was lighted as though by a bright sun; the light lasted several seconds. Another remarked that if a few exploding bombs could have such an effect, it must be terrible to have them drop on a city.

15. My liaison officer at the Alamogordo Air Base, 60 miles away, made the following report:

"There was a blinding flash of light that lighted the entire northwestern sky. In the center of the flash, there appeared to be a huge billow of smoke. The original flash lasted approximately 10 to 15 seconds. As the first flash died down, there arose in the approximate center of where the original flash had occurred an enormous ball of what appeared to be fire and closely resembled a rising sun that was three-fourths above a mountain. The ball of fire lasted approximately 15 seconds, then died down and the sky resumed an almost normal appearance.

"Almost immediately, a third, but much smaller, flash and billow of smoke of a whiteish-orange color appeared in the sky, again lighting the sky for approximately 4 seconds. At the time of the original flash, the field was lighted well enough so that a newspaper could easily have been read. The second and third flashes were of much lesser intensity.

"We were in a glass-enclosed control tower some 70 feet above the ground and felt no concussion or air compression. There was no noticeable earth tremor although reports overheard at the Field during the following 24 hours indicated that some believed that they had both heard the explosion and felt some earth tremor."

16. I have not written a separate report for General Marshall as I feel you will want to show this to him. I have informed the necessary people here of our results. Lord Halifax after discussion with Mr. Harrison and myself stated that he was not sending a full report to his government at this time. I informed him that I was sending this to you and that you might wish to show it to the proper British representatives.

17. We are all fully conscious that our real goal is still before us. The battle test is what counts in the war with Japan.

18. May I express my deep personal appreciation for your congratulatory cable to us and for the support and confidence which I have received from you ever since I have had this work under my charge.

19. I know that Colonel Kyle will guard these papers with his customary extraordinary care.

L. R. GROVES,
Major General, USA

Source: *Foreign Relations of the United States. The Conference of Berlin (The Potsdam Conference), 1945, Volume 2*, 1361–1368. 1960. Washington, D.C.: Government Printing Office.

35. Stafford Warren Report to Leslie Groves on the July 16 Trinity Test, July 21, 1945

Radiologist and physician Colonel Stafford Warren was responsible for health safety at the Alamogordo, New Mexico, Trinity nuclear test site and was present for the test. Five days later, he sent a report on the event to Major General Leslie Groves, the overall director of the Manhattan Project. Knowing the importance of the test, Groves collected as many such reports as he could, each one as comprehensive as the author could make it. Sometimes, this led to meaningless statements such as the reasoning in the first point below (after all, Warren would have had no real involvement with scheduling and would know nothing about it), included simply in an attempt at an appearance of comprehensive reporting. This attempt, however, did make Warren's report more interesting than a simple recording of immediate health consequences would be.

21 July 1945
To: Major Gen. Groves
SUBJECT: Report on Test II at Trinity, 16 July 1945

1. The test was performed two days ahead of the tentative schedule because everything of importance to the test was ready.
2. A study of the weather indicated that a variety of wind conditions at slow speeds going on in general N.W. and N.E. could be expected with different directions and speeds at different levels for 16 and 17 July 1945. These slow winds would be advantageous in localizing the outfall of active material from the cloud to the site and nearby desert areas. They would also dilute the outfall most effectively in the early hours of the life of the cloud when it would help the most. The monitoring problem would be worse, however, because of the wide area covered.
3. In the two days available, the population of the surrounding areas was located by G-2 on large scale maps for a radius of 75 to 100 miles. The deserted areas corresponded fortunately to the most probable courses of the outfall from the cloud as predicted by the directions of the winds at the various altitudes. Troops under Major Palmer were available if monitoring indicated that evacuation was necessary.
4. At zero minus five hours, five cars with Dr. J. Hoffman in charge were stationed with Major Palmer and troops at the outlet road near the east-west highway #380. They were in radio communication with Base Camp and Post #2. Outlying monitor cars were in San Antonio, Roswell, Carrizozo and Fort Summer to cover these areas in case the speed of the cloud was greater than predicted.
5. Dr. Aebersold was in general charge of the monitoring at Base Camp and the three shelters at 10,000 yards, with local telephone and radio communication. There was a technician monitor and doctor in each shelter and at Base Camp.
6. Dr. Hempelmann in charge of all the monitoring program was at S 10,000, the center of communication and final decisions (also Brigadier General Farrell, Dr. Oppenheimer, Dr. Bainbridge, Mr. Hubbard, etc.)
7. This officer acted as liaison in a secondary communication center in Base Camp. Lieutenant Colonel Friedell was located with G-2 at Albuquerque as another communication center via long distance for controlling the field monitoring in case Base Camp communications broke down. All groups were keyed in by identical maps showing preliminary locations of the monitors, their presumed course, the two possible paths of the cloud, WNW and NNE (depending upon the altitude which it reached) houses and nearby ranges, etc.
8. Accessory equipment and other preparations were in keeping with the preliminary plans submitted in the preliminary report.
9. The shot was fired at 0530 on 16 July 1945. The energy developed in the test was several times greater than that expected by scientific group. The cloud column mass and top reached a phenomenal height, variously estimated as 50,000 to 70,000 feet. It remained towering over the northeast corner of the site for several hours. This was sufficient time for the majority of the largest particles to fall out. Various levels were seen to move in different directions. In general the lower one-third drifted eastward, the middle portion to the West and northwest, while the upper third moved northeast. Many small sheets of dust moved independently at all levels and large sheets remained practically in situ. By zero plus 2 hours, the main masses were no longer identifiable except for the very high white mass presumably in the stratosphere.

10. By 0800 hours the monitors reported an area of high intensity in a canyon 20 miles northeast of zero. Since this was beyond the tolerance set and equally high intensities were expected in other areas, four more monitor cars were sent into this northeast area from Base Camp. The roving monitors in this area were each accompanied by a trooper in a 4 wheel drive and authorized to evacuate families if necessary. At no house in this whole north and northeast area between 20 miles and 40 miles from zero was a dangerous intensity found. The highest intensities, fortunately, were only found in deserted regions. The highest found is shown in detail attached #1. Intensities in the deserted canyon were high enough to cause serious physiological effects.

11. The distribution over the countryside was spotty and subject to local winds and contour. It skipped the nearby highway #380 (20 mi. N.E.) except for low intensities which were equalled at twice and three times the distance. It is presumed that the largest outfall occurred in the N.E. quadrant of the site. This can only be explored by horseback at a later date.

12. The monitors all took considerable risks knowingly and many have received exposures of considerable amounts, i.e. 8r total. This is safe within a considerable margin. They should not be exposed to more radiation within the next month.

13. The dust could be measured at low intensities 200 miles north and northeast of the site on the 4th day. (Attached #2) There is still a tremendous quantity of radioactive dust floating in the air.

14. Neither the Base Camp or the shelters were contaminated very much.

15. Partially eviscerated dead wild jack rabbits were found more than 800 yards from zero, presumably killed by the blast. A farm house 3 miles away had doors torn loose and suffered other extensive damage.

16. Details indicating blast, heat, and other effects cannot be worked out until the area around the crater "cools down". It is this officer's opinion, however, that lethal or severe casualties would occur in exposed personnel up to two miles from a variety or combination of causes, ie., blast, heat, ultraviolet and missiles.

   The light intensity was sufficient at nine miles to have caused temporary blindness and this would be longer lasting at shorter distances. Several observers at 20 miles were bothered by a large blind spot for 15 m after the shot. The light together with the heat and ultraviolet radiation would probably cause severe damage to the unprotected eyes at 5–6 miles; damage sufficient to put personnel out of action several days if not permanently. All of the personnel obeyed the safety precautions during the test so that no such injury resulted.

17. A great deal of experience was obtained on the requirements for quick and adequate monitoring. Excellent radio communications, good transportation and better and more rugged meters are required.

18. It is this officer's opinion based on the damage to "Jumbo" (2400 ft), the extent of the glazed sand area (up to 500 ft.), the extent of the cleaned off area (about 1 mile), the farm house (at 3 miles) that this explosion was a great many times more violent than the 100 ton test. "Conservative" estimates by the scientific groups put it at least equivalent to 10,000 tons of T.N.T.

19. While no house area investigated received a dangerous amount, ie, no

more than an accumulated two weeks dose of 60r, the dust outfall from the various portions of the cloud was potentially a very serious hazard over a band almost 30 miles wide extending almost 90 miles northeast of the site.

20. It is this officer's opinion that this site is too small for a repetition of a similar test of this magnitude except under very special conditions. It is recommended that the site be expanded or a larger one, preferably with a radius of at least 150 miles without population, be obtained if this test is to be repeated.

Colonel Stafford L. Warren
Chief of Medical Section
Manhattan District

SLW/fp
cc/ Maj. Gen Groves (2)
    R. Oppenheimer (1)
    Col. Warren (1)

Source: Record Group 77, Records of the Office of the Chief of Engineers, Manhattan Engineer District, TS Manhattan Project Files, Folder 4, "Trinity Test," National Archives.

36. Harry Truman Diary Entry for July 25, 1945

This excerpt from U.S. President Harry Truman's diary for the day when he transmitted his decision to authorize use of atomic bombs against cities in Japan shows that he did not make the decision lightly. Though he had only been aware of the Manhattan Project and the possibility of a deliverable atomic bomb for about three months and was beset by myriad other problems, both domestic and related to wrapping up the war in Europe and resolving the one in the Pacific, he considered carefully his decision concerning the atomic bomb. Whether one agrees with the decision or not, one has to respect that Truman was not willing to evade responsibility for perhaps the single most destructive decision (even if it did, as many have argued, save many American lives) of the twentieth century. Though he had not yet his "The buck stops here" sign on his desk, Truman was already living up to that philosophy. The initial idea, as we see in the diary, was to drop the bomb on a military target. That, as we know, did not happen. Nor was there any warning given to Japan.

We have discovered the most terrible bomb in the history of the world. It may be the fire destruction prophesied in the Euphrates Valley Era, after Noah and his fabulous Ark.

Anyway we "think" we have found the way to cause a disintegration of the atom. An experiment in the New Mexico desert was startling—to put it mildly. Thirteen pounds of the explosive caused the complete disintegration of a steel tower 60 feet high, created a crater 6 feet deep and 1,200 feet in diameter, knocked over a steel tower 1/2 mile away and knocked men down 10,000 yards away. The explosion was visible for more than 200 miles and audible for 40 miles and more.

This weapon is to be used against Japan between now and August 10th. I have told the Sec. of War, Mr. Stimson, to use it so that military objectives and soldiers and sailors are the target and not women and children. Even if the Japs are savages, ruthless, merciless and fanatic, we as the leader of the world for the common welfare cannot drop that terrible bomb on the old capital or the new.

He and I are in accord. The target will be a purely military one and we will issue a warning statement asking the Japs to surrender and save lives. I'm sure they will not do that, but we will have given them the chance. It is certainly a good thing for the world that Hitler's crowd or Stalin's did not discover this atomic bomb. It seems to be the most terrible thing ever discovered, but it can be made the most useful.

Source: Papers of Harry S. Truman, President's Secretary File. Harry S. Truman Presidential Library and Museum. Available online at https://www.trumanlibrary.org/hst/d.htm. Accessed April 30, 2019.

37. Thomas Handy to Carl Spaatz Memorandum, July 25, 1945

General Thomas Handy was deputy chief of staff of the U.S. Army under George Marshall and acting chief of staff in July and August 1945, making him responsible for transmitting President Harry Truman's order to drop the atomic bombs on Hiroshima and Nagasaki. General Carl Spaatz had recently been transferred, after the cessation of warfare in Europe, to take command of the U.S. Strategic Air Forces in the Pacific, making him the commander above Colonel Paul Tibbets of the 509th Composite Group that included the B-29 Superfortresses Enola Gay and Bockscar, Silverplate bombers meant for carrying atomic bombs. This memorandum contains the order to drop the first atomic bomb and any subsequent ones as they became ready.

Memo for General Carl Spaatz
WAR DEPARTMENT
OFFICE OF THE CHIEF OF STAFF
Washington 25, D. C.
25 July 1945

TO: General Carl Spaatz
Commanding General
United States Army Strategic Air Forces

1. The 509 Composite Group, 20th Air Force will deliver its first special bomb as soon as weather will permit visual bombing after about 3 August 1945 on one of the targets: Hiroshima, Kokura, Niigata and Nagasaki. To carry military and civilian scientific personnel from the War Department to observe and record the effects of the explosion of the bomb, additional aircraft will accompany the airplane carrying the bomb. The observing planes will stay several miles distant from the point of impact of the bomb.

2. Additional bombs will be delivered on the above targets as soon as made ready by the project staff. Further instructions will be issued concerning targets other than those listed above.

3. Discussion of any and all information concerning the use of the weapon against Japan is reserved to the Secretary of War and the President of the United States. No communiques on the subject or releases of information will be issued by Commanders in the field without specific prior authority. Any news stories will be sent to the War Department for specific clearance.

4. The foregoing directive is issued to you by direction and with the approval of the Secretary of War and of the Chief of Staff, USA. It is desired that you personally deliver one copy of this directive to General MacArthur and one copy to Admiral Nimitz for their information.

(Sgd) THOS. T. HANDY

THOS. T. HANDY
General, G.S.C.
Acting Chief of Staff

copy for General Groves

Source: Record Group 77, Records of the Office of the Chief of Engineers, Manhattan Engineer District, TS Manhattan Project File '42 to '46, Folder 5B, "(Directives, Memos, Etc. to and from C/S, S/W, etc.)," National Archives.

38. Potsdam Declaration: Proclamation Defining Terms for Japanese Surrender Issued, at Potsdam, July 26, 1945

The Potsdam Declaration offered no hint or warning to the Japanese of the powerful bombs that were being prepared for use against them. Though the phrase "prompt and utter destruction" was used, the implied atomic destruction was never explained to the Japanese. It had been decided that knowledge of the atomic bomb was not yet to be shared, that the demonstration would be destruction of a Japanese city, which one to be determined by weather and other factors. When the Japanese responded to the declaration with silence, the stage was set for the dropping of an atomic bomb first on Hiroshima on August 6, 1945, and then on Nagasaki on August 9.

Potsdam Declaration
Proclamation Defining Terms for
Japanese Surrender Issued, at Potsdam,
July 26, 1945

1. We—the President of the United States, the President of the National Government of the Republic of China, and the Prime Minister of Great Britain, representing the hundreds of millions of our countrymen, have conferred and agree that Japan shall be given an opportunity to end this war.
2. The prodigious land, sea and air forces of the United States, the British Empire and of China, many times reinforced by their armies and air fleets from the west, are poised to strike the final blows upon Japan. This military power is sustained and inspired by the determination of all the Allied Nations to prosecute the war against Japan until she ceases to resist.
3. The result of the futile and senseless German resistance to the might of the aroused free peoples of the world stands forth in awful clarity as an example to the people of Japan. The might that now converges on Japan is immeasurably greater than that which, when applied to the resisting Nazis, necessarily laid waste to the lands, the industry and the method of life of the whole German people. The full application of our military power, backed by our resolve, will mean the inevitable and complete destruction of the Japanese armed forces and just as inevitably the utter devastation of the Japanese homeland.
4. The time has come for Japan to decide whether she will continue to be controlled by those self-willed militaristic advisers whose unintelligent calculations have brought the Empire of Japan to the threshold of annihilation, or whether she will follow the path of reason.
5. Following are our terms. We will not deviate from them. There are no alternatives. We shall brook no delay.
6. There must be eliminated for all time the authority and influence of those who have deceived and misled the people of Japan into embarking on world conquest, for we insist that a new order of peace, security and justice will be impossible until irresponsible militarism is driven from the world.
7. Until such a new order is established and until there is convincing proof that

Japan's war-making power is destroyed, points in Japanese territory to be designated by the Allies shall be occupied to secure the achievement of the basic objectives we are here setting forth.

8. The terms of the Cairo Declaration shall be carried out and Japanese sovereignty shall be limited to the islands of Honshu, Hokkaido, Kyushu, Shikoku and such minor islands as we determine.

9. The Japanese military forces, after being completely disarmed, shall be permitted to return to their homes with the opportunity to lead peaceful and productive lives.

10. We do not intend that the Japanese shall be enslaved as a race or destroyed as a nation, but stern justice shall be meted out to all war criminals, including those who have visited cruelties upon our prisoners. The Japanese Government shall remove all obstacles to the revival and strengthening of democratic tendencies among the Japanese people. Freedom of speech, of religion, and of thought, as well as respect for the fundamental human rights shall be established.

11. Japan shall be permitted to maintain such industries as will sustain her economy and permit the exaction of just reparations in kind, but not those which would enable her to re-arm for war. To this end, access to, as distinguished from control of, raw materials shall be permitted. Eventual Japanese participation in world trade relations shall be permitted.

12. The occupying forces of the Allies shall be withdrawn from Japan as soon as these objectives have been accomplished and there has been established in accordance with the freely expressed will of the Japanese people a peacefully inclined and responsible government.

13. We call upon the government of Japan to proclaim now the unconditional surrender of all Japanese armed forces, and to provide proper and adequate assurances of their good faith in such action. The alternative for Japan is prompt and utter destruction.

Source: U.S. Department of State. 1950. *A Decade of American Foreign Policy: Basic Documents, 1941–1949,* 34–50. Washington, D.C.: Government Printing Office.

---

39. Leslie Groves Memorandum to the U.S. Army Chief of Staff from the Conclusions of the Trinity Test, July 30, 1945

Though General George Marshall was chief of staff of the U.S. Army, General Thomas Handy, his deputy, had temporarily replaced him at the time of the memorandum so would have been the one to receive it. General Groves, by the time he wrote this memo, had recovered from the exhilaration of the days directly after the Trinity Test and could now write a great deal more dispassionately. Now, the incredible power of the bomb was being reduced to numbers and technical details and bureaucratic language.

30 July 1945

MEMORANDUM TO THE CHIEF OF STAFF

1. The following additional conclusions have been drawn from the test in New Mexico with respect to the probable effects of the combat bomb which will be exploded about 1800 feet in the air:

   a. Measured from the point on the ground directly below the explosion the blast should be lethal to at least 1000 feet. Between 2500 and 3500 feet, blast effects should be extremely serious to personnel. Heat and flame should be fatal to about 1500 to 2000 feet.

b. At 10 miles for a few thousandths of a second the light will be as bright as a thousand suns; at the end of a second, as bright as one or possibly two suns. The effect on anyone about a half mile away who looks directly at the explosion would probably be permanent sight impairment; at one mile, temporary blindness; and up to and even beyond ten miles, temporary sight impairment. To persons who are completely unshielded, gamma rays may be lethal to 3500 feet and neutrons to about 2000 feet.

c. No damaging effects are anticipated on the ground from radioactive materials. These effects at New Mexico resulted from the low altitude from which the bomb was set off.

d. Practically all structures in an area of one or two square miles should be completely demolished and a total area of six to seven square miles should be so devastated that the bulk of the buildings would have to have major repairs to make them habitable.

e. At New Mexico tanks could have gone through the immediate explosion area at normal speeds within thirty minutes after the blast. With the explosion at the expected 1800 feet, we think we could move troops through the area immediately preferably by motor but on foot if desired. The units should be preceded by scouts with simple instruments. The nearest exposed personnel should not be nearer to the blast than six miles plus the necessary allowance for bombing inaccuracy and they would require a high order of discipline and special but simple instructions. As an extra precaution, extra special dark glasses might be issued to all commanders of units as large as a platoon. If dropped on the enemy lines, the expected effect on the enemy would be to wipe out his resistance over an area 2000 feet in diameter; to paralyze it over an area a mile in diameter; and to impede it seriously over an area five miles in diameter. Troops which were in deep cave shelters at distances of over a mile should not be seriously affected. Men in slit trenches within 800 feet should be killed by the blast.

2. The energy of the test explosion has been broken down as follows:

Total theoretical energy contained in the bomb at 100% efficiency was [sensitive information deleted]. Of this amount, 21,000 to 24,000 tons were converted into actual energy made up of:

Blast - 10,500 tons minimum, 13,500 maximum

Light - 2500 tons

Waste Heat - 8000 tons, about 4000 of which went into the air and 4000 into the ground. If the explosion had been at the combat altitude of 1800 feet, most of the 4000 that went into the ground would have been converted into blast, making the total blast from 14,000 to 17,000 tons.

3. There is a definite possibility, . . . as we increase our rate of production at the Hanford Engineer Works, with the type of weapon tested that the blast will be smaller due to detonation in advance of the optimum time. But in any event, the explosion should be on the order of thousands of tons. The difficulty arises from an undesirable isotope which is created in greater quantity as the production rate increases.

4. The final components of the first gun type bomb have arrived at Tinian, those of the first implosion type should leave San Francisco by airplane early on 30 July. I see no reason to change our previous readiness predictions on the first three bombs. In September, we should have three or four bombs. One of these will be made from 235 material and will have a smaller effectiveness, about two-thirds that of the test type, but by

November, we should be able to bring this up to full power. There should be either four or three bombs in October, one of the lesser size. In November there should be at least five bombs and the rate will rise to seven in December and increase decidedly in early 1946. By some time in November, we should have the effectiveness of the 235 implosion type bomb equal to that of the tested plutonium implosion type.

5. By mid-October we could increase the number of bombs slightly by changing our design now to one using both materials in the same bomb. I have not made this change because of the ever present possibilities of difficulties in new designs. We could, if it were wise, change our plans and develop the combination bomb. But if this is to be done, it would entail an initial ten-day production setback which would be caught up in about a month's time; unless the decision to change were made before 1 August, in which case it would probably not entail any delay. From what I know of the world situation, it would seem wiser not to make this change until the effects of the present bomb are determined.

L. R. GROVES
Major General, U.S.A.

Source: General Groves to Chief of Staff, "Memorandum to the Chief of Staff," July 30, 1945, U.S. National Archives, MED records, TS Manhattan Project files '42–'46, Folder 5B. National Archives.

40. Charge-Loading Checklist for Little Boy on the Enola Gay, August 1945

The Little Boy bomb, a gun-type nuclear explosive and the direct responsibility of ordnance specialist Captain Deak Parsons, who would fly on the mission over Hiroshima, Japan, as the weaponeer, had been carefully transported to Tinian Island in preparation for a possible strike on Japan. Parsons would have had this list with him on August 6, 1945, when he loaded the Little Boy charge as the Enola Gay flew toward Hiroshima. As important were the instructions for unloading the charge in case, as it says here, of an emergency landing or, unstated, an aborted mission. No one involved wanted an accidental explosion if anything went wrong with the mission. Imagine trying to land a plane loaded with an untested atomic bomb!

Check list for loading charge in plane with special breech plug
(After all D-3 tests are completed)

1. Check that green plugs are installed.
2. Remove rear plate.
3. Insert breech wrench in breech plug.
4. Unscrew breech plug, place on rubber pad.
5. Insert charge, 4 sections, red ends to breech.
6. Insert breech plug and tighten home.
7. Connect firing line.
8. Install armor plate.
9. Install rear plate.
10. Remove and secure catwalk and tools.

Check list for emergency landing.

1. Check that green plugs are installed.
2. Install catwalk.
3. Remove rear plate.
4. Remove armor plate.
   ←------ Disconnect firing line.
5. Insert breech wrench.
6. Unscrew breech plug, (about 16 turns), remove, place on pad
7. Remove charge, 4 sections, place in powder can and secure.
8. Replace breech plug in breech, if there is time.

Source: Atomic Heritage Foundation. Available online at https://www.atomicheritage.org/key-documents/checklist-loading-charge-little-boy-aboard-enola-gay. Accessed April 30, 2019.

41. Memorandum from General Leslie Groves to U.S. Army Chief of Staff George Marshall, August 6, 1945

The U.S. Army recorded its every action—and had through at least two World Wars. It wasn't going to stop now that this one was reaching it explosive conclusion. General Leslie Groves, who had shepherded the Manhattan Project from its first days to this, its day of terrible success, here dispassionately recounts to George Marshall, the architect of Allied victory, the event of the first moments of the atomic age.

6 August 1945

MEMORANDUM TO THE CHIEF OF STAFF

The gun type bomb was ready at Tinian on 31 July awaiting the first favorable weather. The daily 24 hour advance forecasts kept indicating unsatisfactory conditions until 3 August when there was a prediction of possible good weather over the targets for 4 August at 2200Z (5 August 0700 Tinian or 4 August 1800 EWT). Later predictions delayed this a day. At 5 August 0415Z General LeMay finalized the take-off time, final assembly of the bomb proceeded and take-off actually occurred on schedule at 1645Z 5 August. Two B-29's with recording instruments and special scientific observers accompanied the vital plane. The anticipated weather over the targets was not certain to be good but only fair.

One hour prior to the bomb take-off, three B-29's were dispatched for final weather check observations over three of the designated targets. Reports to date do not indicate which three were observed.

Arrangements were made for the vital plane to stage at Iwo Jima to await more favorable weather if that should be deemed desirable. A spare B-29 was dispatched to that point for use as a replacement if that should be necessary.

The target used was Hiroshima, the one reserved target where there was no indication of any POW camp.

The following flash report from the vital plane by Captain Parsons, USN, my chief ordnance expert, was received at Tinian after the attack and relayed to Washington: "Results clearcut, successful in all respects. Visible effects greater than New Mexico test. Conditions normal in airplane following delivery." The plan also radioed "Target at Hiroshima attacked visually 1/10th cloud at 052315Z. No fighters and no flak."

After return of the vital aircraft to base, the message below was sent from Tinian at 0645Z 6 August and received in Washington at 0845Z (4:45 EWT): "Following additional information furnished by Parsons, crews, and observers on return to Tinian at 060500Z. Report delayed until information could be assembled at interrogation of crews and observers. Present at interrogation were Spaatz, Giles, Twining, and Davies.

"Confirmed neither fighter or flak attack and one tenth cloud cover with large open hole directly over target. High speed camera reports excellent record obtained. Other observing aircraft also anticipates good records although films not yet processed. Reconnaissance aircraft taking post-strike photographs have not yet returned.

"Sound—Not appreciably observed.

"Flash—Not so blinding as New Mexico test because of bright sunlight. First there was a ball of fire changing in a few seconds to purple clouds and flames boiling and swirling upward. Flash observed just after airplane rolled out of turn. All agreed light was intensely bright and white cloud rose faster than New Mexico test reaching thirty thousand feet in three minutes it was one-third greater diameter. It mushroomed at the top, broke away from column and the column mushroomed again. Cloud was most turbulent. It went at least to forty thousand feet. Flattening across its top at this level. It was observed from combat airplane three hundred sixty-three nautical miles away with airplane at twenty-five thousand feet. Observation was then limited by haze and not curvature of the earth.

"Blast—There were two distinct shocks felt in combat airplane similar in intensity of close flak bursts. Entire city except outermost ends of dock areas was covered with a dark grey dust layer which joined the cloud column. It was extremely turbulent with flashes of fire visible in the dust. Estimated diameter of this dust layer is at least three miles. One observer stated it looked as though whole town was being torn apart with columns of dust rising out of valleys approaching the town. Due to dust visual observation of structural damage could not be made.

"Parsons and other observers felt this strike was tremendous and awesome even in comparison with New Mexico test. Its effects may be attributed by the Japanese to a huge meteor."

The operational plan provided for three photo planes to cover the target four hours after the drop. No report has yet been received from these.

As of 1020Z, 6 August, G-2 WDGS has not received through FCC or OWI radio intercepts any Japanese broadcasts of exceptional significance.

L.R. Groves,
Major General, USA.

Source: Record Group 77, MED Records, Top Secret Documents, File 5b (copy from microfilm). National Archives.

42. U.S. Government Press Releases on the Occasion of the Hiroshima Bombing and Public Recognition of the Manhattan Project, August 6, 1945

These press releases were carefully prepared by the U.S. Department of War in the weeks before the dropping of the atomic bomb over Hiroshima, Japan, on August 6, 1945. Detailed and surprisingly comprehensive (though lacking, of course, in scientific and security detail), these press releases quickly became the guiding documents for descriptions of the Manhattan Project, their general perspective showing up today in almost every article or book about the project. They have become, one might say, the "received wisdom" about the project, the bedrock information in large part because they were the first. The people who composed them were quite aware that this could happen so developed the press releases with a great deal of care.

42a. White House Press Release on Hiroshima, August 6, 1945

THE WHITE HOUSE
Washington, D.C.
IMMEDIATE RELEASE   August 6, 1945
STATEMENT BY THE PRESIDENT OF THE UNITED STATES

Sixteen hours ago an American airplane dropped one bomb on Hiroshima, an important Japanese Army base. That bomb had more power than 20,000 tons of T.N.T. It had more than two thousand times the blast power of the British "Grand Slam" which is the largest bomb ever yet used in the history of warfare.

The Japanese began the war from the air at Pearl Harbor. They have been repaid many fold. And the end is not yet. With this bomb we have now added a new and revolutionary increase in destruction to supplement the growing power of our armed forces. In their present form these bombs are now in production and even more powerful forms are in development.

It is an atomic bomb. It is a harnessing of the basic power of the universe. The force from which the sun draws its power has been loosed against those who brought war to the Far East.

Before 1939, it was the accepted belief of scientists that it was theoretically possible to release atomic energy. But no one knew any practical method of doing it. By 1942, however, we knew that the Germans were working feverishly to find a way to add atomic energy to the other engines of war with which they hoped to enslave the world. But they failed. We may be grateful to Providence that the Germans got the V-1's and the V-2's late and in limited quantities and even more grateful that they did not get the atomic bomb at all.

The battle of the laboratories held fateful risks for us as well as the battles of the air, land and sea, and we have now won the battle of the laboratories as we have won the other battles.

Beginning in 1940, before Pearl Harbor, scientific knowledge useful in war was pooled between the United States and Great Britain, and many priceless helps to our victories have come from that arrangement. Under that general policy the research on the atomic bomb was begun. With American and British scientists working together we entered the race of discovery against the Germans.

The United States had available the large number of scientists of distinction in the many needed areas of knowledge. It had the tremendous industrial and financial resources necessary for the project and they could be devoted to it without undue impairment of other vital war work. In the United States the laboratory work and the production plants, on which a substantial start had already been made, would be out of reach of enemy bombing, while at that time Britain was exposed to constant air attack and was still threatened with the possibility of invasion. For these reasons Prime Minister Churchill and President Roosevelt agreed that it was wise to carry on the project here. We now have two great plants and many lesser works devoted to the production of atomic power. Employment during peak construction numbered 125,000 and over 65,000 individuals are even now engaged in operating the plants. Many have worked there for two and a half years. Few know what they have been producing. They see great quantities of material going in and they see nothing coming out of these plants, for the physical size of the explosive charge is exceedingly small. We have spent two billion dollars on the greatest scientific gamble in history—we won.

But the greatest marvel is not the size of the enterprise, its secrecy, nor its cost, but the achievement of scientific brains in putting together infinitely complex pieces of knowledge held by many men in different fields of science into a workable plan. And hardly less marvelous has been the capacity of industry to design, and of labor to operate, the machines and methods to do things never done before so that the brain child of many minds came forth in physical shape and performed as it was supposed to do. Both science and industry worked under the direction of the United States Army, which achieved a unique success in managing so diverse a problem in the advancement of knowledge in an amazingly short time. It is doubtful if such another combination could be got together in the world. What has been done is the greatest achievement of organized science in history. It was done under high pressure and without failure.

We are now prepared to obliterate more rapidly and completely every productive enterprise the Japanese have above ground in any city. We shall destroy their docks, their factories, and their communications. Let there be no mistake; we shall completely destroy Japan's power to make war.

It was to spare the Japanese people from utter destruction that the ultimatum of July 26 was issued at Potsdam. Their leaders promptly rejected that ultimatum. If they do not now accept our terms they may expect a rain of ruin from the air, the like of which has never been seen on this earth. Behind this air attack will follow sea and land forces in such numbers and power as they have not yet seen and with the fighting skill of which they are already well aware.

The Secretary of War, who has kept in personal touch with all phases of this project, will immediately make public a statement giving further details.

His statement will give facts concerning the sites of Oak Ridge near Knoxville, Tennessee, and at Richland near Pasco, Washington, and an installation near Santa Fe, New Mexico. Although the workers at the sites have been making materials to be used in producing the greatest destructive force in history they have not themselves been in danger beyond that of many other occupations, for the utmost care has been taken of their safety.

The fact that we can release atomic energy ushers in a new era in man's understanding of nature's forces. Atomic energy may in the future supplement the power that now comes from coal, oil, and falling water, but at present it cannot be produced on a basis to compete with them commercially. Before that comes there must be a long period of intensive research.

It has never been the habit of the scientists of this country or the policy of the Government to withhold from the world scientific knowledge. Normally, therefore, everything about the work with atomic energy would be made public.

But under present circumstances it is not intended to divulge the technical processes of production or all the military applications, pending further examination of possible methods of protecting us and the rest of the world from the danger of sudden destruction. I shall recommend that the Congress of the United States consider promptly the establishment of an appropriate commission to control the production and use of atomic power within the United States. I shall give further consideration and make further recommendations to the Congress as to how atomic power can become a powerful and forceful influence towards the maintenance of world peace.

Source: Public Papers of the Presidents of the United States, Harry S. Truman, 1945–1953. 1966. Document 93. Washington, D.C.: U.S. Government Printing Office.

42b. Henry Stimson's Statement as the Secretary of War, August 6, 1945

WAR DEPARTMENT
Washington, D.C.
IMMEDIATE RELEASE   August 6, 1945
STATEMENT OF THE SECRETARY
OF WAR

The recent use of the atomic bomb over Japan, which was today made known by the

President, is the culmination of years of herculean effort on the part of science and industry working in cooperation with the military authorities. This development which was carried forward by the many thousand participants with the utmost energy and the very highest sense of national duty, with the greatest secrecy and the most imperative of time schedules, probably represents the greatest achievement of the combined efforts of science, industry, labor, and the military in all history.

The military weapon which has been forged from the products of this vast undertaking has an explosive force such as to stagger imagination. Improvements will be forthcoming shortly which will increase by several fold the present effectiveness. But more important for the long-range implications of this new weapon, is the possibility that another scale of magnitude will be evolved after considerable research and development. The scientists are confident that over a period of many years atomic bombs may well be developed which will be very much more powerful than the atomic bombs now at hand. It is abundantly clear that the possession of this weapon by the United States even in its present form should prove a tremendous aid in the shortening of the war against Japan.

The requirements of security do not permit of any revelation at this time of the exact methods by which the bombs are produced or of the nature of their action. However, in accord with its policy of keeping the people of the nation as completely informed as is consistent with national security, the War Department wishes to make known at this time, at least in broad dimension, the story behind this tremendous weapon which has been developed so effectively to hasten the end of the war. Other statements will be released which will give further details concerning the scientific and production aspects of the project and will give proper recognition to the scientists, technicians, and the men of industry and labor who have made this weapon possible.

The chain of scientific discoveries which has led to the atomic bomb began at the turn of the century when radio-activity was discovered. Until 1939 work in this field was world-wide, being carried on particularly in the United States, the United Kingdom, Germany, France, Italy and Denmark.

Before the lights went out over Europe and the advent of war imposed security restrictions, the fundamental scientific knowledge concerning atomic energy from which has been developed the atomic bomb now in use by the United States was widely known in many countries, both Allied and Axis. The war, however, ended the exchange of scientific information on this subject and, with the exception of the United Kingdom and Canada, the status of work in this field in other countries is not fully known, but we are convinced that Japan will not be in a position to use an atomic bomb in this war. While it is known that Germany was working feverishly in an attempt to develop such a weapon, her complete defeat and occupation has now removed that source of danger. Thus it was evident when the war began that the development of atomic energy for war purposes would occur in the near future and it was a question of which nations would control the discovery.

A large number of American scientists were pressing forward the boundaries of scientific knowledge in this fertile new field at the time when American science was mobilized for war. Work on atomic fission was also in progress in the United Kingdom when the war began in Europe. A close connection was maintained between the British investigations and the work here, with a pooling of information on this as on other matters of scientific research of importance for military purposes. It was later agreed between President Roosevelt and Prime Minister Churchill that the project would be most quickly and effectively brought to fruition if all effort were concentrated in the United States, thus ensuring intimate collaboration and also avoiding duplication. As a consequence of this decision, a number of British scientists who had been working on this problem were transferred here in late 1943, and they have from that time participated in the development of the project in the United States.

II.

Late in 1939 the possibility of using atomic energy for military purposes was brought to the attention of President Roosevelt. He appointed a committee to survey the problem. Research which had been conducted on a small scale with Navy funds was put on a full scale basis as a result of the recommendations of various scientific committees. At the end of 1941 the decision was made to go all-out on research work, and the project was put under the direction of a group of eminent American scientists in the Office of Scientific Research and Development, with all projects in operation being placed under contract with the OSRD. Dr. Vannevar Bush, Director of OSRD, reported directly to the President on major developments. Meanwhile President Roosevelt appointed a General Policy Group, which consisted of former Vice President Henry A. Wallace, Secretary of War Henry L. Stimson, General George C. Marshall, Dr. James B. Conant, and Dr. Bush. In June 1942 this group recommended a great expansion of the work and the transfer of the major part of the program to the War Department. These recommendations were approved by President Roosevelt and put into effect. Major General Leslie R. Groves was appointed by the Secretary of War to take complete executive charge of the program and was made directly responsible to him and the Chief of Staff. In order to secure continuing consideration to the military aspects of the program, the President's General Policy Group appointed a Military Policy Committee consisting of Dr. Bush as Chairman with Dr. Conant as his alternate, Lt. General Wilhelm D. Styer, and Rear Admiral William R. Purnell. This Committee was charged with the responsibility of considering and planning military policy relating to the program including the development and manufacture of material, the production of atomic fission bombs, and their use as a weapon.

Although there were still numerous unsolved problems concerning the several theoretically possible methods of producing explosive material, nevertheless, in view of the tremendous pressure of time it was decided in December 1942 to proceed with the construction of large scale plants. Two of these are located at the Clinton Engineer Works in Tennessee and a third is located at the Hanford Engineer Works in the State of Washington. The decision to embark on large scale production at such an early stage was, of course, a gamble, but as is so necessary in war a calculated risk was taken and the risk paid off.

The Clinton Engineer Works is located on a Government reservation of some 59,000 acres eighteen miles west of Knoxville, Tennessee. The large size and isolated location of this site was made necessary by the need for security and for safety against possible, but then unknown, hazards. A Government-owned and operated city, named Oak Ridge, was established within the reservation to accommodate the people working on the project. They live under normal conditions in modest houses, dormitories, hutments, and trailers, and have for their use all the religious, recreational, educational, medical, and other facilities of a modern small city, The total population of Oak Ridge is approximately 78,000 and consists of construction workers and plant operators and their immediate families; others live in immediately surrounding communities.

The Hanford Engineer Works is located on a Government reservation of 430,000 acres in an isolated area fifteen miles northwest of Pasco, Washington. Here is situated a Government-owned and operated town called Richland with a population of approximately 17,000 consisting of plant operators and their immediate families. As in the case of the site in Tennessee, consideration of security and safety necessitated placing this site in an isolated area. Living conditions in Richland are similar to those in Oak Ridge.

A special laboratory dealing with the many technical problems involved in putting the components together into an effective bomb is located in an isolated area in the vicinity of Santa Fe, New Mexico. This laboratory has been planned, organized, and directed by Dr. J. Robert Oppenheimer. The development of the bomb itself has been largely due to his genius and the inspiration and leadership he has given to his associates.

Certain other manufacturing plants much smaller in scale are located in the United States and in Canada for essential production of needed materials. Laboratories at the Universities of Columbia, Chicago, and California, Iowa State College, and at other schools as well as certain industrial laboratories have contributed materially in carrying on research and in developing special equipment, materials, and processes for the project. A laboratory has been established in Canada and a pilot plant for the manufacture of material is being built. This work is being carried on by the Canadian Government with assistance from, and appropriate liaison with, the United States and the United Kingdom.

While space does not permit of a complete listing of the industrial concerns which have contributed so signally to the success of the project, mention should be made of a few. The du Pont de Nemours Company designed and constructed the Hanford installations in Washington and operate them. A special subsidiary of the M. W. Kellogg Company of New York designed one of the plants at Clinton, which was constructed by the J. A. Jones Company and is operated by the Union Carbide and Carbon Company. The second plant at Clinton was designed and constructed by the Stone and Webster Engineering corporation of Boston and is operated by the Tennessee Eastman Company. Equipment was supplied by almost all of the important firms in the United States, including Allis-Chalmers, Chrysler, General Electric, and Westinghouse. These are only a few of the literally thousands of firms, both large and small, which have contributed to the success of the program. It is hoped that one day it will be possible to reveal in greater detail the contributions made by industry to the successful development of this weapon.

Behind these concrete achievements lie the tremendous contributions of American science. No praise is too great for the unstinting efforts, brilliant achievements, and complete devotion to the national interest of the scientists of this country. Nowhere else in the world has science performed so successfully in time of war. All the men of science who have cooperated effectively with industry and the military authorities in bringing the project to fruition merit the very highest expression of gratitude from the people of the nation.

In the War Department the main responsibility for the successful prosecution of the program rests with Major General Leslie R. Groves. His record of performance in securing the effective development of this weapon for our armed forces in so short a period of time has been truly outstanding and merits the very highest commendation.

III.

From the outset extraordinary secrecy and security measures have surrounded the project. This was personally ordered by President Roosevelt and his orders have been strictly complied with. The work has been completely compartmentalized so that while many thousands of people have been associated with the program in one way or another no one has been given more information concerning it than was absolutely necessary to do his particular job. As a result only a few highly placed persons in Government and science know the entire story. It was inevitable, of course, that public curiosity would be aroused concerning so large a project and that citizens would make inquiries of Members of Congress. In such instances the Members of Congress have been most cooperative and have accepted in good faith the statement of the War Department that military security precluded any disclosure of detailed information.

In the appropriation of funds, the Congress has accepted the assurances of the Secretary of War and the Chief of Staff that the appropriations made were absolutely essential to national security. The War Department is confident that the Congress will agree that its faith was not a mistake. Because it has not been possible for Congress to keep a close check on the expenditure of the funds appropriated for the project which to June 30, 1945, amounted to $1,950,000,000, key scientific phases of the work have been reviewed from time to time by eminently qualified scientists and industrial leaders in order to be certain that the expenditures were warranted by the potentialities of the program.

The press and radio of the nation, as in so many other instances, have complied wholeheartedly with the requests of the Office of Censorship that publicity on any phase of this subject be suppressed.

IV.

In order to bring the project to fruition as quickly as possible, it was decided in August 1943 to establish a Combined Policy Committee with the following membership: Secretary of War Henry L. Stimson, Dr. Vannevar Bush, and Dr. James B. Conant, for the United States; Field Marshal Sir John C. Dill and Colonel J. J. Llewellin, for the United Kingdom; and Mr. C. D. Howe, for Canada. The Committee is responsible for the broad direction of the project as between the countries. Interchange of information has been provided for within certain limits. In the field of scientific research and development full interchange is maintained between those working in the same sections of the field; in matters of design, construction and operation of large scale plants information is exchanged only when such exchange will hasten the completion of weapons for use in the present war. All these arrangements are subject to the approval of the Combined Policy Committee. The United States members have had as their scientific adviserRichard C. Tolman; the British members, Sir James Chadwick; and the Canadian member, Dean C. J. Mackenzie.

It was early recognized that in order to make certain that this tremendous weapon would not fall into the hands of the enemy prompt action should be taken to control patents in the field and to secure control over the ore which is indispensable to the process. Substantial patent control has been accomplished in the United States, the United Kingdom, and Canada. In each country all personnel engaged in the work, both scientific and industrial, are required to assign their entire rights to any inventions in this field to their respective governments. Arrangements have been made for appropriate patent exchange in instances where inventions are made by nationals of one country working in the territory of another. Such patent rights, interests, and titles as are exchanged, however, are held in a fiduciary sense subject to settlement at a later date on mutually satisfactory terms. All patent actions taken are surrounded by all safeguards necessary for the security of the project. At the present stage of development of the science of atomic fission, uranium is the ore essential to the production of the weapon. Steps have been taken, and continue to be taken, to assure us of adequate supplies of this mineral.

V.

Atomic fission holds great promise for sweeping developments by which our civilization may be enriched when peace comes, but the overriding necessities of war have precluded the full exploration of peacetime applications of this new knowledge. With the evidence presently at hand, however, it appears inevitable that many useful contributions to the well-being of mankind will ultimately flow from these discoveries when the world situation makes it possible for science and industry to concentrate on these aspects.

The fact that atomic energy can now be released on a large scale in an atomic bomb raises the question of the prospect of using this energy for peaceful industrial purposes. Already in the course of producing one of the elements much energy is being released, not explosively but in regulated amounts. This energy, however, is in the form of heat at a temperature too low to make practicable the operation of a conventional power plant. It will be a matter of much further research and development to design machines for the conversion of atomic energy into useful power. How long this will take no one can predict but it will certainly be a period of many years. Furthermore, there are many economic considerations to be taken into account before we can say to what extent atomic energy will supplement coal, oil, and water as fundamental sources of power in industry in this or any other country. We are at the threshold of a new industrial art which will take many years and much expenditure of money to develop.

Because of the widespread knowledge and interest in this subject even before the war, there is no possibility of avoiding the risks inherent in this knowledge by any long-term policy of secrecy. Mindful of these considerations as well as the grave problems that arise concerning the control of the weapon and the implications of this science for the peace of the world, the Secretary of War, with the approval of the President, has appointed an Interim Committee to consider these matters. Membership of the Committee is as follows: The Secretary of War, Chairman; the Honorable James F. Byrnes, now Secretary of State; the Honorable Ralph A. Bard, former Under Secretary of the Navy; the Honorable William L. Clayton, Assistant Secretary of State; Dr. Vannevar Bush, Director of the Office of Scientific Research and Development and President of the Carnegie Institution of Washington; Dr. James B. Conant, Chairman of the National Defense Research Committee and President of Harvard University; Dr. Karl T. Compton, Chief of the Office of Field Service in the Office of Scientific Research and Development and President of the Massachusetts Institute of Technology; and Mr. George L. Harrison, special Consultant to the Secretary of War and President of the New York Life Insurance Company. Mr. Harrison is alternate Chairman of the Committee.

The Committee is charged with the responsibility of formulating recommendations to the President concerning the post-war organization that should be established to direct and control the future course of the United States in this field both with regard to the research and developmental aspects of the entire field and to its military applications. It will make recommendations with regard to the problems of both national and international control. In its consideration of these questions, the Committee has had the benefit of the views of the scientists who have participated in the project. These views have been brought to the attention of the Committee by an advisory group selected from the leading physicists of the country who have been most active on this subject. This group is composed of Dr. J. R. Oppenheimer, Dr. E. O. Lawrence, Dr. A. H. Compton, and Dr. Enrico Fermi. The Interim Committee has also consulted the representatives of those industries which have been most closely connected with the multitude of problems that have been faced in the production phases of the project. Every effort is being bent toward assuring that this weapon and the new field of science that stands behind it will be employed wisely in the interests of the security of peace-loving nations and the well-being of the world.

Source: Press release by Henry Stimson, August 6, 1945. Ayers Papers, Subject File. Army U.S., Press releases, the atomic bomb and atomic energy. Harry S. Truman Presidential Library and Museum.

42c. Memorandum for the Press from the War Department, August 6, 1945

WAR DEPARTMENT
Bureau of Public Relations
PRESS BRANCH
Tel. – RE 6700
Brs. 3425 and 4860

August 6, 1945

MEMORANDUM FOR THE PRESS:

In response to questions as to the damage accomplished by the atomic bomb dropped on Hiroshima, the War Department announced that it was as yet unable to make an accurate report. Reconnaissance planes state that an impenetrable cloud of dust and smoke covered the target area. As soon as accurate details of the results of the bombing become available, they will be released by the Secretary of War.

END

Source: Hadden, Gavin, ed. 1947. *Manhattan District History*. Book I General, Volume 4, Chapter 8, Part 1. Washington, D.C.: Department of Energy, Office of History and Heritage Resources. Available online at https://www.osti.gov/opennet/manhattan_district. Accessed April 27, 2019.

42d. War Department Press Release on Electromagnetic Uranium Enrichment at Oak Ridge, August 6, 1945

WAR DEPARTMENT
WASHINGTON, D.C.

IMMEDIATE RELEASE

This release is prepared as background information on one of the production areas at Clinton Engineer Works, Oak Ridge, Tenn., and is for use with the story on the Atomic Bomb Project

OAK RIDGE, Tenn. ----- A complicated laboratory apparatus, used in pre-war days to separate light from heavy isotopes of the same element on a sub-microscopic scale, has been transformed under the stimulus of a national emergency into a giant industrial plant to produce the devastating material used in an atomic bomb.

It has been metamorphosed into a plant covering 500 acres. From a mere few feet it has stretched into a length of two miles; instead of sub-microscopic amounts, it turns out uranium 235 (U-235) on a production basis for use against Japan in atomic bombs.

A modern industrial miracle, the plant, as part of the gigantic project known as the Manhattan Engineer District, is situated on a 59,000-acre Government reservation, the Clinton Engineer Works, 18 miles west of Knoxville, which includes the newly-built government-operated town of Oak Ridge with a population of nearly 75,000. The plant is one of two large and one small production units on the area.

Built by the Stone & Webster Engineering Corporation, and operated under government contract by the Tennessee Eastman Corporation, a subsidiary of Eastman Kodak, the plant has a total of 270 buildings of a permanent nature, including five main large chemistry buildings, repair shops, storage, an administration building, two cafeterias, a training school and a host of auxiliary buildings. Its operating personnel totals 24,000.

Construction of the plant began Feb. 2, 1943 and the first units were placed in operation Jan. 27, 1944. The building involved problems of construction and design never before encountered. Since it became the first and only one of its kind in the world, there was <u>no</u> time even to construct a small pilot plant to carry out the methods of separating the uranium atoms under the electromagnetic process as developed by Prof. Ernest O. Lawrence, of the University of California, one of the world's most brilliant experimental physicists, who won the Nobel prize for his invention of the cyclotron, an atom-smashing apparatus.

Credit for the scientific development which made possible a remarkable transmutation from the laboratory into a giant industrial plant in an incredibly short time is largely due to Professor Lawrence, who overcame apparent evidence that the electromagnetic method would <u>not</u> be practical for large scale separation of U-235.

Ripping apart his cyclotron in 1941 and putting the magnet to use in a large mass spectrometer, Professor Lawrence by mid-summer of 1942 had shown that the electromagnetic method might be practical and that a large enough electromagnetic plant might have a critical bearing on the war. Professor Lawrence and his associates were then directed to abandon plans for a pilot plant and re-orient their efforts toward the building of a large industrial plant and placing it in operation in the shortest possible time. Thus followed the production area at Oak Ridge.

Stone & Webster was selected to design and build the plant. General Electric, Westinghouse and Allis-Chalmers were the major suppliers of equipment. The Tennessee Eastman Corporation was picked to operate the plant. Offices were established at the University of California Radiation Laboratory early in 1943. Industrial scientists and engineers worked in closest conjunction with the laboratory's physicists, chemists and engineers to translate data, procedure, techniques and equipment into a practical functioning plant design. Meanwhile, tests of the mechanical and electrical equipment for the plant's installation were carried on at the Radiation Laboratory simultaneously with the construction of the plant at Clinton Engineer Works.

The plant uses a tremendous amount of electric power and this was a compelling reason for its location in the Tennessee valley.

Because of the great scarcity of copper and because time was more precious than gold, millions of pounds of silver were borrowed from the Treasury Department for use as winding coils and bushers for the multitudinous magnets. Silver is as good a conductor of electricity as copper and it is not harmed by the passage of the current. It will be returned after the war is over.

Source: Hadden, Gavin, ed. 1947. *Manhattan District History.* Book I General, Volume 4, Chapter 8, Part 1. Washington, D.C.: Department of Energy, Office of History and Heritage Resources. Available online at https://www.osti.gov/opennet/manhattan_district. Accessed April 27, 2019.

42e. War Department Background Information Press Release on Clinton Engineer Works at Oak Ridge, Tennessee, August 6, 1945

WAR DEPARTMENT
WASHINGTON, D.C.

IMMEDIATE RELEASE

This release is prepared as background information on the town of Oak Ridge, Tenn., the site of the Clinton Engineer Works, one phase of this Government's Atomic Bomb Project.

OAK RIDGE, Tenn. During the past thirty-six months, one of the most remarkable cities in the world has come into being on a site where only oak and pine trees dotting small farms had been before.

In three years, the town of Oak Ridge, 18 miles west of Knoxville, has not only grown from nothing to the fifth largest city in Tennessee, with a population of nearly 75,000, but in the course of this time has managed to become one of the historic cities of America, a town that will ever remain associated with the greatest secret project of World War II.

Oak Ridge is the heart of this Government's Atomic Bomb Project, which, under the camouflaged name of the Manhattan Engineer District, operated by the War Department under the immediate direction of Major General Leslie R. Groves in Washington and Colonel Kenneth D. Nichols at Oak Ridge, succeeded in harnessing atomic energy into the most devastating weapon in history, and in so doing, built a great industrial empire.

Oak Ridge, situated on what is known as Black Oak Ridge, one of five principal oak and pine-covered ridges in the reservation area, was named by Colonel (now Brigadier-General) J. C. Marshall, former District Engineer of the Manhattan District. The name was chosen from among many suggested by workers. General Marshall was succeeded as District Engineer by Colonel Nichols.

Few persons outside of that section of the South in which Oak Ridge is situated and fewer throughout the country knew much about Oak Ridge, even though an industry which was the best-kept secret of the war, was being built around it. In addition to the town's inhabitants, some 200,000 residents of Knoxville knew that Oak Ridge had been built around a vital, secret war project. But they learned to avoid discussions involving secret projects and cooperated in maintaining security. Thousands of workers who had been employed on construction and then left for other parts when they were no longer needed, refrained from overly discussing Oak Ridge and its plants with strangers outside the reservation.

In many respects, Oak Ridge is unique in history. There had been other "hidden" cities, but never one that has grown so swiftly under the pressure of war and secrecy. What is probably most remarkable about Oak Ridge is the fact that the inhabitants themselves, with the exception of a few key men, knew nothing about the city's purpose, what it was built for or what its giant plants were producing. This was not only true of the families of those employed in the plants but also of the workers themselves. The work was so compartmentalized that each worker knew only his own job and had not the slightest inkling of how his part fitted the whole.

Only certain top-ranking scientists, engineers and Army officers knew the full implications of the project, but even in such cases there were limitations. The head of one plant, for instance, was kept completely insulate from other plants where different processes and methods were used.

Not only did the workers not know what they were producing in the mammoth plants that use tremendous amounts of electrical energy, but the vast majority could not be sure they were actually producing anything. They would see huge quantities of material going into the plants but nothing coming out. This created an atmosphere of unreality, in which giant plants operated feverishly day and night to produce nothing that could be seen or touched.

Oak Ridge is the residential center for the workers in one sub-division of the Manhattan Engineer District, known as Clinton Engineer Works. The Clinton Engineer Works covers a high Government reservation of 59,000 acres of which Oak Ridge proper covers more than eight miles. Oak Ridge is the administrative center for the entire Manhattan District, which includes the 631-square-mile Hanford Engineer Works near Pasco, Wash. and other divisions.

The plants at Clinton Engineer Works, where raw material is separated by three different methods, include more than 425 buildings. The town of Oak Ridge has nearly 10,000 family units, 13,000 dormitory spaces, more than 5,000 trailers and more than 16,000 hutment and barracks spaces. Its population of nearly 75,000 makes it the fifth largest in Tennessee, topped only by Memphis, Nashville, Knoxville, and Chattanooga.

The site, acquired in the Autumn of 1942, was chosen because of its accessibility to power and water, its remoteness from the Coast and its isolation. The first family moved into its trailer home on July 3, 1943, and the first house was occupied on July 27 of that year. At the height of its construction period, one thousand houses were built per month.

With the bulldozers, the carpenters, plumbers, and electricians also came books, musical instruments, artists' paint and brushes and all the other paraphernalia of American culture—a culture reflecting every section of the country, for Oak Ridge is an extremely cosmopolitan place, its residents coming from virtually every state in the union.

Simultaneously with the roads and streets, sewers and waterworks went the building of schools, a library, theatres, a hospital, a dental clinic, recreation centers and athletic facilities. By June 1945, the town had one high school and eight elementary schools with another grammar school under construction. At the Spring term of 1945, there were over 11,000 pupils and 317 teachers. The Public Library had around 9,000 books and 10,000 members holding cards. A hospital of 300 beds was built at a cost of over $1,000,000 and a dental service building erected at a cost of $92,000. The total outlay for schools, including several existing rural schools taken over at the start of the work, was $3,700,000.

Hospitalization and medical care is provided through an insurance plan, the worker paying $2 per month for all hospital and medical bills, except home care. Under the direction of Colonel Stafford Warren, formerly professor of Radiology, School of Medicine and Dentistry, University of Rochester, and a staff of Army Doctors, the health, medical and dental facilities ran among the best.

The medical insurance plan is on a voluntary basis and now pays for itself, though it required a subsidy for the first six months. Subscription is by groups, such as chemists, physicists and administrative personnel. The overhead cost is 16 per cent.

More than 300 miles of roads either have been built or improved in the area. Around 55 miles of railroad were built on the project to transport equipment and material. Buses on the area number nearly 350, while an additional 400 buses operate off the area to carry non-resident workers at the project to and from their homes. From July 1944 through June 1945 the on area buses carried 22,252,479 passengers. During June 1945 they carried 2,401,070 passengers.

There are 17 different organized religious bodies at Oak Ridge. At first all worshipped at different times at one Colonial-style little church called Chapel on the Hill which rests against a wooded background. Later, another church building was constructed and a third was in process of being built this summer. A school and theatre auditoriums also are utilized for religious services.

Oak Ridge has 13 supermarkets, nine drug stores and seven theatres. It has 17 major eating facilities, including nine cafeterias, five restaurants and three lunch rooms. There are also a number of minor eating establishments.

Oak Ridge has a high health standard and a low crime record, with hardly any crimes of violence. Its population is probably the youngest age group in the country and has a very high birth rate, believed among the highest in the country.

At the time the War Department took over, there were around 3,750 residents on the land which was taken into the reservation. These were scattered over the entire 59,000 acres, which included the hamlets of Robertsville, Wheat and Scarboro and a large number of small farms on a total of over 800 separate tracts of land.

The area was among the first in Tennessee to be settled and the Government went to great pains to resettle these uprooted families. Many of them took jobs on the site.

The Clinton Engineer Works is bounded on the East, South and West by the tortuously-winding Clinch River for a total distance of 36 miles. Within the reservation, there are five main ridges, running east and west. The northernmost is Black Oak Ridge. Next in order come East Fork Ridge, Pine Ridge, Chestnut Ridge and Haw Ridge, which are wooded with oak and several species of pine trees. The variety of vegetation in this vicinity is said to be wider than anywhere in the United States, the region constituting a meeting ground between northern and southern varieties of flora.

Being near Knoxville, the site is not far from the Great Smoky Mountain area which lies east and southeast of Knoxville. To the west are the Cumberland Mountains. Largest towns beside Knoxville near the area are Clinton, from which the Works derives its name; Herriman and Lenoir City. The project covers part of two counties, Anderson and Roane, with the greater part being in Anderson. It is the heart of the TVA country and is situated about 20 miles from Norris Dam.

The town of Oak Ridge is in the northeastern part of the area about 8 miles from Clinton. One production plant is situated between Pine and Chestnut Ridges. Another area is at the extreme western part of the reservation and is 15 miles from Oak Ridge proper. An experimental plant, the pilot plant for the process at the Hanford Engineer Works, near Pasco, Washington is at the southwestern part of the reservation between Chestnut and Haw ridges. Another process plant is in the area of a huge steam plant.

The total amount of lumber used by the Clinton Engineer Works from the latter part of 1942 to May 1, 1945, was in excess of 200,000,000 board feet, almost the output of the State of Minnesota for an entire year. Around 400,000 cubic yards of concrete were used for foundations and some of the structural frames in the plant areas, or one-eighth the amount of concrete used in Boulder Dam. Around 55,000 cars of material and equipment were shipped to the Clinton Engineer Works from November, 1942 through June, 1945.

During the peak construction period of July and August, 1944, Clinton Engineer Works used 800 pieces of heavy construction equipment, 5,600 of light construction equipment, 2,000 air driver tools, and nearly 6,000 items of automotive equipment, including 1,000 passenger cars, 400 station wagons, 1,300 pick-up trucks, 750 buses and 2,500 construction-type trucks. The total of pieces of equipment used in that period exceeded 14,000 valued at approximately $20,000,000.

Most of the automotive and construction equipment (light and heavy) was obtained from previously-completed war construction jobs by Government transfer, with practically all the major construction pieces obtained from other Corps of Engineer construction jobs.

In July 1945 about 50 per cent of Oak Ridge's population lived in houses and apartments, about 21 per cent in dormitories, another 21 per cent in trailers and about 8 percent in hutments. The houses vary in size but are comfortable, roomy and homey. The Guest House, the town's pleasant two-story Inn, frequently houses many of the world's most distinguished scientists and other persons of note, including Secretary of War Henry L. Stimson during an inspection visit last Spring.

Cultural activities at the project began practically when the first residents moved into their new homes, on which rentals per month range from $22 to $73 for family houses, $10 to $15 monthly per person in dormitories, and $30 to $50 monthly on apartments. The cultural activity includes the Singing Society, the Oak Ridge Community Chorus, the Oak Ridge Community Band and String Orchestra, the Oak Ridge Symphony and the Music Society, which are sponsored by the Oak Ridge Recreation and Welfare Association. There is also the Oak Ridge Artists' Society and a Little Theatre.

Those athletically included formed an Independent Baseball League, Horseshoe Pitching League, Women's Softball League and badminton, tennis, handball, archery and gym groups. Clubs included College Women's, Artist, Chess, Stamp, Duplicate Bridge, Saddle, Model Airplane and state clubs formed by residents from widely scattered parts of the country.

Oak Ridge also has its own weekly newspaper, the Oak Ridge Journal. Like all other cultural and recreational activities at the project, it is backed by the Oak Ridge Reaction and Welfare Association, a non-profit citizens' organization which derives its revenue from self-liquidating recreational enterprises.

Source: Hadden, Gavin, ed. 1947. *Manhattan District History*. Book I General, Volume 4, Chapter 8, Part 1. Washington, D.C.: Department of Energy, Office of History and Heritage Resources. Available online at https://www.osti.gov/opennet/manhattan_district. Accessed April 27, 2019.

42f. Press Release on the Gaseous Uranium Enrichment Plant at Oak Ridge, August 6, 1945

WAR DEPARTMENT
Washington, D.C.
IMMEDIATE RELEASE

This release is prepared as background information on one of the production areas at Clinton Engineer Works, Oak Ridge, Tenn., and is for use with the story on the Atomic Bomb Project.

OAK RIDGE, Tenn. A huge "U"-shaped building housing thousands of complicated pieces of apparatus is the home of the gaseous diffusion process for concentrating uranium (U-235) for use in atomic bombs.

The vast structure and its process equipment represent a scientific and engineering achievement of the first magnitude. It is a monument to the ingenuity and vision of America's top scientists and development engineers, headed by Prof. Harold C. Urey, the discoverer of "heavy water" and Prof. John R. Dunning, both of Columbia University, and P. C. Keith of the Kellex Corporation.

The main building in this vast plant is constructed in the form of a giant letter "U", each side 2,450 feet long, and averaging 400 feet in width and 60 feet in height. The total area of the main building is 5,568,000 square feet.

The plant contains 70 additional buildings, bringing the total area to 600 acres. Those include a conditioning building, a giant in itself, its main floor and basement covering a total ground area of 800,000 square feet. This building "conditions" the equipment before installation. The plant has a repair shop of 400,000 square feet and a special warehouse containing 300,000 different types of spare parts (several hundred of each type).

Development of certain porous barriers necessary in the process was only one of the formidable problems that had to be solved in building this mammoth plant. New types of all kinds of equipment and the most delicate measuring devices were vitally necessary.

As an auxiliary requirement, a huge powerhouse was constructed in the area with a capacity of 238,000 kilowatts, the largest initial single installation of its kind ever built. It has three giant boilers, each producing 750,000 pounds of superheated steam per hour.

A number of the country's leading construction companies participated in the designing and construction of the plant. It was designed by the Kellex Corporation, a subsidiary of the Kellogg Company, and constructed by the J. A. Jones Construction Co. It is operated by the Carbide and Carbon Chemical Corporation. Ford, Bacon and Davis designed and constructed the conditioning building.

Construction of the main process plant started Sept. 10, 1943, and the first units began operating Feb. 20, 1945. The construction forces of this particular phase reached 25,000 on May, 1945. The peak operation force for the process is about 12,000.

Construction of the power plant started June 1, 1943, and began initial operation April 17, 1944. It reached its full generating capacity in July, 1945.

Source: Hadden, Gavin, ed. 1947. *Manhattan District History*. Book I General, Volume 4, Chapter 8, Part 1. Washington, D.C.: Department of Energy, Office of History and Heritage Resources. Available online at https://www.osti.gov/opennet/manhattan_district. Accessed April 27, 2019.

42g. Press Release on the Thermal Diffusion Plant at Oak Ridge, August 6, 1945

WAR DEPARTMENT
Washington, D.C.

IMMEDIATE RELEASE

This release is prepared as background information on one of the production areas at Clinton Engineer works, Oak Ridge, Tenn., and is for use with the story on the Atomic Bomb Project.

OAK RIDGE, Tenn. In addition to two giant plants at the Clinton Engineer Works here which concentrates uranium 235 (U-235) for use in atomic bombs against Japan, there is also a "little plant" which uses the thermal diffusion method for concentrating the raw material.

This plant comprises about 20 structures. The largest building is 525 feet long, 75 feet high and 82 feet wide. The construction was begun July 13, 1944, and completed December 15, 1944. Its first unit started operating, however, on October 13, just three months to a day from the start of construction. Its peak construction force was 1,917 persons and the operating personnel numbered around 2,000.

The research and development work for the plant was done by the United States Naval Research Laboratory and it was designed and constructed by the H. K. Ferguson Company, of Cleveland, Ohio. It is operated by the Fercleve Corporation, an affiliate of the Ferguson Company.

The plant devours many pounds of steam per hour, which is obtained at present from a large power house in the immediate area. An auxiliary steam plant with 12 boilers is now under construction.

The boilers were originally intended for destroyer escorts and were obtained through cooperation of the Navy. They were shipped to Tennessee through inland waterways from Orange, Texas, where they were built.

Source: Hadden, Gavin, ed. 1947. *Manhattan District History*. Book I General, Volume 4, Chapter 8, Part 1. Washington, D.C.: Department of Energy, Office of History and Heritage Resources. Available online at https://www.osti.gov/opennet/manhattan_district. Accessed April 27, 2019.

42h. Press Release on the Hanford Engineer Works, August 6, 1945

WAR DEPARTMENT
Washington, D.C.

IMMEDIATE RELEASE

This release is prepared as background information on the Hanford Engineer Works, one of the phases of the Atomic Bomb Project.

RICHLAND VILLAGE, Wash., -- In this newly-built, pleasant little town 15 miles northwest of Pasco, the inhabitants have good jobs and pleasant Government-owned homes on the banks of the swiftly flowing Columbia River. But when the curtain was lifted on the Atomic Bomb Project, the vast majority of the workers and their families, some 17,000 people, did not have the slightest idea of what they were producing in the gigantic Government plants, some 30 miles away.

Previously no mention was ever made in private conversations of the enormous structures scattered over an area of more than 400,000 acres only a short distance away. Talking to them did not give one the slightest inkling of the reason for existence of the very town they live in, of the force that brought them here from Maine to California.

Hanford Engineer Works, as this particular division of the Project is known, is one of the largest and most unique of the Manhattan Engineer District's war construction units for the production of the raw materials for atomic bombs.

Located in the central portion of the State of Washington, between the Yakima Range and the Columbia River, Hanford Engineer Works lies on an undulating table land containing in the most part an uninhabited region of gray sand, gray-green sagebrush, and dried water courses.

It was constructed in this isolated expanse of wasteland by E. I. du Pont de Nemours & Company, which also has the contract for operating the plant. The scientific research was done under the auspices of Chicago University. The story of its construction and operation is a story of ingenuity, intelligent planning and bold innovations in design and construction in the middle of one of America's greatest deserts. It is a story of action, sacrifice, high morale, and loyal hard-working employees. It is the epic of American industry's and the American workers' answer to the challenge of a great emergency.

The nearest community of any size is Yakima, some 40 miles westward, which has a normal population of about 30,000.

The area owned or controlled through the lease amounts to over 600 square miles. Of this total, 230 square miles are owned by the Government. The remaining property owned is accounted for by certain power and irrigation properties and rights, which were integral with the land and by the acquisition of nearby Richland Village, as a site for a housing development and the administration center.

The manufacturing area is subdivided into three huge areas, and each of these three in turn is again subdivided into sections covering miles of ground. One of the three main areas contains three enormous structures where material is produced. The second area contains three huge chemical plants where the material is purified and concentrated. The third prepares the raw materials.

Before the Project could be built it was first necessary to build housing for the construction workers at Hanford, which mushroomed up practically overnight on the south bank of the Columbia River some eight miles away. This government town grew to 60,000 in the course of two years.

A host of formidable new problems such as science had never faced before had to be overcome in the production of the materials and their chemical purification.

Not only was it necessary to develop an entirely new chemistry for concentrating this material but plants had to be designed for performing all the complicated operations involved by remote control, behind heavy concrete walls to protect the workers completely against even the fear of danger.

When the process was first discovered in March, 1941, and the building of plants for producing it was first contemplated, leaders in chemistry feared that it might take at least five years to develop the chemical methods involved. This would have been too late for use in the war.

Since no more than microgram (one-millionth of a gram) amounts of the material could be made by the methods then available, it became mandatory to work on an extremely small scale of operation, namely, the so-called "ultra-micro scale."

On the basis of those "bits of nothing," the huge chemical plants were designed some 10,000,000,000 times greater in scope.

To do so they had to use a host of chemicals in exact proportions, which meant that they had to be used in quantities of micrograms and fractions of micrograms, within a limit of accuracy of three percent of one microgram.

A human breath weights about 750,000 micrograms, while a dime weights 2,500,000 micrograms.

To achieve this unheard of accuracy in weighing, special laboratory equipment with extremely high sensitivity had to be designed and built.

Work continued on approximately this scale of operation until about January, 1944, at which time milligram amounts became available. Since then the investigations have continued with larger and larger amounts of material. Experiments on a gram scale became possible in March, and experiments on a ten gram scale were begun at the New Mexico Site in July, 1944. After that time the scale became substantially larger.

On the basis of these ultra-micro scale procedures of the Chicago group a pilot plant was built at the Clinton Engineer Works in Tennessee where the chemistry was further developed.

Chemical plants costing many millions of dollars were thus designed, constructed, and put into successful operation on the basis of this early work with only micrograms. This is the first time that a scale up of anything near this amount has been accomplished in an industrial development.

The finished plants at Hanford Engineer Works are huge rectangular structures 800 feet long. They are the most remarkable chemical plants ever conceived or designed by man, where enormous quantities of materials are handled through many successive processes with no human eye ever seeing what actually goes on, except through a complicated series of dials and panels that enable the operators to maintain perfect control of every single operation at all times.

Each operation is performed in a remote cell, and when it is completed the treated material invisibly moves on to the next cell, until at the end of the successive processes the material emerges, ready for the next stage at other plants.

The construction of the Hanford Engineer Works presented innumerable and unprecedented problems which stemmed from several basic requirements established by research and development, engineering design, and policy. The principal factors which created these problems were:

(1) The magnitude of the project.
(2) The distances between the several manufacturing plants to be constructed.
(3) The isolated location of the site.
(4) The time element which demanded that construction proceed without awaiting completion of engineering design or even of the basic research data.
(5) The unusually high quality of construction required in many instances.
(6) The extreme and rigid requirements of military security.

The magnitude of the work of construction is indicated by the following general items selected at random:
- Excavation amounted to 25,000,000 cubic yards of earth, a quantity approximately 1/4 of the earth moved in the construction of the Fort Peck Dam, the largest earth dam ever constructed.
- A total of 40,000 car loads of material were received on the site equivalent to a train 333 miles long which is greater than the distance from Chicago to Louisville.
- More than 780,000 cubic yards of concrete were placed which amount is approximately equal to 390 miles of concrete highway 20 ft. wide by 6 inches thick.
- Excluding railroad rail and special steels, about 40,000 tons of steel were used in building construction which is equivalent approximately to the displacement of a battleship.
- About 1,500,000 concrete blocks and 750,000 cement bricks were used in plant construction or sufficient to build a one foot by six foot wall over 30 miles long.
- More than 11,000 poles were required for the electric power and lighting systems or approximately the number required to build a single pole power line from Chicago to St. Louis.
- More than 8500 major pieces of construction equipment were used.
- Approximately 345 miles of permanent plant roads were constructed on the site which is about the distance from Pittsburgh to Richmond.

The necessity for separating the several areas by relatively great distances from each other and from inhabited areas imposed abnormal problems for transportation of men and materials. These distances are emphasized by the fact that 340,000,000 passenger miles of bus transportation were furnished during the construction phase of the work. This is approximately equivalent to the transportation of 110,000 persons across the United States.

The isolation of the site from any existing centers of population presented serious problems with respect to many phases of construction. Those problems were related primarily to the procurement, transportation, housing, feeding, health, morale, and retention of a maximum total construction force of about 45,000 persons which number was reached in June of 1944.

The urgent need for placing the plant in operation at the earliest possible date precluded the possibility of delaying the start of construction work. In many instances, construction work was in progress during periods when basic research had not been fully developed. Consequently, the burden of construction planning, scheduling, and procurement was extremely great.

Source: Hadden, Gavin, ed. 1947. *Manhattan District History.* Book I General, Volume 4, Chapter 8, Part 1. Washington, D.C.: Department of Energy, Office of History and Heritage Resources. Available online at https://www.osti.gov/opennet/manhattan_district. Accessed April 27, 2019.

42i. Press Release on the Development of the Los Alamos site, August 6, 1945

WAR DEPARTMENT
Washington, D.C.
IMMEDIATE RELEASE
Townsite Established
Near Laboratory

Decision to locate the Atomic Bomb Project Laboratory on a mesa an hour's drive from Santa Fe, N. M., meant that it was necessary for the Army Engineers to construct an entirely new town to house the workers and their families. Primary reason for selection of the isolated site was security.

When the Army took over the property early in 1943 there were a few buildings which had been occupied by the Los Alamos Boys' School. New buildings began going up at once. Today there are 37 in the main technical area and about 200 others on the property used for the Project itself. Three hundred buildings containing 620 family units also were constructed, as well as military barracks, hospital buildings and structures for administrative offices.

Dr. J. R. Oppenheimer, one of the foremost physicists in the country and director of the laboratory, came to the site during early stages of construction. Other scientists and technical workers followed soon after.

Scientific groups which had been working on the project elsewhere in the country moved in rapidly, bringing their equipment with them. The Harvard cyclotron was in operation six weeks after it had reached the site.

Nearest railroad facilities are at Albuquerque and Santa Fe. This made it necessary to truck everything from those cities, at least. The road from Santa Fe is a tortuous one, and in the beginning, the last 18 miles were not paved. This was bad enough for passenger cars, and presented a particularly tough problem in hauling heavy loads.

Today the community has more than 7,000 residents. Slightly less than two thirds are civilian men, women and children and the remainder military personnel. The post commandant is Col. Gerald R. Tyler.

First need of arriving personnel was housing. Various types were constructed, to meet different needs. There are three-room prefabricated, individual houses; three room apartments, eight to a building, and four and five room apartments, four in a two-story unit. There are some hutments, Quonset-type huts and government and personally-owned trailers.

Dormitories have been constructed for unmarried personnel, or persons who do not have their families with them. Rents, for family groups, are based on earnings. Apartments are unfurnished and family groups ordinarily bring their furniture with them, although some items of government furniture have been available.

The community is not unlike any other community of similar population in the United States.

Housewives shop for food for daily meals at an Army commissary where ration points are just as important as elsewhere and a "trading post" offers items needed in every-day life and there are the usual Post Exchange stores.

Personnel living in dormitories eat in mess halls, or in a large cafeteria. There is also a dining room with waitress service.

A "town council" of eight elected members serves in an advisory capacity, meeting with representatives of the project and of the Commanding Officer. There is a school board, appointed by Col. Tyler and Dr. Oppenheimer, which oversees operation of an accredited elementary school and high school. There also is a nursery school for younger children, to permit wives to work on the project.

There is plenty of opportunity for outdoor recreation. The summer months offer a chance to play golf on a nine-hole course built by volunteer labor, or to engage in baseball or tennis. In winter there are skiing and skating. A number of residents own horses.

Two theaters provide movies and a small, local radio station broadcasts news of interest to the community and musical programs. There also is a free library.

A modern fire department is on duty and there is a post hospital.

Groups with kindred interests have been formed. There is a little theater organization as well as singing societies, dance groups, etc. Since a great many of the scientific and technical workers have the same interests there is considerable social activity.

The community may be isolated, but the personnel has not given up living as any American group would anywhere else in the nation.

Source: Hadden, Gavin, ed. 1947. *Manhattan District History*. Book I General, Volume 4, Chapter 8, Part 1. Washington, D.C.: Department of Energy, Office of History and Heritage Resources. Available online at https://www.osti.gov/opennet/manhattan_district. Accessed April 27, 2019.

43. Leaflet Dropped on Japanese Cities, Possibly Starting Slightly Prior to the Nagasaki Bombing, August 9, 1945

Leafletting from the air had long been a part of the Allied war effort, and the run-up to the Hiroshima and Nagasaki bombings was no different. This leaflet was one of a number dropped on Japanese cities during that chaotic time. There is no record that this or any of the others had any impact, but the war effort ethos that had built up over the last four years ensured that every possibility be covered.

ATTENTION JAPANESE PEOPLE
EVACUATE YOUR CITIES

Because your military leaders have rejected the thirteen part surrender declaration, two momentous events have occurred in the last few days.

The Soviet Union, because of this rejection on the part of the military has notified your Ambassador Sato that it has declared war on your nation. Thus, all powerful countries of the world are now at war against you.

Also because of your leaders' refusal to accept the surrender declaration that would enable Japan to honorably end this useless war, we have employed our atomic bomb.

A single one of our newly developed atomic bombs is actually the equivalent in explosive power to what 2000 of our giant B-29s could have carried on a single mission. Radio Tokyo has told you that with the first use of this weapon of total destruction, Hiroshima was virtually destroyed.

Before we use this bomb again and again to destroy every resource of the military by which they are prolonging this useless war, petition the Emperor now to end the war. Our President has outlined for you the thirteen consequences of an honorable surrender. We urge that you accept these consequences and begin the work of building a new, better, and peace loving Japan.

Act at once or we shall resolutely employ this bomb and all our other superior weapons to promptly and forcefully end the war.

EVACUATE YOUR CITIES

Source: Translation of leaflet dropped on the Japanese, August 6, 1945. Miscellaneous Historical Documents Collection, 258. Harry S. Truman Presidential Library and Museum.

44. Excerpt of Assistant Chief of Staff Summary of Activities, August 9, 1945

Even those who knew of the power of the new bombs as a result of the Trinity Test were sobered by the power witnessed through the destruction of Hiroshima and Nagasaki. Yes, the ability to destroy an entire city in a matter of days had already been proven with the bombings of Dresden, Germany, during the previous February, but at no time before had anyone expected that a single bomb could devastate entire modern cities so easily.

No. 307
By Auth.   A. C. of St., G-2
Date   9 Aug 1945
                         WAR DEPARTMENT
                          Office of A. C. of S., G-2
               "Magic"—Far East Summary

1. Hiroshima-Japanese Reports on Atomic Bomb Attack:

   a. At 2155I on 7 Aug the 12th Flying Div (Hq Ozuki, 80 m. SW of Hiroshima) sent to the Air General Army at Tokyo the following report, entitled "Eyewitness Account (and Estimates Heard) of the Sixth Air Army, and of this Division, in regard to the Bombing of Hiroshima (#2 Report)":

   "(1) Report on the bomb used (an estimate) and resulting conditions: A violent, large, special-type bomb, giving the appearance of magnesium, was dropped over the center of the city of Hiroshima this morning by a formation of three or four planes (it is also said that there was only one plane; some say that the bomb was attached to a parachute). It is estimated that, after being dropped from a plane, the bomb exploded as a certain altitude above the ground (500 to 1,000 meters). There was a blinding flash and a violent blast. (Over the center of the city the flash and the blast were almost simultaneous, but in the vicinity of the airfield the blast came two or three seconds later.) Then a mass of white smoke billowed up into the air.

"(2) The flash was instantaneous, burning objects in the immediate vicinity, burning the exposed parts of people's bodies as far as three kilometers away, and setting fire to their thin clothing.

"(3) The blast leveled completely or partially as many as 60,000 houses within a radius of three kilometers, and smashed glass blocks, etc.

"(4) Losses: The majority of the houses within the city were completely or partially leveled. The conflagration spread all over, and many important areas were destroyed by fire. The majority of government buildings were either leveled or destroyed by fire. Many people were injured by burns from the flash and by objects shattered by the blast, particularly by glass fragments, and as far as was observed, [word missing] one third of the residents were either seriously or slightly injured.

"(5) Countermeasures:

"(a) Personnel, aircraft, etc. have been moved underground. (Partially underground [word missing] walls, if they are strong, are all right.)

"(b) We must keep a strict watch even for a small number of planes.

"(c) Planes must be dispersed and their tanks emptied.

"(d) The height of the planes should be lowered (even if it be only the height of the wheels) and the ailerons fixed in place. Walls or valleys should be used to protect planes on the ground."

b. Available parts of a later report from the 12th Flying Div, sent out at 1000I on the 8th, include the following:

(1) "Because conflagration broke out suddenly and the spread of the fire was rapid, we think that 70 or 80 per cent of the people in the city were casualties."

(2) "As a result of the horrible catastrophes brought about by the recent air raid, there appears to be a gradual increase in the circulation of wild and fantastic rumors. Moreover, there have been an increasing number of cases in which the fighting spirit of victims or eyewitnesses has been broken. However, in this prefecture the mobile police officials are doing everything in their power to [words missing] the spread of such frenzied rumors, and are using every means at their disposal to provide against this in advance. In order to calm the people's fears, they are particularly stressing the fact that, even in the recent air raid, those who took refuge immediately in the safe underground shelters escaped injury completely."

c. A Japanese Navy report, transmitted from Kure at 1124I on the 8th but apparently prepared somewhat earlier, includes the following statements:

(1) "The concussion was beyond imagination, demolishing practically every house in the city."

(2) "Present estimate of damage: About 80 per cent of the city was wiped out (destroyed or burned). Only a portion of the western section escaped the disaster. Casualties have been estimated at 100,000 persons."

(3) "Relief squads have been dispatched to the area to assist the Army in rescue operations. About 1,000 Army troops and 10,000 [word missing] medical supplies were moved in by dawn on the 7th." . . .

Source: Record Group 457, Summaries of Intercepted Japanese Messages ("Magic" Far East Summary, March 20, 1942–October 2, 1945), Box 7, SRS 491–547. National Archives.

45. Harry Truman Radio Report, August 9, 1945

Although there had been much ballyhoo over the last few days, there had yet to be anything directly from the president to the people concerning what all Americans now knew was not only the most dramatic and destructive end to a war the world had ever seen but also heralded a new age of much danger and potential. So, as soon as he had returned to Washington, D.C., from the Potsdam conference, Harry Truman sat down at the microphone to address the American people. As one sees in the transcript below, he felt the need to reassure and to explain that structures were being put in place to assure international cooperation and to prevent any necessity of atomic weapons being used again.

My fellow Americans:

I have just returned from Berlin, the city from which the Germans intended to rule the world. It is a ghost city. The buildings are in ruins, its economy and its people are in ruins.

Our party also visited what is left of Frankfurt and Darmstadt. We flew over the remains of Kassel, Magdeburg, and other devastated cities. German women and children and old men were wandering over the highways, returning to bombed-out homes or leaving bombed out cities, searching for food and shelter.

War has indeed come home to Germany and to the German people. It has come home in all the frightfulness with which the German leaders started and waged it.

The German people are beginning to atone for the crimes of the gangsters whom they placed in power and whom they wholeheartedly approved and obediently followed.

We also saw some of the terrific destruction which the war had brought to the occupied countries of Western Europe and to England.

How glad I am to be home again! And how grateful to Almighty God that this land of ours has been spared!

We must do all we can to spare her from the ravages of any future breach of the peace. That is why, though the United States wants no territory or profit or selfish advantage out of this war, we are going to maintain the military bases necessary for the complete protection of our interests and of world peace. Bases which our military experts deem to be essential for our protection, and which are not now in our possession, we will acquire. We will acquire them by arrangements consistent with the United Nations Charter.

No one can foresee what another war would mean to our own cities and our own people. What we are doing to Japan now—even with the new atomic bomb—is only a small fraction of what would happen to the world in a third World War.

That is why the United Nations are determined that there shall be no next war.

That is why the United Nations are determined to remain united and strong. We can never permit any aggressor in the future to be clever enough to divide us or strong enough to defeat us.

That was the guiding spirit in the conference at San Francisco.

That was the guiding spirit in the conference of Berlin.

That will be the guiding spirit in the peace settlements to come.

In the conference of Berlin, it was easy for me to get along in mutual understanding and friendship with Generalissimo Stalin, with Prime Minister Churchill, and later with Prime Minister Attlee.

Strong foundations of good will and cooperation had been laid by President Roosevelt. And it was clear that those foundations rested upon much more than the personal friendships of three individuals. There was a fundamental accord and agreement upon the objectives ahead of us.

Two of the three conferees of Teheran and Yalta were missing by the end of this conference. Each of them was sorely missed. Each had done his work toward winning this war. Each had made a great contribution toward establishing and maintaining a lasting world peace. Each of them seems to have been ordained to lead his country in its hour of greatest need. And so thoroughly had they done their jobs that we were able to carry on and to reach many agreements essential to the future peace and security of the world.

The results of the Berlin conference have been published. There were no secret agreements or commitments—apart from current military arrangements.

And it was made perfectly plain to my colleagues at the conference that, under our Constitution, the President has no power to make any treaties without ratification by the Senate of the United States.

I want to express my thanks for the excellent services which were rendered at this conference by Secretary of State Byrnes, and which were highly commended by the leaders of the other two powers. I am thankful also to the other members of the American delegation—Admiral Leahy and Ambassadors Harriman, Davies, and Pauley—and to the entire American staff. Without their hard work and sound advice the conference would have been unable to accomplish as much as it did.

The conference was concerned with many political and economic questions. But there was one strictly military matter uppermost in the minds of the American delegates. It was the winning of the war against Japan. On our program, that was the most important item.

The military arrangements made at Berlin were of course secret. One of those secrets was revealed yesterday, when the Soviet Union declared war on Japan.

The Soviet Union, before she had been informed of our new weapon, agreed to enter the war in the Pacific. We gladly welcome into this struggle against the last of the Axis aggressors our gallant and victorious ally against the Nazis.

The Japs will soon learn some more of the other military secrets agreed upon at Berlin. They will learn them firsthand—and they will not like them.

Before we met at Berlin, the United States Government had sent to the Soviet and British Governments our ideas of what should be taken up at the conference. At the first meeting our delegation submitted these proposals for discussion. Subjects were added by the Soviet and British Governments, but in the main the conference was occupied with the American proposals.

Our first nonmilitary agreement in Berlin was the establishment of the Council of Foreign Ministers.

The Council is going to be the continuous meeting ground of the five principal governments, on which to reach common understanding regarding the peace settlements. This does not mean that the five governments are going to try to dictate to, or dominate, other nations. It will be their duty to apply, so far as possible, the fundamental principles of justice underlying the Charter adopted at San Francisco.

Just as the meeting at Dumbarton Oaks drew up the proposals to be placed before the conference at San Francisco, so this Council of Foreign Ministers will lay the groundwork for future peace settlements. This preparation by the Council will make possible speedier, more orderly, more efficient, and more cooperative peace settlements than could otherwise be obtained.

One of the first tasks of the Council of Foreign Ministers is to draft proposed treaties of peace with former enemy countries—Italy, Rumania, Bulgaria, Hungary, and Finland.

These treaties, of course, will have to be passed upon by all the nations concerned. In our own country the Senate will have to ratify them. But we shall begin at once the necessary preparatory work. Adequate study now may avoid the planting of the seeds of future wars.

I am sure that the American people will agree with me that this Council of Foreign Ministers will be effective in hastening the day of peace and reconstruction.

We are anxious to settle the future of Italy first among the former enemy countries. Italy was the first to break away from the Axis. She helped materially in the final defeat of Germany. She has now joined us in the war against Japan. She is making real progress toward democracy.

A peace treaty with a democratic Italian government will make it possible for us to receive Italy as a member of the United Nations.

The Council of Foreign Ministers will also have to start the preparatory work for a German peace settlement. But its final acceptance will have to wait until Germany has developed a government with which a peace treaty can be made. In the meantime, the conference of Berlin laid down the specific political and economic principles under which Germany will be governed by the occupying powers.

Those principles have been published. I hope that all of you will read them.

They seek to rid Germany of the forces which have made her so long feared and hated, and which have now brought her to complete disaster. They are intended to eliminate Nazis, armaments, war industries, the German General Staff and all its military tradition. They seek to rebuild democracy by control of German education, by reorganizing local government and the judiciary, by encouraging free speech, free press, freedom of religion, and the right of labor to organize.

German industry is to be decentralized in order to do away with concentration of economic power in cartels and monopolies. Chief emphasis is to be on agriculture and peaceful industry. German economic power to make war is to be eliminated. The Germans are not to have a higher standard of living than their former victims, the people of the defeated and occupied countries of Europe.

We are going to do what we can to make Germany over into a decent nation, so that it may eventually work its way from the economic chaos it has brought upon itself, back into a place in the civilized world.

The economic action taken against Germany at the Berlin conference included another most important item—reparations.

We do not intend again to make the mistake of exacting reparations in money and then lending Germany the money with which to pay. Reparations this time are to be paid in physical assets from those resources of Germany which are not required for her peacetime subsistence.

The first purpose of reparations is to take out of Germany everything with which she can prepare for another war. Its second purpose is to help the devastated countries to bring about their own recovery by means of the equipment and material taken from Germany.

At the Crimea conference a basis for fixing reparations had been proposed for initial discussion and study by the Reparations Commission. That basis was a total amount of reparations of twenty billions of dollars. Of this sum, one half was to go to Russia, which had suffered more heavily in the loss of life and property than any other country.

But at Berlin the idea of attempting to fix a dollar value on the property to be removed from Germany was dropped. To fix a dollar value on the share of each nation would be a sort of guarantee of the amount each nation would get—a guarantee which might not be fulfilled.

Therefore, it was decided to divide the property by percentages of the total amount available. We still generally agreed that Russia should get approximately half of the total for herself and Poland, and that the remainder should be divided among all the other nations entitled to reparations.

Under our agreement at Berlin, the reparations claims of the Soviet Union and Poland are to be met from the property located in the zone of Germany occupied by the Soviet Union, and from the German assets in Bulgaria, Finland, Hungary, Rumania and East Austria. The reparations claims of all the other countries are to be met from property located in the western zones of occupation in Germany, and from the German assets in all other countries. The Soviet waives all claim to gold captured by the Allied troops in Germany.

This formula of taking reparations by zones will lead to less friction among the Allies than the tentative basis originally proposed for study at Yalta.

The difficulty with this formula, however, is that the industrial capital equipment not necessary for German peace economy is not evenly divided among the zones of occupation. The western zones have a much higher percentage than the eastern zone, which is mostly devoted to agriculture and to the production of raw materials. In order to equalize the distribution and to give Russia and Poland their fair share of approximately 50 percent, it was decided that they should receive, without any reimbursement, 10 percent of the capital equipment in the western zones available for reparations.

As you will note from the communique, a further 15 percent of the capital equipment in the western zones not necessary for Germany's peace economy is also to be turned over to Russia and Poland. But this is not free. For this property, Poland and Russia will give to the western zones an equal amount in value in food, coal, and other raw materials. This 15 percent, therefore, is not additional reparations for Russia and Poland. It is a means of maintaining a balanced economy in Germany and providing the usual exchange of goods between the eastern part and the western part.

It was agreed at Berlin that the payment of reparations, from whatever zones taken, should always leave enough resources to enable the German people to subsist without sustained support from other nations.

The question of Poland was a most difficult one. Certain compromises about Poland had already been agreed upon at the Crimea conference. They obviously were binding upon us at Berlin.

By the time of the Berlin conference, the Polish Provisional Government of National Unity had already been formed; and it had been recognized by all of us. The new Polish Government had agreed to hold free and unfettered elections as soon as possible, on the basis of universal suffrage and the secret ballot.

In acceptance—in accordance with the Crimea agreement, we did seek the opinion of the Polish Provisional Government of National Unity with respect to its western and northern boundaries.

They agreed, as did we all, that the final determination of the borders could not be accomplished at Berlin, but must await the peace settlement. However, a considerable portion of what was the Russian zone of occupation in Germany was turned over to Poland at the Berlin conference for administrative purposes until the final determination of the peace settlement.

Nearly every international agreement has in it the element of compromise. The agreement on Poland is no exception. No one nation can expect to get everything that it wants. It is a question of give and take—of being willing to meet your neighbor half-way.

In this instance, there is much to justify the action taken. The agreement on some line—even provisionally—was necessary to enable the new Poland to organize itself, and to permit the speedier withdrawal of the armed forces which had liberated her from the Germans. In the area east of the Curzon line there are over 3,000,000 Poles who are to be returned to Poland. They need room, room to settle. The new area in the West was formerly populated by Germans. But most of them have already left in the face of the invading Soviet Army. We were informed that there were only about a million and a half left.

The territory the Poles are to administer will enable Poland better to support its population. It will provide a short and more easily defensible frontier between Poland and Germany. Settled by Poles, it will provide a more homogeneous nation.

The Three Powers also agreed to help bring about the earliest possible return to Poland of all Poles who wish to return, including soldiers, with the assurance that they would have all the rights of other Polish citizens.

The action taken at Berlin will help carry out the basic policy of the United Nations toward Poland—to create a strong, independent, and prosperous nation with a government to be selected by the people themselves.

It was agreed to recommend that in the peace settlement a portion of East Prussia should be turned over to Russia. That, too, was agreed upon at Yalta. It will provide the Soviet Union, which did so much to bring about victory in Europe, with an ice-free port at the expense of Germany.

At Yalta it was agreed, you will recall, that the three governments would assume a common responsibility in helping to reestablish in the liberated and satellite nations of Europe governments broadly representative of democratic elements in the population. That responsibility still stands. We all recognize it as a joint responsibility of the three governments.

It was reaffirmed in the Berlin Declarations on Rumania, Bulgaria, and Hungary. These nations are not to be spheres of influence of any one power. They are now governed by Allied control commissions composed of representatives of the three governments which met at Yalta and Berlin. These control commissions, it is true, have not been functioning completely to our satisfaction; but improved procedures were agreed upon at Berlin. Until these states are reestablished as members of the international family, they are the joint concern of all of us.

The American delegation was much disturbed over the inability of the representatives of a free press to get information out of the former German satellite nations. The three governments agreed at Berlin that the Allied press would enjoy full freedom from now on to report to the world upon all developments in Rumania, Bulgaria, Hungary, and Finland. The same agreement was reaffirmed also as to Poland.

One of the persistent causes for wars in Europe in the last two centuries has been the selfish control of the waterways of Europe. I mean the Danube, the Black Sea Straits, the Rhine, the Kiel Canal, and all the inland waterways of Europe which border upon two or more states.

The United States proposed at Berlin that there be free and unrestricted navigation of these inland waterways. We think this is important to the future peace and security of the world. We proposed that regulations for such navigation be provided by international authorities.

The function of the agencies would be to develop the use of the waterways and assure equal treatment on them for all nations. Membership on the agencies would include the United States, Great Britain, the Soviet Union, and France, plus those states which border on the waterways.

Our proposal was considered by the conference and was referred to the Council of Ministers. There, the United States intends to press for its adoption.

Any man who sees Europe now must realize that victory in a great war is not something you win once and for all, like victory in a ball game. Victory in a great war is something that must be won and kept won. It can be lost after you have won it—if you are careless or negligent or indifferent.

Europe today is hungry. I am not talking about Germans. I am talking about the people of the countries which were overrun and devastated by the Germans, and particularly about the people of Western Europe. Many of them lack clothes and fuel and tools and shelter and raw materials. They lack the means to restore their cities and their factories.

As the winter comes on, the distress will increase. Unless we do what we can to help, we may lose next winter what we won at such terrible cost last spring. Desperate men are liable to destroy the structure of their society to find in the wreckage some substitute for hope. If we let Europe go cold and hungry, we may lose some of the foundations of order on which the hope for worldwide peace must rest.

We must help to the limits of our strength. And we will.

Our meeting at Berlin was the first meeting of the great Allies since victory was won in Europe. Naturally our thoughts now turn to the day of victory in Japan.

The British, Chinese, and United States Governments have given the Japanese people adequate warning of what is in store for them. We have laid down the general terms on which they can surrender. Our warning went unheeded; our terms were rejected. Since then the Japanese have seen what our atomic bomb can do. They can foresee what it will do in the future.

The world will note that the first atomic bomb was dropped on Hiroshima, a military base. That was because we wished in this first attack to avoid, insofar as possible, the killing of civilians. But that attack is only a warning of things to come. If Japan does not surrender, bombs will have to be dropped on her war industries and, unfortunately, thousands of civilian lives will be lost. I urge Japanese civilians to leave industrial cities immediately, and save themselves from destruction.

I realize the tragic significance of the atomic bomb.

Its production and its use were not lightly undertaken by this Government. But we knew that our enemies were on the search for it. We know now how close they were to finding it. And we knew the disaster which would come to this Nation, and to all peace-loving nations, to all civilization, if they had found it first.

That is why we felt compelled to undertake the long and uncertain and costly labor of discovery and production.

We won the race of discovery against the Germans.

Having found the bomb we have used it. We have used it against those who attacked us without warning at Pearl Harbor, against those who have starved and beaten and executed American prisoners of war, against those who have abandoned all pretense of obeying international laws of warfare. We have used it in order to shorten the agony of war, in order to save the lives of thousands and thousands of young Americans.

We shall continue to use it until we completely destroy Japan's power to make war. Only a Japanese surrender will stop us.

The atomic bomb is too dangerous to be loose in a lawless world. That is why Great Britain, Canada, and the United States, who have the secret of its production, do not intend to reveal that secret until means have been found to control the bomb so as to protect ourselves and the rest of the world from the danger of total destruction.

As far back as last May, Secretary of War Stimson, at my suggestion, appointed a committee upon which Secretary of State Byrnes served as my personal representative, to prepare plans for the future control of this bomb. I shall ask the Congress to cooperate to the end that its production and use be controlled, and that its power be made an overwhelming influence towards world peace.

We must constitute ourselves trustees of this new force—to prevent its misuse, and to turn it into the channels of service to mankind.

It is an awful responsibility which has come to us.

We thank God that it has come to us, instead of to our enemies; and we pray that He may guide us to use it in His ways and for His purposes.

Our victory in Europe was more than a victory of arms.

It was a victory of one way of life over another. It was a victory of an ideal founded on the rights of the common man, on the dignity of the human being, on the conception of the State as the servant—and not the master—of its people.

A free people showed that it was able to defeat professional soldiers whose only moral arms were obedience and the worship of force.

We tell ourselves that we have emerged from this war the most powerful nation in the world—the most powerful nation, perhaps, in all history. That is true, but not in the sense some of us believe it to be true.

The war has shown us that we have tremendous resources to make all the materials for war. It has shown us that we have skillful workers and managers and able generals, and a brave people capable of bearing arms.

All these things we knew before.

The new thing—the thing which we had not known—the thing we have learned now and should never forget, is this: that a society of self-governing men is more powerful, more enduring, more creative than any other kind of society, however disciplined, however centralized.

We know now that the basic proposition of the worth and dignity of man is not a sentimental aspiration or a vain hope or a piece of rhetoric. It is the strongest, most creative force now present in this world.

Now let us use that force and all our resources and all our skills in the great cause of a just and lasting peace!

The Three Great Powers are now more closely than ever bound together in determination to achieve that kind of peace. From Teheran, and the Crimea, from San Francisco and Berlin—we shall continue to march together to a lasting peace and a happy world!

Source: *Public Papers of the Presidents of the United States: Harry S. Truman, Containing the Public Messages, Speeches and Statements of the President April 12 to December 31, 1945*, 212. 1961.Washington, D.C.: U.S. Government Printing Office.

46. Henry Stimson Press Release, August 9, 1945

The interactions with the press since the dropping of the bomb on Hiroshima had been carefully scripted; documents and press releases had been prepared in the weeks prior, held in readiness until the event actually occurred. Even when events, such as a meeting with the president, threw the War Department slightly off script, the PR officers refused to break step. So, they released Stimson's notes as this memorandum for the press.

WAR DEPARTMENT
Bureau of Public Relations
PRESS BRANCH
Tel. – RE 6700
Brs. 3425 and 4860
August 9, 1945

MEMORANDUM FOR THE PRESS:

The Secretary of War, the Honorable Henry L. Stimson, today made the following statement:

The press conference this morning was cancelled owing to an engagement which I had at the White House. I had expected to make some general reflections at the conference in reference to the atomic bomb, and certain specific comment in reference to questions which had been asked. My general reflections were as follows:

Great events have happened. The world is changed and it is time for sober thought. It is natural that we should take satisfaction in the achievements of our science, our industry, and our Army in creating the atomic bomb, but any satisfaction we may feel must be overshadowed by deeper emotions.

The result of the bomb is so terrific that the responsibility of its possession and its use must weigh heavily on our minds and on our hearts. We believe that its use will save the lives of American soldiers and bring more quickly to an end the horror of this war which the Japanese leaders deliberately started. Therefore, the bomb is being used.

No American can contemplate what Mr. Churchill has referred to as "this terrible means of maintaining the rule of law in the world" without a determination that after this war is over this great force shall be used for the welfare and not the destruction of mankind.

My specific statement is as follows:

A great many questions have been asked about the effect of the Atomic Bomb and the Declaration of War by Russia on our military strategy and the size of the Army.

The War Department will, of course, appraise the military situation and the size of the Army in the light of the successful use of the bomb and the new Declaration of War. These possibilities have been in our minds for many months. We shall also give heed to any new factors which may develop from day to day. But we shall not do our duty if we plan for the reduction of the Army by even one man below the number which we believe may be needed for the complete defeat of Japan with the least possible loss of American lives.

My further comments on this subject will be found in a reply on the same subject which I have sent to Senator Johnson.

END

Source: Hadden, Gavin, ed. 1947. *Manhattan District History*. Book I General, Volume 4, Chapter 8, Part 1. Washington, D.C.: Department of Energy, Office of History and Heritage Resources. Available online at https://www.osti.gov/opennet/manhattan_district. Accessed April 27, 2019.

47. Memorandum by General Leslie Groves to Chief of Staff George Marshall, with Marshall's Note to Halt Bombings, August 10, 1945

Imagining the death of probably another hundred thousand civilians were a third atomic bomb to be dropped, President Harry Truman decided that he could not continue the bombings unless absolutely necessary. Coming from the meeting where Truman announced that he was stopping the bombings unless he, personally, gave the OK for continuation, Marshall received this memo from General Groves. He took the occasion to effectively stop preparation for a future bombing, noting on the memo that it was now on hold.

WAR DEPARTMENT WASHINGTON
10 August 1945

MEMORANDUM TO: Chief of Staff.

The next bomb of the implosion type had been scheduled to be ready for delivery on the target on the first good weather after 24 August 1945. We have gained 4 days in manufacture and expect to ship from New Mexico on 12 or 13 August the final components. Providing there are no unforeseen difficulties in manufacture, in transportation to the theatre or after arrival in the theatre, the bomb should be ready for delivery on the first suitable weather after 17 or 18 August.

[signature]
L. R. Groves,
Major General, USA.

[Handwritten over bottom third of paper:]
8/10/45
It is not to be released over Japan without express authority from the President.
G C Marshall

Source: Record Group 77: Records of the Office of the Chief of Engineers, 1789–1999, Series: General Correspondence, 1940–1950. File Unit: 25Q. Item: Memorandum from Major General Leslie Groves to Army Chief of Staff about the Availability of Another Atomic Bomb, 8/10/1945. National Archives.

48. Press Release on Security Measures Protecting the Secret of the Atomic Bomb, August 10, 1945

One of the things that worried the army was the American reaction to revelation of the secret project that had been going on right in their midst. Would they feel they had been lied to or deceived? Or could they be convinced that, even if they had been, it had all been in their best interest? The War Department, as part of the propaganda blitz following the Hiroshima bombing, made sure that this issue was addressed, too.

FUTURE RELEASE
PLEASE NOTE DATE
WAR DEPARTMENT
Bureau of Public Relations
PRESS BRANCH
Tel. - RE 6700
Brs. 3425 and 4850

FUTURE RELEASE
FOR RELEASE SUN-
DAY, AUGUST 12, 1945
For Radio Broadcast after
9:00 P.M., EWT, Saturday, August 11, 1945
ELABORATE SECURITY MEASURES
PROTECTED SECRET OF ATOMIC
BOMB

An intelligence and security organization which operated under such severe and stringent regulations that even representatives of the Federal Bureau of Investigation were required to have special passes for entry into the various installations throughout the country, protected the atomic bomb secret in the three-year period it took to reach the project's objective.

In a release today giving official recognition to the Military Intelligence personnel who pursued their activities anonymously and who played the major part in controlling the intelligence and security aspects of the atomic bomb project, the War Department gave in general outline the story of how the war's best-kept secret was kept. At the same time, the War Department emphasized that security of the project was still of highest importance on all information not officially released.

As an organization within an organization, the Military Intelligence Division of the Manhattan Engineer District was organized under the direct personal supervision of Major General Leslie R. Groves, officer in charge of the atomic bomb project, who was directed by personal letter in 1942 from President Roosevelt to take "extraordinary" steps to maintain security and secrecy.

The organization which General Groves directed to operate as an independent agency outside of G-2 and specifically as a separate unit under the Manhattan District was set up when General Groves selected from the Military Intelligence Division of the War Department two officers to act with and for him in establishing intelligence and security policies. These officers, both of whom have made extraordinary records in the Intelligence Division, were Colonel John Lansdale, Jr., of Cleveland, Ohio, and Lieutenant Colonel W. A. Consodine, of Newark, New Jersey.

They in turn handpicked a group of Intelligence Officers and Agents for what was to be the most difficult security job of all time. This detachment of officers and agents was then assigned to Colonel K. D. Nichols, District Engineer of the Manhattan Engineer District, with Major H. K. Calvert, of Oklahoma City in charge. Major Calvert was later transferred to London to handle foreign intelligence for the project, and Lieutenant Colonel W. B. Parsons, of Seattle, Washington, took command of the detachment.

In an extraordinary departure from usual Army channels, this detachment was responsible directly only to General Groves and Colonel Nichols. Members of the detachment were spread throughout this country from Washington to California and from Maine to Florida with their headquarters at Oak Ridge, Tennessee, site of the Clinton Engineer Works. Red tape was cut, short cuts were taken, formalities done away with. "Protect the Project" became the watchword of the group.

Personnel at all project installations were screened exclusively by the District's Intelligence Division for the elimination of undesirables. Security and secrecy agreements were executed by all and exhaustive loyalty investigations were made of key persons. Elaborate precautions were taken against espionage and sabotage. Every known method to insure production and shipment security was taken advantage of.

Information was compartmentalized so that each person knew only such information as was needed to do his or her part of the job. Army officers themselves were cognizant of only their particular phase of the work. A security of information program was instituted to develop individual responsibility and military police were specially trained for internal and perimeter control of all installations.

As the operations of the Intelligence and Security Division developed, the bulk of the intelligence matters were developed under the supervision of General Groves' Washington office and the security program developed under the supervision of the District Engineer at Oak Ridge. There was complete coordination on both phases.

In a statement, Colonel Nichols declared:

"Regardless of the rank of those connected with Military Intelligence, each member did his part and did it well. The magnificent security job that was done could not have been accomplished without the wholehearted support of all concerned. The G-2 Division of the War Department, the Security and Intelligence Divisions of all nine service commands, office of Naval Intelligence, FBI, and each and every loyal American citizen who worked for the Manhattan District contributed to the success of the security of this project. In fact, America itself gave security to its own greatest project."

END

DISTRIBUTION: Aa, Af, B, Da, Dd, Dg, Dm, E., Ea, N.
8-10-45
1:15 P.M.

Source: Hadden, Gavin, ed. 1947. *Manhattan District History*. Book I General, Volume 4, Chapter 8, Part 1. Washington, D.C.: Department of Energy, Office of History and Heritage Resources. Available online at https://www.osti.gov/opennet/manhattan_district. Accessed April 27, 2019.

49. Japanese Request for Surrender, Transmitted August 10, 1945

With the confirmation, through the Nagasaki bombing, that Hiroshima had been no fluke, the Japanese government was in no position to do anything but sue for peace. They started the process the day after the Nagasaki bombing with messages to the United States sent through Swiss and Swedish intermediaries.

TOP SECRET ULTRA

VJ-1

On 10 August, at 0120 hours Z time, the following message from the Japanese Foreign Ministry was transmitted to Stockholm and Berne:

> "In accordance with the will of the Emperor, who is desirous of saving humanity from the catastrophe of war, the Imperial Government has decided to request that the intentions of the Imperial Government be transmitted to the principal belligerent countries as stated in supplementary circular number 648 paren English text as given in supplementary wire 649 paren and also to transmit the gist of this directly to the Soviet Government through the Soviet Ambassador in Tokyo. In this connection, it is requested that the minister in Switzerland inform at once the U.S. Government and the Government of China and that the minister in Sweden inform Great Britain and Soviet Russia, and that the countries to which you are respectively accredited lend their assistance in obtaining an immediate answer. Please wire back the results at once."

The text of circular 648, mentioned in the above communication, reads as follows:

> "The Japanese Government, being desirous of freeing mankind from the horrors of war and of bringing about an immediate peace, recently requested the good offices of the government of the Soviet Union, which was at that time neutral in the Greater East Asia War, in accordance with the will of his majesty the Emperor. Unfortunately, however, our efforts in this direction saw no fruition.
> Accordingly, in accordance with the will of his Majesty the Emperor, we would now like to cease our participation in the war and bring about a state of peace immediately.
> We have made the following decision. The Japanese Government accepts the joint declaration decided upon and published in common by the leaders of the United States, Great Britain and China—in which declaration it later developed that the Soviet Union had had a part—on the condition that the stipulations of that declaration do not include any demand for alteration of the authority of the Emperor to rule the state.
> The Imperial Government is most anxious to have this made clear to the government to which you are accredited at once, and that there be no error in the above understanding.
> The Imperial Government has the honor to request the Swedish Government to transmit this at once to Great Britain and to the Soviet Union."

TOP SECRET ULTRA

Source: Record Group 457, Records of the National Security Agency/Central Security Service, "Magic" Diplomatic Summaries 1942–1945, Box 18. National Archives.

50. J. Robert Oppenheimer Letter to Henry Stimson, August 17, 1945

This warning from the most important scientist in the United States to one of the prime shapers of American foreign and nuclear policy, though heartfelt and, as it turned out, perceptive, fell on deaf ears. Even if they already knew they couldn't, the leaders of the United States would try as hard as they could to maintain a hegemony over atomic technology. That, of course, failed: It would be only a short four years and almost two weeks from the date of this letter until the Soviet Union exploded its own atomic bomb.

F: To the Secretary of War

August 17, 1945

Dear Mr. Secretary

The Interim Committee has asked us to report in some detail on the scope and program of future work in the field of atomic energy. One important phase of this work is the development of weapons; and since this is the problem which has dominated our war time activities, it is natural that in the field our ideas should be most definite and clear, and that we should be most confident of answering adequately the questions put to us by the committee. In examining these questions we have, however, come on certain quite general conclusions, whose implications for national policy would seem to be both more immediate and more profound than those of the detailed technical recommendations to be submitted. We, therefore, think it appropriate to present them to you at this time.

1. We are convinced that weapons quantitatively and qualitatively far more effective than now available will result from further work on these problems. This conviction is motivated not alone by analogy with past developments, but by specific projects to improve and multiply the existing weapons, and by the quite favorable technical prospects of the realization of the super bomb.
2. We have been unable to devise or propose effective military countermeasures for atomic weapons. Although we realize that future work may reveal possibilities at present obscure to us, it is our firm opinion that no military countermeasures will be found which will be adequately effective in preventing the delivery of atomic weapons. The detailed technical report in preparation will document these conclusions, but hardly alter them.
3. We are not only unable to outline a program that would assure to this nation for the next decades hegemony in the field of atomic weapons; we are equally unable to insure that such hegemony, if achieved, could protect us from the most terrible destruction.
4. The development, in the years to come, of more effective atomic weapons, would appear to be a most natural element in any national policy of maintaining our military forces at great strength, nevertheless we have grave doubts that this further development can contribute essentially or permanently to the prevention of war. We believe that the safety of this nation—as opposed to its ability to inflict damage on an enemy power—cannot lie wholly or even primarily in its scientific or technical prowess. It can be based only on making future wars impossible. It is our unanimous and urgent recommendation to you that, despite the present incomplete exploitation of technical possibilities in this field, all steps be taken, all necessary international arrangements be made, to this one end.
5. We should be most happy to have you bring these views to the attention of other members of the Government, or of the American people, should you wish to do so.

Very sincerely,

J. R. Oppenheimer

For the Panel

Source: Secretary of War, August 17, 1945. J. Robert Oppenheimer papers, 1799–1980, Manuscript Division, Library of Congress.

51. Norman Ramsey Undated Letter to J. Robert Oppenheimer, Probably About August 22, 1945

Physicist Norman Ramsey had been pried away from work for the War Department in Washington, D.C., to work at Los Alamos on the Manhattan Project. He was part of the group personally selected and recruited by J. Robert Oppenheimer. Like Leó Szilárd and many others, he was thinking of the future of the bomb even before the first one was exploded, though from a different perspective. In this letter, handwritten and, one assumes, hand delivered, he writes of what he believed needed to be done before another Fat Man bomb (which he had worked on) be used and what he knew of the Nagasaki raid.

<u>Secret</u>

Dear Robert:

This is another lengthy long hand letter with copies to no one. Unfortunately the only means of communication with you in which I have any real influence are these personally delivered letters. All significant developments here which are reportable by telecon have been so reported. Nevertheless it is clear from the message we have received from Y that these reports are not being forwarded to Y [Los Alamos] from Washington. In one case we received a number of questions from Y almost all of which were answered in those separate telecons which were transmitted three, four, and five days respectively earlier than your questions. Two of these messages were explicitly addressed to you. If it should become necessary to continue our operations, it is in my opinion essential that communication between here and Y be drastically improved, perhaps with direct uncensored transmission of messages being authorized. I apologize for the failure of information from here to reach you, but both [illegible] surprising if the 509th lost the Green Hornet C-54's now that the war is over and transportation is so jammed. Without these we would probably have to wait quite a while for even a boat. Also some people are worried about reservation of moving vans away from site Y.

Our experience in the delivery of the fat man has convinced almost all of us of the importance of one much needed improvement. It is in my opinion essential that any atomic bomb to be used in any fair quantity must be capable of being completely protected against even a slight possibility of a nuclear explosion being detonated by fire in take off of the aircraft. This will be particularly true later when atomic bombs are available in sufficient quantity that one can not safely gamble the safety of the base on merely the low probability of a fire on a single takeoff and when one can afford even a small loss of reliability to ensure the protection of the home base. Only twice since I have been here have I been even slightly worried or nervous but both of these times the intensity of my worry made up for the relative calm of the other periods. One of the bad times was during the two hour interval between the scheduled time of the report from Ashworth on the Nagasaki raid and the time of the actual report. However, the worst period was that between the time the B-29 engines with the fat man were cranked up and the time the plane was well clear of the island. The night before the takeoff four planes in succession crashed in takeoff at the other end of the island—in fact the situation got so bad a mission of 100 planes was cancelled after only 30 got off the ground. Since I have been here I have watched several fires resulting from crashes. By actual timing a very intense gasoline fire continues for over twenty minutes. Six of eight fire engines working on such a fire don't even make a dent. After witnessing such fires and after having sweated out one FM [Fat Man] atomic bomb take off, I can't urge too strongly the importance of complete nuclear safety in take off for future models. The only sure ways I have been able to think of is a trap door model with a cylindrical plug through the HE [high explosive] so that the active material can be inserted in flight or the insertion of neutral material in the open space of a non-Christy. I realize the difficulty of this especially with a non-Christy model. However, I feel that this feature is so important that with future great abundance of active material even a loss in efficiency and reliability to achieve it is justified. The one FM take off has been my most unpleasant experience since joining the project.

I also think that serious thought should be given to the means whereby from now on the United States can remain in a state of readiness in which an atomic bomb could be delivered to any place in the world on a moment's notice. To establish a base similar to our present one at Tinian would take a long time. My own preference would be to have the main base in the United States with all equipment necessary for establishing a forward base being air transportable and being held in reserve along with the necessary air transports at the U.S. base. This would be especially applicable if the units could be made completely safe against a possible nuclear explosion resulting from a crash. In this case I would strongly recommend assembly and loading at the U.S. base with only staging occurring at the advanced base. As more material becomes available we could afford a sacrifice in reliability to achieve this and could even avoid the need for a loading pit at the advanced base by having all planes including the spare ones carry units.

LeMay and Tibbets have been proposing some post war Air Force proposals to send to Eaker. You'd better make sure that there are properly coordinated with future bomb development plans before the Air Force goes too far. At present their proposals (which I believe have not yet been sent in) call for the establishment of an atomic bomb wing based in the Palm Springs-Victorville area and capable of delivering atomic bombs to any place in the world. This location would be all right if Y moves to Pasadena but I at least have heard nothing official on such a move. I suggest that you watch out that the tail does not wag the dog and that the future location of Project Y is not determined by an Air Force action.

I am sure by now that you have heard the full story on the Hiroshima mission, but in case you have not been fully informed about the Nagasaki one, I shall summarize it. Our original schedule called for take off on the morning of 11 August local time (10 August Washington time). However on the evening of 7 August we concluded that we could safely move the date to 10 August. When we proposed this to Tibbets he said it was too bad we could not advance the date still another day since good weather was forecast for 9 August with at least five days of bad weather forecast to follow. We agreed to try with the understanding we might miss our schedule since we were unwilling to speed any operation which might conceivably affect either safety or reliability. Finally at 11 PM on August 8 the unit was in the plane and completely & thoroughly checked out. Take off was at about 300 AM. We all aged ten years until the plane cleared the Island. We were scheduled to receive a strike report at 10:30 AM 9 August, but all we had until 1230 was very the very worried query from the fastax [aircraft with high-speed cameras] ship, "Did the strike plane abort?" Finally we received the message from Ashworth that the secondary target had been bombed largely by radar and that at least technically the unit functioned even better than Hiroshima although there was some doubt as to the location of the bomb. We learned later that the strike plane had its first trouble in making its rendezvous with the fastax plane. Although it was supposed to wait not over fifteen minutes at the rendezvous point at the coast of Japan it kept seeing approaching B-29's on another mission each one of which it would think initially was the fastax plane. In this way the strike plane actually lost 50 minutes. It then made three attempts to bomb the primary target, but on each occasion a cloud interfered. This took another fifty minutes. As its fuel was then getting lower it then went to Nagasaki, making a necessary shortcut which carried it over enemy territory most of the way instead of over the usual water routes. It was then clear that there was enough gas for only one run and not enough gas to carry the unit on to Okinawa (Iwo [Jima] was closed in with bad weather). It was therefore decided to drop either by radar or visually. A radar run was made in the course of which the bombardier got one visual check. The bomb was released & hit apparently approximately over the Mitsubishi steel works. However, it was days later before the weather cleared enough for good photo recon pictures to be taken so that we could learn what a really lucky shot it was. The drop was far away from the aiming point but was at probably an even better position than the aiming point since at the time of the selection of the aiming point it was not certain that the extent of the destruction would be as good as that actually obtained. The bomb apparently detonated somewhat north of the Mitsubishi Steel and Arms Works. All other factories and buildings on the Urahami River from the Nakajima Gawa River through the Mitsubishi Urahami Ordnance Plant were destroyed. The distance from the northernmost factory that was destroyed to the southern boundary of complete destruction was about three miles and damage might have occurred north of the Urahami Ordnance Plant if any buildings had been there. Although only 44% of the city was destroyed by the official record this is due to the unfavorable shape of the city and not to the location of the bomb detonation. The most conspicuously factory section of the city was the section destroyed. Good pressure records were obtained on the mission and copies of these curves are being forwarded to you by Alvarez. No fastax pictures were obtained due to the failure of that plane to make its rendezvous. The fastax film from Hiroshima is being forwarded by Waldman for further study at Y. A complete set of photo recon pictures of both Hiroshima and Nagasaki before and after the strike is being forwarded to you by Baker (directly I hope but Kirkpatrick may insist that your set go through Groves first). That Nagasaki picture is of very poor quality since the original negative is now in Washington. The extent of the damage is much clearer on prints made from the original negative.

I think that on the whole things have gone remarkably well. Up to 19 August this was the most successful and best managed field party that I have ever seen or heard of. Everyone did a really excellent job and the whole organization worked beautifully as a unit. Unfortunately, the orders requiring us to stop [assembly work] on after 20 August made a bad anti-climax. However, since then we have tried to make the best of a sad situation. I hope that you can do something to get us home. Everyone deserves at least this much of a reward.

I'm sorry that this letter has been so tediously long.

Sincerely,
Norman

Source: Library of Congress, J. Robert Oppenheimer Papers, Box 60, Ramsey, Norman.

52. Transcript of Telephone Conversation between General Leslie Groves and Lieutenant Colonel Charles E. Rea, August 25, 1945

Wartime can warp one's sensibilities, especially about the enemy and about public relations. This telephone conversation, horrifying in its insensitivity concerning the painful deaths still occurring at Hiroshima and Nagasaki in Japan, depicts not so much the callousness of the speakers, though that is certainly evident, but the remorseless logic of a system that had been set up for one goal—victory—and that could not stop even once that was achieved.

MEMORANDUM of Telephone Conversation between General Groves and Lt. Col. Rea, Oak Ridge Hospital, 9:00 a.m., 25 August 1945.

G: " . . . which fatally burned 30,000 victims during the first two weeks following its explosion."

R: Ultra-violet—is that the word?

G: Yes.

R: That's kind of crazy.

G: Of course, it's crazy—a doctor like me can tell that. "The death toll at Hiroshima and at Nagasaki, the other Japanese city blasted atomically, is still rising, the broadcast said. Radio Tokyo described Hiroshima as a city of death. 90% of its houses, in which 250,000 had lived, were instantly crushed." I don't understand the 250,000 because it had a much bigger population a number of years ago before the war started, and it was a military city. "Now it is peopled by ghost parade, the living doomed to die of radioactivity burns."

R: Let me interrupt you here a minute. I would say this: I think it is good propaganda. The thing is these people got good and burned—good thermal burns.

G: That's the feeling I have. Let me go on here and give you the rest of the picture. "So painful are these injuries that sufferers plead: 'Please kill me,' the broadcast said. No one can ever completely recover."

R: This has been in our paper, too, last night.

G: Then it goes on: "Radioactivity caused by the fission of the uranium used in atomic bombs is taking a toll of mounting deaths and causing reconstruction workers in Hiroshima to suffer various sicknesses and ill health."

R: I would say this: You yourself, as far as radioactivity is concerned, it isn't anything immediate, it's a prolonged thing. I think what these people have, they just got a good thermal burn, that's what it is. A lot of these people, first of all, they don't notice it much. You may get burned and you may have a little redness, but in a couple of days you may have a big blister or a sloughing of the skin, and I think that is what these people have had.

G: That is brought out a little later on. Now it says here: "A special news correspondent of the [Japanese] said that three days after the bomb fell, there were 30,000 dead, and two weeks later the death toll had mounted to 60,000 and is continuing to rise." One thing is they are finding the bodies.

R: They are getting the delayed action of the burn. For instance, at the Coconut Grove, they didn't all die at once, you know—they were dying for a month afterward.

G: Now then, he says—this is the thing I wanted to ask you about particularly—"An examination of soldiers working on reconstruction projects one week after the bombing showed that their white corpuscles had diminished by half and a severe deficiency of red corpuscles."

R: I read that, too—I think there's something hookum about that.

G: Would they both go down?

R: They may, yes—they may, but that's awfully quick, pretty terrifically quick. Of course, it depends—but I wonder if you aren't getting a good dose of propaganda.

G: Of course, we are getting a good dose of propaganda, due to the idiotic performance of the scientists and another one who is also on the project, and the newspapers and the radio wanting news.

R: Of course, those [Japanese] scientists over there aren't so dumb either and they are making a play on this, too. They evidently know what the possibility is. Personally, I discounted an awful lot of it, as it's too early, and in the second place, I think that a lot of these deaths they are getting are just delayed thermal burns.

G: You see what we are faced with. Matthias is having trouble holding his people out there.

R: Do you want me to get you some real straight dope on this, just how it affects them, and call you back in just a bit?

G: That's true—that's what I want. Did you also see anything about the Geiger counter? It says that the fact that the uranium had permeated into the ground has been easily ascertained by using a Geiger counter and it has been disclosed that the uranium used in the atomic bomb is harmful to human bodies. Then it talks about this, which is just the thing that we thought—The majority of injured persons received burns from powerful ultra-violet rays and those within a two-kilometer radius from the center received burns two or three times, which, I suppose, is second or third degree. Those within three to four kilometers received burns to the extent that their skin is burned bright red, but if these burns are caused by ultra-violet, they hardly felt the heat, at that time. Later, however, blisters formed resulting in dropsy.

R: That's why I say it's got to be a thermal burn.

G: Then they talk about the burned portions of the bodies are infected from the inside.

R: Well, of course, any burn is potentially an infected wound. We treat any burn as an infected wound. I think you had better get the anti-propagandists out.

G: We can't, you see, because the whole damage has been done by our own people. There is nothing we can do except sit tight. The reason I am calling you is because we can't get hold of Ferry and because I might be asked at any time and I would like to be able to answer. Did you see about the Army men who had received burns on reconstruction? "Examination of 33 servicemen, of whom 10 had received burns in reconstruction projects, one week after the bombing took place, showed those with burns had 3150 white corpuscles and others, who were apparently healthy, had 3800, compared to the ordinary healthy person who has 7,000 to 8,000." This is a drastic decrease. Comes over from Tokyo. On the other hand, servicemen with burns had only 3,000,000 red corpuscles and others apparently healthy had just a little bit more when compared to 4,500,000 to 5,000,000 in the ordinary healthy person. What is that measured by?

R: You go by cubic millimeters. I would say this right off the bat. Anybody with burns, the red count goes down after a while, and the white count may go down, too, just from an ordinary burn. I can't get too excited about that.

G: We are not bothered a bit, excepting for what they are trying to do is create sympathy. The sad part of it all is that an American started them off.

R: Let me look it up and I'll give you some straight dope on it.

G: This is the kind of thing that hurts us—"The Japanese, who were reported today by Tokyo radio, to have died mysteriously a few days after the atomic bomb blast, probably were victims of a phenomenon which is well known in the great radiation laboratories of America." That, of course, is what does us the damage.

R: I would say this: You will have to get some big-wig to put a counter-statement in the paper.

Source: Department of Energy OpenNet. http://www.osti.gov/opennet. Accessed May 14, 2019.

53. Message from General Thomas Farrell to General Leslie Groves on Nagasaki Damage, September 14, 1945

The members of the Manhattan Project wanted to know as much as they could about the impact of the bombs. General Thomas Farrell, who was Manhattan Project head General Leslie Groves's top aide, was sent to Japan to lead the effort to learn as much as possible about the impact of the bomb. The message below was meant to keep Groves up-to-date on what Farrell and his team were learning.

**WAR DEPARTMENT
CLASSIFIIED MESSAGE CENTER
INCOMING CLASSIFIED MESSAGE**
SECRET IVI
OPERATIONAL PRIORITY

From: Commander in Chief Army Forces Pacific Advance Yokohama, Japan
To: Commander in Chief Army Forces Pacific Administration Manila Philippines
Nr: CAX 51948   14 September 1945

From GHQ CINCAFPAC Adv to WARCOS info 313th Bomb Wing Tinian pass to Ashworth cite CAX 51948, N8N pls pass the info.

Message for Groves from Farrel [sic].

We finished preliminary inspection of Nagasaki today. In many ways the effects of the explosion there are more spectacular and startling than Hiroshima. One gets the impression of a much greater power of the blast. The destruction of heavy industrial buildings, gas storage tanks, and many reinforced concrete structures within a 2000 foot radius indicate the greater power. The destruction of the huge steel works by blast and fire and the destruction of the torpedo works by blast alone gives outstanding proof of the enormous amount of blast energy released. In all cases the steel frames and buildings are pushed away from the point of detonation. The larger distance of destruction of worker houses indicates <u>a blast energy about twice</u> that at Hiroshima.

The rugged terrain including steep hills and deep ravines provided much shielding but the blast turned and followed the ravines so that the damage extended in a greater or lesser degree to the entire city. The blow was struck in an area largely industrial and left a large part of the residential area more or less standing.

Because of the fact Nagasaki is still alive and functioning while Hiroshima is flat and dead.

Point of burst was determined from directional effects of charging on telephone poles. Approximate position is 1000 feet northeast of center of stadium. Japanese state burst was at 500 meters. All distances hereafter given from point on ground below our estimated point of burst. Preliminary survey of blast shows radius of complete demolition of Japanese worker homes 8000 feet. Roofs collapsed, walls smashed but partly standing for all workers homes up to two miles radius except in special cases where local topography gave exceptional shielding. Some roof damage to tiles of heavy type observed up to three miles. Plaster and glass damage to much greater distances. Many excellent examples of thin brick walled structures, thick brick walls concrete, and reinforced concrete structures have been found and are being studied. Nine inch reinforced concrete walls destroyed to 2000 feet. Brick smokestacks displaced, cracked, and overturned up to 4000 feet. A prison was demolished at a distance of 1000 feet. Its walls were of eight inch concrete. Northern Ordnance factory, distance 4000 feet, was stripped of corrugated iron walls and roof, window sash were pushed out, and framework destroyed and overturned.

These structures were of light type of steel frame construction. South factory similarly destroyed, but in addition was covered by fire. Fire damage is heavy in region from prefectural office in south of northern Ordnance factory. Length of burned area three miles, width 6000 feet in northern part of city. Hills north, east, and west of this scorched by radiant heat at distance of 7000 feet.

The Japanese official report that any one who entered the blast area from outside after the explosion has become sick.

Warren and Nolan have not yet arrived from Hiroshima due to bad weather and poor transportation. Warren's party coming by water have not yet reached Nagasaki. A Naval doctor on board the hospital ship Haven has taken samples of dirt, wood and metal from all over the blast area and has made a check for radio activity. No evidence was disclosed of any radioactivity in the materials collected. Report will be sent to you as soon as Warren can make a detailed check.

The Japanese report no destruction to shipping in the harbor except minor damage to superstructures including broken glass. At time of explosion there were about 100 ships and small boats in the harbor of which about 1/3 were over 100 tons in size. No destructive wave was produced. There was not crater under the point of bursts and no fusing of the ground. Japanese officials state that the reported crater near the harbor area was the result of earlier bombings in July.

The following is a brief summary of the Japanese official report of the explosion. At a radius of one kilometer all were killed, those outside by burning, those inside by falling timber and burning. Between one kilo and two kilos radius almost all persons were killed by either concussion or head. All buildings were knocked down and burned. Between two kilos and four kilos about half were killed and about half wounded by burning or missiles. Nearly all buildings were destroyed. Between four kilos and eight kilos about half wounded and half remained uninjured. About half buildings destroyed. Between eight kilos and fifteen kilos few were wounded. Glass was broken and tiles loosened.

Areas behind hills were protected. Casualties rptd and dead 19,743, missing 1,927, wounded 40,993. Houses blasted and burned 11,494, houses blasted not burned 2,652, houses half burned 150 and houses half blasted 5,291. At least 50,000 houses which includes practically every home in Nagasaki had at least minor damage such as broken glass. 10 large factories were destroyed. 19 schools and colleges were destroyed. One prison completely destroyed and burned. At least 15 other major bldgs were destroyed and great damage was done to telephone, telegraph, public water supply, railways and ships of all kinds. Detailed rpts of the explosion by Japanese officials give a story quite close to what we would expect from our knowledge of the operation. The population of Nagasaki at the time of the blast is reported at approximately 280,000. Wounded are now dying at the rate of 20 per day. The Japanese report a considerable number have died up to September 1st who did not seem to be wounded originally.

I will bring you further details on Hiroshima and Nagasaki.

I expect to return to the States by air as soon as I can get transportation. Kirkpatrick will return to the states in a few days.

End.

Note: This message received by AGWAR as retransmission from CINCAFPAC Admin under DTG 141845Z.
ACTION: Gen Groves
INFO: Gen Arnold; Gen Hull; Gen Bissell; C of S
CM-IN-12071 (15 Sep 45) DTG fpc 141203Z
SECRET

Source: Record Group 77, Tinian Files, April–December 1945, Box 17, Envelope B. National Archives.

54. Press Release of President Harry Truman's Request for Press Assistance in Assuring Secrecy on the Manhattan Project, September 14, 1945

Even after all of the publicity, much of it government promoted, surrounding the Hiroshima and Nagasaki bombings in Japan and the unveiling of the Manhattan Project, the need for secrecy concerning nuclear issues remained—something even those who wanted to shift responsibility for nuclear arms and power to the international community appreciated. However, the idea that a U.S. president could actually send American newspaper editors a message and expect not only for the message itself to be kept secret but for the editors to cooperate with the government on keeping secret aspects of one of the biggest stories of a generation would be beyond belief, today. At that time, coming at the end of four years of necessary government secrecy in wartime, such cooperation was not only expected but found.

WAR DEPARTMENT
Bureau of Public Relations

PRESS BRANCH
Tel. - RE 6700
Brs. 3425 and 4860
September 14, 1945

C O N F I D E N T I A L - - N O T F O R
P U B L I C A T I O N
N O T E T O E D I T O R S

The following memorandum is CONFIDENTIAL and NOT FOR PUBLICATION:

The President of the United States today made the following request for the cooperation of American editors and broadcasters and the public in protecting the secret of the atomic bomb. The President said that his action was in the national interest and not with any idea of imposing censorship upon the press or radio.

The request, herewith communicated to you in confidence, is as follows:

"In the interest of the highest national security, editors and broadcasters are requested to withhold information (beyond the official releases) without first consulting with the War Department, concerning scientific processes, formulas, and mechanics of operation and techniques employed in the operational use of the atomic bomb; location, procurement and consumption of uranium stocks; quality and quantity of production of these bombs; their physics and characteristics; and information as to the relative importance of the various methods or plants, or of their relative functions or efficiencies."

DISTRIBUTION: A, B, C, D, E, F, L, M, N.

Source: Hadden, Gavin, ed. 1947. *Manhattan District History*. Book I General, Volume 4, Chapter 8, Part 1. Washington, D.C.: Department of Energy, Office of History and Heritage Resources. Available online at https://www.osti.gov/opennet/manhattan_district. Accessed April 27, 2019.

55. J. Robert Oppenheimer's Speech to the Association of Los Alamos Scientists, November 2, 1945

Perhaps the best known of the fathers of the atomic bomb, Oppenheimer had been instrumental in the success of the Manhattan Project from his perch at the Los Alamos Laboratory in New Mexico. In this talk to fellow scientists months after the war had ended, Oppenheimer said that they all had "to re-consider the relations between science and common sense," echoing Leó Szilárd's earlier concerns that there can be too much concentration on science and not enough on its place in the world—its consequences. Also in this talk, Oppenheimer raises concerns about the "unilateral responsibility for the handling of atomic weapons" the United States was assuming, a course he assumed, correctly, as it would turn out, that would prove unsustainable.

Speech to the Association of Los
Alamos Scientists
J. Robert Oppenheimer
Los Alamos, New Mexico
November 2, 1945

I am grateful to the Executive Committee for this chance to talk to you. I should like to talk tonight—if some of you have long memories perhaps you will regard it as justified—as a fellow scientist, and at least as a fellow worrier about the fix we are in. I do not have anything very radical to say, or anything that will strike most of you with a great flash of enlightenment. I don't have anything to say that will be of an immense encouragement. In some ways I would have liked to talk to you at an earlier date—but I couldn't talk to you as a Director. I could not talk, and will not tonight talk, too much about the practical political problems which are involved. There is one good reason for that—I don't know very much about practical politics. And there is another reason, which has to some extent restrained me in the past. As you know, some of us have been asked to be technical advisors to the Secretary of War, and through him to the President. In the course of this we have naturally discussed things that were on our minds and have been made, often very willingly, the recipient of confidences; it is not possible to speak in detail about what Mr. A thinks and Mr. B doesn't think, or what is going to happen next week, without violating these confidences. I don't think that's important. I think there are issues which are quite simple and quite deep, and which involve us as a group of scientists—involve us more, perhaps than any other group in the world. I think that it can only help to look a little at what our situation is—at what has happened to us—and that this must give us some honesty, some insight, which will be a source of strength in what may be the not-too-easy days ahead. I would like to take it as deep and serious as I know how, and then perhaps come to more immediate questions in the course of the discussion later. I want anyone who feels like it to ask me a question and if I can't answer it, as will often be the case, I will just have to say so.

What has happened to us—it is really rather major, it is so major that I think in some ways one returns to the greatest developments of the twentieth century, to the discovery of relativity, and to the whole development of atomic theory and its interpretation in terms of complementarity, for analogy. These things, as you know, forced us to re-consider the relations between science and common sense. They forced on us the recognition that the fact that we were in the habit of talking a certain language and using certain concepts did not necessarily imply that there was anything in the real world to correspond to these. They forced us to be prepared for the inadequacy of the ways in which human beings attempted to deal with reality, for that reality. In some ways I think these virtues, which scientists quite reluctantly were forced to learn by the nature of the world they were studying, may be useful even today in preparing us for somewhat more radical views of what the issues are than would be natural or easy for people who had not been through this experience.

But the real impact of the creation of the atomic bomb and atomic weapons—to understand that one has to look further back, look, I think, to the times when physical science was growing in the days of the renaissance, and when the threat that science offered was felt so deeply throughout the Christian world. The analogy is, of course, not perfect. You may even wish to think of the days in the last century when the theories of evolution seemed a threat to the values by which men lived. The analogy is not perfect because there is nothing in atomic weapons—there is certainly nothing that we have done here or in the physics or chemistry that immediately preceded our work here—in which any revolutionary ideas were involved. I don't think that the conceptions of nuclear fission have strained any man's attempts to understand them, and I don't feel that any of us have really learned in a deep sense very much from following this up. It is in a quite different way. It is not an idea—it is a development and a reality—but it has in common with the early days of physical science the fact that the very existence of science is threatened, and its value is threatened. This is the point that I would like to speak a little about.

I think that it hardly needs to be said why the impact is so strong. There are three reasons: one is the extraordinary speed with which things which were right on the frontier of science were translated into terms where they affected many living people, and potentially all people. Another is the fact, quite accidental in many ways, and connected with the speed, that scientists themselves played such a large part, not merely in providing the foundation for atomic weapons, but in actually making them. In this we are certainly closer to it than any other group. The third is that the thing we made—partly because of the technical nature of the problem, partly because we worked hard, partly because we had good breaks—really arrived in the world with such a shattering reality and suddenness that there was no opportunity for the edges to be worn off.

In considering what the situation of science is, it may be helpful to think a little of what people said and felt of their motives in coming into this job. One always has to worry that what people say of their motives is not adequate. Many people said different things, and most of them, I think, had some validity. There was in the first place the great concern that our enemy might develop these weapons before we did, and the feeling—at least, in the early days, the very strong feeling—that without atomic weapons it might be very difficult, it might be an impossible, it might be an incredibly long thing to win the war. These things wore off a little as it became clear that the war would be won in any case. Some people, I think, were motivated by curiosity, and rightly so; and some by a sense of adventure, and rightly so. Others had more political arguments and said, "Well, we know that atomic weapons are in principle possible, and it is not right that the threat of their unrealized possibility should hang over the world. It is right that the world should know what can be done in their field and deal with it." And the people added to that that it was a time when all over the world men would be particularly ripe and open for dealing with this problem because of the immediacy of the evils of war, because of the universal cry from everyone that one could not go through this thing again, even a war without atomic bombs. And there was finally, and I think rightly, the feeling that there was probably no place in the world where the development of atomic weapons would have a better chance of leading to a reasonable solution, and a smaller chance of leading to disaster, than within the United States. I believe all these things that people said are true, and I think I said them all myself at one time or another.

But when you come right down to it the reason that we did this job is because it was an organic necessity. If you are a scientist you cannot stop such a thing. If you are a scientist you believe that it is good to find out how the world works; that it is good to find out what the realities are; that it is good to turn over to mankind at large the greatest possible power to control the world and to deal with it according to its lights and its values.

There has been a lot of talk about the evil of secrecy, of concealment, of control, of security. Some of that talk has been on a rather low plane, limited really to saying that it is difficult or inconvenient to work in a world where you are not free to do what you want. I think that the talk has been justified, and that the almost unanimous resistance of scientists to the imposition of control and secrecy is a justified position, but I think that the reason for it may lie a little deeper. I think that it comes from the fact that secrecy strikes at the very root of what science is, and what it is for. It is not possible to be a scientist unless you believe that it is good to learn. It is not good to be a scientist, and it is not possible, unless you think that it is of the highest value to share your knowledge, to share it with anyone who is interested. It is not possible to be a scientist unless you believe that the knowledge of the world, and the power which this gives, is a thing which is of intrinsic value to humanity, and that you are using it to help in the spread of knowledge, and are willing to take the consequences. And, therefore, I think that this resistance which we feel and see all around us to anything which is an attempt to treat science of the future as though it were rather a dangerous thing, a thing that must be watched and managed, is resisted not because of its inconvenience—I think we are in a position where we must be willing to take any inconvenience—but resisted because it is based on a philosophy incompatible with that by which we live, and have learned to live in the past.

There are many people who try to wiggle out of this. They say the real importance of atomic energy does not lie in the weapons that have been made; the real importance lies in all the great benefits which atomic energy, which the various radiations, will bring to mankind. There may be some truth in this. I am sure that there is truth in it, because there has never in the past been a new field opened up where the real fruits of it have not been invisible at the beginning. I have a very high confidence that the fruits—the so-called peacetime applications—of atomic energy will have in them all that we think, and more. There are others who try to escape the immediacy of this situation by saying that, after all, war has always been very terrible; after all, weapons have always gotten worse and worse; that this is just another weapon and it doesn't create a great change; that they are not so bad; bombings have been bad in this war and this is not a change in that—it just adds a little to the effectiveness of bombing; that some sort of protection will be found. I think that these efforts to diffuse and weaken the nature of the crisis make it only more dangerous. I think it is for us to accept it as a very grave crisis, to realize that these atomic weapons which we have started to make are very terrible, that they involve a change, that they are not just a slight modification: to accept this, and to accept with it the necessity for those transformations in the world which will make it possible to integrate these developments into human life. As scientists I think we have perhaps a little greater ability to accept change, and accept radical change, because of our experiences in the pursuit of science. And that may help us—that, and the fact that we have lived with it—to be of some use in understanding these problems.

It is clear to me that wars have changed. It is clear to me that if these first bombs—the bomb that was dropped on Nagasaki—that if these can destroy ten square miles, then that is really quite something. It is clear to me that they are going to be very cheap if anyone wants to make them; it is clear to me that this is a situation where a quantitative change, and a change in which the advantage of aggression compared to defense—of attack compared to defense—is shifted, where this quantitative change has all the character of a change in quality, of a change in the nature of the world. I know that whereas wars have become intolerable, and the question would have been raised and would have been pursued after this war, more ardently than after the last, of whether there was not some method by which they could be averted. But I think the advent of the atomic bomb and the facts which will get around that they are not too hard to make—that they will be universal if people wish to make them universal, that they will not constitute a real drain on the economy of any strong nation, and that their power of destruction will grow and is already incomparably greater than that of any other weapon—I think these things create a new situation, so new that there is some danger, even some danger in believing, that what we have is a new argument for arrangements, for hopes, that existed before this development took place. By that I mean that much as I like to hear advocates of a world federation, or advocates of a United Nations organization, who have been talking of these things for years—much as I like to hear them say that here is a new argument, I think that they are in part missing the point, because the point is not that atomic weapons constitute a new argument. There have always been good arguments. The point is that atomic weapons constitute also a field, a new field, and a new opportunity for realizing preconditions. I think when people talk of the fact that this is not only a great peril, but a great hope, this is what they should mean. I do not think they should mean the unknown, though sure, value of industrial and scientific virtues of atomic energy, but rather the simple fact that in this field, because it is a threat, because it is a peril, and because it has certain special characteristics, to which I will return, there exists a possibility of realizing, of beginning to realize, those changes which are needed if there is to be any peace.

Those are very far-reaching changes. They are changes in the relations between nations, not only in spirit, not only in law, but also in conception and feeling. I don't know which of these is prior; they must all work together, and only the gradual interaction of one on the other can make a reality. I don't agree with those who say the first step is to have a structure of international law. I don't agree with those who say the only thing is to have friendly feelings. All of these things will be involved. I think it is true to say that atomic weapons are a peril which affect everyone in the world, and in that sense a completely common problem, as common a problem as it was for the Allies to defeat the Nazis. I think that in order to handle this common problem there must be a complete sense of community responsibility. I do not think that one may expect that people will contribute to the solution of the problem until they are aware of their ability to take part in the solution. I think that it is a field in which the implementation of such a common responsibility has certain decisive advantages. It is a new field, in which the position of vested interests in various parts of the world is very much less serious than in others. It is serious in this country, and that is one of our problems. It is a new field, in which the role of science has been so great that it is to my mind hardly thinkable that the international traditions of science, and the fraternity of scientists, should not play a constructive part. It is a new field, in which just the novelty and the special characteristics of the technical operations should enable one to establish a community of interest which might almost be regarded as a pilot plant for a new type of international collaboration. I speak of it as a pilot plant because it is quite clear that the control of atomic weapons cannot be in itself the unique end of such operation. The only unique end can be a world that is united, and a world in which war will not occur. But those things don't happen overnight, and in this field it would seem that one could get started, and get started without meeting those insuperable obstacles which history has so often placed in the way of any effort of cooperation.

Now, this is not an easy thing, and the point I want to make, the one point I want to hammer home, is what an enormous change in spirit is involved. There are things which we hold very dear, and I think rightly hold very dear; I would say that the word democracy perhaps stood for some of them as well as any other word. There are many parts of the world in which there is no democracy. There are other things which we hold dear, and which we rightly should. And when I speak of a new spirit in international affairs I mean that even to these deepest of things which we cherish, and for which Americans have been willing to die—and certainly most of us would be willing to die—even in these deepest things, we realize that there is something more profound than that; namely, the common bond with other men everywhere. It is only if you do that that this makes sense; because if you approach the problem and say, "We know what is right and we would like to use the atomic bomb to persuade you to agree with us," then you are in a very weak position and you will not succeed, because under those conditions you will not succeed in delegating responsibility for the survival of men. It is a purely unilateral statement; you will find yourselves attempting by force of arms to prevent a disaster.

I want to express the utmost sympathy with the people who have to grapple with this problem and in the strongest terms to urge you not to underestimate its difficulty. I can think of an analogy, and I hope it is not a completely good analogy: in the days in the first half of the nineteenth century there were many people, mostly in the North, but some in the South, who thought that there was no evil on earth more degrading than human slavery, and nothing that they would more willingly devote their lives to than its eradication. Always when I was young I wondered why it was that when Lincoln was President he did not declare that the war against the South, when it broke out, was a war that slavery should be abolished, that this was the central point, the rallying point, of that war. Lincoln was severely criticized by many of the Abolitionists as you know, by many then called radicals, because he seemed to be waging a war which did not hit the thing that was most important. But Lincoln realized, and I have only in the last months come to appreciate the depth and wisdom of it, that beyond the issue of slavery was the issue of the community of the people of the country, and the issue of the Union. I hope that today this will not be an issue calling for war; but I wanted to remind you that in order to preserve the Union Lincoln had to subordinate the immediate problem of the eradication of slavery, and trust—and I think if he had had his way it would have gone so—to the conflict of these ideas in a united people to eradicate it.

These are somewhat general remarks and it may be appropriate to say one or two things that are a little more programmatic, that are not quite so hard to get one's hands on. That is, what sort of agreement between nations would be a reasonable start. I don't know the answer to this, and I am very sure that no a priori answer should be given, that it is something that is going to take constant working out. But I think it is a thing where it will not hurt to have some reasonably concrete proposal. And I would go a step further and say of even such questions as the great question of secrecy—which perplexes scientists and other people—that even this was not a suitable subject for unilateral action. If atomic energy is to be treated as an international problem, as I think it must be, if it is to be treated on the basis of an international responsibility and an international common concern, the problems of secrecy are also international problems. I don't mean by that that our present classifications and our present, in many cases inevitably ridiculous, procedures should be maintained. I mean that the fundamental problem of how to treat this peril ought not to be treated unilaterally by the United States, or by the United States in conjunction with Great Britain.

The first thing I would say about any proposals is that they ought to be regarded as interim proposals, and that whenever they are made it be understood and agreed that within a year or two years—whatever seems a reasonable time—they will be reconsidered and the problems which have arisen, and the new developments which have occurred, will cause a rewriting. I think the only point is that there should be a few things in these proposals which will work in the right direction, and that the things should be accepted without forcing all of the changes, which we know must ultimately occur, upon people who will not be ready for them. This is anyone's guess, but it would seem to me that if you took these four points, it might work: first, that we are dealing with an interim solution, so recognized. Second, that the nations participating in the arrangement would have a joint atomic energy commission, operating under the most broad directives from the different states, but with a power which only they had, and which was not subject to review by the heads of State, to go ahead with those constructive applications of atomic energy which we would all like to see developed— energy sources, and the innumerable research tools which are immediate possibilities. Third, that there would be not merely the possibility of exchange of scientists and students; that very, very concrete machinery more or less forcing such exchange should be established, so that we would be quite sure that the fraternity of scientists would be strengthened and that the bonds on which so much of the future depends would have some reinforcement and some scope. And fourth, I would say that no bombs be made. I don't know whether these proposals are good ones, and I think that anyone in this group would have his own proposals. But I mention them as very simple things, which I don't believe solve the problem, and which I want to make clear are not the ultimate or even a touch of the ultimate, but which I think ought to be started right away; which I believe—though I know very little of this— may very well be acceptable to any of the nations that wish to become partners with us in this great undertaking.

One of the questions which you will want to hear more about, and which I can only partly hope to succeed in answering, is to what extent such views—essentially the view that the life of science is threatened, the life of the world is threatened, and that only [by] a profound revision of what it is that constitutes a thing worth fighting for and a thing worth living for can this crisis be met—to what extent these views are held by other men. They are certainly not held universally by scientists; but I think they are in agreement with all of the expressed opinions of this group, and I know that many of my friends here see pretty much eye to eye. I would speak especially of Bohr, who was here so much during the difficult days, who had many discussions with us, and who helped us reach the conclusion that [it was] not only a desirable solution, but that it was the unique solution, that there were no other alternatives.

I would say that among scientists there are certain centrifugal tendencies which seem to me a little dangerous, but not very. One of them is the attempt to try, in this imperiled world, in which the very function of science is threatened, to make convenient arrangements for the continuance of science, and to pay very little attention to the preconditions which give sense to it. Another is the tendency to say we must have a free science and a strong science, because this will make us a strong nation and enable us to fight better wars. It seems to me that this is a profound mistake, and I don't like to hear it. The third is even odder, and it is to say, "Oh give the bombs to the United Nations for police purposes, and let us get back to physics and chemistry." I think none of these are really held very widely, but they show that there are people who are desperately trying to avoid what I think is the most difficult problem. One must expect these false solutions, and overeasy solutions, and these are three which pop up from time to time.

As far as I can tell in the world outside there are many people just as quick to see the gravity of the situation, and to understand it in terms not so different from those I have tried to outline. It is not only among scientists that there are wise people and foolish people. I have had occasion in the last few months to meet people who had to do with the Government—the legislative branches, the administrative branches, and even the judicial branches, and I have found many in whom an understanding of what this problem is, and of the general lines along which it can be solved, is very clear. I would especially mention the former Secretary of War, Mr. Stimson, who, perhaps as much as any man, seemed to appreciate how hopeless and how impractical it was to attack this problem on a superficial level, and whose devotion to the development of atomic weapons was in large measure governed by his understanding of the hope that lay in it that there would be a new world. I know this is a surprise, because most people think that the War Department has as its unique function the making of war. The Secretary of War has other functions.

I think this is another question of importance: that is, what views will be held on these matters in other countries. I think it is important to realize that even those who are well informed in this country have been slow to understand, slow to believe that the bombs would work, and then slow to understand that their working would present such profound problems. We have certain interests in playing up the bomb, not only we here locally, but all over the country, because we made them, and our pride is involved. I think that in other lands it may be even more difficult for an appreciation of the magnitude of the thing to take hold. For this reason, I'm not sure that the greatest opportunities for progress do not lie somewhat further in the future than I had for a long time thought.

There have been two or three official statements by the President which defined, as nearly as they're in some measure inevitable contradictions made possible, the official policy of the Government. And I think that one must not be entirely discouraged by the fact that there are contradictions, because the contradictions show that the problem is being understood as a difficult one, is temporarily being regarded as an insoluble one. Certainly you will notice, especially in the message to Congress, many indications of a sympathy with, and an understanding of, the views which this group holds, and which I have discussed briefly tonight. I think all of us were encouraged at the phrase "too revolutionary to consider in the framework of old ideas." That's about what we all think. I think all of us were encouraged by the sense of urgency that was frequently and emphatically stressed. I think all of us must be encouraged by the recognition, the official recognition by the Government of the importance—of the overriding importance—of the free exchange of scientific ideas and scientific information between all countries of the world. It would certainly be ridiculous to regard this as a final end, but I think that it would also be a very dangerous thing not to realize that it is a precondition. I am myself somewhat discouraged by the limitation of the objective to the elimination of atomic weapons, and I have seen many articles—probably you have, too—in which this is interpreted as follows: "Let us get international agreement to outlaw atomic weapons and then let us go back to having a good, clean war." This is certainly not a very good way of looking at it. I think, to say it again, that if one solves the problems presented by the atomic bomb, one will have made a pilot plant for solution of the problem of ending war.

But what is surely the thing which must have troubled you, and which troubled me, in the official statements was the insistent note of unilateral responsibility for the handling of atomic weapons. However good the motives of this country are—I am not going to argue with the President's description of what the motives and the aims are—we are 140 million people, and there are two billion people living on earth. We must understand that whatever our commitments to our own views and ideas, and however confident we are that in the course of time they will tend to prevail, our absolute—our completely absolute—commitment to them, in denial of the views and ideas of other people, cannot be the basis of any kind of agreement.

As I have said, I had for a long time the feeling of the most extreme urgency, and I think maybe there was something right about that. There was a period immediately after the first use of the bomb when it seemed most natural that a clear statement of policy, and the initial steps of implementing it, should have been made; and it would be wrong for me not to admit that something may have been lost, and that there may be tragedy in that loss. But I think the plain fact is that in the actual world, and with the actual people in it, it has taken time, and it may take longer, to understand what this is all about. And I am not sure, as I have said before, that in other lands it won't take longer than it does in this country. As it is now, our only course is to see what we can do to bring about an understanding on a level deep enough to make a solution practicable, and to do that without undue delay.

One may think that the views suggested in the President's Navy Day speech are not entirely encouraging, that many men who are more versed than we in the practical art of statesmanship have seen more hope in a radical view, which may at first sight seem visionary, than in an approach on a more conventional level.

I don't have very much more to say. There are a few things which scientists perhaps should remember, that I don't think I need to remind us of; but I will, anyway. One is that they are very often called upon to give technical information in one way or another, and I think one cannot be too careful to be honest. And it is very difficult, not because one tells lies, but because so often questions are put in a form which makes it very hard to give an answer which is not misleading. I think we will be in a very weak position unless we maintain at its highest the scrupulousness which is traditional for us in sticking to the truth, and in distinguishing between what we know to be true from what we hope may be true.

The second thing I think it right to speak of is this: it is everywhere felt that the fraternity between us and scientists in other countries may be one of the most helpful things for the future; yet it is apparent that even in this country not all of us who are scientists are in agreement. There is no harm in that; such disagreement is healthy. But we must not lose the sense of fraternity because of it; we must not lose our fundamental confidence in our fellow scientists.

I think that we have no hope at all if we yield in our belief in the value of science, in the good that it can be to the world to know about reality, about nature, to attain a gradually greater and greater control of nature, to learn, to teach, to understand. I think that if we lose our faith in this we stop being scientists, we sell out our heritage, we lose what we have most of value for this time of crisis.

But there is another thing: we are not only scientists; we are men, too. We cannot forget our dependence on our fellow men. I mean not only our material dependence, without which no science would be possible, and without which we could not work; I mean also our deep moral dependence, in that the value of science must lie in the world of men, that all our roots lie there. These are the strongest bonds in the world, stronger than those even that bind us to one another, these are the deepest bonds—that bind us to our fellow men.

Source: Papers of the Federation of American Scientists, Box 21, Folder 4, Department of Special Collections, University of Chicago Library.

56. The Effects of the Atomic Bombs: Excerpt from U.S. Strategic Bombing Survey Summary Report (Pacific War), Washington, D.C., July 1, 1946

Less than a year after the Pacific war ended, the U.S. government sought to assess the effects upon Japan of the major bombing campaign mounted in the later years of the war. The survey covered both the physical impact and casualties and the effect on morale. It provided a graphic account of the explosions of nuclear devices over both Hiroshima and Nagasaki. It was too soon, however, to assess the long-term impact of the nuclear explosions upon the health of the survivors.

EFFECTS OF THE ATOMIC BOMBS
On 6 August and 9 August 1945, the first two atomic bombs to be used for military purposes were dropped on Hiroshima and Nagasaki respectively. One hundred thousand people were killed, 6 square miles or over 50 percent of the built-up areas of the two cities were destroyed. The first and crucial question about the atomic bomb thus was answered practically and conclusively; atomic energy had been mastered for military purposes and the overwhelming scale of its possibilities had been demonstrated. A detailed examination of the physical, economic, and morale effects of the atomic bombs occupied the attention of a major portion of the Survey's staff in Japan in order to arrive at a more precise definition of the present capabilities and limitations of this radically new weapon of destruction.

Eyewitness accounts of the explosion all describe similar pictures. The bombs exploded with a tremendous flash of blue-white light, like a giant magnesium flare. The flash was of short duration and accompanied by intense glare and heat. It was followed by a tremendous pressure wave and the rumbling sound of the explosion. This sound is not clearly recollected by those who survived near the center of the explosion, although it was clearly heard by others as much as fifteen miles away. A huge snow-white cloud shot rapidly into the sky and the scene on the ground was obscured first by a bluish haze and then by a purple-brown cloud of dust and smoke.

Such eyewitness accounts reveal the sequence of events. At the time of the explosion, energy was given off in the forms of light, heat, radiation, and pressure. The complete band of radiations, from X- and gamma-rays, through ultraviolet and light rays to the radiant heat of infra-red rays, travelled with the speed of light. The shock wave created by the enormous pressures built up almost instantaneously at the point of explosion but moved out more slowly, that is at about the speed of sound. The superheated gases constituting the original fire ball expanded outward and upward at a slower rate.

The light and radiant heat rays accompanying the flash travelled in a straight line and any opaque object, even a single leaf of a vine, shielded objects lying behind it. The duration of the flash was only a fraction of a second, but it was sufficiently intense to cause third degree burns to exposed human skin up to a distance of a mile. Clothing ignited, though it could be quickly beaten out, telephone poles charred, thatch-roofed houses caught fire. Black or other dark-colored surfaces of combustible material absorbed the heat and immediately charred or burst into flames; white or light-colored surfaces reflected a substantial portion of the rays and were not consumed. Heavy black clay tiles which are an almost universal feature of the roofs of Japanese houses bubbled at distances up to a mile. Test of samples of this tile by the National Bureau of Standards in Washington indicates that temperatures in excess of 1,800° C. must have been generated in the surface of the tile to produce such an effect. The surfaces of granite blocks exposed to the flash scarred and spoiled at distances up to almost a mile. In the immediate area of ground zero (the point on the ground immediately below the explosion), the heat charred corpses beyond recognition.

Penetrating rays such as gamma-rays exposed X-ray films stored in the basement of a concrete hospital almost a mile from ground zero. Symptoms of their effect on human beings close to the center of the explosion, who survived other effects thereof, were generally delayed for two or three days. The bone marrow and as a result the process of blood formation were affected. The white corpuscle count went down and the human processes of resisting infection were destroyed. Death generally followed shortly thereafter.

The majority of radiation cases who were at greater distances did not show severe symptoms until 1 to 4 weeks after the explosion. The first symptoms were loss of appetite, lassitude and general discomfort. Within 12 to 48 hours, fever became evident in many cases, going as high as 104° to 105° F., which in fatal cases continued until death. If the fever subsided, the patient usually showed a rapid disappearance of other symptoms and soon regained his feeling of good health. Other symptoms were loss of white blood corpuscles, loss of hair, and decrease in sperm count.

Even though rays of this nature have great powers of penetration, intervening substances filter out portions of them. As the weight of the intervening material increases the percentage of the rays penetrating goes down. It appears that a few feet of concrete, or a somewhat greater thickness of earth, furnished sufficient protection to humans, even those close to ground zero, to prevent serious after effects from radiation.

The blast wave which followed the flash was of sufficient force to press in the roofs of reinforced concrete structures and to flatten completely all less sturdy structures. Due to the height of the explosion, the peak pressure of the wave at ground zero was no higher than that produced by a near miss of a high-explosive bomb, and decreased at greater distances from ground zero. Reflection and shielding by intervening hills and structures produced some unevenness in the pattern. The blast wave, however, was of far greater extent and duration than that of a high-explosive bomb and most reinforced-concrete structures suffered structural damage or collapse up to 700 feet at Hiroshima and 2,000 feet at Nagasaki. Brick buildings were flattened up to 7,300 feet at Hiroshima and 8,500 feet at Nagasaki. Typical Japanese houses of wood construction suffered total collapse up to approximately 7,300 feet at Hiroshima and 8,200 feet at Nagasaki. Beyond these distances structures received less serious damage to roofs, wall partitions, and the like. Glass windows were blown out at distances up to 5 miles. The blast wave, being of longer duration than that caused by high-explosive detonations, was accompanied by more flying debris. Window frames, doors, and partitions which would have been shaken down by a near-miss of a high-explosive bomb were hurled at high velocity through those buildings which did not collapse. Machine tools and most other production equipment in industrial plants were not directly damaged by the blast wave, but were damaged by collapsing buildings or ensuing general fires.

The above description mentions all the categories of the destructive action by the atomic-bomb explosions at Hiroshima and Nagasaki. There were no other types of action. Nothing was vaporized or disintegrated; vegetation is growing again immediately under the center of the explosions; there are no indications that radio-activity continued after the explosion to a sufficient degree to harm human beings.

Let us consider, however, the effect of these various types of destructive action on the cities of Hiroshima, and Nagasaki and their inhabitants.

Hiroshima is built on a broad river delta; it is flat and little above sea level. The total city area is 26 square miles but only 7 square miles at the center were densely built up. The principal industries, which had been greatly expanded during the war, were located on the periphery of the city. The population of the city had been reduced from approximately 340,000 to 245,000 as a result of a civilian defense evacuation program. The explosion caught the city by surprise. An alert had been sounded but in view of the small number of planes the all-clear had been given. Consequently, the population had not taken shelter. The bomb exploded a little northwest of the center of the built-up area. Everyone who was out in the open and was exposed to the initial flash suffered serious burns where not protected by clothing. Over 4 square miles in the center of the city were flattened to the ground with the exception of some 50 reinforced concrete buildings, most of which were internally gutted and many of which suffered structural damage. Most of the people in the flattened area were crushed or pinned down by the collapsing buildings or flying debris. Shortly thereafter, numerous fires started, a few from the direct heat of the flash, but most from overturned charcoal cooking stoves or other secondary causes. These fires grew in size, merging into a general conflagration fanned by a wind sucked into the center of the city by the rising heat. The civilian-defense organization was overwhelmed by the completeness of the destruction, and the spread of fire was halted more by the air rushing toward the center of the conflagration than by efforts of the fire-fighting organization.

Approximately 60,000 to 70,000 people were killed, and 50,000 were injured. Of approximately 90,000 buildings in the city, 65,000 were rendered unusable and almost all the remainder received at least light superficial damage. The underground utilities of the city were undamaged except where they crossed bridges over the rivers cutting through the city. All of the small factories in the center of the city were destroyed. However, the big plants on the periphery of the city were almost completely undamaged and 94 percent of their workers unhurt.

These factories accounted for 74 percent of the industrial production of the city. It is estimated that they could have resumed substantially normal production within 30 days of the bombing, had the war continued. The railroads running through the city were repaired for the resumption of through traffic on 8 August, 2 days after the attack.

Nagasaki was a highly congested city built around the harbor and up into the ravines and river valleys of the surrounding hills. Spurs of these hills coming down close to the head of the bay divide the city roughly into two basins. The built-up area was 3.4 square miles of which 0.6 square miles was given over to industry. The peak wartime population of 285,000 had been reduced to around 230,000 by August 1945, largely by pre-raid evacuations. Nagasaki had been attacked sporadically prior to 9 August by an aggregate of 136 planes which dropped 270 tons of high explosives and 53 tons of incendiary bombs. Some 2 percent of the residential buildings had been destroyed or badly damaged; three of the large industrial plants had received scattered damage. The city was thus comparatively intact at the time of the atomic bombing.

The alarm was improperly given and therefore few persons were in shelters. The bomb exploded over the northwest portion of the city; the intervening hills protected a major portion of the city lying in the adjoining valley. The heat radiation and blast actions of the Nagasaki bomb were more intense than those of the bomb dropped over Hiroshima. Reinforced-concrete structures were structurally damaged at greater distances; the heavy steel-frame industrial buildings of the Mitsubishi steel works and the arms plant were pushed at crazy angles away from the center of the explosion. Contrary to the situation at Hiroshima, the majority of the fires that started immediately after the explosion resulted from direct ignition by the flash.

Approximately 40,000 persons were killed or missing and a like number injured. Of the 52,000 residential buildings in Nagasaki 14,000 were totally destroyed and a further 5,400 badly damaged. Ninety-six percent of the industrial output of Nagasaki was concentrated in the large plants of the Mitsubishi Co. which completely dominated the town. The arms plant and the steel works were located within the area of primary damage. It is estimated that 58 percent of the yen value of the arms plant and 78 percent of the value of the steel works were destroyed. The main plant of the Mitsubishi electric works was on the periphery of the area of greatest destruction. Approximately 25 percent of its value was destroyed. The dockyard, the largest industrial establishment in Nagasaki and one of the three plants previously damaged by high-explosive bombs, was located down the bay from the explosion. It suffered virtually no new damage. The Mitsubishi plants were all operating, prior to the attack, at a fraction of their capacity because of a shortage of raw materials. Had the war continued, and had the raw material situation been such as to warrant their restoration, it is estimated that the dockyard could have been in a position to produce at 80 percent of its full capacity within 3 to 4 months; that the steel works would have required a year to get into substantial production; that the electric works could have resumed some production within 2 months and been back at capacity within 6 months; and that restoration of the arms plant to 60 to 70 percent of former capacity would have required 15 months.

Some 400 persons were in the tunnel shelters in Nagasaki at the time of the explosion. The shelters consisted of rough tunnels dug horizontally into the sides of hills with crude, earth-filled blast walls protecting the entrances. The blast walls were blown in but all the occupants back from the entrances survived, even in those tunnels almost directly under the explosion. Those not in a direct line with the entrance were uninjured. The tunnels had a capacity of roughly 100,000 persons. Had the proper alarm been sounded, and these tunnel shelters been filled to capacity, the loss of life in Nagasaki would have been substantially lower.

The Survey has estimated that the damage and casualties caused at Hiroshima by the one atomic bomb dropped from a single plane would have required 220 B-29s carrying 1,200 tons of incendiary bombs, 400 tons of high-explosive bombs, and 500 tons of anti-personnel fragmentation bombs, if conventional weapons, rather than an atomic bomb, had been used. One hundred and twenty-five B-29s carrying 1,200 tons of bombs would have been required to approximate the damage and casualties at Nagasaki. This estimate pre-supposed bombing under conditions similar to those existing when the atomic bombs were dropped and bombing accuracy equal to the average attained by the Twentieth Air Force during the last 3 months of the war.

As might be expected, the primary reaction of the populace to the bomb was fear, uncontrolled terror, strengthened by the sheer horror of the destruction and suffering witnessed and experienced by the survivors. Prior to the dropping of the atomic bombs, the people of the two cities had fewer misgivings about the war than people in other cities and their morale held up after it better than might have been expected. Twenty-nine percent of the survivors interrogated indicated that after the atomic bomb was dropped they were convinced that victory for Japan was impossible. Twenty-four percent stated that because of the bomb they felt personally unable to carry on with the war. Some 40 percent testified to various degrees of defeatism. A greater number (24 percent) expressed themselves as being impressed with the power and scientific skill which underlay the discovery and production of the atomic bomb than expressed anger at its use (20 percent). In many instances, the reaction was one of resignation.

The effect of the atomic bomb on the confidence of the Japanese civilian population outside the two cities was more restricted. This was in part due to the effect of distance, lack of understanding of the nature of atomic energy, and the impact of other demoralizing experiences. . . .

Source: U.S. Strategic Bombing Survey Summary Report, Pacific War, July 1, 1946. Washington, D.C.: Government Printing Office.

57. Eben Ayers Diary on Memories by Harry Truman of the Atomic Bomb, August 6, 1951

Imagine how the decision to drop the atomic bomb on Japan in the first months of his presidency must have weighed on Harry Truman's mind, probably for the rest of his life even after his generally successful time in office. White House staff member Eben Ayers recollects here a time, six years after the fact, when Truman reminisced about his knowledge of the situation when he made his decision, knowledge that, this passage shows, was extremely limited and at least a little bit inaccurate.

August 6, 1951

On Saturday, August 4th, I saw the President at this office at 10:40 AM and he told me about his first knowledge and connection with the atomic bomb development.

He said that his first connection with it was when he was serving in the Senate as a Member of the Appropriations Committee and the first appropriation for the atomic project came before the Committee. The appropriation request did not disclose the nature of the project and shortly afterward the President, in his investigation of the war effort, ordered an investigator to go down to Oak Ridge.(?) Immediately afterward he said Secretary of War Stimson called him and said he wanted to come over and see the President. The President said he offered to go over to Stimson's office and they got together. Stimson did not tell the President what the project was but did tell him that it concerned the most top secret in the Government and they wanted to go ahead without disclosing any information. On Stimson's assurances, the President called off his investigator and did not go further into the matter.

Immediately after he became President— the President recalls that it was, he thought, the day after he was sworn in, James F. Byrnes, who had been Director of War Mobilization and Fred M. Vinson, who was to succeed him, came to see him and told him for the first time about the project and its purpose. On April____, Stimson had an appointment with the President and at that time he told Mr. Truman all about the project. Stimson later described this in his book, "An Active Service in Peace and War".

The President said that on July 16th, while he was at Potsdam for the conference with Churchill and Stalin, the message was received that the first test of the bomb had been made at Alamogordo, New Mexico, and had been successful. He said it was an almost "ecstatic" message and told how the explosion of the bomb had made a hole in the earth 1200 feet in diameter, had melted the steel tower from which the bomb was dropped and fused the sand on the desert floor about the scene.

"Then," the President said Stimson and I began to discuss the use of the bomb. It was my suggestion that we pick out a place to drop it as near a war plant as possible so as not to injure any more people than necessary. He said he conferred not only with Stimson but with Byrnes and Admiral Leahy and the decision was reached to drop the bombs on Hiroshima and Nagasaki. The President said that the military leaders believed, up to that time, that it would require an army of at least a million Americans to defeat Japan and they told the President, in answer to his inquiries that they estimated there would be about 25% casualties. He said he asked what the population of Hiroshima was and his recollection was that they said about 60,000. He said that he felt and said it was far better to kill 60,000 Japanese than to have 250,000 Americans killed and he, therefore, ordered the dropping of the bomb on Hiroshima and Nagasaki.

Source: Eben A. Ayers Papers, Box 21. Harry S. Truman Presidential Library and Museum. Available online at https://www.trumanlibrary.org/whistlestop/study_collections/bomb/large/documents/fulltext.php?fulltextid=21. Accessed May 4, 2019.

58. President Harry Truman's Later Thoughts in Letters, August 5, 1963 and August 4, 1964

No matter how often he would affirm his belief that he had made the right decision in ordering the atomic attacks on Hiroshima and Nagasaki, the decision always weighed heavily in President Harry Truman's mind. In these two letters, written almost exactly eighteen and nineteen years after Hiroshima, Truman revisits that decision.

August 5, 1963

Dear Kup:

I appreciated most highly your column of July 30th, a copy of which you sent me.

I have been rather careful not to comment on the articles that have been written on the dropping of the bomb for the simple reason that the dropping of the bomb was completely and thoroughly explained in my Memoirs, and it was done to save 125,000 youngsters on the American side and 125,000 on the Japanese side from getting killed and that is what it did. It probably also saved a half million youngsters on both sides from being maimed for life.

You must always remember that people forget, as you said in your column, that the bombing of Pearl Harbor was done while we were at peace with Japan and trying our best to negotiate a treaty with them.

All you have to do is to go out and stand on the keel of the Battleship in Pearl Harbor with the 3,000 youngsters underneath it who had no chance whatever of saving their lives. That is true of two or three other battleships that were sunk in Pearl Harbor. Altogether, there were between 3,000 and 6,000 youngsters killed at that time without any declaration of war. It was plain murder.

I knew what I was doing when I stopped the war that would have killed a half million youngsters on both sides if those bombs had not been dropped. I have no regrets and, under the same circumstances, I would do it again—and this letter is not confidential.

Sincerely yours,

Harry S. Truman.

Source: Harry S. Truman to Irv Kupcinet, August 5, 1963. Truman Papers, Post-Presidential File. *Chicago Sun-Times*. Harry S. Truman Presidential Library and Museum.

August 4, 1964

Dear Mrs. Klein:

In response to yours of the 28th of July, the matter about which you wrote me—the atomic bomb—is one that is of interest to most people. The only reason the atomic bomb was used was because it was a weapon of war.

While I was on the way home from Potsdam I sent a message to the Japanese Government asking them to surrender unconditionally and I hoped that would end the war. They refused and then I ordered the bombs dropped on Hiroshima and Nagasaki, just as I would have used the long gun as the Germans did in the first World War.

The dropping of those bombs ended the war and that was the objective. There is nothing to take home with you to sleep with—it was a means to end the war and save 250,000 men from being killed on our side and that many on the Japanese side, plus twice that many being injured for life. You will find this information in my Memoirs and in any other documents.

I have never worried about the dropping of the bomb. It was just a means to end the war and that is what was accomplished.

Sincerely yours,

Harry S. Truman.

Source: Harry S. Truman to Mrs. Haydon Klein, Jr., August 4, 1964. Truman Papers, Post-Presidential File. Klein. Harry S. Truman Presidential Library and Museum.

59. Eyewitness Accounts

The importance of the eyewitness accounts, especially of the Trinity Test at Alamogordo, New Mexico, of the first nuclear explosions on earth cannot be overstated. The world of 1945 was one of destruction, brought to populations all over the world through words, pictures, radio, and film. People were used to death on a large scale—the firebombing of Dresden, Germany, for example, in February 1945 had killed more than 20,000 people, and millions of Jews, it was becoming known as the camps were liberated, had perished in German concentration camps in what was soon to become known generally as the Holocaust. Not pictures alone, be they still or moving, with or without sound recordings, could capture the human reactions, the human awe and amazement, the way words can. They say that a picture is worth a thousand words, but sometimes words express more that is both ethereal and damning than image and sound alone can ever encompass.

59a. Trinity

Luis Alvarez's Eyewitness Account of the Trinity Test, Monday, 5:30 a.m.—16 July 1945

I was kneeling between the pilot and co-pilot in B-29 No. 384 and observed the explosion through the pilot's window on the left side of the plane. We were about 20 to 25 miles from the site and the cloud cover between us and the ground was approximately 7/10. About 30 seconds before the object was detonated the clouds obscured our vision of the point so that we did not see the initial stages of the ball of fire. I was looking through crossed polaroid glasses directly at the site. My first sensation was one of intense light covering my whole field of vision. This seemed to last for about 1/2 second after which I noted an intense orange red glow through the clouds. Several seconds later it appeared that a second spherical red ball appeared but it is probable that this apparent phenomenon was caused by the motion of the airplane bringing us to a position where we could see through the cloud directly at the ball of fire which had been developing for the past few seconds. This fire ball seemed to have a rough texture with irregular black lines dividing the surface of the sphere into a large number of small patches of reddish orange. This thing disappeared a few seconds later and what seemed to be a third ball of fire appeared again and I am now convinced that this was all the same fire ball which I saw on two separate occasions through a new hole in the undercast.

When this "third ball" disappeared the light intensity dropped considerably and within another 20 seconds or so the cloud started to push up through the undercast. It first appeared as a parachute which was being blown up by a large electric fan. After the hemispherical cap had emerged through the cloud layer one could see a cloud of smoke about 1/3 the diameter of the "parachute" connecting the bottom of the hemisphere with the undercast. This had very much the appearance of a large mushroom. The hemispherical structure was creased with "longitude lines" running from the pole to the equator. In another minute the equatorial region had partially caught up with the poles giving a flattened out appearance to the top of the structure. In the next few minutes the symmetry of the structure was broken up by wind currents at various altitudes so the shape of the cloud cannot be described in any geometrical manner. In about 8 minutes the top of the cloud was at approximately 40,000 feet as close as I could estimate from our altitude of 24,000 feet and this seemed to be the maximum altitude attained by the cloud. I did not feel the shock wave hit the plane but the pilot felt the reaction on the rudder through the rudder pedals. Some of the other passengers in the plane noted a rather small shock at the time but it was not apparent to me.

I am attaching two sketches of the cloud which I made at the times noted. Mr. Glenn Fowler had made several sketches earlier in the development.

Luis W. Alvarez

Source: Record Group 227, OSRD-S1 Committee, Box 82, Folder 6, "Trinity." ARC identifier 594933. Transcription by Gene Dannen. National Archives.

Enrico Fermi's Eyewitness Report on the Trinity Test, July 16, 1945

My Observations During the Explosion at Trinity on July 16, 1945 - E. Fermi

On the morning of the 16th of July, I was stationed at the Base Camp at Trinity in a position about ten miles from the site of the explosion.

The explosion took place at about 5:30 A.M. I had my face protected by a large board in which a piece of dark welding glass had been inserted. My first impression of the explosion was the very intense flash of light, and a sensation of heat on the parts of my body that were exposed. Although I did not look directly towards the object, I had the impression that suddenly the countryside became brighter than in full daylight. I subsequently looked in the direction of the explosion through the dark glass and could see something that looked like a conglomeration of flames that promptly started rising. After a few seconds the rising flames lost their brightness and appeared as a huge pillar of smoke with an expanded head like a gigantic mushroom that rose rapidly beyond the clouds probably to a height of 30,000 feet. After reaching its full height, the smoke stayed stationary for a while before the wind started dissipating it.

About 40 seconds after the explosion the air blast reached me. I tried to estimate its strength by dropping from about six feet small pieces of paper before, during, and after the passage of the blast wave. Since, at the time, there was no wind I could observe very distinctly and actually measure the displacement of the pieces of paper that were in the process of falling while the blast was passing. The shift was about 2 1/2 meters, which, at the time, I estimated to correspond to the blast that would be produced by ten thousand tons of T.N.T.

Source: Record Group 227, OSRD-S1 Committee, Box 82, Folder 6, "Trinity." National Archives. Transcription and document scan by Gene Dannen.

O. R. Frisch's Eyewitness Report on the July 16, 1945 Trinity Test

I watched the explosion from a point said to be about 20 (or 25) miles away and about north of it, together with the members of the coordinating council. Fearing to be dazzled and to be burned by ultraviolet rays, I stood with my back to the gadget, and behind the radio truck. I looked at the hills, which were visible in the first faint light of dawn (0530 M.W. Time). Suddenly and without any sound, the hills were bathed in brilliant light, as if somebody had turned the sun on with a switch. It is hard to say whether the light was less or more brilliant than full sunlight, since my eyes were pretty well dark adapted. The hills appeared kind of flat and colourless like a scenery seen by the light of a photographic flash, indicating presumably that the retina was stimulated beyond the point where intensity discrimination is adequate. The light appeared to remain constant for about one or two seconds (probably for the same reason) and then began to diminish rapidly. After that I turned round and tried to look at the light source but found it still too bright to keep my eyes on it. A few short glances gave me the impression of a small very brilliant core much smaller in appearance than the sun, surrounded by decreasing and reddening brightness with no definite boundary, but not greater than the sun. After some seconds I could keep my eye on the thing and it now looked like a pretty perfect red ball, about as big as the sun, and connected to the ground by a short gray stem. The ball rose slowly, lengthening its stem and getting gradually darker and slightly larger. A structure of darker and lighter irregularities became visible, making the ball look somewhat like a raspberry. Then its motion slowed down and it flattened out, but still remained connected to the ground by its stem, looking more than ever like the trunk of an elephant. Then a hump grew out of its top surface and a second mushroom grew out of the top of the first one, slowly penetrating the highest cloud layers. As the red glow died out it became apparent that the whole structure, in particular the top mushroom, was surrounded by a purplish blue glow. A minute or so later the whole top mushroom appeared to glow feebly in this colour, but this was no longer easy to see, in the increasing light of dawn.

A very striking phenomenon was the sudden appearance of a white patch on the underside of the cloud layer just above the explosion; the patch spread very rapidly, like a pool of spilt milk, and a second or two later, a similar patch appeared and spread on another cloud layer higher up. They marked no doubt the impact of the blast wave on the cloud layers. They appeared, I believe, before the red ball bad started to flatten out.

When I thought it was soon time for the blast to arrive, I sat on the ground, still facing the explosion, and put my fingers in my ears. Despite that, the report was quite respectable and was followed by a long rumbling, not quite like thunder but more regular, like huge noisy wagons running around in the hills.

Source: *Foreign Relations of the United States.* 1960. Potsdam, vol. 2, 1371. Washington: Government Printing Office.

Kenneth Greisen's Eyewitness Account of the Trinity Test, July 16, 1945

July 21, 1945
To: Lt. Taylor
From: K. Greisen
Subject: Eye-witness account of Trinity shot

A group of us were lying on the ground just outside of base camp (10 miles from the charge), and received time signals over the radio, warning us when the shot would occur. I was personally nervous, for my group had prepared and installed the detonators, and if the shot turned out to be a dud, it might possibly be our fault. We were pretty sure we had done our job well, but there is always some chance of a slip.

At minus about 15 seconds I put my head close to the ground, turned to look away from the tower, and put up a shield between my head and the tower. I probably also closed my eyes briefly just before the shot. Suddenly I felt heat on the side of my head toward the tower, opened my eyes and saw a brilliant yellow-white light all around. The heat and light were as though the sun had just come out with unusual brilliance. About a second later I turned to look at the tower through the dark welding glass. A tremendous cloud of smoke was pouring upwards, some parts having brilliant red and yellow colors, like clouds at sunset. These parts kept folding over and over like dough in a mixing bowl. At this time I believe I exclaimed, "My god, it worked!" and felt a great relief.

When the intensity of the light had diminished, I put away the glass and looked toward the tower directly. At about this time I noticed a blue color surrounding the smoke cloud. Then someone shouted that we should observe the shock wave travelling along the ground. The appearance of this was a brightly lighted circular area, near the ground, slowly spreading out towards us. The color was yellow.

At what I presume was about 50 seconds after the shot, the ground shock and sound reached us almost simultaneously. The noise lasted for a long time, echoing back and forth from the hills. I noticed no sharp crack, but a rumbling sound as of thunder. After the brilliant optical display we had seen, the ground shock and noise were disappointing. No damage occurred, and we were not at all severely shaken.

Between the appearance of light and the arrival of the sound, there was loud cheering in the group around us. After the noise was over, we all went about congratulating each other and shaking hands. I believe we were all much more shaken up by the shot mentally than physically.

The permanence of the smoke cloud was one thing that surprised me. After the first rapid explosion, the lower part of the cloud seemed to assume a fixed shape and to remain hanging motionless in the air. The upper part meanwhile continued to rise, so that after a few minutes it was at least five miles high. It slowly assumed a zigzag shape because of the changing wind velocity at different altitudes. The smoke had pierced a cloud early in its ascent, and seemed to be completely unaffected by the cloud.

Source: Record Group 227, OSRD-S1 Committee, Box 82, Folder 6, "Trinity." National Archives. Transcription and document scan by Gene Dannen.

Edwin M. McMillan's Eyewitness Account of the Trinity Test, July 16, 1945

19 July 1945

IMPRESSIONS OF TRINITY TEST

I shall try to describe the Trinity test as seen from the "Hill Station", twenty miles from the event. None of my estimates of times or magnitudes can be considered very accurate, as I have found by comparison with others a wide variation, illustrating the difficulty of personal judgement without instruments.

The shot went off at about 5:30 a.m., just before sunrise. I was watching the shot through a piece of dark glass such as is used in welders' helmets. An exceedingly bright light appeared and expanded very rapidly. I was aware of a sensation of heat on my face and hands, which lasted about a second. After about two seconds, I took the glass away. The sky and surrounding landscape were brightly illuminated, but not as strongly as in full sunlight. The "ball of fire" was still too bright for direct observation, but it could be seen to be rising and expanding and slowly fading out. At some time during this stage, the layers of clouds visible above the explosion evaporated, forming a hole which rapidly got bigger.

At about thirty seconds, the general appearance was similar to a goblet; the ball I estimated to be about a mile in diameter and about four miles above the ground, glowing with a dull red; a dark stem connected it with the ground, and spread out in a thin dust layer that extended to a radius of about six miles. When the red glow faded out a most remarkable effect made its appearance. The whole surface of the ball was covered with a purple luminescence, like that produced by the electrical excitation of air, and caused undoubtedly by the radioactivity of the material in the ball. This was visible for about five seconds; by this time the sunlight was becoming bright enough to obscure luminous effects.

At some time near the end of the luminescence (I am not sure whether it was before or after) a great cloud broke out of the top of the ball and rose very rapidly to a height of about eight miles, expanding to a rather irregular shape several times as large as the ball. At about two minutes, the blast came. It was remarkably sharp, being more of a "crack" than a "boom". I did not feel any earth shock.

The later stages of motion of the cloud consisted of a slow drifting in the wind, showing the existence of several different wind directions at different altitudes. A current at a few hundred feet carrying the lower part of the "stem" toward the North 10,000 station was particularly striking. The cloud was a different color than the ordinary clouds through which it passed, having a brownish tinge; this could be caused by nitrogen dioxide formed from air by the intense ionization.

The whole spectacle was so tremendous and one might almost say fantastic that the immediate reaction of the watchers was one of awe rather than excitement. After some minutes of silence, a few people made remarks like, "Well, it worked," and then conversation and discussion became general. I am sure that all who witnessed this test went away with a profound feeling that they had seen one of the great events of history.

Edwin M. McMillan

Source: Record Group 227, OSRD-S1 Committee, Box 82, Folder 6, "Trinity." National Archives. Transcription and document scans by Gene Dannen.

Philip Morrison's Eyewitness Account of the Trinity Test, July 16, 1945

Observations of the Trinity Shot
July 16, 1945
P. Morrison

I observed the Trinity shot looking toward Zero from a position on the south bank of the base camp reservoir directly beside the larger water tank. There were three distinct stages in the process I saw, which I describe consecutively as follows:

1. Instantaneous glow and ball of fire

At time T = -45 seconds I lay prone facing Zero wearing ordinary sun glasses and holding in one hand a stop watch and in the other the welding glass issued by the stockroom. I watched the second-hand until T = -5 seconds when I lowered my head onto the sand bank in such a way that a slight rise in the ground completely shielded me from Zero. I placed the welding glass over the right lens of my sun glasses, the left lens of which was covered by an opaque cardboard shield. I counted seconds and at zero began to raise my head just over the protecting rise. During this motion the gadget went off while I was looking at it or possibly a small fraction of a second before. What I saw first was a brilliant violet glow entering my eyes by reflection from the ground and from the surroundings generally. I had not raised my head quite enough to provide a clear vision of Zero. Immediately after this brilliant violet flash, which was somewhat blinding, I observed through the welding glass, centered at the direction of the tower an enormous and brilliant disk of white light. The sensation lasted for such a short time and the light was so great that I cannot be sure of the shape observed. I remember it only as a well-marked vaguely round pattern. This disk was a true white in color, even through the welding glass which makes the sun's disk distinctly deep green. On subsequently looking at the noon sun through these glasses I have been led to estimate this initial stage of the gadget as corresponding to a color much whiter or bluer and a brightness several times greater than that of the noon sun. I felt a strong sensation of heat on the exposed skin of face and arms, lasting for several seconds and at least as intense as the direct noon sun.

It should be noted that my eyes were adapted to twilight or perhaps even to somewhat brighter light because of the use of the radio dial light I had made just previous to the T -45 second signal.

2. Growth of the mushroom

For a time which I guess to be less than two seconds the bright disk produced an after effect in my eyes which spoiled the details of the following process. I quickly realized that my vision was improving, that the image was becoming much fainter and less white. I then took off the welding glass and several seconds later the sun glasses as well. Beginning at T = +2 to 3 seconds, I observed the somewhat yellowed disk beginning to be eaten into from below by dark obscuring matter. Meanwhile the whole surface of the plain was covered with matter being thrown up into the air as the motion continued outward from Zero. In a matter of a few seconds more the disk had nearly stopped growing horizontally and was beginning to extend in a vertical direction while its appearance had transformed into that of a bright glowing distinctly red column of flame mixed with swirling obscuring matter. The column looked rather like smoke and flame rising from an oil fire. This turbulent red column rose straight up several thousand feet in a few seconds growing a mushroom-like head of the same kind. This mushroom was fully developed and the whole glowing structure complete at about 15,000 feet altitude. I do not recall whether this stage was reached before or after the arrival of the shock. At T +30 I realized the shock was due very soon and I huddled closer to the ground in anticipation of a severe shock. The arrival of the air shock at T +45 on my stop-watch came as an anti-climax. I noticed two deep thuds which sounded rather like a kettle drum rhythm being played some distance away. I remember the sound as being without any important high frequency components as cracks, etc. There was no earth tremor perceptible to me at any time. The ground on which I was lying was a very loosely packed dike of mud.

3. Appearance of the smoke cloud

After the passage of the shock I stood up to watch the end of the mushroom. The red glow died out and the mushroom appeared as a column of smoke or cloud hanging over Zero. In a matter of another minute or so the smoke had arranged itself in three rather well defined oblique clouds forming roughly a vertical Z. The lowest cloud was quite well defined, and stretched north at a slight angle. At a couple of thousand feet, it appeared to bend around almost double and to stretch about southeast for a somewhat greater distance. This second cloud again seemed broken off rather sharply and a large cloud gradually spread with less and less well defined shape from the upper end of the second step. This process was nearly complete when the upper cap was spread over most of the bowl at a height of about 30,000 feet. There was a strong impression of definite layers in the wind structure, and there were even some water vapor clouds which seemed to mark the boundaries between winds of different directions. The completion of this stage took many minutes until finally the cloud was rather well dispersed toward north 10,000 at a rather low level, had overspread at an intermediate level all the way to the Oscuro mountains, and on a higher level was drifting slowly south and southeast.

Other observations:

After T = +50 seconds, I distinctly smelled upon standing up a faint but marked odor of ozone or corona discharge ionization.

At T +15 minutes or more I observed Zero through a battery commander's periscope set of 8-power. Not much detail was visible in this region. A sort of dust haze seemed to cover the area. A remarkable amount of heat shimmer was noticed on the horizon directly above the Zero area. It was shortly after this that I saw the Jumbo tower was missing.

Size and distance figures mentioned here are based on judgments of angular size and the assumption of 18,000 yards distance from Zero to base camp.

Source: Record Group 227, OSRD-S1 Committee, Box 82, Folder 6, "Trinity." National Archives. Transcription and document scans by Gene Dannen.

Robert Serber's Eyewitness Account of the Trinity Test, July 16, 1945

I viewed the test, with the Coordinating Committee expedition, from a point about twenty miles away. At the instant of the explosion I was looking directly at it, with no eye protection of any kind. I saw first a yellow glow, which grew almost instantly into an overwhelming white flash, so intense that I was completely blinded. There was a definite sensation of heat. The brilliant illumination seemed to last for about three to five seconds, changing to yellow and then to red; at this stage it appeared to have a radius of about twenty degrees. The first thing I succeeded in seeing after being blinded by the flash looked like a dark violet column several thousand feet high. This column must actually have been quite bright, or I would not have been able to distinguish it. By twenty or thirty seconds after the explosion I was regaining normal vision. At a height of perhaps twenty thousand feet, two or three thin horizontal layers of shimmering white cloud were formed, perhaps due to condensation in the negative phase of the shock wave. Some time later, the noise of the explosion reached us. It had the quality of distant thunder, but was louder. The sound, due to reflections from nearby hills, returned and repeated and reverberated for several seconds, very much like thunder. A column of white smoke appeared over the point of the explosion, rising very rapidly, and spreading slightly as it rose. In a few seconds it reached cloud level, and the clouds in the immediate neighborhood seemed to evaporate and disappear. The column continued to rise and spread to a height of about twice the cloud level. There was no appearance of mushrooming at any height. A smoke cloud also was spreading near ground level.

The grandeur and magnitude of the phenomenon were completely breath-taking.

Robert Serber

Source: Record Group 227, OSRD-S1 Committee, Box 82, Folder 6, "Trinity." National Archives. Transcription and document scans by Gene Dannen.

Maurice M. Shapiro's Eyewitness Account of the Trinity Test, July 16, 1945

INTER-OFFICE MEMORANDUM

DATE: 23 July 1945

TO: Captain T. O. Jones
FROM: Maurice M. Shapiro
SUBJECT: Observations of the Trinity Test

During the Trinity test, I was stationed about 20 miles away, with the members of the Coordinating Council.

At the time of the initial flash of light my eyes were not protected, and I was momentarily blinded, much as one would be in emerging suddenly from a dark room into bright sunlight. After a couple of seconds I regained sufficient sight to see the entire sky (in the direction of Trinity) aglow with an orange hue. This glow disappeared after a second or two, and then I saw a column of dark gases rising toward the overhanging clouds. Several people near me commented on the violet color of the cloud of gas, but I observed no such color, presumably because of the initial effect on my eyes. I estimated the width (or diameter) of the column of gas as roughly 1/5 mile. After a few minutes this column rose to a height which I judged to be 8 or 10 miles high, and then it spread laterally. There were a few small puffs of white vapor, which I interpreted as arising from a "cloud-chamber effect" (supersaturation followed by condensation of moisture).

The shock wave from the explosion arrived at about one and a half minutes after the flash of light, and I heard it as a sharp report. Although I had expected it, the intensity of the blast startled me. My impression at the time was that an enemy observer stationed about 20 miles from the scene of delivery would be deeply impressed, to say the least.

Maurice M. Shapiro

MMS:fs
cc: 2-File

Source: Record Group 227, OSRD-S1 Committee, Box 82, Folder 6, "Trinity." National Archives. Transcription and document scans by Gene Dannen.

Cyril S. Smith's Eyewitness Account of the Trinity Test, July 16, 1945

INTER-OFFICE MEMORANDUM

DATE: July 25, 1945

TO: Lieutenant Taylor
FROM: C. S. Smith
SUBJECT: Trinity Shot

You requested me to write a brief description of the Trinity shot. Since this took place over a week ago my impressions have undoubtedly been modified very considerably by subsequent discussion and many features have faded from memory.

I was located at the base camp, behind a five foot embankment near the water tanks at T=0. I was facing away from the shot, somewhat bent down below the top of the bank. In addition, my eyes were partly covered by a welder's glass. For a time estimated as two seconds (though it may have been less) I was watching the ground through the corner of my eye. Even though this was lighted by reflection from the clouds, it was intensely bright and apparently free from color. Since the shot there has been some discussion of the duration of this intense light, but it is definitely my recollection that I opened and closed my eyes several times and waited for the light to decrease in intensity before turning to face the reaction zone directly. Even after the estimated 2 seconds the light was still intense enough to be clearly seen through the welder's glass but there was no direct ball of fire or structure or any symmetry, this part of the phenomenon evidently having ceased.

The appearance of a turbulent gas apparently undergoing combustion was quite surprising. It looked not much different from the film of the 100 ton shot or any large fire, for instance an oil tank fire or the Graf Zeppelin. After another second or two I removed the welder's glass and looked directly. As the main light became less intense, the bluish ionization zone became visible, extending to a diameter almost twice that of the area where there was incandescence. I noticed a dust cloud travelling near the ground, and at some stage (I am not sure whether early or late in the proceedings, but it was definitely illuminated by the shot) I noticed a ring, supposedly of moisture condensed by the rarefaction wave, at a level slightly below the clouds. This ring did not spread, but once formed seemed to remain stationary.

At the instant after the shot, my reactions were compounded of relief that "it worked"; consciousness of extreme silence, and a momentary question as to whether we had done more than we intended. Practically none of the watchers made any vocal comment until after the shock wave had passed and even then the cheers were not intense or prolonged. The elation of most observers seemed to increase for a period of 30 minutes afterwards, as they had a chance to absorb the significance of the achievement.

The rising of the cloud of reaction products to above the cloud level seems to have proceeded rapidly but in a normal fashion. It was noticeable that there were a number of rough projections, indicating high local turbulence. Shortly after the smoke column with its mushroom top was formed, wind currents distorted it into a jagged or corkscrew appearance. There was a dust cloud over the ground, extending for a considerable distance. A cloud, whether of dust or moisture particles, hung close to the ground and slowly drifted east into the hills, persisting for over an hour.

The obvious fact that all of the reaction products were not proceeding upward in a neat ball but were lagging behind and being blown by low altitude winds over the ground in the direction of inhabited areas produced very definite reflection that this is not a pleasant weapon we have produced. Later reflections were on the manner of defense against it and the realization that a city is henceforth not the place in which to live.

I repeat that no attention should be paid to any comment made in this report, since the described events occurred many days ago.

Cyril Stanley Smith

CSS:bc
cc:
Hawkins
File

Source: Record Group 227, OSRD-S1 Committee, Box 82, Folder 6, "Trinity." National Archives. Transcription and document scans by Gene Dannen.

Victor Weisskopf's Eyewitness Report on the Trinity Test, July 16, 1945

INTER-OFFICE MEMORANDUM
DATE: July 24, 1945
TO: Lt.   Taylor
FROM: V. Weisskopf
SUBJECT: EYE WITNESS ACCOUNT

You have asked me to submit to you an eye witness account of the explosion. I was located at base camp and watched the phenomenon from a little ridge about 100 yds. east of the water tower. Groups of observers had arranged small wooden sticks at a distance of 10 yds. from our observation place in order to estimate the size of the explosion. They were arranged so that their distance corresponded to 1000 ft. at zero point. I looked at the explosion through the dark glass, but I have provided for an indirect view of the landscape in order to see the deflected light.

When the explosion went off, I was first dazzled by this indirect light which was much stronger than I anticipated, and I was not able to concentrate upon the view through the dark glass and missed, therefore, the first stages of the explosion. When I was able to look through the dark glass I saw flames and smoke of an estimated diameter of 1000 yds. which was slowly decreasing in brightness seemingly due to more smoke development. At the same time it rose slightly above the surface. After about three seconds its intensity was so low I could remove the dark glass and look at it directly. Then I saw a reddish glowing smoke ball rising with a thick stem of dark brown color. This smoke ball was surrounded by a blue glow which clearly indicated a strong radioactivity and was certainly due to the gamma rays emitted by the cloud into the surrounding air. At that moment the cloud had about 1000 billions of curies of radioactivity whose radiation must have produced the blue glow.

The first two or three seconds, I felt very strongly the heat radiation all over the exposed parts of my body. The part of my retina which was exposed to the indirect light from the surrounding mountains was completely blinded and I could feel traces of the after image 30 minutes after the shock.

The reddish cloud darkened after about 10 or 20 seconds and rose rather rapidly leaving behind a thick stem of dark brown smoke. After this, I remember having seen a white hemisphere rising above the clouds in continuation of the breakthrough of the explosion cloud through the ordinary cloud level.

The path of the shock wave through the clouds was plainly visible as an expanding circle all over the sky where it was covered by clouds.

After about 45 seconds the sound wave arrived and it struck me as being much weaker than anticipated.

V. Weisskopf

VW:jsh
cc:Hawkins

Source: Record Group 227, OSRD-S1 Committee, Box 82, Folder 6, "Trinity." National Archives. Transcription and document scans by Gene Dannen.

59b. Hiroshima

John Siemes's Eyewitness Account of Atomic Bomb Over Hiroshima, August 6, 1945

Up to August 6th, occasional bombs, which did no great damage, had fallen on Hiroshima. Many cities roundabout, one after the other, were destroyed, but Hiroshima itself remained protected. There were almost daily observation planes over the city but none of them dropped a bomb. The citizens wondered why they alone had remained undisturbed for so long a time. There were fantastic rumors that the enemy had something special in mind for this city, but no one dreamed that the end would come in such a fashion as on the morning of August 6th.

August 6th began in a bright, clear, summer morning. About seven o'clock, there was an air raid alarm which we had heard almost every day and a few planes appeared over the city. No one paid any attention and at about eight o'clock, the all-clear was sounded. I am sitting in my room at the Novitiate of the Society of Jesus in Nagatsuke; during the past half year, the philosophical and theological section of our Mission had been evacuated to this place from Tokyo. The Novitiate is situated approximately two kilometers from Hiroshima, half-way up the sides of a broad valley which stretches from the town at sea level into this mountainous hinterland,

and through which courses a river. From my window, I have a wonderful view down the valley to the edge of the city.

Suddenly—the time is approximately 8:14—the whole valley is filled by a garish light which resembles the magnesium light used in photography, and I am conscious of a wave of heat. I jump to the window to find out the cause of this remarkable phenomenon, but I see nothing more than that brilliant yellow light. As I make for the door, it doesn't occur to me that the light might have something to do with enemy planes. On the way from the window, I hear a moderately loud explosion which seems to come from a distance and, at the same time, the windows are broken in with a loud crash. There has been an interval of perhaps ten seconds since the flash of light. I am sprayed by fragments of glass. The entire window frame has been forced into the room. I realize now that a bomb has burst and I am under the impression that it exploded directly over our house or in the immediate vicinity.

I am bleeding from cuts about the hands and head. I attempt to get out of the door. It has been forced outwards by the air pressure and has become jammed. I force an opening in the door by means of repeated blows with my hands and feet and come to a broad hallway from which open the various rooms. Everything is in a state of confusion. All windows are broken and all the doors are forced inwards. The bookshelves in the hallway have tumbled down. I do not note a second explosion and the fliers seem to have gone on. Most of my colleagues have been injured by fragments of glass. A few are bleeding but none has been seriously injured. All of us have been fortunate since it is now apparent that the wall of my room opposite the window has been lacerated by long fragments of glass.

We proceed to the front of the house to see where the bomb has landed. There is no evidence, however, of a bomb crater; but the southeast section of the house is very severely damaged. Not a door nor a window remains. The blast of air had penetrated the entire house from the southeast, but the house still stands. It is constructed in a Japanese style with a wooden framework, but has been greatly strengthened by the labor of our Brother Gropper as is frequently done in Japanese homes. Only along the front of the chapel which adjoins the house, three supports have given way (it has been made in the manner of Japanese temple, entirely out of wood.)

Down in the valley, perhaps one kilometer toward the city from us, several peasant homes are on fire and the woods on the opposite side of the valley are aflame. A few of us go over to help control the flames. While we are attempting to put things in order, a storm comes up and it begins to rain. Over the city, clouds of smoke are rising and I hear a few slight explosions. I come to the conclusion that an incendiary bomb with an especially strong explosive action has gone off down in the valley. A few of us saw three planes at great altitude over the city at the time of the explosion. I, myself, saw no aircraft whatsoever.

Perhaps a half-hour after the explosion, a procession of people begins to stream up the valley from the city. The crowd thickens continuously. A few come up the road to our house. We give them first aid and bring them into the chapel, which we have in the meantime cleaned and cleared of wreckage, and put them to rest on the straw mats which constitute the floor of Japanese houses. A few display horrible wounds of the extremities and back. The small quantity of fat which we possessed during this time of war was soon used up in the care of the burns. Father Rektor who, before taking holy orders, had studied medicine, ministers to the injured, but our bandages and drugs are soon gone. We must be content with cleansing the wounds.

More and more of the injured come to us. The least injured drag the more seriously wounded. There are wounded soldiers, and mothers carrying burned children in their arms. From the houses of the farmers in the valley comes word: "Our houses are full of wounded and dying. Can you help, at least by taking the worst cases?" The wounded come from the sections at the edge of the city. They saw the bright light, their houses collapsed and buried the inmates in their rooms. Those that were in the open suffered instantaneous burns, particularly on the lightly clothed or unclothed parts of the body. Numerous fires sprang up which soon consumed the entire district. We now conclude that the epicenter of the explosion was at the edge of the city near the Jokogawa Station, three kilometers away from us. We are concerned about Father Kopp who that same morning, went to hold Mass at the Sisters of the Poor, who have a home for children at the edge of the city. He had not returned as yet.

Toward noon, our large chapel and library are filled with the seriously injured. The procession of refugees from the city continues. Finally, about one o'clock, Father Kopp returns, together with the Sisters. Their house and the entire district where they live has burned to the ground. Father Kopp is bleeding about the head and neck, and he has a large burn on the right palm. He was standing in front of the nunnery ready to go home. All of a sudden, he became aware of the light, felt the wave of heat and a large blister formed on his hand. The windows were torn out by the blast. He thought that the bomb had fallen in his immediate vicinity. The nunnery, also a wooden structure made by our Brother Gropper, still remained but soon it is noted that the house is as good as lost because the fire, which had begun at many points in the neighborhood, sweeps closer and closer, and water is not available. There is still time to rescue certain things from the house and to bury them in an open spot. Then the house is swept by flame, and they fight their way back to us along the shore of the river and through the burning streets.

Soon comes news that the entire city has been destroyed by the explosion and that it is on fire. What became of Father Superior and the three other Fathers who were at the center of the city at the Central Mission and Parish House? We had up to this time not given them a thought because we did not believe that the effects of the bomb encompassed the entire city. Also, we did not want to go into town except under pressure of dire necessity, because we thought that the population was greatly perturbed and that it might take revenge on any foreigners which they might consider spiteful onlookers of their misfortune, or even spies.

Father Stolte and Father Erlinghagen go down to the road which is still full of refugees and bring in the seriously injured who have sunken by the wayside, to the temporary aid station at the village school. There iodine is applied to the wounds but they are left uncleansed. Neither ointments nor other therapeutic agents are available. Those that have been brought in are laid on the floor and no one can give them any further care. What could one do when all means are lacking? Under those circumstances, it is almost useless to bring them in. Among the passersby, there are many who are uninjured. In a purposeless, insensate manner, distraught by the magnitude of the disaster most of them rush by and none conceives the thought of organizing help on his own initiative. They are concerned only with the welfare of their own families. It became clear to us during these days that the Japanese displayed little initiative, preparedness, and organizational skill in preparation for catastrophes. They failed to carry out any rescue work when something could have been saved by a cooperative effort, and fatalistically let the catastrophe take its course. When we urged them to take part in the rescue work, they did everything willingly, but on their own initiative they did very little.

At about four o'clock in the afternoon, a theology student and two kindergarten children, who lived at the Parish House and adjoining buildings which had burned down, came in and said that Father Superior LaSalle and Father Schiffer had been seriously injured and that they had taken refuge in Asano Park on the river bank. It is obvious that we must bring them in since they are too weak to come here on foot.

Hurriedly, we get together two stretchers and seven of us rush toward the city. Father Rektor comes along with food and medicine. The closer we get to the city, the greater is the evidence of destruction and the more difficult it is to make our way. The houses at the edge of the city are all severely damaged. Many have collapsed or burned down. Further in, almost all of the dwellings have been damaged by fire. Where the city stood, there is a gigantic burned-out scar. We make our way along the street on the river bank among the burning and smoking ruins. Twice we are forced into the river itself by the heat and smoke at the level of the street.

Frightfully burned people beckon to us. Along the way, there are many dead and dying. On the Misasi Bridge, which leads into the inner city we are met by a long procession of soldiers who have suffered burns. They drag themselves along with the help of staves or are carried by their less severely injured comrades . . . an endless procession of the unfortunate.

Abandoned on the bridge, there stand with sunken heads a number of horses with large burns on their flanks. On the far side, the cement structure of the local hospital is the only building that remains standing. Its interior, however, has been burned out. It acts as a landmark to guide us on our way.

Finally we reach the entrance of the park. A large proportion of the populace has taken refuge there, but even the trees of the park are on fire in several places. Paths and bridges are blocked by the trunks of fallen trees and are almost impassable. We are told that a high wind, which may well have resulted from the heat of the burning city, has uprooted the large trees. It is now quite dark. Only the fires, which are still raging in some places at a distance, give out a little light.

At the far corner of the park, on the river bank itself, we at last come upon our colleagues. Father Schiffer is on the ground pale as a ghost. He has a deep incised wound behind the ear and has lost so much blood that we are concerned about his chances for survival. The Father Superior has suffered a deep wound of the lower leg. Father Cieslik and Father Kleinsorge have minor injuries but are completely exhausted.

While they are eating the food that we have brought along, they tell us of their experiences. They were in their rooms at the Parish House—it was a quarter after eight, exactly the time when we had heard the explosion in Nagatsuke—when came the intense light and immediately thereafter the sound of breaking windows, walls and furniture. They were showered with glass splinters and fragments of wreckage. Father Schiffer was buried beneath a portion of a wall and suffered a severe head injury. The Father Superior received most of the splinters in his back and lower extremity from which he bled copiously. Everything was thrown about in the rooms themselves, but the wooden framework of the house remained intact. The solidity of the structure which was the work of Brother Gropper again shone forth.

They had the same impression that we had in Nagatsuke: that the bomb had burst in their immediate vicinity. The Church, school, and all buildings in the immediate vicinity collapsed at once. Beneath the ruins of the school, the children cried for help. They were freed with great effort. Several others were also rescued from the ruins of nearby dwellings. Even the Father Superior and Father Schiffer despite their wounds, rendered aid to others and lost a great deal of blood in the process.

In the meantime, fires which had begun some distance away are raging even closer, so that it becomes obvious that everything would soon burn down. Several objects are rescued from the Parish House and were buried in a clearing in front of the Church, but certain valuables and necessities which had been kept ready in case of fire could not be found on account of the confusion which had been wrought. It is high time to flee, since the oncoming flames leave almost no way open. Fukai, the secretary of the Mission, is completely out of his mind. He does not want to leave the house and explains that he does not want to survive the destruction of his fatherland. He is completely uninjured. Father Kleinsorge drags him out of the house on his back and he is forcefully carried away.

Beneath the wreckage of the houses along the way, many have been trapped and they scream to be rescued from the oncoming flames. They must be left to their fate. The way to the place in the city to which one desires to flee is no longer open and one must make for Asano Park. Fukai does not want to go further and remains behind. He has not been heard from since. In the park, we take refuge on the bank of the river. A very violent whirlwind now begins to uproot large trees, and lifts them high into the air. As it reaches the water, a waterspout forms which is approximately 100 meters high. The violence of the storm luckily passes us by. Some distance away, however, where numerous refugees have taken shelter, many are blown into the river. Almost all who are in the vicinity have been injured and have lost relatives who have been pinned under the wreckage or who have been lost sight of during the flight. There is no help for the wounded and some die. No one pays any attention to a dead man lying nearby.

The transportation of our own wounded is difficult. It is not possible to dress their wounds properly in the darkness, and they bleed again upon slight motion. As we carry them on the shaky litters in the dark over fallen trees of the park, they suffer unbearable pain as the result of the movement, and lose dangerously large quantities of blood. Our rescuing angel in this difficult situation is a Japanese Protestant pastor. He has brought up a boat and offers to take our wounded up stream to a place where progress is easier. First, we lower the litter containing Father Schiffer into the boat and two of us accompany him. We plan to bring the boat back for the Father Superior. The boat returns about one-half hour later and the pastor requests that several of us help in the rescue of two children whom he had seen in the river. We rescue them. They have severe burns. Soon they suffer chills and die in the park.

The Father Superior is conveyed in the boat in the same manner as Father Schiffer. The theology student and myself accompany him. Father Cieslik considers himself strong enough to make his way on foot to Nagatsuke with the rest of us, but Father Kleinsorge cannot walk so far and we leave him behind and promise to come for him and the housekeeper tomorrow. From the other side of the stream comes the whinny of horses who are threatened by the fire. We land on a sand spit which juts out from the shore. It is full of wounded who have taken refuge there. They scream for aid for they are afraid of drowning as the river may rise with the sea, and cover the sand spit. They themselves are too weak to move. However, we must press on and finally we reach the spot where the group containing Father Schiffer is waiting.

Here a rescue party had brought a large case of fresh rice cakes but there is no one to distribute them to the numerous wounded that lie all about. We distribute them to those that are nearby and also help ourselves. The wounded call for water and we come to the aid of a few. Cries for help are heard from a distance, but we cannot approach the ruins from which they come. A group of soldiers comes along the road and their officer notices that we speak a strange language. He at once draws his sword, screamingly demands who we are and threatens to cut us down. Father Laures, Jr., seizes his arm and explains that we are German. We finally quiet him down. He thought that we might well be Americans who had parachuted down. Rumors of parachutists were being bandied about the city. The Father Superior who was clothed only in a shirt and trousers, complains of feeling freezing cold, despite the warm summer night and the heat of the burning city. The one man among us who possesses a coat gives it to him and, in addition, I give him my own shirt. To me, it seems more comfortable to be without a shirt in the heat.

In the meantime, it has become midnight. Since there are not enough of us to man both litters with four strong bearers, we determine to remove Father Schiffer first to the outskirts of the city. From there, another group of bearers is to take over to Nagatsuke; the others are to turn back in order to rescue the Father Superior. I am one of the bearers. The theology student goes in front to warn us of the numerous wires, beams and fragments of ruins which block the way and which are impossible to see in the dark. Despite all precautions, our progress is stumbling and our feet get tangled in the wire. Father Kruer falls and carries the litter with him. Father Schiffer becomes half unconscious from the fall and vomits. We pass an injured man who sits all alone among the hot ruins and whom I had seen previously on the way down.

On the Misasa Bridge, we meet Father Tappe and Father Luhmer, who have come to meet us from Nagatsuke. They had dug a family out of the ruins of their collapsed house some fifty meters off the road. The father of the family was already dead. They had dragged out two girls and placed them by the side of the road. Their mother was still trapped under some beams. They had planned to complete the rescue and then to press on to meet us. At the outskirts of the city, we put down the litter and leave two men to wait until those who are to come from Nagatsuke appear. The rest of us turn back to fetch the Father Superior.

Most of the ruins have now burned down. The darkness kindly hides the many forms that lie on the ground. Only occasionally in our quick progress do we hear calls for help. One of us remarks that the remarkable burned smell reminds him of incinerated corpses. The upright, squatting form which we had passed by previously is still there.

Transportation on the litter, which has been constructed out of boards, must be very painful to the Father Superior, whose entire back is full of fragments of glass. In a narrow passage at the edge of town, a car forces us to the edge of the road. The litter bearers on the left side fall into a two meter deep ditch which they could not see in the darkness. Father Superior hides his pain with a dry joke, but the litter which is now no longer in one piece cannot be carried further. We decide to wait until Kinjo can bring a hand cart from Nagatsuke. He soon comes back with one that he has requisitioned from a collapsed house. We place Father Superior on the cart and wheel him the rest of the way, avoiding as much as possible the deeper pits in the road.

About half past four in the morning, we finally arrive at the Novitiate. Our rescue expedition had taken almost twelve hours. Normally, one could go back and forth to the city in two hours. Our two wounded were now, for the first time, properly dressed. I get two hours sleep on the floor; some one else has taken my own bed. Then I read a Mass in gratiarum actionem, it is the 7th of August, the anniversary of the foundation of our society. Then we bestir ourselves to bring Father Kleinsorge and other acquaintances out of the city.

We take off again with the hand cart. The bright day now reveals the frightful picture which last night's darkness had partly concealed. Where the city stood everything, as far as the eye could reach, is a waste of ashes and ruin. Only several skeletons of buildings completely burned out in the interior remain. The banks of the river are covered with dead and wounded, and the rising waters have here and there covered some of the corpses. On the broad street in the Hakushima district, naked burned cadavers are particularly numerous. Among them are the wounded who are still alive. A few have crawled under the burnt-out autos and trams. Frightfully injured forms beckon to us and then collapse. An old woman and a girl whom she is pulling along with her fall down at our feet. We place them on our cart and wheel them to the hospital at whose entrance a dressing station has been set up. Here the wounded lie on the hard floor, row on row. Only the largest wounds are dressed. We convey another soldier and an old woman to the place but we cannot move everybody who lies exposed in the sun. It would be endless and it is questionable whether those whom we can drag to the dressing station can come out alive, because even here nothing really effective can be done. Later, we ascertain that the wounded lay for days in the burnt-out hallways of the hospital and there they died.

We must proceed to our goal in the park and are forced to leave the wounded to their fate. We make our way to the place where our church stood to dig up those few belongings that we had buried yesterday. We find them intact. Everything else has been completely burned. In the ruins, we find a few molten remnants of holy vessels. At the park, we load the housekeeper and a mother with her two children on the cart. Father

Kleinsorge feels strong enough, with the aid of Brother Nobuhara, to make his way home on foot. The way back takes us once again past the dead and wounded in Hakushima. Again no rescue parties are in evidence. At the Misasa Bridge, there still lies the family which the Fathers Tappe and Luhmer had yesterday rescued from the ruins. A piece of tin had been placed over them to shield them from the sun. We cannot take them along for our cart is full. We give them and those nearby water to drink and decide to rescue them later. At three o'clock in the afternoon, we are back in Nagatsuka.

After we have had a few swallows and a little food, Fathers Stolte, Luhmer, Erlinghagen and myself, take off once again to bring in the family. Father Kleinsorge requests that we also rescue two children who had lost their mother and who had lain near him in the park. On the way, we were greeted by strangers who had noted that we were on a mission of mercy and who praised our efforts. We now met groups of individuals who were carrying the wounded about on litters. As we arrived at the Misasa Bridge, the family that had been there was gone. They might well have been borne away in the meantime. There was a group of soldiers at work taking away those that had been sacrificed yesterday.

More than thirty hours had gone by until the first official rescue party had appeared on the scene. We find both children and take them out of the park: a six-year old boy who was uninjured, and a twelve-year old girl who had been burned about the head, hands and legs, and who had lain for thirty hours without care in the park. The left side of her face and the left eye were completely covered with blood and pus, so that we thought that she had lost the eye. When the wound was later washed, we noted that the eye was intact and that the lids had just become stuck together. On the way home, we took another group of three refugees with us. They first wanted to know, however, of what nationality we were. They, too, feared that we might be Americans who had parachuted in. When we arrived in Nagatsuka, it had just become dark.

We took under our care fifty refugees who had lost everything. The majority of them were wounded and not a few had dangerous burns. Father Rektor treated the wounds as well as he could with the few medicaments that we could, with effort, gather up. He had to confine himself in general to cleansing the wounds of purulent material. Even those with the smaller burns are very weak and all suffered from diarrhea. In the farm houses in the vicinity, almost everywhere, there are also wounded. Father Rektor made daily rounds and acted in the capacity of a painstaking physician and was a great Samaritan. Our work was, in the eyes of the people, a greater boost for Christianity than all our work during the preceding long years.

Three of the severely burned in our house died within the next few days. Suddenly the pulse and respirations ceased. It is certainly a sign of our good care that so few died. In the official aid stations and hospitals, a good third or half of those that had been brought in died. They lay about there almost without care, and a very high percentage succumbed. Everything was lacking: doctors, assistants, dressings, drugs, etc. In an aid station at a school at a nearby village, a group of soldiers for several days did nothing except to bring in and cremate the dead behind the school.

During the next few days, funeral processions passed our house from morning to night, bringing the deceased to a small valley nearby. There, in six places, the dead were burned. People brought their own wood and themselves did the cremation. Father Luhmer and Father Laures found a dead man in a nearby house who had already become bloated and who emitted a frightful odor. They brought him to this valley and incinerated him themselves. Even late at night, the little valley was lit up by the funeral pyres.

We made systematic efforts to trace our acquaintances and the families of the refugees whom we had sheltered. Frequently, after the passage of several weeks, some one was found in a distant village or hospital but of many there was no news, and these were apparently dead. We were lucky to discover the mother of the two children whom we had found in the park and who had been given up for dead. After three weeks, she saw her children once again. In the great joy of the reunion were mingled the tears for those whom we shall not see again.

The magnitude of the disaster that befell Hiroshima on August 6th was only slowly pieced together in my mind. I lived through the catastrophe and saw it only in flashes, which only gradually were merged to give me a total picture. What actually happened simultaneously in the city as a whole is as follows: As a result of the explosion of the bomb at 8:15, almost the entire city was destroyed at a single blow. Only small outlying districts in the southern and eastern parts of the town escaped complete destruction. The bomb exploded over the center of the city. As a result of the blast, the small Japanese houses in a diameter of five kilometers, which compressed 99% of the city, collapsed or were blown up. Those who were in the houses were buried in the ruins. Those who were in the open sustained burns resulting from contact with the substance or rays emitted by the bomb. Where the substance struck in quantity, fires sprang up. These spread rapidly.

The heat which rose from the center created a whirlwind which was effective in spreading fire throughout the whole city. Those who had been caught beneath the ruins and who could not be freed rapidly, and those who had been caught by the flames, became casualties. As much as six kilometers from the center of the explosion, all houses were damaged and many collapsed and caught fire. Even fifteen kilometers away, windows were broken. It was rumored that the enemy fliers had spread an explosive and incendiary material over the city and then had created the explosion and ignition. A few maintained that they saw the planes drop a parachute which had carried something that exploded at a height of 1,000 meters. The newspapers called the bomb an "atomic bomb" and noted that the force of the blast had resulted from the explosion of uranium atoms, and that gamma rays had been sent out as a result of this, but no one knew anything for certain concerning the nature of the bomb.

How many people were a sacrifice to this bomb? Those who had lived through the catastrophe placed the number of dead at at least 100,000. Hiroshima had a population of 400,000. Official statistics place the number who had died at 70,000 up to September 1st, not counting the missing . . . and 130,000 wounded, among them 43,500 severely wounded. Estimates made by ourselves on the basis of groups known to us show that the number of 100,000 dead is not too high. Near us there are two barracks, in each of which forty Korean workers lived. On the day of the explosion, they were laboring on the streets of Hiroshima. Four returned alive to one barracks and sixteen to the other. 600 students of the Protestant girls' school worked in a factory, from which only thirty to forty returned. Most of the peasant families in the neighborhood lost one or more of their members who had worked at factories in the city. Our next door neighbor, Tamura, lost two children and himself suffered a large wound since, as it happened, he had been in the city on that day. The family of our reader suffered two dead, father and son; thus a family of five members suffered at least two losses, counting only the dead and severely wounded. There died the Mayor, the President of the central Japan district, the Commander of the city, a Korean prince who had been stationed in Hiroshima in the capacity of an officer, and many other high ranking officers. Of the professors of the University, thirty-two were killed or severely injured. Especially hard hit were the soldiers. The Pioneer Regiment was almost entirely wiped out. The barracks were near the center of the explosion.

Thousands of wounded who died later could doubtless have been rescued had they received proper treatment and care, but rescue work in a catastrophe of this magnitude had not been envisioned; since the whole city had been knocked out at a blow, everything which had been prepared for emergency work was lost, and no preparation had been made for rescue work in the outlying districts. Many of the wounded also died because they had been weakened by under-nourishment and consequently lacked in strength to recover. Those who had their normal strength and who received good care slowly healed the burns which had been occasioned by the bomb. There were also cases, however, whose prognosis seemed good who died suddenly. There were also some who had only small external wounds who died within a week or later, after an inflammation of the pharynx and oral cavity had taken place. We thought at first that this was the result of inhalation of the substance of the bomb. Later, a commission established the thesis that gamma rays had been given out at the time of the explosion, following which the internal organs had been injured in a manner resembling that consequent upon Roentgen irradiation. This produces a diminution in the numbers of the white corpuscles.

Only several cases are known to me personally where individuals who did not have external burns later died. Father Kleinsorge and Father Cieslik, who were near the center of the explosion, but who did not suffer burns became quite weak some fourteen days after the explosion. Up to this time small incised wounds had healed normally, but thereafter the wounds which were still unhealed became worse and are to date (in September) still incompletely healed. The attending physician diagnosed it as leucopania. There thus seems to be some truth in the statement that the radiation had some effect on the blood. I am of the opinion, however, that their generally undernourished and weakened condition was partly responsible for these findings. It was noised about that the ruins of the city emitted deadly rays and that workers who went there to aid in the clearing died, and that the central district would be uninhabitable for some time to come. I have my doubts as to whether such talk is true and myself and others who worked in the ruined area for some hours shortly after the explosion suffered no such ill effects.

None of us in those days heard a single outburst against the Americans on the part of the Japanese, nor was there any evidence of a vengeful spirit. The Japanese suffered this terrible blow as part of the fortunes of war . . . something to be borne without complaint. During this, war, I have noted relatively little hatred toward the allies on the part of the people themselves, although the press has taken occasion to stir up such feelings. After the victories at the beginning of the war, the enemy was rather looked down upon, but when allied offensive gathered momentum and especially after the advent of the majestic B-29's, the technical skill of America became an object of wonder and admiration.

The following anecdote indicates the spirit of the Japanese: A few days after the atomic bombing, the secretary of the University came to us asserting that the Japanese were ready to destroy San Francisco by means of an equally effective bomb. It is dubious that he himself believed what he told us. He merely wanted to impress upon us foreigners that the Japanese were capable of similar discoveries. In his nationalistic pride, he talked himself into believing this. The Japanese also intimated that the principle of the new bomb was a Japanese discovery. It was only lack of raw materials, they said, which prevented its construction. In the meantime, the Germans were said to have carried the discovery to a further stage and were about to initiate such bombing. The Americans were reputed to have learned the secret from the Germans, and they had then brought the bomb to a stage of industrial completion.

We have discussed among ourselves the ethics of the use of the bomb. Some consider it in the same category as poison gas and were against its use on a civil population. Others were of the view that in total war, as carried on in Japan, there was no difference between civilians and soldiers, and that the bomb itself was an effective force tending to end the bloodshed, warning Japan to surrender and thus to avoid total destruction. It seems logical to me that he who supports total war in principle cannot complain of war against civilians. The crux of the matter is whether total war in its present form is justifiable, even when it serves a just purpose. Does it not have material and spiritual evil as its consequences which far exceed whatever good that might result? When will our moralists give us a clear answer to this question?

Source: The Atomic Bombings of Hiroshima and Nagasaki. Manhattan Engineer District, June 29, 1946. Appendix. Available online at http://www.gutenberg.org/cache/epub/685/pg685-images.html. Accessed May 5, 2019.

59c. Nagasaki
William Laurence's Eyewitness Account of Atomic Bomb Over Nagasaki, August 9, 1945

Eyewitness Account of Atomic
Bomb Over Nagasaki
William L. Laurence
WAR DEPARTMENT
Bureau of Public Relations
PRESS BRANCH
FUTURE RELEASE
FOR RELEASE SUNDAY, SEPTEMBER 9, 1945
**EYE WITNESS ACCOUNT
ATOMIC BOMB MISSION OVER
NAGASAKI**

NOTE TO EDITORS:
The following release was written by William L. Laurence, Science writer for the New York Times, and Special Consultant to the Manhattan Engineer District and former Pulitzer Prize winner. The story can be released with or without the use of Mr. Laurence's name.
WITH THE ATOMIC BOMB MISSION TO JAPAN, AUGUST 9 (DELAYED)—We

are on our way to bomb the mainland of Japan. Our flying contingent consists of three specially designed B-29 Superforts, and two of these carry no bombs. But our lead plane is on its way with another atomic bomb, the second in three days, concentrating its active substance, and explosive energy equivalent to 20,000, and under favorable conditions, 40,000 tons of TNT.

We have several chosen targets. One of these is the great industrial and shipping center of Nagasaki, on the western shore of Kyushu, one of the main islands of the Japanese homeland.

I watched the assembly of this man-made meteor during the past two days, and was among the small group of scientists and Army and Navy representatives privileged to be present at the ritual of its loading in the Superfort last night, against a background of threatening black skies torn open at intervals by great lightning flashes.

It is a thing of beauty to behold, this "gadget." In its design went millions of man-hours of what is without a doubt the most concentrated intellectual effort in history. Never before had so much brain-power been focused on a single problem.

This atomic bomb is different from the bomb used three days ago with such devastating results on Hiroshima.

I saw the atomic substance before it was placed inside the bomb. By itself it is not at all dangerous to handle. It is only under certain conditions, produced in the bomb assembly, that it can be made to yield up its energy, and even then it gives up only a small fraction of its total contents, a fraction, however, large enough to produce the greatest explosion on earth.

The briefing at midnight revealed the extreme care and the tremendous amount of preparation that had been made to take care of every detail of the mission, in order to make certain that the atomic bomb fully served the purpose for which it was intended. Each target in turn was shown in detailed maps and in aerial photographs. Every detail of the course was rehearsed, navigation, altitude, weather, where to land in emergencies. It came out that the Navy had submarines and rescue craft, known as "Dumbos" and "Super Dumbos," stationed at various strategic points in the vicinity of the targets, ready to rescue the fliers in case they were forced to bail out.

The briefing period ended with a moving prayer by the Chaplain. We then proceeded to the mess hall for the traditional early morning breakfast before departure on a bombing mission.

A convoy of trucks took us to the supply building for the special equipment carried on combat missions. This included the "Mae West," a parachute, a life boat, an oxygen mask, a flak suit and a survival vest. We still had a few hours before take-off time but we all went to the flying field and stood around in little groups or sat in jeeps talking rather casually about our mission to the Empire, as the Japanese home islands are known hereabouts.

In command of our mission is Major Charles W. Sweeney, 25, of 124 Hamilton Avenue, North Quincy, Massachusetts. His flagship, carrying the atomic bomb, is named "The Great Artiste," but the name does not appear on the body of the great silver ship, with its unusually long, four-bladed, orange-tipped propellers. Instead it carried the number "77," and someone remarks that it is "Red" Grange's winning number on the Gridiron.

Major Sweeney's co-pilot is First Lieutenant Charles D. Albury, 24, of 252 Northwest Fourth Street, Miami, Florida. The bombardier upon whose shoulders rests the responsibility of depositing the atomic bomb square on its target, is Captain Kermit K. Beahan, of 1004 Telephone Road, Houston, Texas, who is celebrating his twenty-seventh birthday today.

Captain Beahan has been awarded the Distinguished Flying Cross, the Air Medal, and one Silver Oak Leaf Cluster, the Purple Heart, the Western Hemisphere Ribbon, the European Theater ribbon and two battle stars. He participated in the first heavy bombardment mission against Germany from England on August 17, 1942, and was on the plane that transported General Eisenhower from Gibraltar to Oran at the beginning of the North African invasion. He has had a number of hair-raising escapes in combat.

The Navigator on "The Great Artiste" is Captain James F. Van Pelt, Jr., 27, of Oak Hill, West Virginia. The flight engineer is Master Sergeant John D. Kuharek, 32, of 1054 22nd Avenue, Columbus, Nebraska. Staff Sergeant Albert T. De Hart of Plainview, Texas, who celebrated his thirtieth birthday yesterday, is the tail gunner; the radar operator is Staff Sergeant Edward K. Buckley, 32, of 529 East Washington Street, Lisbon, Ohio. The radio operator is Sergeant Abe M. Spitzer, 33, of 655 Pelham Parkway, North Bronx, New York; Sergeant Raymond Gallagher, 23, of 5727 South Mozart Street, Chicago, Illinois, is assistant flight engineer.

The lead ship is also carrying a group of scientific personnel, headed by Commander Frederick L. Ashworth, U.S.N., one of the leaders in the development of the bomb. The group includes Lieutenant Jacob Beser, 24, of Baltimore, Maryland, an expert on airborne radar.

The other two Superforts in our formation are instrument planes, carrying special apparatus to measure the power of the bomb at the time of explosion, high speed cameras and other photographic equipment.

Our Superfort is the second in line. Its Commander is Captain Frederick C. Bock, 27, of 300 West Washington Street, Greenville, Michigan. Its other officers are Second Lieutenant Hugh C. Ferguson, 21, of 247 Windermere Avenue, Highland Park, Michigan, pilot; Second Lieutenant Leonard A. Godfrey, 24, of 72 Lincoln Street, Greenfield, Massachusetts, navigator; and First Lieutenant Charles Levy, 26, of 1954 Spencer Street, Philadelphia, Pennsylvania, bombardier.

The enlisted personnel of this Superfort are the following: Technical Sergeant Roderick F. Arnold, 28, of 130 South Street, Rochester, Michigan, flight engineer; Sergeant Ralph D. Curry, 20, of 1101 South 2nd Avenue, Hoopeston, Illinois, radio operator; Sergeant William C. Barney, 22, of Columbia City, Indiana, radar operator; Corporal Robert J. Stock, 21, of 415 Downing Street, Fort Wayne, Indiana, assistant flight engineer; and Corporal Ralph D. Belanger, 19, of Thendara, New York, tail gunner.

The scientific personnel of our Superfort includes: Staff Sergeant Walter Goodman, 22, of 1956 74th Street, Brooklyn, New York, and Lawrence Johnson, graduate student at the University of California, whose home is at Hollywood, California.

The third Superfort is commanded by Major James Hopkins, 1311 North Queen Street, Palestine, Texas. His officers are Second Lieutenant John E. Cantlon, 516 North Takima Street, Tacoma, Washington, pilot; Second Lieutenant Stanley C. Steinke, 604 West Chestnut Street, West Chester, Pennsylvania, navigator; and Second Lieutenant Myron Faryna, 16 Elgin Street, Rochester, New York, bombardier.

The crew are Technical Sergeant George L. Brabenec, 9727 South Lawndale Avenue, Evergreen, Illinois; Sergeant Francis X. Dolan, 30-60 Warrent Street, Elmhurst,

New York; Corporal Richard F. Cannon, 160 Carmel Road, Buffalo, New York; Corporal Martin G. Murray, 7356 Dexter Street, Detroit, Michigan, and Corporal Sidney J. Bellamy, 529 Johnston Avenue, Trenton, New Jersey.

On this Superfort are also two distinguished observers from Great Britain, whose scientists played an important role in the development of the Atomic Bomb. One of these is Group Captain G. Leonard Cheshire, famous RAF pilot, who is now a member of the British Military Mission to the United States. The other is Dr. William G. Penney, Professor of Applied Mathematics London University, one of the group of eminent British scientists which has been working at the "Y-Site" near Santa Fe, New Mexico, on the enormous problems involved in taming the Atom.

Group Captain Cheshire, whose rank is the equivalent of that of Colonel in the AAF, was designated as an observer of the Atomic Bomb in action by Winston Churchill when he was still Prime Minister. He is now the official representative of Prime Minister Attlee.

We took off at 3:50 this morning and headed northwest on a straight line for the Empire. The night was cloudy and threatening, with only a few stars here and there breaking through the overcast. The weather report had predicted storms ahead part of the way but clear sailing for the final and climactic stages of our odyssey.

We were about an hour away from our base when the storm broke. Our great ship took some heavy dips through the abysmal darkness around us, but it took these dips much more gracefully than a large commercial airliner, producing a sensation more in the nature of a glide than a "bump" like a great ocean liner riding the waves. Except that in this case the air waves were much higher and the rhythmic tempo of the glide much faster.

I noticed a strange eerie light coming through the window high above in the Navigator's cabin and as I peered through the dark all around us I saw a startling phenomenon. The whirling giant propellers had somehow become great luminous discs of blue flame. The same luminous blue flame appeared on the plexiglass windows in the nose of the ship, and on the tips of the giant wings it looked as though we were riding the whirlwind through space on a chariot of blue fire.

It was, I surmised, a surcharge of static electricity that had accumulated on the tips of the propellers and on the dielectric material in the plastic windows. One's thoughts dwelt anxiously on the precious cargo in the invisible ship ahead of us. Was there any likelihood of danger that this heavy electric tension in the atmosphere all about us may set it off?

I express my fears to Captain Bock, who seems nonchalant and imperturbed at the controls. He quickly reassures me:

"It is a familiar phenomenon seen often on ships. I have seen it many times on bombing missions. It is known as St. Elmo's Fire."

On we went through the night. We soon rode out the storm and our ship was once again sailing on a smooth course straight ahead, on a direct line to the Empire.

Our altimeter showed that we were traveling through space at a height of 17,000 feet. The thermometer registered an outside temperature of 33 degrees below zero centigrade (about 30 below Fahrenheit). Inside our pressurized cabin the temperature was that of a comfortable air-conditioned room, and a pressure corresponding to an altitude of 8,000 feet. Captain Bock cautioned me, however, to keep my oxygen mask handy in case of emergency. This, he explained, may mean either something going wrong with the pressure equipment inside the ship or a hole through the cabin by flak.

The first signs of dawn came shortly after 5:00 o'clock. Sergeant Curry, who had been listening steadily on his earphones for radio reports while maintaining a strict radio silence himself, greeted it by rising to his feet and gazing out the window. "It's good to see the day," he told me. "I get a feeling of claustrophobia hemmed in in this cabin at night."

He is a typical American youth, looking even younger than his 20 years. It takes no mind reader to read his thoughts.

"It's a long way from Hoopeston, Illinois," I find myself remarking.

"Yep," he replies, as he busies himself decoding a message from outer space.

"Think this atomic bomb will end the war?" he asks hopefully.

"There is a very good chance that this one may do the trick," I assure him, "but if not then the next one or two surely will. Its power is such that no nation can stand up against it very long."

This was not my own view. I had heard it expressed all around a few hours earlier before we took off. To anyone who had seen this man-made fireball in action, as I had less than a month ago in the desert of New Mexico, this view did not sound over-optimistic.

By 5:50 it was real light outside. We had lost our lead ship but Lieutenant Godfrey, our Navigator, informs me that we had arranged for that contingency. We have an assembly point in the sky above the little island of Yakoshima, southeast of Kyushu, at 9:10. We are to circle there and wait for the rest of our formation.

Our genial Bombardier, Lieutenant Levy, comes over to invite me to take his front row seat in the transparent nose of the ship and I accept eagerly. From that vantage point in space, 17,000 feet above the Pacific, one gets a view of hundreds of miles on all sides, horizontally and vertically. At that height the vast ocean below and the sky above seem to merge into one great sphere. I was on the inside of that firmament, riding above the giant mountains of white cumulous clouds, letting myself be suspended in infinite space. One hears the whirl of the motors behind one, but soon becomes insignificant against the immensity all around and is before long swallowed by it. There comes a point where space also swallows time, and one lives through eternal moments filled with an oppressive loneliness, as though all life had suddenly vanished from the earth and you are only one left, a lone survivor traveling endlessly through interplanetary space.

My mind soon returns to the mission I am on. Somewhere beyond these vast mountains of white clouds ahead of me there lies Japan, the land of our enemy. In about four hours from now one of its cities, making weapons of war for use against us will be wiped off the map by the greatest weapon ever made by man. In one-tenth of a millionth of a second, a fraction of time immeasurable by any clock, a whirlwind from the skies will pulverize thousands of its buildings and tens of thousands of its inhabitants.

Our weather planes ahead of us are on their way to find out where the wind blows. Half an hour before target time we will know what the winds have decided.

Does one feel any pity or compassion for the poor devils about to die? Not when one thinks of Pearl Harbor and of the death march on Bataan.

Captain Bock informs me that we are about to start our climb to bombing altitude.

He manipulates a few knobs on his control panel to the right of him and I alternately watch the white clouds and ocean below me and the altimeter on the Bombardier's panel. We reached our altitude at 9:00 o'clock. We were then over Japanese waters, close to their mainland. Lieutenant Godfrey motioned to me to look through his radar scope. Before me was the outline of our assembly point. We shall soon meet our lead ship and proceed to the final stage of our journey.

We reached Yakoshima at 9:12 and there, about 4,000 feet ahead of us, was "The Great Artiste" with its precious load. I saw Lieutenant Godfrey and Sergeant Curry strap on their parachutes and I decided to do likewise.

We started circling. We saw little towns on the coastline, heedless of our presence. We kept on circling, waiting for the third ship in our formation.

It was 9:?? when we began heading for the coastline. Our weather scouts had sent us code messages, deciphered by Sergeant Curry, informing us that both the primary target as well as the secondary were clearly visible.

The winds of destiny seemed to favor certain Japanese cities that must remain nameless. We circled about them again and again and found no opening in the thick umbrella of clouds that covered them. Destiny chose Nagasaki as the ultimate target.

We had been circling for some time when we noticed black puffs of smoke coming through the white clouds directly at us. There were 15 bursts of flak in rapid succession, all too low. Captain Bock changed his course. There soon followed eight more bursts of flak, right up to our altitude, but by this time we were too far to the left.

We flew southward down the channel and at 11:33 crossed the coastline and headed straight for Nagasaki about a hundred miles to the west. Here again we circled until we found an opening in the clouds. It was 12:01 and the goal of our mission had arrived.

We heard the pre-arranged signal on our radio, put on our ARC welder's glasses and watched tensely the maneuverings of the strike ship about half a mile in front of us.

"There she goes!" someone said. Out of the belly of the Artiste what looked like a black object came downward.

Captain Bock swung around to get out of range, but even though we were turning away in the opposite direction, and despite the fact that it was broad daylight in our cabin, all of us became aware of a giant flash that broke through the dark barrier of our ARC welder's lenses and flooded our cabin with an intense light.

We removed our glasses after the first flash but the light still lingered on, a bluish-green light that illuminated the entire sky all around. A tremendous blast wave struck our ship and made it tremble from nose to tail. This was followed by four more blasts in rapid succession, each resounding like the boom of cannon fire hitting our plane from all directions.

Observers in the tail of our ship saw a giant ball of fire rise as though from the bowels of the earth, belching forth enormous white smoke rings. Next they saw a giant pillar of purple fire, 10,000 feet high, shooting skyward with enormous speed.

By the time our ship had made another turn in the direction of the atomic explosion the pillar of purple fire had reached the level of our altitude. Only about 45 seconds had passed. Awe-struck, we watched it shoot upward like a meteor coming from the earth instead of from outer space, becoming ever more alive as it climbed skyward through the white clouds. It was no longer smoke, or dust, or even a cloud of fire. It was a living thing, a new species of being, born right before our incredulous eyes.

At one stage of its evolution, covering missions of years in terms of seconds, the entity assumed the form of a giant square totem pole, with its base about three miles long, tapering off to about a mile at the top. Its bottom was brown, its center was amber, its top white. But it was a living totem pole, carved with many grotesque masks grimacing at the earth.

Then, just when it appeared as though the thing has settled down into a state of permanence, there came shooting out of the top a giant mushroom that increased the height of the pillar to a total of 45,000 feet. The mushroom top was even more alive than the pillar, seething and boiling in a white fury of creamy foam, sizzling upwards and then descending earthward, a thousand old faithful geysers rolled into one.

It kept struggling in an elemental fury, like a creature in the act of breaking the bonds that held it down. In a few seconds it had freed itself from its gigantic stem and floated upward with tremendous speed, its momentum carrying into the stratosphere to a height of about 60,000 feet.

But no sooner did this happen when another mushroom, smaller in size than the first one, began emerging out of the pillar. It was as though the decapitated monster was growing a new head.

As the first mushroom floated off into the blue it changed its shape into a flower-like form, its giant petal curving downward, creamy white outside, rose-colored inside. It still retained that shape when we last gazed at it from a distance of about 200 miles.

END

DISTRIBUTION: Aa, Af, E, Dn, Dd, Dm, N.
9-7-45
5:00 P.M

Source: Hadden, Gavin, ed. 1947. *Manhattan District History*. Book I General, Volume 4, Chapter 8, Part 1. Washington, D.C.: Department of Energy, Office of History and Heritage Resources. Available online at https://www.osti.gov/opennet/manhattan_district. Accessed April 27, 2019.

60. War Department Press Release, Calendar of Important Events, October 30, 1946

Even after the war, the U.S. government tried to control the narrative of the emerging story of the Manhattan Project—right down to the timeline. The propaganda succeeded; much of what is popularly known about the project stems from the government's efforts.

WAR DEPARTMENT
Public Relations Division
PRESS SECTION
Tel. RE 6700.
Brs. 2528 and 4860

FOR RELEASE WEDNESDAY A.M.,
OCTOBER 30, 1946

CALENDAR
OF IMPORTANT EVENTS
IN THE DEVELOPMENT OF ATOMIC
ENERGY
1938 to 1946

Background information for use at any time in connection with observance of December 2 as significant anniversary of atomic energy.

JANUARY 1939	Confirmation and interpretation in U.S. of discovery of fission of Uranium abroad in November 1938. Implications: the release of energy, the production of radioactive atomic species, and the possibility of a neutron chain reaction.
OCTOBER 11, 1939	President Roosevelt apprised of potentialities of uranium fission. Appoints "Advisory Committee on Uranium."
FEBRUARY 1940	First transfer of funds from Army and Navy to Advisory Committee on Uranium.

APRIL 1940	American scientists propose voluntary censorship on atomic matters.
JUNE 1940	Advisory Committee on Uranium placed under National Defense Research Council.
MAY 1941	E. O. Lawrence, CIT, reports plutonium (discovered late in 1940) is formed by neutron capture and two successive changes in atomic structure of uranium 238, and that plutonium undergoes fission.
JULY 1941	First graphite and uranium lattice structure set up at Columbia University to study neutron emission,
NOVEMBER 1941	Review Committee reports favorably on possibility of an atomic bomb of great strength. Estimates between three and four years needed to produce a bomb. Dr. Vannevar Bush and associates decide that possibilities of the atomic bomb justify greater effort and that the existing NDRC set-up was not equipped to handle such a program. Therefore responsibility was transferred to the Office of Scientific Research and Development.
DECEMBER 1941	Top Policy Group recommends further fundamental research and engineering planning of pilot plants; also that the Army should be brought in when full scale construction was ready to start. Dr. Conant, following recommendations of the Top Policy Group, emphasizes that an all out effort at this time was justified by the military value of atomic bombs and that all efforts must be concentrated in this direction.
JANUARY 1942	Columbia and Princeton groups moved to University of Chicago; Lawrence continues electromagnetic methods study at CIT; research on gaseous diffusion method continues at Columbia; centrifuge work continues at University of Virginia and Standard Oil Development Laboratory in Bayway, New Jersey; Navy continues research on thermal diffusion method.
JUNE 13, 1942	Bush and Conant send a report to Top Policy Group stressing that there were four equally promising methods of separating the U-235 from U-238, that graphite uranium and heavy water uranium pile methods of producing plutonium seemed likely to succeed, that production plants for all methods should be started, and that the Army should be brought in to the project. President Roosevelt initialed and approved this report on June 17, 1942.
JUNE 18, 1942	Colonel J. C, Marshall, Corps of Engineers, instructed to form a new district in the Corps of Engineers labeled for security purposes the DSM Project

	(Development of Substitute Materials).		and development contracts from OSRD.
AUGUST 13, 1942	The Manhattan District Officially established and designated.	OCTOBER 1943	U-235 separation by electromagnetic process starts.
SEPTEMBER 17, 1942	Major General (then Brigadier General) Leslie R, Groves placed in charge of all Army activities relating to the DSM Project.	NOVEMBER 1943	Pile at Clinton operating.
		JANUARY 1944	Experimental amounts of U-235 from electromagnetic process shipped to Los Alamos. First shipments of usable amounts made in March 1944.
SEPTEMBER 23, 1942	A Military Policy Committee named, consisting of Dr. Bush, Dr. Conant, General Styer, Admiral Purnell and with General Groves as executive officer in charge of the work.		
		MARCH 1944	By this time several grams of plutonium had been delivered by Clinton.
		SEPTEMBER 1944	First pile at Hanford operating,
SEPTEMBER 1942	Oak Ridge selected as site for Clinton Engineer Works.	JULY 16, 1945	First Atomic Explosion, Alamogordo, New Mexico.
NOVEMBER 1942	Site selected for bomb development—Los Alamo, New Mexico.	JULY 26, 1945	Potsdam Surrender Ultimatum to Japan.
		JULY 29, 1945	Japan rejects Potsdam Ultimatum.
DECEMBER 2, 1942	First nuclear chain reacting pile at the Metallurgical Laboratory at the University of Chicago. (Date suggested by General Groves as significant anniversary to be observed in connection with United States Atomic Energy Development).	AUGUST 6, 1945	Hiroshima, Japan, bombed.
		AUGUST 9, 1945	Nagasaki, Japan, bombed.
		AUGUST 14, 1945	Japan offers to surrender. . . .
DECEMBER 1942	Hanford, Washington, selected as site for new facilities for plutonium production.		
MAY 1943	Manhattan District takes over all remaining research		

Source: Hadden, Gavin, ed. 1947. *Manhattan District History.* Book I General, Volume 4, Chapter 8, Part 1. Washington, D.C.: Department of Energy, Office of History and Heritage Resources. Available online at https://www.osti.gov/opennet/manhattan_district. Accessed April 27, 2019.

Perspective Essays

Was the United States justified in dropping atomic bombs on Hiroshima and Nagasaki? This question burned in many American minds over the decades after the end of the Second World War. It is one that cannot be answered by a study of the Manhattan Project alone, but on the other hand, it cannot be intelligently addressed without knowledge of that project and the course of the war that sparked it. There is no definitive answer to the question, though many have heartfelt opinions on it, but it remains one whose answers in each heart determine attitudes toward the contemporary world and issues from international politics to powering our homes.

By the summer of 1945, America's participation in World War II had been dragging on for nearly four years. The war in Europe had ended in May with the surrender of Nazi Germany, but the United States and Japan continued to slug it out in a brutal campaign in the Pacific. The American public was war weary and wanted the conflict to end. At the time, U.S. military planners were girding themselves for a potentially brutal campaign to assault and subdue the Japanese home islands, an endeavor that was expected to bring heavy U.S. casualties. Presented with an opportunity to end the war quickly, President Harry S. Truman authorized the use of atomic bombs against Japan. The Japanese death toll from the bombings was shockingly high. Some 70,000 people died almost instantly at Hiroshima on August 6, and more than 70,000 people died at Nagasaki on August 9; perhaps as many as 200,000 more were injured or later died from radiation poisoning or cancer. Japan surrendered unconditionally on August 15. But was the use of the atomic bomb justified? Were there other ways in which the Japanese might have been compelled to capitulate? And were there other motives at play in employing the atomic bombs?

In the first of three perspective essays, Dr. Conrad C. Crane argues that the use of atomic bombs was justified and was merely a natural extension of bombing tactics that had already been implemented, including the firebombing of German and Japanese cities that had killed tens of thousands of civilians. Thus, discussions concerning the use of the bombs revolved around how to employ them rather than if they should be employed in the first place. Dr. Spencer C. Tucker contends that the use of the atomic bombs was justified, as the United States did not have conclusive proof that Japan was ready to surrender unconditionally. Furthermore, a land invasion would have resulted in unacceptably high numbers of casualties. Dr. J. Samuel Walker takes issue with the arguments made by both traditionalists and revisionists, pointing out errors and oversimplifications made on both extremes of the debate. Instead, he opts for a middle ground that rejects the "atomic bomb or invasion" dichotomy. He argues that dropping the bombs was necessary to end the war quickly and save thousands (although not hundreds of thousands) of American lives, but it was not the only feasible alternative to an all-out invasion of the Japanese home islands. Finally, Dr. Gar Alperovitz is firm in his view that dropping the bombs was unnecessary and, further, that many if not most of the top U.S. military leaders are on record as having strongly agreed that it was unnecessary. He contends that Japan was on the brink of surrendering and that a coordinated Soviet attack, along with a readily acceptable modification of the surrender terms as advised by U.S. intelligence and other officials, would likely have brought an end to the war well before an invasion could begin. He also argues that U.S. policy makers elected to employ the bombs to intimidate the Soviet leadership.

Background Essay

The U.S. bombing of the Japanese city of Hiroshima on August 6, 1945, was the first use of an atomic bomb in warfare. On July 25, 1945, commander of U.S. Strategic Air Forces General Carl Spaatz received orders to employ the 509th Composite Group, Twentieth Air Force, in a "special bomb" attack on selected target cities in Japan, specifically Hiroshima, Kokura, Niigata, or Nagasaki. Following Japanese rejection of conditions promulgated by the Potsdam Proclamation on July 26, a declaration threatening Japan with total destruction if unconditional surrender was not accepted, U.S. President Harry S. Truman authorized use of the special bomb.

Assembled in secret and loaded on the Boeing B-29 Superfortress Enola Gay, the bomb consisted of a core of uranium isotope 235 shielded by several hundred pounds of lead encased in explosives designed to condense the uranium and initiate a fission reaction. Known as "Little Boy," the bomb possessed a force equivalent to 12,500 tons of TNT (12.5 kilotons).

The Enola Gay, commanded by Colonel Paul Tibbets, departed Tinian early on August 6, accompanied to Japan by two B-29s assigned as scientific and photographic observers. The flight to Japan was uneventful, and Tibbets was informed at 7:47 a.m. by weather planes that Hiroshima was clear for bombing. Japan's eighth largest city (with about 245,000 residents in August 1945), Hiroshima was an important port of southern Honshu and headquarters of the Japanese Second Army.

The Enola Gay arrived over the city at an altitude of 31,600 feet and dropped the bomb at 8:15:17 a.m. local time. After a descent of some nearly six miles, the bomb detonated 43 seconds later some 1,890 feet over a clinic and about 800 feet from the aiming point, Aioi Bridge. The initial fireball expanded to 110 yards in diameter, generating heat in excess of 300,000 degrees centigrade, with core temperatures over 50 million degrees centigrade. At the clinic directly beneath the explosion, the temperature was several thousand degrees. The immediate concussion destroyed almost everything within two miles of ground zero. The resultant mushroom cloud rose to 50,000 feet and was observed by B-29s more than 360 miles away. After 15 minutes, the atmosphere dropped radioactive "black rain," adding to the death and destruction.

Four square miles of Hiroshima's heart disappeared in seconds, including 62,000 buildings. More than 71,000 Japanese died, another 20,000 were wounded, and 171,000 were left homeless. Some estimates place the number of killed at more than 200,000. About one-third of those killed instantly were soldiers. Most elements of the Japanese Second General Army were at physical training on the grounds of Hiroshima Castle when the bomb exploded. Barely 900 yards from the explosion's epicenter, the castle and its residents were vaporized. Also killed was an American prisoner of war in the exercise area. Radiation sickness began the next day and added to the death toll over several years.

Truman released a statement on August 7 describing the weapon and calling on Japan to surrender, but most Japanese leaders ignored his message as propaganda. Following the Japanese refusal to surrender, on August 8 the Twentieth Air Force headquarters directed that on the following day the second atomic bomb on Tinian Island be dropped on another Japanese city. Kokura was designated as the primary target, with Nagasaki, a city of some 230,000 persons, the alternate.

Early on August 9, the Boeing B-29 Superfortress bomber Bockscar (sometimes written as *Bock's Car*), commanded by Major Charles Sweeney, departed Tinian. Again, two other B-29s accompanied it as scientific and photographic observer aircraft. Bockscar carried a plutonium nuclear-fission bomb nicknamed "Fat Man." Its payload was greater than that of the Hiroshima bomb. The plutonium-238 isotope core consisted of two melon-shaped hemispheres surrounded by a ring of explosive charges designed to drive the sections together, achieving critical mass and a chain reaction releasing 22 kilotons of energy in a millionth of a second.

Sweeney flew Bockscar to Kokura but found it overcast and circled for 10 minutes, then decided to divert to Nagasaki, which was also partly obscured by clouds. A break in the clouds allowed a visual bomb run rather than employing radar. The aiming point was the Mitsubishi shipyards.

The bomb was dropped from 31,000 feet at 11:02 a.m. local time and detonated 53 seconds later, approximately 1,500 feet over the city, destroying everything within a 1,000-yard radius. An intense blue-white explosion pushed up a pillar of fire 10,000 feet, followed by a mushroom cloud to 60,000 feet.

Although the bomb exploded 8,500 feet from its intended aiming point, it leveled one-third of the city. Called the "Red Circle of Death," the fire and blast area within the Urakami Valley section destroyed more than 18,000 homes and killed 74,000 people. Another 75,000 were injured, with many of these dying from wounds or complications. Blast forces traveling in excess of 9,000 miles per hour damaged buildings three miles away, and the concussion was felt 40 miles from the epicenter. Ashes of death from the mushroom cloud spread radiation poisoning, killing those not taken outright within 1,000 yards of the epicenter. The bomb might have killed thousands more, but it detonated away from the city center in a heavy industrial area, vaporizing three of Nagasaki's largest war factories.

Critically low on fuel, the Bockscar landed on Okinawa, its gas tanks virtually empty, then flew back to Tinian. Included in the instrument bundle dropped from the observation plane was a letter addressed to Japanese physicist professor F. Sagane (Sagane Ryokichi) urging immediate surrender and threatening continued atomic destruction of Japanese cities. Written by three American physicists, the letter was a bluff, as no other atomic bombs were then ready. Nonetheless, the second atomic attack, coupled with the August 8 declaration of war against Japan by the Soviet Union, provided Japanese Emperor Hirohito with the excuse to end the war.

Mark E. Van Rhyn

Perspective Essay #1: The Decision to Employ the Bomb

Although there were extensive consultations about the employment of the atomic bomb, discussions always focused on how to use the new weapon rather than whether to use it. Its employment was a natural extension of bombing tactics already in use, including the firebombing of German and Japanese cities in which civilians perished in the tens of thousands.

Intelligence reports revealed that Germany was working to develop an atomic weapon, so during the first years of the top-secret Manhattan Project, military planners assumed that an American-made bomb would be used against the Germans. Germany surrendered before the U.S. bomb could be successfully tested, however. In the spring and summer of 1945, the primary aim of Allied decision makers was to achieve the surrender of Japan as quickly as possible at the lowest cost in lives, and all involved assumed that if the Manhattan Project could produce a workable weapon, it would be expended against an enemy target.

It could be argued that the decision to use the atomic bomb was made on December 6, 1941, when the first funds were approved for its development. At the time, American leaders assumed that the new invention would be a legitimate weapon in the war, and they never questioned that assumption afterward.

Although President Franklin D. Roosevelt's key advisers on the project concluded in May 1943 that the first operational bomb should be dropped on Japan, the choice of targets really did not receive systematic attention until two years later. A special Target Committee for the Manhattan Project began meeting in April 1945, and by the next month it had produced a short list of target cities, including Kyoto and Hiroshima. On May 31, the blue-ribbon Interim Committee appointed by Secretary of War Henry L. Stimson began meeting to discuss how best to use the new weapon. A suggestion made to try a warning and noncombat demonstration was quickly rejected. First, if this failed, it might serve to stiffen Japanese resolve rather than forcing surrender. Second, at the time, there were only two or three bombs under development; if one failed or did not impress the Japanese, this left only one or two bombs in the American arsenal. The committee thus recommended that the bomb be dropped without warning on a target that would have the largest possible psychological impact.

On July 16, 1945, the United States successfully detonated the world's first atomic bomb in the desert near Alamogordo, New Mexico. Eventually, military planners came up with a target list of Hiroshima, Kokura, Kyoto, and Niigata. Stimson persuaded the planners to substitute Nagasaki for the shrine city of Kyoto and then presented the list to President Harry S. Truman in late July. Truman approved the directive without consulting anyone and wrote in his diary that the bomb would be used between July 25 and August 10. The new weapon offered the possibility of ending the war sooner, and he saw no compelling reason not to employ it. Despite some historians' claims to the contrary, there was no reliable evidence of any imminent Japanese collapse or surrender. Although some leaders did perceive a display of the atomic bomb's power as a potential tool to intimidate the Soviet Union in the future, this was a secondary benefit of its employment and not a factor in operational decision-making.

No single government document shows Truman's decision to use the bomb, but there were two relevant military directives from the joint chiefs of staff to the U.S. Army Air Forces. The first, to Army Air Forces Commander General Henry "Hap" Arnold on July 24, designated the four possible targets. The next day a similar order to General Carl Spaatz, commanding U.S. Strategic Air Forces in the Pacific, added a date: "after about August 3, 1945." That document also directed that other bombs were to be delivered against targets as soon as they were ready. On the basis of these orders, Spaatz selected Hiroshima and then Kokura to be the targets for the first and second atomic missions. Cloud cover on the day of the second raid caused the shift to the secondary target of Nagasaki.

Some critics have questioned why there was not more deliberation about whether to use the terrible new weapon. The main concern for decision makers was to win the war quickly while avoiding a costly invasion of the Japanese mainland or losing public support for unconditional surrender. Under the conditions in 1945, which had already produced fire raids that had killed far more Japanese civilians than did the attacks on Hiroshima and Nagasaki, no U.S. president or general could have failed to employ the atomic bomb.

Conrad C. Crane

Perspective Essay #2: Dropping the Bomb Saved Lives

Dropping the atomic bombs on Japan saved the lives of hundreds of thousands of U.S. soldiers and was the only way to end the war quickly. In the summer of 1945, American planners hoped that a naval blockade and a strategic bombing campaign of the Japanese home islands would bring the war to an end. The prospects for an actual invasion appeared dim, as Japanese leaders made major preparations to defend against such an attack. In light of the heavy casualties sustained by U.S. forces in the invasions of Iwo Jima and Okinawa earlier that year, the U.S. joint chiefs of staff were reluctant to carry out Operation Downfall, the planned land invasion of Japan. The Japanese military had one million soldiers, 3,000 kamikaze aircraft, and 5,000 suicide boats available to defend its home islands. Civilians were also being prepared to fight to the death. With the U.S. invasion scheduled for November 1, 1945, and well aware that the cost of such an enterprise was likely to be high, the joint chiefs of staff pressed President Franklin D. Roosevelt at the February 1945 Yalta Conference to persuade the Soviet Union to enter the war against Japan at any cost.

Following the successful test detonation of an atomic bomb at Alamogordo, New Mexico, on July 16, 1945, sharp debate arose among advisers to U.S. President Harry S. Truman (who had succeeded Roosevelt as president on the latter's death in April) regarding whether to employ the new weapon against Japan. The terror threshold had already been passed in the firebombing of Japanese cities. Indeed, the most destructive single air raid in history was not the atomic bombing of Hiroshima or Nagasaki but rather the firebombing of Tokyo on the night of March 9–10, 1945. This was total war. It was always assumed that the bomb would be used if it became available. American planners believed that employing the bomb would in all likelihood bring the war to a speedy end, saving many American lives. It would also mean that the United States would not have to share occupation of Japan with the Soviet Union, and hopefully it would deter Soviet leader Joseph Stalin from future aggression. The atomic bomb was thus essentially a psychological weapon rather than a purely military tool, the use of which was designed to influence Japanese political leaders. Dropping it appeared to be the only way to realize the American goal of unconditional surrender.

Revisionist historians have held that the Japanese government was trying desperately to leave the war and that employing the bomb was unnecessary. Intercepts of diplomatic messages indicated, however, that Japan had not yet reached the decision to surrender when the first bomb was dropped. While Emperor Hirohito and his principal advisers had concluded that Japan could not win the war, they still held out hope for a negotiated settlement and believed that a last decisive battle would force the Allies to grant more favorable peace terms.

Post–atomic bomb estimates have claimed the possibility of up to one million casualties in a U.S. invasion of Japan. However, historian Ray Skates concludes in his authoritative study, *The Invasion of Japan: Alternative to the Bomb* (1998), that Operation Olympic, the first phase of the invasion of Japan (the conquest of the island of Kyushu planned for November 1945), would alone have taken two months and resulted in 75,000 to 100,000 U.S. casualties. Such losses, while they would not have affected the outcome of the war, might indeed have brought about the political goals sought by the Japanese leaders for more favorable surrender terms.

Prolonging the war would have meant a significantly higher cost in Japanese lives than those actually killed in the atomic bombings. During the war the Japanese lost 323,495 dead on the home front, the vast majority of them from air attack. With continued strategic bombing this total would have swelled, and many other Japanese would simply have died of starvation. By August 1945, Japan's largest cities had been largely burned out. Waterborne transportation had been interdicted by airborne mining and submarines, and the Japanese nation was close to starvation. The reduced food supply was highly dependent on railroad distribution, and the railroads would have been the next major strategic bombing target. In effect, dropping the bomb resulted in a net saving of both Japanese and American lives.

The first bomb fell on Hiroshima on August 6, 1945. On August 8, the Soviet Union declared war on Japan, with Stalin honoring to the day his pledge at Yalta to enter the war against Japan "two or three months after the defeat of Germany," which had occurred on May 8, 1945. On August 9, a second atomic bomb fell on Nagasaki.

After prolonged meetings with his advisers, Hirohito made the decision for peace. The U.S. dropping of the atomic bombs enabled him to take this difficult step in the face of a sharply divided cabinet. Even so, his decision was not without danger, for fanatics determined to fight on to the end plotted to assassinate the emperor to prevent announcement of the decision. To forestall this, Hirohito communicated the decision over radio. On the afternoon of August 15, 1945, in a voice never heard before by the Japanese people, Hirohito told his people that Japan would accept the Potsdam Declaration and surrender. In so doing, he specifically mentioned the atomic bomb: "Moreover, the enemy has begun to employ a new and most cruel bomb, the power of which to do damage is indeed incalculable, taking the toll of many innocent lives."

World War II had come to an end, and the atomic bomb played a major role in it, saving both Japanese and American lives.

Spencer C. Tucker

Perspective Essay #3: A Necessary Action to End the War

The simple answer to the question "Was the United States justified in dropping the atomic bomb on Hiroshima and Nagasaki in World War II?" is *yes,* the United States was justified in using atomic bombs to end World War II in the Pacific at the earliest possible moment. The answer to a closely related question—"Was the use of the bomb necessary?"—is more ambiguous. In my view, the answer to this question is yes, it was necessary in some ways, and no, it was not necessary in other ways.

By the summer of 1945, after three and a half years of cruel and bloody war, American leaders knew that Japan was defeated. It was running desperately short of vital supplies and faced the prospect of mass starvation. But this did not mean that Japan was ready to surrender. Although its leaders recognized that they could not win the war, they fought on in hopes of securing surrender terms that they would find acceptable. President Harry S. Truman and his advisers considered various methods of forcing the Japanese to surrender including, in the worst case, an invasion of the Japanese home islands that would claim the lives of large numbers of U.S. soldiers, sailors, and marines. The invasion, if it became necessary, was scheduled to begin around November 1, 1945.

The success of the Manhattan Project in building atomic bombs that became available for the first time in the summer of 1945 greatly eased the dilemma that Truman faced. Here, he hoped, was a means to force the Japanese to quit the war without having to confront the ghastly prospect of an invasion or risk the major drawbacks of the other possible but highly uncertain alternatives. The alternatives included continuing the firebombing of Japanese cities that had already caused massive destruction and loss of life, modifying the U.S. demand for unconditional surrender by allowing the emperor to remain on his throne, and waiting for Soviet entry into the war against Japan. Those options might have brought about a Japanese surrender, but they ran the risks of prolonging the war in the first two cases and expanding Soviet influence in East Asia in the third.

Although some Japanese leaders sought to persuade Emperor Hirohito to surrender, he vacillated while the war continued. Therefore, the use of the atomic bomb was essential and justified to compel Japan to capitulate promptly. The shock of the bombing of Hiroshima, followed immediately by a Soviet attack on Japanese forces in Manchuria, finally convinced Hirohito that the war must end quickly. After agonizing deliberations in Tokyo, the Japanese government surrendered on the sole condition that the institution of the emperor be preserved.

For many years after the end of World War II, Americans embraced the view that the use of the bomb was necessary because the only alternative was an invasion of Japan that would have cost hundreds of thousands of American lives. But this categorical position has been discredited by the opening of new American and Japanese sources. They show that neither the president nor top military advisers regarded an invasion as inevitable. Further, Truman was not told by his most trusted advisers that an invasion, if it became necessary, would cost hundreds of thousands of lives. The idea that Truman had to choose between the bomb and an invasion to defeat Japan is a myth that took hold in the United States after World War II.

Truman was committed to ending the war as soon as possible, saving as many American lives as he could. He did not need estimates of potential losses in the hundreds of thousands to authorize the use of the bomb, and in fact there is no contemporaneous evidence that he received projections of such staggering losses. For Truman, his advisers, and the vast majority of the American people, ending the war and sparing the lives of a smaller but far from inconsequential number of Americans was ample reason to drop atomic bombs. The Japanese government could have avoided the terrible effects of the atomic bombs by electing to surrender sooner than it did, but Japan was too divided and too indecisive to take the proper action.

There are many uncertainties and complexities surrounding the end of World War II. But the answer to the fundamental question of whether the use of the bomb on Hiroshima and Nagasaki was necessary appears to be yes and no. Yes, it was necessary to end the war as quickly as possible. And yes, it was necessary to save the lives of American troops, perhaps numbering in the several thousands. But no, the bomb probably was not necessary to end the war within a fairly short time without an invasion, because Japan was in such dire straits. And no, it was not necessary to save the lives of hundreds of thousands of American troops.

J. Samuel Walker

Perspective Essay #4: Dropping the Bombs Was Not Justified

The United States was not justified in using atomic bombs against Japanese cities in 1945. U.S. and British intelligence had already advised that Japan was likely to surrender when the Soviet Union entered the war in early August and on terms that, in fact, would have been very close to those ultimately accepted by the United States. There are also reasons to believe that the decision had as much to do with geopolitics connected with the Soviet Union as it did with the war against Japan.

The conventional wisdom that the atomic bomb saved one million lives is so widespread that most Americans have not paused to ponder something rather striking to anyone seriously concerned with the issue: most American military leaders did not think that the bombings were either necessary or justified, and many were morally offended by what occurred at Hiroshima and Nagasaki.

Here is how General Dwight D. Eisenhower reacted on July 30, 1945, when he was told by Secretary of War Henry L. Stimson that the atomic bomb would be used: "During his recitation of the relevant facts, I had been conscious of a feeling of depression and so I voiced to him my grave misgivings, first on the basis of my belief that Japan was already defeated and that dropping the bomb was completely unnecessary, and secondly because I thought that our country should avoid shocking world opinion by the use of a weapon whose employment was, I thought, no longer mandatory as a measure to save American lives." In another public statement the man who later became president was blunt: "It wasn't necessary to hit them with that awful thing."

General Curtis LeMay, the tough Army Air Forces general and hawk who directed the firebombing of Tokyo and other Japanese cities, was also dismayed. Shortly after the bombings, he stated that "The war would have been over in two weeks.... The atomic bomb had nothing to do with the end of the war at all." And Fleet Admiral Chester W. Nimitz, commander in chief of the Pacific Fleet, went public with this statement: "The Japanese had, in fact, already sued for peace. . . . The atomic bomb played no decisive part, from a purely military standpoint, in the defeat of Japan."

The reasons these and many, many military leaders felt this way are both clear and instructive: Japan was essentially defeated, its navy at the bottom of the ocean; its air force was limited by fuel, equipment, and other shortages; its army was facing defeat on all fronts; and its cities were subjected to bombing that was all but impossible to challenge. With Germany out of the war, the United States and Britain were about to bring their full power to bear on what was left of the Japanese military. Moreover, the Soviet Army was getting ready to attack on the Asian mainland.

American intelligence had broken Japanese codes and had advised as early as April 1945 that although a hard-line faction wished to continue the war, the expected Soviet Union attack, roughly in the first week of August, would likely force Japan to surrender as long as assurances were given concerning the fate of the emperor. Combined U.S. and British intelligence reaffirmed this advice a month before the bombings. One reason this option using the shock of the Soviet attack and giving assurances to the emperor appeared highly likely to work was that Japanese leaders feared the political consequences of Soviet power. Moreover, there was also little to lose: an invasion could not in any event begin until November, three months after the Soviet attack. If the war did not end as expected, the bomb could still be used.

Instead, the United States rushed to employ two bombs on August 6 and August 9 at almost exactly the time that the Soviet attack was scheduled. Numerous studies suggest that this was done in part because they "preferred," as Pulitzer Prize–winning historian Martin Sherwin has put it, to end the war in this way. Although the available evidence is not as yet absolutely conclusive, impressing the Soviets also appears to have been a factor.

Many military leaders were offended not only because the bombs were used in these circumstances but also because they were used against Japanese cities, essentially civilian targets. William D. Leahy, President Truman's friend, his chief of staff, and a five-star admiral who presided over meetings of both the U.S. joint chiefs of staff and the combined U.S.–British chiefs of staff, wrote after the war that "the use of this barbarous weapon at Hiroshima and Nagasaki was of no material assistance in our war against Japan. The Japanese were already defeated and ready to surrender. . . . [I]n being the first to use it, we . . . adopted an ethical standard common to the barbarians of the Dark Ages."

President Richard Nixon would recall that "[General Douglas] MacArthur once spoke to me very eloquently about it, pacing the floor of his apartment in the Waldorf. He thought it a tragedy that the Bomb was ever exploded. MacArthur believed that the same restrictions ought to apply to atomic weapons as to conventional weapons, that the military objective should always be limited damage to noncombatants. . . . MacArthur, you see, was a soldier. He believed in using force only against military targets, and that is why the nuclear thing turned him off."

Gar Alperovitz

References

Alperovitz, Gar. 1994. *Atomic Diplomacy: Hiroshima and Potsdam; The Use of the*

Atomic Bomb and the American Confrontation with Soviet Power. New York: Simon & Schuster.

Asada, Sadao. 1997. "The Mushroom Cloud and National Psyches: Japanese and American Perceptions of the Atomic-Bomb Decision, 1945–1995." In Laura Hein and Mark Selden, eds. *Living with the Bomb: American and Japanese Cultural Conflicts in the Nuclear Age,* 173–201. Armonk, NY: East Gate Book.

Bernstein, Barton. 1983. "The Dropping of the A-Bomb." *Center Magazine* (March–April): 7–15.

Bix, Herbert. 1996. "Japan's Delayed Surrender: A Reinterpretation." In Michael J. Hogan, ed. *Hiroshima in History and Memory,* 197–225. Cambridge, U.K.: Cambridge University Press.

Bywater, Hector C. 1991. *The Great Pacific War: A Historic Prophecy Now Being Fulfilled.* Boston: Houghton Mifflin.

Craig, William. 1967. *The Fall of Japan.* New York: Dial.

Frank, Richard B. 1999. *Downfall: The End of the Japanese Empire.* New York: Random House.

Giangreco, D. M. 2009. *Hell to Pay: Operation Downfall and the Invasion of Japan, 1945–47.* Annapolis, MD: Naval Institute Press.

Hasegawa, Tsuyoshi. 2005. *Racing the Enemy: Stalin, Truman and the Surrender of Japan.* Cambridge, MA: Harvard University Press.

Hogan, Michael J. 1996. *Hiroshima in History and Memory.* Cambridge, U.K.: Cambridge University Press.

Kagan, Donald. 1995. "Why America Dropped the Bomb." *Commentary* 100 (September): 17–23.

Maddox, Robert James. 1995. *Weapons for Victory: The Hiroshima Decision Fifty Years Later.* Columbia: University of Missouri Press.

Malloy, Sean L. 2008. *Atomic Tragedy: Henry L. Stimson and the Decision to Use the Bomb against Japan.* Ithaca, NY: Cornell University Press.

Merrill, Dennis. 1995. *Documentary History of the Truman Presidency.* Vol. 1 of *The Decision to Drop the Atomic Bomb on Japan.* Bethesda, MD: University Publications of America.

Miscamble, Wilson D. 2011. *The Most Controversial Decision: Truman, the Atomic Bombs, and the Defeat of Japan.* New York: Cambridge University Press.

Mosley, Leonard. 1966. *Hirohito, Emperor of Japan.* Englewood Cliffs, NJ: Prentice Hall.

Newman, Robert P. 1995. *Truman and the Hiroshima Cult.* East Lansing: Michigan State University Press.

Rotter, Andrew J. 2008. *Hiroshima: The World's Bomb.* Oxford: Oxford University Press.

Schaffer, Ronald. 1985. *Wings of Judgment: American Bombing in World War II.* New York: Oxford University Press.

Sherwin, Martin J. 2003. *A World Destroyed: Hiroshima and Its Legacies.* Stanford, CA: Stanford University Press.

Skates, John Ray. 1998. *The Invasion of Japan: Alternative to the Bomb.* Columbia: University of South Carolina Press.

Spector, Ronald H. 1987. *Eagle against the Sun: The American War with Japan.* New York: Free Press.

Toland, John. 2001. *The Rising Sun: The Decline and Fall of the Japanese Empire, 1936–1945.* New York: Penguin.

Wainstock, Dennis D. 1996. *The Decision to Drop the Atomic Bomb.* Westport, CT: Praeger.

Walker, J. Samuel. 1997. *Prompt and Utter Destruction: Truman and the Use of Atomic Bombs against Japan.* 2nd ed. Chapel Hill: University of North Carolina Press.

Walker, J. Samuel. 2005. "Recent Literature on Truman's Atomic Bomb Decision: A Search for Middle Ground." *Diplomatic History* 29 (April): 311–334.

Watt, D. C. 2001. *How War Came: The Immediate Origins of the Second World War, 1938–1939*. London: Pimlico.

Wilmot, H. P. 1991. *The Great Crusade: A New Complete History of the Second World War*. New York: Free Press.

Zeiler, Thomas W. 2004. *Unconditional Defeat: Japan, America, and the End of World War II*. Wilmington, DE: Scholarly Resources.

Chronology

1905
Albert Einstein proposes his Theory of Relativity.

1930
Ernest Lawrence of the University of California, Berkeley, builds the first cyclotron.

1931
Harold Urey discovers deuterium, or heavy hydrogen.

1932
E. T. S. Walton and John Crockcroft split the atom, providing proof of Albert Einstein's Theory of Relativity.

1932
The neutron is discovered by James Chadwick.

September 12, 1933
Leó Szilárd posits the possibility of a nuclear chain reaction.

1934
Enrico Fermi achieves nuclear fission for the first time.

1935
University of Chicago physicist Arthur Jeffrey Dempster discovers the uranium isotope U-235.

December 17, 1938
Otto Hahn and Fritz Strassmann, working in Nazi Germany, discover that the collision of a neutron with a uranium nucleus will produce barium as one of its by-products.

1939
Lise Meitner and Otto Frisch announce their Theory of Nuclear Fission.

January 26, 1939
Niels Bohr announces the discovery of fission to American scientists at George Washington University.

January 29, 1939
Robert Oppenheimer contemplates military possibilities of nuclear fission.

August 2, 1939
Albert Einstein signs a letter, written primarily by Leó Szilárd, to President Franklin Roosevelt on the use of uranium as a source of energy and advising the president to authorize research into using nuclear fission as a weapon. It would not reach Roosevelt until October 11, 1939.

September 1, 1939
Germany invades Poland, the first hostile event in what would soon be known as World War II.

October 11, 1939
President Franklin Roosevelt becomes aware of the August 2, 1939, Leó Szilárd letter over Albert Einstein's signature and immediately authorizes the formation of the Committee on Uranium.

October 21, 1939
The Advisory Committee on Uranium meets for the first time.

November 1, 1939
The Advisory Committee on Uranium recommends the purchase of uranium oxide for fission research.

March 2, 1940
John Dunning, at Columbia University, is able to verify Niels Bohr's hypothesis on fission.

March 1940
John Dunning demonstrates that fission is produced in uranium-235 and not often in the bulk of uranium made up of uranium-238.

March 1940
Otto Frisch and Rudolf Peierls send the Frisch-Peierls Memorandum to Mark Oliphant. They hypothesize that as little as one pound of enriched uranium might be enough to create the explosion of an atomic bomb.

April 10, 1940
Sir Henry Tizard establishes the MAUD Committee in England for investigating creation of an atomic bomb.

May 21, 1940
George Kistiakowsky posits that isotope separation can be achieved through gaseous diffusion.

June 12, 1940
President Franklin Roosevelt authorizes creation of the National Defense Research Committee and names Vannevar Bush as its head. The NDRC replaces and includes the Advisory Committee on Uranium.

February 23, 1941
Glenn Seaborg and Arthur Wahl demonstrate the existence of plutonium.

March 28, 1941
Seaborg demonstrates that plutonium is fissionable.

June 28, 1941
Vannevar Bush becomes head of the Office of Scientific Research and Development, replaced by James Conant at the National Defense Research Committee, which is reduced to an advisory role.

July 2, 1941
The MAUD Committee Report, concluding that it may be possible to construct an atomic bomb, is distributed.

October 9, 1941
President Franklin Roosevelt authorizes development of an atomic weapon.

December 6, 1941
President Franklin Roosevelt gives authorization for creation of the Manhattan Engineering District with the expressed purpose of creation of an atomic bomb.

December 7, 1941
Japan attacks Pearl Harbor at Hawaii. The Unite States enters the war.

December 18, 1941
The S-1 Section of the Office of Scientific Research and Development meets for the first time.

January 19, 1942
President Franklin Roosevelt formalizes authorization of an atomic bomb project.

January 24, 1942
Arthur Compton decides that work on plutonium should be concentrated at the University of Chicago.

June 19, 1942
The S-1 Executive Committee is formed, consisting of Vannevar Bush as chair along with James Conant, Arthur Compton, Ernest Lawrence, and Harold Urey. It replaced the S-1 Section.

June 25, 1942
Stone & Webster is selected as contractor by the S-1 Committee for what will be known as the Clinton Engineer Works.

Summer, 1942
J. Robert Oppenheimer leads a conference at the University of California, Berkeley, on design possibilities for an atomic bomb.

August 16, 1942
James Marshall becomes district engineer of a new Manhattan Engineering District.

September 23, 1942
Colonel Leslie Groves is promoted to brigadier general and assigned to head the Manhattan Project.

September 29, 1942
The site that will be known as Oak Ridge is acquired by the U.S. Army Corps of Engineers.

October 19, 1942
General Leslie Groves appoints J. Robert Oppenheimer as coordinator of scientific research at what will eventually be the facilities at Los Alamos, New Mexico.

December 2, 1942
Enrico Fermi produces the first controlled nuclear fission reaction at the University of Chicago.

January 16, 1943
General Leslie Groves approves development of a site at Hanford, Washington.

February 18, 1943
Construction begins on the huge electromagnetic separation plant for uranium enrichment at the Clinton Engineer Works, Oak Ridge.

April 1, 1943
The facilities at Los Alamos, New Mexico, are established.

May 5, 1943
The Military Policy Committee of the Manhattan Engineering District names Japan as the primary target for the atomic bomb.

June 2, 1943
Construction begins at Oak Ridge of a gaseous diffusion plant for uranium enrichment.

August 13, 1943
Kenneth Nichols assigned as chief engineer of the Manhattan Engineer District and initiates move of all activities to Oak Ridge.

August 19, 1943
The Quebec Agreement is signed by President Franklin Roosevelt and Prime Minister Winston Churchill.

September 8, 1943
The Combined Policy Committee, formed through the Quebec Agreement, convenes for the first time.

October 10, 1943
Construction begins at Hanford, Washington, of a nuclear reactor.

March 11, 1944
A beta calutron commences operation at Oak Ridge.

May 9, 1944
The first aqueous homogeneous reactor goes critical at Los Alamos.

September 2, 1944
In an accident at Los Alamos, New Mexico, two chemists are killed while attempting to repair a clogged uranium enrichment device.

December 17, 1944
The 509th Composite Group is formed.

April 12, 1945
President Franklin Roosevelt dies. Vice President Harry Truman becomes the 33rd president of the United States.

April 27, 1945
The Target Committee of what is now known, though still secretly, as the Manhattan Project selects the Japanese cities of Kyoto, Hiroshima, Kokura, and Niigata as possible targets for the atomic bomb.

May 8, 1945
Germany surrenders, ending the war in the European Theater.

May 25, 1945
Leó Szilárd tries to warn President Harry Truman about the dangers of atomic weapons.

July 1, 1945
Leó Szilárd circulates a petition to convince President Harry Truman to refrain from using the atomic bomb in Japan.

July 16, 1945
Trinity Test at Alamogordo, New Mexico, takes place, the first atomic detonation on Earth.

July 21, 1945
President Harry Truman issues orders authorizing use of atomic bombs.

July 26, 1945
The Potsdam Declaration calls for the unconditional surrender of Japan.

July 28, 1945
Japan rejects the Potsdam Declaration.

August 6, 1945
The United States bombs Hiroshima using a uranium bomb, killing close to 100,000 people immediately.

August 9, 1945
The United States again bombs a Japanese city with an atomic weapon. The initial target, Kokura, was rejected due to weather conditions, and the bomb was dropped over Nagasaki instead.

August 9, 1945
President Harry Truman addresses the United States on the use of atomic weapons.

September 2, 1945
Japan formally announces its surrender.

Bibliography

Ahnfeldt, Arnold Lorentz, ed. 1966. *Radiology in World War II*. Washington, D.C.: Office of the Surgeon General, Department of the Army.

Albright, Joseph, and Marcia Kinstel. 1997. *Bombshell: The Secret Story of America's Unknown Atomic Spy Conspiracy*. New York: Times Books.

Alperovitz, Gar, and Sanho Tree. 1996. *The Decision to Use the Atomic Bomb*. New York: Vintage.

Anderson, C. E. 2016. *Keep Your Ducks in a Row! The Manhattan Project Hanford, Washington*. New York: Page Publishing.

Atomic Heritage Foundation. 2012. *A Guide to the Manhattan Project in New Mexico*. Washington, D.C.: Atomic Heritage Foundation.

Baker, Richard D., Siegfried S. Hecker, and Delbert R. Harbur. 1983. "Plutonium: A Wartime Nightmare but a Metallurgist's Dream." *Los Alamos Science* 4, no. 7: 142–151.

Bernstein, Barton J. 1976. "The Uneasy Alliance: Roosevelt, Churchill, and the Atomic Bomb, 1940–1945." *The Western Political Quarterly* 29, no. 2: 202–230.

Bernstein, Barton J. 1988. "Four Physicists and the Bomb: The Early Years, 1945–1950." *Historical Studies in the Physical and Biological Sciences* 18, no. 2: 231–263.

Bernstein, Jeremy. 1995. *Hitler's Uranium Club: The Secret Recordings at Farm Hall*. College Park, MD: American Institute of Physics.

Bernstein, Jeremy. 2004. *Oppenheimer: Portrait of an Enigma*. Lanham, MD: Ivan R. Dee Publishing.

Bethe, Hans A. 1991. *The Road from Los Alamos*. New York: Simon & Schuster.

Bird, Kai, and Martin Sherwin. 2005. *American Prometheus. The Triumph and Tragedy of J. Robert Oppenheimer*. New York: Alfred A. Knopf.

Bowen, Lee. 1959. *Project Silverplate 1943–1946*. Vol. 1 of *A History of the Air Force Atomic Energy Program*. The U.S. Air Force Historical Division.

Bundy, McGeorge. 1988. *Danger and Survival: Choices About the Bomb in the First Fifty Years*. New York: Random House.

Campbell, Richard H. 2005. *The Silverplate Bombers: A History and Registry of the Enola Gay and Other B-29s Configured to Carry Atomic Bombs*. Jefferson, NC: McFarland & Company.

Cantelon, Philip L., Robert G. Hewlett, and Robert C. Williams, eds. 1984. *The American Atom: A Documentary History of Nuclear Policies from the Discovery of Fission to the Present, 1939–1984*. Philadelphia: University of Pennsylvania Press.

Cassidy, David. 2004. *J. Robert Oppenheimer and the American Century*. Baltimore, MD: Johns Hopkins University Press.

Clark, Ronald W. 1965. *Tizard*. London: Phoenix House.

Compton, Arthur. 1956. *Atomic Quest*. New York: Oxford University Press.

Conant, J. 2005. *109 East Palace: Robert Oppenheimer and the Secret City of Los Alamos*. New York: Simon & Schuster.

Craig, William. 1967. *The Fall of Japan: A Chronicle of the End of an Empire*. New York: Dial.

Dvorak, Darrell F. 2013. "The First Atomic Bomb Mission: Trinity B-29 Operations Three Weeks Before Hiroshima." *Air Power History* 60, no. 4 (winter): 4–17.

Ermenc, Joseph J., ed. 1989. *Atomic Bomb Scientists: Memoirs, 1939–1945*. Westport, CT and London: Meckler.

Fermi, Laura. 1987. *Atoms in the Family: My Life with Enrico Fermi*. In *History of Modern Physics, 1800–1950*, vol. 9. College Park, MD: American Institute of Physics.

Feynman, Richard. 1984. *Surely You're Joking, Mr. Feynman! (Adventures of a Curious Character)*. New York: W. W. Norton.

Fine, Lenore, and Jesse A. Remington.1972. *The Corps of Engineers: Construction in the United States*. Washington, D.C.: U.S. Army Center of Military History.

Freeman, Lindsey A. 2015. *Longing for the Bomb: Oak Ridge and Atomic Nostalgia*. Chapel Hill: University of North Carolina Press.

Frisch, David H. 1970. "Scientists and the Decision to Bomb Japan." *Bulletin of the Atomic Scientists* 26, no. 6: 107–115.

Gerber, Michele. 2007. *On the Home Front: The Cold War Legacy of the Hanford Nuclear Site*. 3rd ed. Lincoln, NE: Bison Books.

Gilbert, Keith V. 1969. *History of the Dayton Project*. Miamisburg, OH: Mound Laboratory, Atomic Energy Commission.

Goodchild, Peter. 1980. *J. Robert Oppenheimer: Shatterer of Worlds*. London: BBC Books.

Goodchild, Peter. 2004. *Edward Teller: The Real Dr. Strangelove*. Cambridge, MA: Harvard University Press.

Gosling, F. G. 1994. *The Manhattan Project: Making the Atomic Bomb*. Washington, D.C.: U.S. Department of Energy.

Goudsmit, Samuel A. 1947. *Alsos*. New York: Henry Schuman.

Gowing, Margaret. 1964. *Britain and Atomic Energy, 1935–1945*. London: Macmillan Publishing.

Grodzins, Morton, and Eugene Rabinowitch, eds. 1963. *The Atomic Age: Scientists in National and World Affairs*. New York: Basic Book Publishing.

Groves, Leslie. 1962. *Now It Can Be Told: The Story of the Manhattan Project*. New York: Harper & Row.

Hacker, Barton C. 1987. *The Dragon's Tail: Radiation Safety in the Manhattan Project, 1942–1946*. Berkeley: University of California Press.

Hales, Peter. 1997. *Atomic Spaces. Living on the Manhattan Project*. Urbana and Chicago: University of Illinois Press.

Ham, Paul. 2014. *Hiroshima Nagasaki: The Real Story of the Atomic Bombings and Their Aftermath*. New York: Thomas Dunne Books.

Hanford Cultural and Historic Resources Program, U.S. Department of Energy. 2002. *History of the Plutonium Production Facilities, 1943–1990*. Richland, WA: Hanford Site Historic District.

Hansen, Chuck. 1995a. *Volume I: The Development of U.S. Nuclear Weapons. Swords of Armageddon: U.S. Nuclear Weapons Development since 1945*. Sunnyvale, CA: Chukelea Publications.

Hansen, Chuck. 1995b. *Volume V: U.S. Nuclear Weapons Histories. Swords of Armageddon: U.S. Nuclear Weapons Development since 1945*. Sunnyvale, CA: Chukelea Publications.

Harder, Robert. 2015. *The Three Musketeers of the Army Air Forces*. Annapolis, MD: Naval Institute Press.

Hargittai, Istvan. 2010. *Judging Edward Teller: A Closer Look at One of the Most*

Influential Scientists of the Twentieth Century. Amherst, NY: Prometheus Books.

Hasegawa, Tsuyoshi. 2005. *Racing the Enemy: Stalin, Truman, and the Surrender of Japan.* Cambridge, MA: Belknap Press.

Hawkins, David. 1946. *Manhattan District History, Project Y, the Los Alamos Project. Vol. I: Inception until August 1945.* Los Alamos, NM: Los Alamos Scientific Laboratory of the University of California.

Hawkins, David, Edith C. Truslow, and Ralph C. Smith. 1961. *Manhattan District History, Project Y, the Los Alamos Project.* Los Angeles: Tomash Publishers.

Herken, Gregg. 2002. *Brotherhood of the Bomb. The Tangled Lives and Loyalties of Robert Oppenheimer, Ernest Lawrence, and Edward Teller.* New York: Holt.

Hersey, John. 1946. *Hiroshima.* New York: Knopf.

Hershberg, James. 1993. *James B. Conant: Harvard to Hiroshima and the Making of the Nuclear Age.* New York: Knopf.

Hewlett, Richard G., and Oscar E. Anderson. 1962. *The New World, 1939–1946.* University Park: Pennsylvania State University Press.

Hewlett, Richard G., and Francis Duncan. 1969. *Atomic Shield, 1947–1952. A History of the United States Atomic Energy Commission.* University Park: Pennsylvania State University Press.

Hoddeson, Lillian, Paul W. Henriksen, Roger A. Meade, and Catherine L. Westfall. 1993. *Critical Assembly: A Technical History of Los Alamos during the Oppenheimer Years, 1943–1945.* New York: Cambridge University Press.

Hogan, Michael J. 1996. *Hiroshima in History and Memory.* Cambridge, U.K.: Cambridge University Press.

Holloway, David. 1994. *Stalin and the Bomb: The Soviet Union and Atomic Energy, 1939–1956.* New Haven, CT: Yale University Press.

Home, R. W., and Morris F. Low. 1993. "Postwar Scientific Intelligence Missions to Japan." *Isis* 84, no. 3 (September): 527–537.

Hornblum, Allen. 2010. *The Invisible Harry Gold: The Man Who Gave the Soviets the Atom Bomb.* New Haven, CT: Yale University Press.

Hounshell, D., and J. Smith. 1988. *Science and Corporate Strategy: Du Pont R&D, 1902–1980.* New York: Cambridge University Press.

Howes, Ruth H., and Caroline Herzenberg. 1999. *Their Day in the Sun: Women of the Manhattan Project.* Philadelphia: Temple University Press.

Hughes, Jeff. 2002. *The Manhattan Project: Big Science and the Atom Bomb.* New York: Columbia University Press.

Hunner, Jon. 2004. *Inventing Los Alamos: The Growth of an Atomic Community.* Norman: University of Oklahoma Press.

Johnson, Charles W., and Charles O. Jackson. 1981. *City Behind A Fence: Oak Ridge, Tennessee, 1942–1946.* Knoxville: University of Tennessee Press.

Jones, Vincent. 1985. *Manhattan: The Army and the Bomb.* Washington, D.C.: U.S. Army Center of Military History.

Jungk, Robert, and James Cleugh, trans. 1958. *Brighter than a Thousand Suns: A Personal History of the Atomic Scientists.* New York: Harvest Books.

Kelly, Cynthia C., ed. 2007. *The Manhattan Project.* New York: Black Dog & Leventhal.

Kiernan, Denise. 2013. *The Girls of Atomic City: The Untold Story of the Women Who Helped Win World War II.* New York: Simon & Schuster.

Krauss, Robert, and Amelia Krauss, eds. 2005. *The 509th Remembered: A History of the 509th Composite Group as Told by the Veterans that Dropped the Bombs on Japan.* Wichita, KS: 509th Press.

Lanouette, William, and Bela Silard. 1992. *Genius in the Shadows: A Biography of Leo Szilard: The Man Behind the Bomb.* New York: Scribner.

Libby, Leona Marshall. 1979. *Uranium People*. New York: Scribner.

Los Alamos Scientific Laboratory. 2017. *Los Alamos: Beginning of an Era, 1943–1945, Covering Military and Scientific Realities, Designing the Bomb, Trinity, Trial Run, Fission Bombs, H-bomb, and Thermonuclear Program History*. Los Alamos, NM: Los Alamos Scientific Laboratory.

MacKenzie, D., and G. Spinardi. 1995. "Tacit Knowledge, Weapons Design, and the Uninvention of Nuclear Weapons." *The American Journal of Sociology* 101, no. 1: 44–99.

MacLeod, Roy M., ed. 2000. *Science and the Pacific War: Science and Survival in the Pacific, 1939–1945*. Boston: Kluwer.

Malloy, Sean L. 2008. *Atomic Tragedy: Henry L. Stimson and the Decision to Use the Bomb Against Japan*. Ithaca, NY: Cornell University Press.

Mason, Katrina. *Children of Los Alamos: An Oral History of the Town Where the Atomic Age Began*. Farmington Hills, MI: Twayne.

Miscamble, Wilson D. 2011. *The Most Controversial Decision: Truman, the Atomic Bombs, and the Defeat of Japan*. New York: Cambridge University Press.

Moss, Norman. 1987. *Karl Fuchs: The Man Who Stole the Atom Bomb*. New York: St. Martin's Press.

Ndiaye, Pap A. Elborg Forster, trans. 2006. *Nylon and Bombs: DuPont and the March of Modern America*. Baltimore, MD: Johns Hopkins University Press.

Nichols, Kenneth D. 1987. *The Road to Trinity: A Personal Account of How America's Nuclear Policies Were Made*. New York: William Morrow and Company.

Norris, Robert S. 2002. *Racing for the Bomb. General Leslie R. Groves, The Manhattan Project's Indispensable Man*. South Royalton, VT: Steerforth Press.

Phelps, Stephen. 2010. *The Tizard Mission: The Top-Secret Operation that Changed the Course of World War II*. Yardley, PA: Westholme.

Powers, Thomas. 1993. *Heisenberg's War: The Secret History of the German Bomb*. New York: Knopf.

Reed, C. 2014. *The History and Science of the Manhattan Project*. Berlin: Springer Verlag.

Rhodes, Richard. 1986. *The Making of the Atomic Bomb*. New York: Simon & Schuster.

Rhodes, Richard. 2002. "'A Great and Deep Difficulty': Niels Bohr and the Atomic Bomb." *Symposium on "The Copenhagen Interpretation: Science and History on Stage"*: Washington, D.C.: National Museum of Natural History of the Smithsonian Institution.

Rosenberg, D. 1983. "The Origins of Overkill: Nuclear Weapons and American Strategy, 1945–1960." *International Security* 7, no. 4: 3–71.

Ruhoff, John, and Pat Fain. 1962. "The First Fifty Critical Days." *Mallinckrodt Uranium Division News* 7. St. Louis: Mallinckrodt Incorporated.

Seaborg, Glenn, Ronald Kathren, and Jerry Gough. 1994. *The Plutonium Story: The Journals of Professor Glenn T. Seaborg 1939–1946*. Columbus, OH: Battelle Press.

Selden, Kyoko, and Mark Selden, eds. 1990. *The Atomic Bomb: Voices from Hiroshima and Nagasaki*. Armonk, NY: M. E. Sharp.

Serber, Charlotte, and Jane Wilson. 2008. *Standing By and Making Do: Women of Wartime Los Alamos*. Los Alamos, NM: Los Alamos Historical Society.

Serber, Robert. 1992. *The Los Alamos Primer. The First Lectures on How to Build an Atomic Bomb*. Berkeley: University of California Press.

Smyth, Henry DeWolf. 1945. *Atomic Energy for Military Purposes: The Official Report on the Development of the Atomic Bomb under the Auspices of the United States Government, 1940–1945*. Princeton, NJ: Princeton University Press.

Steeper, Nancy. 2005. *Gatekeeper to Los Alamos: Dorothy Scarritt McKibbin*. Los Alamos, NM: Los Alamos Historical Society.

Steinberg, D. Leah. 2016. *Raised in the Shadow of the Bomb*. n. p.: Deborah Leah Steinberg.

Stimson, H. 1947. "The Decision to Use the Atomic Bomb." *Harper's Magazine* (February).

Stoff, Michael, Jonathan Fanton, and Hal Williams. 1990. *The Manhattan Project: A Documentary Introduction to the Atomic Age*. New York: McGraw-Hill.

Sweeney, Michael S. 2001. *Secrets of Victory: The Office of Censorship and the American Press and Radio in World War II*. Chapel Hill: University of North Carolina Press.

Szanton, Andrew. 1992. *The Recollections of Eugene P. Wigner*. New York: Plenum.

Thayer, H. 1996. *Management of the Hanford Engineer Works in World War II. How the Corps, DuPont and the Metallurgical Laboratory Fast Tracked the Original Plutonium Works*. New York: American Society of Civil Engineers Press.

Thorpe, C., and S. Shapin. 2000. "Who Was J. Robert Oppenheimer? Charisma and Complex Organization." *Social Studies of Science* 30, no. 4: 545–590.

Trauger, Donald. 2002. *Horse Power to Nuclear Power: Memoir of an Energy Pioneer*. Franklin, TN: Hillsboro Press.

Ulam, Stanislaw. 1976. *Adventures of a Mathematician*. New York: Scribner.

United States Atomic Energy Commission. 1954. *In the Matter of J. Robert Oppenheimer: Transcript of Hearing Before Personnel Security Board Washington, D.C., April 12, 1954, Through May 6, 1954*. Washington, D.C.: U.S. Government Printing Office.

Villa, Brian L. 1981. "Chapter 11: Alliance Politics and Atomic Collaboration, 1941–1943." In Sidney Aster, ed. *The Second World War as a National Experience*. n.p.: The Canadian Committee for the History of the Second World War, Department of National Defence.

Walker, J. Samuel. 1997. *Prompt and Utter Destruction: Truman and the Use of Atomic Bombs Against Japan*. Chapel Hill: University of North Carolina Press.

West, Nigel. 2004. *Mortal Crimes: Soviet Penetration of the Manhattan Project*. New York: Enigma Books.

Wilcox, Robert. 1985. *Japan's Secret War: Japan's Race Against Time to Build Its Own Atomic Bomb*. New York: William Morrow and Company.

Williams, Mary H. 1960. *Chronology 1941–1945*. Washington, D.C.: Office of the Chief of Military History, Department of the Army.

Williams, Robert. 1987. *Klaus Fuchs: Atom Spy*. Cambridge, MA: Harvard University Press.

Zimmerman, David. 1996. *Top Secret Exchange: The Tizard Mission and the Scientific War*. Montreal: McGill-Queen's University Press.

About the Editor and Contributors

Editor

Dr. Aaron Barlow
Professor
New York City College of Technology
City University of New York

Contributors

Dr. Gar Alperovitz
Lionel R. Bauman Professor of Political Economy
University of Maryland

Dr. William J. Astore
Professor of History
Pennsylvania College of Technology

Dr. Aaron Barlow
Professor
New York City College of Technology
City University of New York

Dr. Michael B. Barrett
Professor of History
The Citadel

Dr. Conrad C. Crane
Chief of Historical Services
Army Heritage and Education Center

Amanda de la Garza
Independent Scholar

Ryan E. Doltz
Independent Scholar

John C. Fredriksen
Independent Scholar

Harry Henderson
Independent Scholar

Kathleen G. Hitt
Independent Scholar

Lt. Col. Jonathan P. Klug
Professor of History
Fellow
Military History, ABC-CLIO

William McGuire
Independent Scholar

Dr. Paul G. Pierpaoli Jr.
Fellow
Military History, ABC-CLIO

Dr. Priscilla Roberts
Associate Professor of Business
Codirector, Asia-Pacific Business Research Centre

City University of Macau
Taipa, Macao Special Administrative Region of China

Dr. Elizabeth D. Schafer
Independent Scholar

Dr. Eric G. Swedin
Professor of History
Weber State University

Dr. Grenetta Thomassey
Independent Scholar

Dr. Spencer C. Tucker
Senior Fellow
Military History, ABC-CLIO

Dr. Mark E. Van Rhyn
History Instructor
Louisiana School for Math, Science, and the Arts

James Erik Vik
Independent Scholar

Dr. J. Samuel Walker
Historian

Leslie Wheeler
Independent Scholar

Dr. Hedley P. Willmott
Honorary Research Associate
Greenwich Maritime Institute
United Kingdom

Index

Page numbers in *italics* refer to photographs; numbers following "Doc." refer to primary documents; and **boldface** page numbers refer to main entries.

Adamson, Keith, 1
Advisory Committee on Uranium (S-1 Executive Committee), **1–2**
    Briggs, Lyman, director of, 1, 8, 59, 83–84, 173 (Doc. 22)
    creation of scientific subcommittee, 1
    first meeting, 1, 8
    initial members, 1
    renamed S-1 Committee, 1, 8
    report to Roosevelt on possibility of chain reaction, 1
    S-1 Committee replaced with S-1 Executive Committee, 2
    S-1 Executive Committee used as code reference for atomic bomb, 2
    second meeting, 1
    subsumed under NDRC Committee on Uranium, 1
Alamogordo Bombing and Gunnery Range, **2–3**, 34, 51
    choice of site, 2
    Groves memorandum on Trinity Test, 208–214 (Doc. 34)
    War Department Trinity Test press release (July 16, 1945), 204 (Doc. 33)
    See also Trinity Test; Trinity Test, eyewitness accounts
Albury, Charles, 7, *7*, 304
Alsos Mission, **3–4**
    capture of Otto Hahn, 4
    capture of Werner Heisenberg, 4
    composition of, 3
    cooperation with T-Force, 3–4
    disbanding of, 4
    mandate of, 3
    name of, 3
    named as tribute to Leslie Groves, 3
    and Strassmann, Fritz, 89
Arnold, Henry "Hap," 5–6, 33, 100, 317
Ashworth, Frederick, *7*, 8, 79, 260, 262, 305
Attlee, Clement R., 3, 77, 248, 306
Ayers, Eben, diary on memories by Truman of atomic bomb (August 6, 1951), 282–283 (Doc. 57)
    on Truman's first connection with Manhattan Project, 282
    on Truman's being told of Manhattan Project, 282
    on Truman's decision to use the atomic bomb, 282

B-29 bombers, 7, 304, 305, 308
    The Great Artiste (Superfortress Silverplate), 7, 304, 305, 308
    number of Superfortresses produced, 33
    role of Superfortresses, 33
    Superfortress Silverplates, 32–34
    Superfortresses, 32–33

B-29 bombers (*cont.*)
  See also B-29 raids against Japan; Bockscar; Enola Gay
B-29 raids against Japan, **5–6**
  atomic bombs dropped on Hiroshima and Nagasaki (*see also* Fat Man; Little Boy), 6
  charge-loading checklist for Little Boy on Enola Gay, 222–223 (Doc. 40)
  first raid on Tokyo, 6
  and 509th Composite Group, 6, 32–34, 43, 90, 117, 218 (Doc. 37)
  incendiary raids on Tokyo and other cities, 6, 102, 313, 316, 317, 319, 320
  Iwo Jima landing strip, 73
  Operation Matterhorn, 5
  and Project Alberta, 78
  psychological warfare campaign, 6
  Ramsey memorandum on dangers from accidental detonations (July 9, 1945), 203 (Doc. 32)
  Saipan and Tinian airbases for, 72
  and Sweeney, Charles, 90–91, 92, 315
  and Tibbets, Paul, 102–103, 314
  and Wendover Army Air Field, 117
  XX Bomber Command, 5–6
  XXI Bomber Command, 6, 176 (Doc. 24)
Bard, Ralph
  Interim Committee member, 45
  memorandum to Stimson, 191–192 (Doc. 29)
Beahan, Kermit K., 7, 8, 57, 305
Beams, Jesse, 1
Beser, Jacob, 7, 8, 26, 305
Bock, Frederick, 7
Bockscar, **7–8**
  bombing of Nagasaki, 57–58, 91–92, 315
  crew, 7–8
  crew of, 7–8
  exhibited at National Museum of the U.S. Air Force (Dayton, Ohio), 7, 92
  ground crew, 8
Bohr, Niels, 25, 34, 35, 41, 53
  and Oppenheimer's security concerns, 160 (Doc. 16)
  and Roosevelt-Churchill "Aide Memoire" (September 18, 1944), 164 (Doc. 19)
Bohr, Niels, memorandum to Roosevelt on atomic weapons (July 1944), 162–164 (Doc. 18)
  on common security among nations, 163–164
  on prospect of international nuclear competition, 162–163
Bowen, Harold G., 1, 59
Breit, Gregory, 1
Breit-Wigner formula, 118
Briggs, Lyman, **8–9**
  appointed by Roosevelt to head Advisory Committee on Uranium, 1, 8, 59, 83–84
  and Compton report, 134 (Doc. 6)
  director of Advisory Committee on Uranium, 1, 8, 59, 173 (Doc. 22)
  director of National Bureau of Standards, 8, 58, 98
  early years and education, 8
  and Einstein's fourth letter to Roosevelt, 173 (Doc. 22)
  removal from Advisory Committee on Uranium, 59
  S-1 Executive Committee member, 2
Buckley, Edward K., 7, 8, 305
Bush, Vannevar, **9–10**
  "As We May Think" (*Atlantic Monthly* essay), 9
  Combined Policy Committee member, 159 (Doc. 15), 230 (Doc. 42b)
  director of National Defense Research Committee, 1, 9, 66, 104, 326
  early years and education, 9
  and Groves-Conant letter to Oppenheimer (February 25, 1943), 146–148 (Doc. 10)
  head of Office of Scientific Research and Development, 1, 9, 59–60, 66, 205 (Doc. 33), 228 (Doc. 42b), 326
  Interim Committee member, 45, 232 (Doc. 42b)

Military Policy Committee member, 147 (Doc. 10), 228 (Doc. 42b)
replacement of Uranium Advisory Committee with S-1 Committee, 1, 59
"Science: The Endless Frontier" (report), 9
and Trinity Test, 207 (Doc. 33), 213 (Doc. 34)
Bush, Vannevar, letter to Roosevelt (March 9, 1942), 143–144 (Doc. 8)
on communication of policy, international relations, and technical aspects, 144
on pilot plant stage, 144
on recent developments, 144
Bush-Conant memoranda to Henry Stimson (September 30, 1944), 165–171 (Doc. 20)
cover letter, 165
on dangers of partial secrecy and international armament race, 166–167, 170
on future military potentialities of atomic bombs, 165–166, 168–169
on impossibility of postwar secrecy, 166, 170
on industrial applications of atomic energy, 168
on present military potentialities of atomic bombs, 165, 167–168
on proposed international exchange of information, 167, 171
on temporary present advantage of United States and Britain, 166, 169–170
Byrnes, James Francis, **10–11**
appointed to Supreme Court by Roosevelt, 10
as "assistant president" to Roosevelt, 10
career in U.S. Congress and Senate, 10
early years and education, 10
governor of South Carolina, 11
Interim Committee member, 10, 45, 232 (Doc. 42b), 253 (Doc. 45)
at Potsdam Conference, 10, 77, 248 (Doc. 45)
secretary of state under Truman, 10–11
and Truman's learning of Manhattan Project, 282 (Doc. 57)
at Yalta Conference, 10

Caron, George R. "Bob," 26
Chadwick, James, 231
MAUD Committee member, 53
MAUD Committee Report edited by, 140
neutron discovered by, 325
and Oppenheimer's security concerns, 160 (Doc. 16)
Churchill, Sir Winston L. S., **13–14**
"Aide Memoire" (with Roosevelt; September 18, 1944), 164 (Doc. 19)
and Atlantic Charter, 14
death and legacy of, 14
and "Destroyers-for-Bases" deal with Roosevelt, 14
early years and education, 13
First Lord of the Admiralty and World War I, 13
First Lord of the Admiralty and World War II, 13
Minister of Munitions under Lloyd George, 13
at Potsdam Conference, 14, 77, 110, 248 (Doc. 45)
Prime Minister (1940–1945) and World War II, 13–14, 77, 81, 84, 111, 119
and Quebec Agreement, 14, 81, 158–160 (Doc. 15), 327
at Quebec Conference, 14, 81
resignation of, 14, 77
and Tube Alloys project, 14, 84, 111
on use of atomic bomb as means of maintaining rule of law, 255 (Doc. 46)
at Yalta Conference, 84
Clayton, Frederick D., 8, 305
Clayton, William, 45, 232 (Doc. 42b)
Clinton Engineer Works, **15–16**

Clinton Engineer Works (*cont.*)
   Clinton Pile nuclear reactor (also X-10 Pile or X-10 Graphite Reactor), 15, 55, 76, 105, 113
   construction of by U.S. Army Corps of Engineers, 15, 42, 65, 115, 327
   descriptions of in War Department press releases, 228–229 (Doc. 42b), 233–234 (Doc. 42d), 234–238 (Doc. 42e)
   first self-sustaining chain reaction at, 76
   gaseous uranium enrichment used at, 37
   K-25 gaseous diffusion plant, 16
   known as Manhattan District, 15
   location, 15, 65
   S-50 thermal diffusion plant, 16
   second Oak Ridge petition to Truman signed by scientific personnel of, 201–202 (Doc. 31g)
   Stone & Webster as contractor for, 229 (Doc. 42b), 233 (Doc. 42d), 327
   Wigner, Eugene Paul, as director of research and development at, 118
   Y-12 Electromagnetic Separation Plant, 15–16
Clinton Engineer Works, War Department background information press release (August 6, 1945), 234–238 (Doc. 42g)
   construction, 236, 237
   cultural activities for residents, 237–238
   hospitals and medical care, 236
   location and geography, 236–237
   plants, 235
   religious bodies and churches, 236
   resettlement of uprooted families, 236
   residential center for workers, 235–236
   roads and railroads, 236
   schools and teachers, 236
   secrecy, 234–235
   uniqueness, 235
   workers, 235
Clinton Engineer Works, War Department press release on electromagnetic enrichment (August 6, 1945), 233–234 (Doc. 42d)
   contracting and construction, 234–235
   and Lawrence, Ernest O., 233
   location, 234
   plant construction, 233
   prewar use, 233
   size, 233
   use of silver, 234
Clinton Engineer Works, War Department press release on gaseous uranium enrichment (August 6, 1945), 238–239 (Doc. 42f)
   construction and design, 239
   construction timetable, 239
   main building, 238
Clinton Engineer Works, War Department press release on thermal diffusion plant at (August 6, 1945), 239 (Doc. 42g)
   on research and development, 239
   on structures, 239
   on use of steam, 239
Cockcroft, John, **16–17**
   early years and education, 17
   head of Canadian Atomic Energy Project, 16–17
   MAUD Committee member, 16, 53
   Nobel Prize awarded to, 17
Compton, Arthur Holly, **17–18**
   Advisory Committee on Uranium member, 1
   Atomic Quest: A Personal Narrative, 18
   Compton effect, 17
   director of Manhattan Project's Metallurgical Laboratory, 18
   early career, 17
   early years and education, 17
   The Freedom of Man, 18
   The Human Meaning of Science, 18
   Interim Committee member, 45, 190–191 (Doc. 28)
   NASA orbiting gamma ray observatory named after, 18
   Nobel Prize in Physics awarded to, 17, 18

Index | 341

S-1 Executive Committee member, 2, 327
Secondary Radiation Produced by X-Rays, 18
University of Chicago chosen as Met Lab site by, 55, 327
X-Rays and Electrons, 17–18
Compton report (National Academy of Sciences Committee on Atomic Fission), 134–140 (Doc. 6)
    on competition for control of chain reaction, 135
    on need for large-scale atomic fission program, 134–135
    on possible military applications of atomic fission, 135–136
    on progress toward securing chain reaction, 136–137
    recommended budget, 138–139
    recommended personnel, 139
Conant, James Bryant, **19–20**
    Combined Policy Group member, 230 (Doc. 42b)
    early life and education, 19
    and founding of National Science Foundation, 19
    General Policy Group member, 228 (Doc. 42b)
    Interim Committee member, 45, 232 (Doc. 42b)
    letter from Oppenheimer on properties of uranium, 144–146 (Doc. 9)
    Military Policy Group member, 228 (Doc. 42b), 310–311 (Doc. 60)
    National Defense Research Committee member and chair, 1, 59, 66, 326
    Office of Scientific Research and Development chair, 19
    and Oppenheimer's security concerns, 160 (Doc. 16)
    president of Harvard, 19
    S-1 Executive Committee member, 2, 327
    Shaping Educational Policy, 19
    Slums and Suburbs, 19
    Trinity Test observed by, 19, 206–207 (Doc. 33), 213 (Doc. 34)
    and War Department's timeline of important events, 310–311 (Doc. 60)
    See also Bush-Conant memoranda to Henry Stimson; Groves-Conant letter to Oppenheimer
Cooper, Jean S., 27
Critical mass, **20**
    and autocatalytic methods, 154–155 (Doc. 11)
    bullet subcritical mass, 99
    definition of in nuclear physics, 20
    and detonation, 151 (Doc. 11)
    and effect of tamper on efficiency, 151 (Doc. 11)
    and Fat Man bomb, 57, 315
    Frisch-Peierls Memorandum on, 132 (Doc. 5)
    and implosion-type weapons, 45
    MAUD Committee Report on, 141 (Doc. 7)
    and mechanics of shooting, 153–154 (Doc. 11)
    subcritical mass, 20, 99
    supercritical mass, 39, 45, 50, 103
    Szilárd's and Fermi's determination of, 20
    target subcritical mass, 99
    use of term in popular culture, 20

DeHart, Albert R., 7, 8, 305
Dempster, Jeffrey, 114
Deuterium (heavy hydrogen), 135, 138, 166, 168, 325
Development of Substitute Materials, **21**
    creation of, 310–311 (Doc. 60)
    first name of Manhattan Project, 15, 21
    renamed Manhattan Engineering District, 21, 115
Duffy, Frank D., 27
Duzenbury, Wyatt E., 26

Einstein, Albert, **23–24**
   Advisory Committee on Uranium member, 1, 23–24
   $E = mc^2$ equation, 23, 54
   early years and education, 23–24
   emigration from Germany to U.S., 23
   excluded from Manhattan Project, 24
   photon theory of light, 18
   and Szilárd, Leó, 92, 93, 94
   Theory of Relativity, 23, 325
   world government advocacy, 24
   See also Einstein-Szilárd Letter
Einstein, Albert, fourth letter to Roosevelt (March 25, 1945), 173–174 (Doc. 22)
   introduction of Szilárd, 173
   on Szilárd's concerns, 173
Einstein-Szilárd Letter, **24–25,** 126–127 (Doc. 3), 325
   background, 24, 63, 126
   delayed delivery to Roosevelt, 24, 83
   impact of, 24, 59, 83, 94, 326
   and possibility of nuclear chain reaction, 126
   proposed purchase of uranium sources, 126–127
   Roosevelt's response to (October 19, 1939), 127 (Doc. 4)
   and Szilárd, Leó, 94
   and Teller, Edward, 24
   and Wigner, Eugene, 24, 94
Eisenhower, Dwight D., 62, 67, 100, 320
Electromagnetic uranium enrichment, **25**
   Clinton Engineer Works Y-12 cauldrons used for, 15–16, 25, 327
   funded by S-1 Committee, 25
   gaseous uranium enrichment as more efficient than, 37
   and Lawrence, Ernest, 25, 67, 310 (Doc. 60)
   and Oliphant, Mark, 25, 67
   used for Little Boy bomb, 25
   War Department press release on (August 6, 1945), 233–234 (Doc. 42d)
Enola Gay, **26–27**
   bombing of Hiroshima, 43–44, 91, 314
   charge-loading checklist for Little Boy on (August 1945), 222–223 (Doc. 40)
   crew, 26
   Great Artiste's support for, 7
   ground crew, 26–27
   Little Boy loaded onto, 43, *50,* 314
   naming of, 26, 102
   Parsons, William S. "Deak," weaponeer on, 26, 103, 172 (Doc. 21), 193–194 (Doc. 30)
   range of, 26
   return from bombing Hiroshima, *26*
   Smithsonian Institution's exhibit of, 92
   Tibbets, Paul, captain of, 26, *101,* 102, 314
   See also Hiroshima, bombing of; Little Boy
Farrell, Thomas, 103, 104
   early life and education, 103
   and setting date of Trinity Test, 193 (Doc. 30)
   Tinian Joint Chiefs member, 103
Farrell, Thomas, message to Groves on Nagasaki damage (September 14, 1945), 265–276 (Doc. 53)
   on comparison with Hiroshima damage, 265–266
   on point of burst and distances of impact, 266–267
   rate of dying wounded, 267
   on shipping and harbor damage, 266
Fat Man, *29,* **29–30**
   implosion-type nuclear weapon, 29
   naming of, 29
   postwar Operations Crossroads test, 30
   shape of, 29
   size and weight, 30
   See also Bockscar; Nagasaki, bombing of
Ferebee, Thomas, 26
Fermi, Enrico, **30–32**
   achieves nuclear fission for first time, 325

Advisory Committee on Uranium
member, 1
B Reactor at Hanford designed by, 42
and Chicago Pile 1 (CP-1) self-sustaining
nuclear reaction, 18, 20, 30–31, 55, 63,
76, 92, 105, 106, 113, 327
at control panel of a particle accelerator,
31
early years and education, 30
and Einstein-Szilárd Letter, 23, 94, 118,
126 (Doc. 3)
emigration from Italy to U.S., 30
eyewitness to Trinity Test (July 16,
1945), 206 (Doc. 33), 285 (Doc. 59a)
Fermi Statistics, 30
first American experiment in nuclear
fission by, 74
and hydrogen (thermonuclear) bomb, 31
Interim Committee scientific panel
member, 45, 190–191 (Doc. 28)
and Oppenheimer's security concerns
(November 2, 1943), 160 (Doc. 16)
and Pegram, George Braxton, 73–74
and Szilárd, Leó, 92
Firebombing
of Dresden, 245 (Doc. 44), 316, 317
of Tokyo and other Japanese cities, 6,
102, 313, 316, 317, 319, 320
Fissile material, **32**
and critical mass, 20
and nuclear fission, 63
subset of fissionable material, 32
three primary types, 32
and transmutation of uranium to
plutonium, 105
509th Composite Group, **32–34**
activation of, 33–34
and B-29 aircraft, 32–33
C-54 "Green Hornet" aircraft, 34, 79,
260 (Doc. 51)
deployment of, *33,* 34, 43, 314
and Project Alberta, 34
proposal and formation of, 33, 328
purpose of, 33

and Sweeney, Charles, 90
Tibbets, Paul W., commander, 32, 34
training at Wendover Army Air Field,
33, 101, 117
Franck, James, 94
Franck, James, report of the Committee on
Political and Social Problems:
Manhattan Project "Metallurgical
Laboratory" (June 11, 1945), 182–190
(Doc. 27)
on armaments race, 183–186
defense of development of new weapons,
184
on impossibility of postwar secrecy, 189
on methods of international control of
nuclear weapons, 188–189
optimistic view of prospect of
international agreement concerning
nuclear weapons, 186–188
pessimistic view of prospect of
international agreement concerning
nuclear weapons, 187
on prospect of international agreement
concerning nuclear weapons, 186–188
on taxpayer investment in nuclear
weapon development, 188
on uniqueness of nuclear power, 182–183
Frisch, Otto, **34–35**
early years and education, 34
emigration from Germany to England, 34
eyewitness to Trinity Test (July 16,
1945), 285–286 (Doc. 59a)
and MAUD Committee, 53
nuclear fission theorized by, 25, 34, 63,
89, 325
See also Frisch-Peierls Memorandum
Frisch-Peierls Memorandum, **35–36**, 128–
134 (Doc. 5)
on assembly of parts, 132
background, 35, 128
on chain reaction, 131–132
on civilian deaths, 129
contents, 35, 114, 326
on critical mass, 128, 132

Frisch-Peierls Memorandum (*cont.*)
   and detection staff needed for radioactive effects, 130
   and Frisch, Otto, 34
   impact of, 35, 36
   "Memorandum on the Properties of a Radioactive 'Super-bomb'" (March 1940), 128–130 (Doc. 5a)
   and Oliphant, Mark, 35, 67
   "On the Construction of a 'Super-bomb' based on a Nuclear Chain Reaction in Uranium" (March 1940), 130–134 (Doc. 5b)
   and Peierls, Rudolf, 75
   on possibility of parallel research in other countries, 129–130
   and radiation, 130, 133–134
   on strategic advantages of super-bomb, 129
   and Tizard Mission, 104

Gallagher, Raymond, 7, 8, 305
Gaseous uranium enrichment, **37**
   initial development of, 37
   process of, 37
   used at Oak Ridge S-50 and K-25 facilities, 16, 37
   War Department press release on (August 6, 1945), 238–239 (Doc. 42f)
Gerken, Rudolph H., 8
Greisen, Kenneth, eyewitness account of Trinity Test (July 16, 1945), 284–285 (Doc. 59a)
   on balls of light, 284
   on mushroom cloud, 284–285
Groves, Leslie Richard, **38–39**
   Alsos Mission named as tribute to, 3
   construction of Pentagon supervised by, 38
   and creation of Manhattan Engineer District, 1
   early years and education, 38
   head of Manhattan Project, 1, 2, 38, 103, 327
   Oak Ridge site chosen by, 65
   Oppenheimer recruited by, 68, 327
   and Trinity Test, 2, *38,* 106, 108
Groves, Leslie Richard, memorandum to Marshall, with Marshall's note to halt bombing (August 10, 1945), 255–256 (Doc. 47)
   on expected date of delivery of third bomb, 255
   Marshall's note to halt bombing, 255
Groves, Leslie Richard, memorandum to Stimson on Trinity Test (July 18, 1945), 208–214 (Doc. 34)
   on crater from explosion, 209–210
   description of cloud, 209, 210
   on destruction of steel tower, 210
   Groves' impressions of test's high points, 213–214
   on news reporting of test, 211
   on radioactivity, 210
   on scientists' reactions to test, 211–212
   on success of test, 209
   on weather, 210–211
Groves, Leslie Richard, memorandum to U.S. Army Chief of Staff George Marshall (August 6, 1945), 223–224 (Doc. 41)
   on bombing of Hiroshima, 223
   on preparation for bombing, 223
   on return of aircraft to base, 223
   on sound, flash, and blast of bomb, 223–224
Groves, Leslie Richard, memorandum to U.S. Army Chief of Staff on conclusions of Trinity Test (July 30, 1945), 220–222 (Doc. 39)
   on brightness and visibility of blast, 221
   on damage to physical structures, 221
   on energy of explosion, 221
   on lethality of blast, 220
   on movement of troops through blast area, 221
   on number of bombs, 221–222
   on radioactive effects, 221
   on size of explosion, 221

Groves, Leslie Richard, office diary on setting test date (July 2, 1945), 192–194 (Doc. 30)
  Groves, Leslie Richard, response to Szilárd petition against use of atomic bomb (July 4, 1945), 198 (Doc. 31d)
  Lindemann, Frederick, Lord Cherwell, response to Groves (July 12, 1945), 198–199
  request for information on Lord Cherwell's discussion with Szilárd, 198
Groves, Leslie Richard, transcript of telephone conversation with Charles E. Rea (August 25, 1945), 263–265 (Doc. 52)
  on burn victims, 263
  on delayed reactions and deaths from burns, 263–264
  on infection from burns, 264–265
Groves-Conant letter to Oppenheimer (February 25, 1943), 146–148 (Doc. 10)
  on role of Commanding Officer, 148
  on role of Military Policy Committee, 147–148
  on role of Scientific Director, 148
  on role of Office of Scientific Research and Development, 147
  on timetable of atomic bomb project, 147
  written on stationary of OSRD, 146
Gunn, Ross, 1
Gun-type fission weapon, **39,** 45
  conventional explosive bomb compared with, 39
  danger of spontaneous fission from, 105
  definition of, 39
  Little Boy bomb as, 39, 49, 100
  Thin Man bomb as, 30, 99
  uranium-powered, 39

Hahn, Otto, **41**
  and Alsos Mission, 4
  development of nuclear fission, 25, 34, 35, 41, 53, 54, 89, 125 (Doc. 2), 325
  early years and education, 41
  and MAUD Committee, 53
  and Meitner, Lise, 53, 54
  Nobel Prize in Chemistry awarded to, 41
  suspicions regarding, 41
Haider, Robert M., 8
Handy, Thomas, memorandum to Spaatz (July 25, 1945), 218–219 (Doc. 37)
  on order of bombs to be dropped, 218
  on secrecy of information, 218
Hanford, Washington, **41–42**
  B Reactor, 41, 42, 55
  choice of site, 42
  construction of Hanford Engineer Works, 41–42
  D Reactor, 41, 42
  F Reactor, 41, 42
  and Los Alamos Laboratory, 51
  and Metallurgical Laboratory, 55
  size and workforce, 42
  and U.S. Army Corps of Engineers, 115
  See also War Department press release on Hanford Engineer Works
Hansell, Haywood, 6
Heavy hydrogen (deuterium), 135, 138, 166, 168, 325
Heisenberg, Werner, 4, 75
Hiroshima, bombing of, **42–44**
  destruction and casualties, 44
  impact on warfare, 44
  initial fireball, 43–44
  length of mission, 44
  mushroom cloud, *43,* 44
  orders for, 43
  See also Siemes, John, eyewitness account of atomic bomb over Hiroshima
Hiroshima, press release on security measures protection secrecy of (August 10, 1945), 256–257 (Doc. 48)
Hiroshima, U.S. government press releases on (August 6, 1945), 224–232 (Doc. 42a-42c)
  on Clinton Engineer Works, 228–229
  on Combined Policy Committee, 230–231

Hiroshima (*cont.*)
  on compartmentalization of project work, 230
  on Hanford Engineer Works, 229
  history of Manhattan Project, 228
  on Interim Committee, 232
  on Los Alamos Laboratory, 229
  on new era of nuclear energy, 226, 231
  on Potsdam ultimatum, 226
  on theoretic possibility of atomic energy, 225
  on scientific cooperation with Great Britain and Canada, 225, 227
  See also press releases under Clinton Engineer Works
Hirst, Hugo, Szilárd's letter to (March 17, 1934), 123–124 (Doc. 1)
Hoover, Gilbert, 1
Hoover, Herbert
  appointment of Henry Stimson as secretary of state, 88
  presidential election loss of 1932, 83

Implosion-type nuclear weapon, **45**
  definition of, 45
  Fat Man bomb as, 29, 45, 50, 51, 105, 106
  gun-type nuclear weapon compared with, 45
  plutonium-powered, 45
Interim Committee, **45–46**
  creation of, 45
  first meeting, 45
  members, 45
  Oppenheimer letter to Stimson (August 17, 1945), 258–259 (Doc. 50)
  purpose of, 46, 316
  science committee members, 46, 190–191 (Doc. 28)
Interim Committee's Science Committee report to Stimson on use of atomic bomb in wartime (August 17, 1945), 46, 190–191 (Doc. 28)
  on differing opinions of scientific experts regarding use of atomic weapons, 191
  on international exchange of information, 191
  on proprietary rights, 191

Jackson, John E., 27
Jeppson, Morris R., 26

Kapitsa, Pyotr, 16
Kuharek, John, 7, 8, 305
Kurti, Nicholas, 37

Laurence, William Leonard, **47**
  controversy regarding, 47
  early years and education, 47
  emigration to U.S. from Lithuania, 47
  eyewitness to bombing of Nagasaki, 47
  eyewitness to Trinity Test, 47
  Pulitzer Prizes awarded to, 47
Laurence, William, eyewitness to bombing of Nagasaki (August 9, 1945), 303–309 (Doc. 59c)
  on assembly of bomb, 304
  on crew and personnel, 304–306
  on dropping the bomb, 308
  on mushroom cloud, 309
  on pole of purple fire, 308–309
  on seeing St. Elmo's Fire, 306
Lawrence, Ernest Orlando, **47–49**
  cyclotron invented by, 18, 25, 47, 48, 233 (Doc. 42d)
  early years and education, 47
  Interim Committee scientific panel member, 45, 190–191 (Doc. 28)
  Nobel Prize in Physics awarded to, 47, 48
  postwar opposition to atomic bomb testing programs, 49
  S-1 Executive Committee member, 2
LeMay, Curtis E.
  in charge of strategic air operations against Japan, 6, 90
  on effect of using atomic bombs, 320–321
  finalizing of take-off time for Hiroshima attack, 223 (Doc. 41)

incendiary raid on Tokyo (February 1945), 102
post-war Air Force atomic bomb proposals, 261 (Doc. 51)
Lesniewski, John J., 27
Lewis, Robert A., 26
Little Boy, **49–51**
    charge-loading checklist for, 222–223 (Doc. 40)
    design and construction, 49–50
    first use in hostilities, 50
    as gun-type fission weapon, 39, 49, 100
    loaded onto Enola Gay, *50*
    weight of, 49
Los Alamos Laboratory, **51–52**

Mackenzie King, William Lyon, 81, 158 (Doc. 15)
Maltese Falcon (novel and film), 29, 45, 99
Manhattan Engineer District
    creation of, 1, 326
    location and size of (described in War Department press release), 233 (Doc. 42d)
    Marshall, James, as district engineer of, 327
    Military Intelligence Division, 256–257 (Doc. 48)
    Military Policy Committee, 327
    name of, 234 (Doc. 42e)
    Nichols, Kenneth, assigned chief engineer of, 327
    Oppenheimer as head of, 144
    renamed from Development of Substitute Materials, 21, 115
Markley, Leonard W., 26
MAUD Committee, **53–54**
    chair and members, 53
    creation of, 35, 36, 67, 326
    and Frisch-Peierls Memorandum, 35, 67
    name of, 53
    and Oliphant, Mark, 53, 59, 67, 74, 75
    report, 1
    split into MAUD Technical Committee and MAUD Policy Committee, 53

and Tizard, Henry, 36, 53, 75, 326
and Tizard Mission, 104
"Use of Uranium as a Source of Power" report, 53
"Use of Uranium in a Bomb" report, 1, 53, 59, 60, 74, 104, 111, 141–143 (Doc. 7)
McCaleb, Walter F., 26
McMillan, Edwin M., eyewitness account of Trinity Test (July 16, 1945), 287 (Doc. 59a)
    on ball of fire, 287–288
    on cloud, 288
    viewing location, 287
McNamee, Robert L., 8
Meitner, Lise, **54**
    early years and education, 54
    and Frisch, Otto, 34
    and Frisch-Peierls Memorandum, 35
    and Hahn, Otto, 41
    nuclear fission theorized by, 25, 34, 63, 89, 325
Metallurgical Laboratory, **54–55**
    Chicago Pile 1 (CP-1) self-sustaining nuclear reaction, 18, 20, 30–31, 55, 63, 76, 92, 105, 106, 113, 327
    Compton, Arthur Holly, director of, 18
    at University of Chicago, 54–55, 63, 113, 118
    See also Franck, James, report of the Committee on Political and Social Problems: Manhattan Project "Metallurgical Laboratory"
Mohler, Fred L., 1
Morrison, Philip, eyewitness account of Trinity Test (July 16, 1945), 288–290 (Doc. 59a)
    on appearance of smoke cloud, 289–290
    on growth of mushroom cloud, 289
    on initial glow and flash, 288–289
    viewing location, 288
Murphree, Eger, 2

Nagasaki, bombing of, **57–58**
    background, 57
    destruction from, 57, *58*

Nagasaki, bombing (*cont.*)
   eyewitness account of (August 9, 1945), 303–309 (Doc. 59c)
   impact on ending World War II, 58
   leaflet dropped on Japanese cities prior to (August 9, 1945), 58, 244–245 (Doc. 43)
   length of mission, 57
   message from Farrell to Groves on damage from (September 14, 1945), 265–267 (Doc. 53)
   order for, 57
National Bureau of Standards, **58–59,** 60
   Briggs, Lyman, director of, 8, 58, 98
National Defense Research Committee, **59–60**
   creation of, 1, 9, 59
   divisions, committees, and panels, 60
   original members, 59
   role in Manhattan Project, 60
   superseded as funding agency by Office of Scientific Research and Development, 60, 66
Nelson, Richard H., 26
Neumann, John von, **60–62,** 117
   appointed by Eisenhower to Atomic Energy Commission, 62
   early years and education, 61
   postwar career, 62
   von Neumann computers, 61
Nuclear chain reaction, **62–63**
   and Chicago Pile 1 (CP-1) self-sustaining nuclear reaction, 18, 20, 30–31, 55, 63, 76, 92, 105, 106, 113, 327
   process of, 62–63
   Szilárd, Leó, and creation of first nuclear chain reaction, 20, 63, 92, 94, 325
Nuclear reactor, **63–64**
   at Clinton Engineer Works, 15, 63
   at Hanford Engineer Works, 41, 42, 63
   at University of Chicago, 63, 94

Oak Ridge, Tennessee, **65–66**
   acquired by U.S. Army Corps of Engineers, 15, 42, 65, 115
   See also entries under Clinton Engineer Works
Office of Scientific Research and Development, **66–67**
   Bush, Vannevar, head of, 1, 9, 59–60, 66, 228 (Doc. 42b), 326
   creation of, 66
   superseded National Defense Research Committee as funding agency, 60, 66
Oliphant, Mark, **67**
   and electromagnetic uranium enrichment, 25, 67
   and Frisch-Peierls Memorandum, 35, 67
   and MAUD Committee, 53, 59, 67, 74, 75
Olivi, Fred J., 7, 8
Olson, Harold R., 27
Operation Alsos. *See* Alsos Mission
Oppenheimer, Julius Robert, **67–68**
   and development of gun-type nuclear weapon, 99
   director of Los Alamos Laboratory, 51, 68
   early years and education, 67–68
   Interim Committee scientific panel member, 45, 190–191 (Doc. 28)
   letter from Groves on personal safety (July 29, 1943), 157–158 (Doc. 14)
   letter from Ramsay (undated), 260–263 (Doc. 51)
   and McCarthyism, 68
   and Neumann, John von, 61
   postwar career, 68
   recruited by Groves, 68
   Teller's testimony against, 98
   and Trinity Test, 2, 106
   at Trinity Test site, *38*
   See also Groves-Conant letter to Oppenheimer
Oppenheimer, Julius Robert, letter to Conant on properties of uranium (November 30, 1942), 144–146 (Doc. 9)
   on personnel, 146
   on purity goals, 144–146

Oppenheimer, Julius Robert, letter to
    Groves (October 6, 1944), 172–174
    (Doc. 21)
  on necessity of testing, 172
  on Parsons, William, 172
Oppenheimer, Julius Robert, letter to
    Groves on aliases (November 2, 1943),
    160 (Doc. 16)
  on new names (aliases) for Bohr and
    other British scientists, 160
  on using real names when making phone
    calls to team members, 160
Oppenheimer, Julius Robert, letter to
    Stimson (August 17, 1945), 258–259
    (Doc. 50)
  on future improvements given further
    research, 259
  on importance of war prevention, 259
  on inability to devise countermeasures
    against atomic weapons, 259
  report of Interim Committee scientific
    panel, 259
Oppenheimer, Julius Robert, memorandum
    on Test of implosion gadget (February
    16, 1944), 161–162 (Doc. 17)
Oppenheimer, Julius Robert, memorandum
    to Groves on Los Alamos (April 30,
    1943), 156 (Doc. 12)
Oppenheimer, Julius Robert, speech to
    Association of Los Alamos Scientists
    (November 2, 1945), 268–277 (Doc.
    55)
  on change in warfare, 271–272
  on dangerous tendencies of scientists,
    274–275
  on fraternity of scientists, 276–277
  on impact of creation of the atomic
    bomb, 269–273
  on official government statements,
    275–276

Pacific Theater: World War II, **69–73**
  1941–1943, 69–71
  1943–1944, 71–72
  1945, 72–73

  See also Hiroshima, bombing of;
    Nagasaki, bombing of
Parsons, William S. "Deak"
  Project Alberta commander, 79, 103, 104
  weaponeer of Enola Gay, 26, 43, 172
    (Doc. 21), 193–194 (Doc. 30), 222–
    223 (Doc. 40)
Pegram, George Braxton, **73–74**
  Advisory Committee on Uranium
    member, 1
  Advisory Committee on Uranium
    scientific subcommittee member, 1
  attendance of first meeting of Tube
    Alloys project, 74
  at Columbia University, 74
Peierls, Rudolf, **75–76**
  early years and education, 75–76
  suspicions regarding, 75
  See also Frisch-Peierls Memorandum
Plutonium, **76–77**
  Pu-239, 20, 32, 39, 42, 49, 55, 63, 76, 105,
    114
  Pu-240, 39, 51, 76, 99, 105
  Pu-241, 76
  Pu-248, 76
  and Thin Man bomb, 39, 49, 51, 76, 105
  transmutation of uranium into, 105–106
Porter, John, 27
Potsdam Conference, **77–78**
  and British elections, 77
  code name "Terminal," 77
  complex legacy of, 78
  dates of, 77
  representatives at, 77
  and Trinity Test, 3, 108, 110
  Truman radio report on (August 9,
    1945), 247–254 (Doc. 45)
Potsdam Declaration, 43, 77, 89, 91, 101,
    102, 219–220 (Doc. 38), 314, 328
Project Alberta, **78–79**
  and Los Alamos Laboratory, 51
  Parsons, William S., commander of, 79,
    103, 104
  purpose of, 34, 78
Purnell, William R., 103, 104, 194 (Doc. 30)

350 | Index

Quebec Conference, 1st, **81–82**
   attendees, 81
   Quebec Agreement, 14, 37, 81–82, 158–160 (Doc. 15), 327

Ramsey, Norman, letter to Oppenheimer (undated), 260–263 (Doc. 51)
   on protection against detonation during take-off, 260
   summary of Nagasaki mission, 261–262
   on U.S. readiness to produce and deliver an atomic bomb, 261
Ramsey, Norman, memorandum to Oppenheimer on dangers from accidental detonations (July 9, 1945), 203 (Doc. 32)
Roberts, Richard B., 1
Rommel, Erwin, 121
Roosevelt, Eleanor, 83, 109
Roosevelt, Franklin D., **83–85**
   appointed of Briggs to head National Bureau of Standards, 8, 83–84
   appointment of Byrnes as secretary of state, 10
   appointment of Stimson as secretary of war, 89
   atomic weapon development authorized by, 326, 327
   Bohr Memorandum to (July 1944), 162–164 (Doc. 18)
   Bush letter to (March 9, 1942), 143–144 (Doc. 8)
   death of, 84, 328
   early years and education, 83
   Einstein's fourth letter to (March 25, 1945), 173–174 (Doc. 22)
   fireside chats, 83
   Manhattan Engineering District authorized by, 326
   National Defense Research Committee authorized by, 326
   Office of Scientific Research and Development authorized by, 66
   and Quebec Agreement, 81, 327
   at Quebec Conference, 81
   response to Einstein (October 19, 1939), 127 (Doc. 4)
   role model for Stimson, 87
   Roosevelt-Churchill "Aide Memoire" (July 1944), 164 (Doc. 19)
   Truman as vice-president under, 109
   and World War II Pacific Theater, 70
   at Yalta Conference, 84, 317
   See also Einstein-Szilárd Letter
Roosevelt, Theodore, 87

S-1 Executive Committee. *See* Advisory Committee on Uranium
Sachs, Alexander
   Advisory Committee on Uranium member, 1
   delivery and summarization of Einstein-Szilárd letter to Roosevelt, 23, 24, 83
   and Roosevelt's reply to Einstein-Szilárd letter, 127
Serber, Robert, **87**
   atomic bombs named by, 29, 87, 99
   early years and education, 87
   "Los Alamos Primer" from lectures (April 1943), 87, 148–156 (Doc. 11)
Serber, Robert, eyewitness account of Trinity Test, 290 (Doc. 59a)
   on initial flash, 290
   on mushroom cloud, 290
   viewing location, 290
Shapiro, Maurice, M, eyewitness account of Trinity Test (July 16, 1945), 291 (Doc. 59a)
   on initial flash, 291
   on cloud-chamber effect, 291
   on shock, 291
   viewing location, 291
Shumard, Robert H., 26
Siemes, John, eyewitness account of atomic bomb over Hiroshima (August 6, 1945), 293–303 (Doc. 59b)
   on burned horses, 296
   on crowd of people after blast, 294–295

on damage to house and other structures, 294, 295, 296
on delayed death from burns, 302
on fires, 297
on funeral processions, 300–301
on initial light, 294
on magnitude of disaster, 301
on refugees, 301
on spirit of Japanese people, 302–303
on transportation of wounded, 297–300
Simon, Francis, 37
Smith, Cyril S., eyewitness account of Trinity Test (July 16, 1945), 291–292 (Doc. 59a)
on initial light, 291
on ionization zone, 292
on mushroom cloud, 292
on reaction products, 292
viewing location, 291
Spitzer, Abe M., 7, *8,* 305
Stalin, Joseph, 3, 14, 77, 84, 110, 119
death of, 121
declaration of war on Japan, 318
inept generalship of, 119
knowledge of Manhattan Project, 110
at Potsdam Conference, 3, 14, 77, 282 (Doc. 57)
Truman on, 218 (Doc. 36), 247–248 (Doc. 45)
at Yalta Conference, 84
Stiborki, Joe S., 26
Stimson, Henry Lewis, **87–89**
appointed secretary of state by Hoover, 88
appointed secretary of war (1911), 88
appointed secretary of war by Roosevelt (1940), 88
and Ayers diary on memories of Truman (August 6, 1951), 282 (Doc. 57)
Bard's Memorandum to (June 27, 1945), 191–192 (Doc. 29)
early years and education, 87
governor general of the Philippines, 88
informed of successful Trinity Test, 108

Interim Committee created by, 45
letter to Truman on Manhattan Project (April 24, 1945), 174 (Doc. 23)
and Marshall, George, *88,* 89
McCloy's Memorandum on meeting with Marshall and Stimson regarding objectives toward Japan (Mary 29, 1945), 181–182 (Doc. 26)
notification of Eisenhower of use of atomic bomb, 320
Oppenheimer letter to (August 17, 1945), 258–259 (Doc. 50)
oversight of Manhattan Project, 89
and target list for atomic bombing, 316
Truman informed of Manhattan Project by, 89, 110, 180–181 (Doc. 23)
See also Bush-Conant memoranda to Henry Stimson
Stimson, Henry Lewis, memorandum to Truman on campaign against Japan (May 16, 1945), 180–181 (Doc. 25)
on diplomacy, 180
on Japanese forces in China, 180
on sparing civilian populations, 180
Stimson, Henry Lewis, press releases on bombing of Hiroshima, 226–232 (Doc. 42b)
on Clinton Engineer Works, 228–229
on Combined Policy Committee, 230–231
on compartmentalization of project work, 230
on Hanford Engineer Works, 229
history of Manhattan Project, 228
on Interim Committee, 232
on Los Alamos Laboratory, 229
on new era of nuclear energy, 226, 231
on Potsdam ultimatum, 226
on scientific cooperation with Great Britain and Canada, 227
Stimson, Henry Lewis, telephone conversation with Truman (June 17, 1943), 157 (Doc. 13)

Strassmann, Fritz, **89–90**
  and Alsos Mission, 89
  development of nuclear fission, 25, 34, 35, 41, 53, 54, 89, 125 (Doc. 2), 325
  early life and education, 89
  Nazis' suspicions regarding, 89
Strauss, Lewis, Szilárd's letter to (January 25, 1939), 125 (Doc. 2)
Sweeney, Charles, **90–92**
  commander of Bockscar B-29 bomber, 7, 8, 57, 90–92, 102, 315
  commander of The Great Artiste B-29 bomber, 7, 304
Szilárd, Leó, **92–95**
  attendance at first meeting of Advisory Committee on Uranium, 1, 8
  Council for a Livable World founded by, 95
  creation of first nuclear chain reaction, 20, 63, 92, 94, 325
  early years and education, 92–93
  and Einstein's fourth letter to Roosevelt (March 25, 1945), 173 (Doc. 22)
  emigration from Germany when Hitler came to power, 93
  laboratory space arranged by George Braxton Pegram for, 74
  in London, 93
  move to U.S., 93–94
  postulation of development of atomic bomb, 25
  and report of Committee on Political and Social Problems: Manhattan Project "Metallurgical Laboratory," Doc. 27
  See also Szilárd petition to Harry Truman against use of atomic bomb; Szilárd-Einstein letter
Szilárd, Leó, letter to Hirst (March 17, 1934), 123–124 (Doc. 1)
  on new sources of energy, 124
  on recommendation of *The World Set Free* (H. G. Wells), 124
Szilárd, Leó, letter to Strauss (January 25, 1939), 125–126 (Doc. 2)
  on potential for atomic bomb, 125
  on work of Otto Hahn, 125
Szilárd petition to Harry Truman against use of atomic bomb, 55, 94, 195–292 (Doc. 31), 328
  cover letter (July 4, 1945), 196–197 (Doc. 31b)
  final petition (July 17, 1945), 199–201 (Doc. 31f)
  first version (July 3, 1945), 195–196 (Doc. 31a)
  Groves' response to (July 4, 1945), 198–199 (Doc. 31d)
  Oak Ridge addendum to (July 13, 1945), 199 (Doc. 31e)
  second Oak Ridge petition (July 1945), 201–202 (Doc. 31g)
  Teller's reply to (July 4, 1945), 197–198 (Doc. 31c)

Teller, Edward, **97–98**
  attendance at first meeting of Advisory Committee on Uranium, 1, 8
  awards granted to, 98
  early years and education, 97
  and Einstein-Szilárd letter, 24, 94, 97, 126
  as "father of the hydrogen bomb," 97–98
  and Lawrence Livermore Laboratory (University of California, Berkeley), 98
  and memorandum by Oppenheimer on test of implosion gadget (February 16, 1944), 161–162 (Doc. 17)
  politics of, 98
  reply to Leó Szilárd's petition letter (July 4, 1945), 197–198 (Doc. 31c)
  testimony against J. Robert Oppenheimer, 98
Thermal diffusion uranium enrichment, **98–99**
  process of, 98–99
  and thermophoresis, 98
Thin Man, 29–30, **99–100**

gun-type fission weapon, 39
naming of, 29, 39, 87, 99
and plutonium impurity, 39, 49, 51, 76, 105
researched at Los Alamos Laboratory, 51
shape of, 33
Thin Man (film series), 29, 39, 99
Tibbets, Paul, **100–103**
  509th Composite Group commander, 32, 34
  captain of Enola Gay, 26, *101,* 101–102, 314
  Distinguished Service Cross awarded to, 102
  early life and education, 100
  naming of Enola Gay, 26, 102
  and Sweeney, Charles, 90, 91, 92
  Wendover training site chosen by, 117
  witness to postwar Bikini Atoll tests, 102
Tinian Joint Chiefs, **103–104**
  Farrel, Thomas, 103, 104, 192–195 (Doc. 30), 265–267 (Doc. 53)
  mission of, 103
  Parsons, William S. "Deak," 26, 43, 103, 104, 172 (Doc. 21), 192–195 (Doc. 30), 222–223 (Doc. 40)
  Purnell, William R., 103, 104, 192–195 (Doc. 30)
Tizard, Henry, 36, 53, 67, 75, 104
  and creation of MAUD Committee, 36, 326
Tizard Mission, **104–105**
  and Cockcroft, John, 16
  and MAUD Committee, 104
  purpose of, 104
  success of, 104
Tolman, Richard C., 29, 59, 194 (Doc. 30)
Transmutation of uranium into plutonium, **105–106**
  first case of, 105
  as major goal of Manhattan Project, 105
  process of, 105
Trinity Test, **106–109**

date of, 107, 192–195 (Doc. 30)
eyewitness accounts, 284–293 (Doc. 59a)
Groves and Oppenheimer at site of, *38*
Groves Memorandum to Stimson on (July 18, 1945), 208–214 (Doc. 34)
Groves Memorandum to U.S. Army Chief of Staff from conclusions of (July 30, 1945), 220–222 (Doc. 39)
and Oppenheimer Memorandum on test of an implosion gadget (February 16, 1944), 161–162 (Doc. 17)
and press secrecy, 108
site, 3, 107
War Department press release on (July 16, 1945), 203–208 (Doc. 33)
Warren Report to Groves on (July 21, 1945), 214–217 (Doc. 35)
Truman, Harry, **109–110**
  advisors on use of atomic bomb, 38, 318–320
  authorization to use atomic bombs, 43, 69, 73, 91, 102, 110, 316–317, 320
  Ayers, Eben, diary entry on memories by Truman on atomic bomb (August 6, 1951), 282–283 (Doc. 57)
  Byrnes, James Francis, secretary of state under, 10–11
  diary entry (July 25, 1945), 217–218 (Doc. 36)
  federal government experience and vice-presidency, 109
  informed of Manhattan Project, 89, 110
  later thoughts in letters on use of atomic bombs (August 5, 1963 and August 4, 1964), 283–283 (Doc. 58)
  letter from Stimson on Manhattan Project (April 24, 1945), 174 (Doc. 23)
  memorandum from Stimson on campaign against Japan (May 16, 1945), 180–181 (Doc. 25)
  at Potsdam Conference, 3, 14, 77, 110
  radio report giving reassurance to American people (August 9, 1945), 247–254 (Doc. 45)

Truman, Harry (*cont.*)
   request for press secrecy on Manhattan Project (September 14, 1945), 267–268 (Doc. 54)
   and "Science: The Endless Frontier" (report by Vannevar Bush), 9
   succession to presidency after Roosevelt's death, 10, 84, 109
   telephone conversation with Stimson (June 17, 1943), 157 (Doc. 13)
   and Trinity Test, 108
Tse-ven Soong, 81
Tube Alloys, 74, **111**
   absorbed into Manhattan Project, 67
   Akers, Wallace, head of, 111
   and Churchill, Winston L. S., 14, 84, 111
   and development of gaseous uranium enrichment, 37
   and Frisch-Peierls Memorandum, 34, 35, 75
   and MAUD Committee, 36, 111
   and Tizard Mission, 104
Tuve, Merle, 1

University of Chicago, **113**
   Chicago Pile 1 (CP-1) self-sustaining nuclear reaction, 18, 20, 30–31, 55, 63, 76, 92, 105, 106, 113, 327
   Metallurgical Laboratory (Met Lab), 54–55, 63, 113, 118, 182–190 (Doc. 27)
   uranium-235 identified at, 114
   See also Compton, Arthur Holly; Fermi, Enrico; Szilárd, Leó, Wigner, Eugene Paul
Uranium enrichment, **113–114**
   processes of, 114
   role in atomic bomb development, 113–114
   See also Electromagnetic uranium enrichment; Gaseous uranium enrichment; Thermal diffusion uranium enrichment
Uranium-235, **114**
   active component of Little Boy bomb, 16, 49, 50, 51, 114
   and electromagnetic uranium enrichment, 25
   first identified, 114
   as fissile material, 32
   and Frisch-Peierls Memorandum, 36, 75
   and gaseous uranium enrichment, 37
   and gun-type fission weapons, 39
   and nuclear chain reactions, 63
   and thermal diffusion uranium enrichment, 98
   and transmutation of uranium into plutonium, 105
Urey, Harold C.
   Advisory Committee on Uranium member, 1
   Advisory Committee on Uranium scientific subcommittee member, 1
   and Compton report, 138–138 (Doc. 6)
   discovery of deuterium (heavy hydrogen), 325
   and discovery of "heavy water," Doc. 238 (Doc. 42e)
   S-1 Executive Committee member, 2, 327
   and Tube Alloys project, 74
U.S. Army Corps of Engineers, **114–115**
   Clinton Engineer Works at Oak Ridge built by, 15, 42, 65, 115
   creation of, 114
   Groves, Leslie Richard, chief of, 38
   initial purpose of, 114
   notable accomplishments, 115
U.S. Strategic Bombing Survey Summary Report, excerpts on effects of atomic bombs (July 1, 1946), 277–281 (Doc. 56)

Van Kirk, Theodore "Dutch," 26
Van Pelt, James F., 7, 8, 305

Walton, Ernest T. S., 16, 17, 325
War Department press release on calendar of important events (October 30, 1946), 309–311 (Doc. 60)

War Department press release on Hanford
　　Engineer Works (August 6, 1945),
　　240–243 (Doc. 42h)
　　acquisition of property, 240
　　challenges for construction, 242
　　construction, 240–241
　　housing for construction workers, 241
　　isolation of site, 242
　　magnitude of construction, 242
　　secrecy of project, 240
　　and ultra-micro scale operations, 241
　　Yakima community, 240
Warren, Stafford, report to Groves on Trinity
　　Test (July 21, 1945), 215–217 (Doc. 35)
　　on light intensity from blast, 216
　　on power of blast, 216
　　recommendation of larger site for future
　　　tests, 217
　　on weather, 215
Weisskopf, Victor, eyewitness account of
　　Trinity Test (July 16, 1945), 292–293
　　(Doc. 59a)
　　on initial light, 293
　　on smoke cloud, 293
　　viewing location, 292
Wendover Army Air Field, **117**
　　location of, 117
　　training of 509th Composite Group at,
　　　33, 101, 117
White Sands Missile Range, 3. *See also*
　　Alamogordo Bombing and Gunnery
　　Range

Wigner, Eugene Paul, **117–119**
　　attendance at first meeting of Advisory
　　　Committee on Uranium, 1, 8
　　Breit-Wigner formula, 118
　　early years and education, 117
　　and Met Lab, 55
　　move from Germany to U.S., 118
　　Nobel Prize in Physics awarded to, 117,
　　　118
　　and Szilárd petition to Truman against
　　　use of atomic bomb, 55, 201
　　　(Doc. 31f)
　　and Szilárd-Einstein letter, 23, 24, 126
　　　(Doc. 3)
　　university professorships, 118
Willoughby, John L., 8
World War II, **119–121**
　　aftermath and legacy, 121
　　attack on Pearl Harbor, 119–120
　　Battle of Midway, 120
　　early phases, 119
　　in Europe, 120–121
　　German Balkan blitzkrieg, 119
　　German invasion of Poland, 119
　　Italian Campaign, 121
　　Operation Torch, 120–121
　　Pacific Theater, 69–73
　　Soviet invasion of Poland, 119
　　U.S. entry, 119–120
　　U.S. production supplies, 120
　　See also Hiroshima, bombing of;
　　　Nagasaki, bombing of

About the Editor

Aaron Barlow, PhD, is a professor of English at the New York City College of Technology of the City University of New York. He is author or editor of numerous books and articles. His most recent publications are Greenwood's *The Depression Era: A Historical Exploration of Literature* (2016) and Praeger's *Doughboys on the Western Front: Memories of American Soldiers in the Great War* (2016). Barlow earned his doctorate in English from the University of Iowa.